Communicating with the Multicultural Consumer

PETER LANG
New York • Washington, D.C./Baltimore • Bern
Frankfurt am Main • Berlin • Brussels • Vienna • Oxford

Barbara Mueller

Communicating with the Multicultural Consumer

Theoretical and Practical Perspectives

PETER LANG
New York • Washington, D.C./Baltimore • Bern
Frankfurt am Main • Berlin • Brussels • Vienna • Oxford

Library of Congress Cataloging-in-Publication Data

Mueller, Barbara.
Communicating with the Multicultural consumer: theoretical
and practical perspectives / Barbara Mueller.
p. cm.
Includes bibliographical references and index.
1. Market segmentation—United States. 2. Minority consumers—United States.
3. Multiculturalism—United States. 4. Advertising—United States.
5. Business ethics—United States. I. Title.
HF5415.127.M84   658.8'02—dc22   2007013527
ISBN 978-1-4331-0204-2 (hardcover)
ISBN 978-0-8204-8119-7 (paperback)

Bibliographic information published by **Die Deutsche Bibliothek**.
Die Deutsche Bibliothek lists this publication in the "Deutsche
Nationalbibliografie"; detailed bibliographic data is available
on the Internet at http://dnb.ddb.de/.

Cover design by Clear Point Designs

The paper in this book meets the guidelines for permanence and durability
of the Committee on Production Guidelines for Book Longevity
of the Council of Library Resources.

© 2008 Peter Lang Publishing, Inc., New York
29 Broadway, 18th floor, New York, NY 10006
www.peterlang.com

To Juergen and Sophie, with love.

Table of Contents

List of Figures

List of Tables

Preface

Over just the past few decades, America's demographic profile has changed profoundly. Today, Hispanics number 41.3 million, officially making them the largest ethnic group in the country. Indeed, by some counts, the United States is considered the second largest Spanish-speaking nation in the world. Hispanics constitute 14.2% of the U.S. population; African Americans constitute 12.8%, and Asian Americans constitute 4.2%—collectively representing over 30% of the total U.S. population. And the U.S. census population projections estimate that these three groups will comprise half of the total U.S. population by the year 2050. Unfortunately, the pace of growth of these ethnic groups far exceeds the level of knowledge and understanding of these populations among marketing and advertising professionals. Ethnic marketing and advertising are still very much in the infancy stage. Rose notes,

> There is no question that the ethnic markets in general, and the Hispanic market in particular, should become increasingly important to both advertising and public relations professionals and agencies. As such, it must be presumed that communication practitioners cannot continue to do business as usual. Nor can communication

students planning to work in today's multi-ethnic world survive without understanding ethnic marketing better. (2002, p. 2)

This textbook was written to help prepare future marketers and advertisers to function more effectively in an increasingly diverse U.S. society. It is
specifically designed for upper-division undergraduate and graduate students
in specialized courses dealing with advertising and marketing to multicultural
consumers. However, it is also an effective supplemental text for introductory
advertising, marketing, or mass communication courses seeking to expand
coverage of multiethnic issues. The text should also prove useful to current
practitioners of advertising, whether on the client side or within the advertising agency, who find themselves needing to communicate with an ethnic
audience with which they are unfamiliar. Finally, researchers of multicultural
markets will find it to be a valuable resource.

This book introduces the student, practitioner, and researcher to the challenges and difficulties in developing and implementing communications
programs for ethnic markets. While advertising is the major focus, the author
recognizes that an integrated marketing communications approach is critical
to competing successfully for the multicultural customer. In order to communicate effectively with ethnic audiences, marketers must coordinate not only
advertising, direct marketing, sales promotions, personal selling, and public
relations efforts, but the other aspects of the marketing mix as well. Therefore,
the basics of marketing to the three largest ethnic groups—Hispanics, African
Americans, and Asian Americans—are also reviewed.

Every attempt has been made to provide a balance of theoretical and
practical perspectives. Using current examples and case studies, *Communicating
with the Multicultural Consumer: Theoretical and Practical Perspectives* addresses
the key issues that advertisers must keep in mind to create effective communications programs for ethnic consumers. The text comprises a total of eight
chapters. In chapter 1, factors influencing the growth of multicultural markets
are examined. Chapter 2 highlights the roles that product, price, distribution,
and promotion play in selling to Hispanics, blacks, and Asians. Chapter 3 is
devoted to developing sensitivity to the various cultural factors that impact
multicultural marketing efforts. Here, the concepts of assimilation and acculturation are explored, as is the influence of culture on both verbal and nonverbal communication. Chapters 4 through 6 provide profiles of Hispanic,
African American, and Asian American consumers. Topics covered in each
chapter include understanding a specific coculture's ethnic identity, unifying
factors, income and buying power, and shopping behavior; where to reach
each segment in terms of geographic concentrations; how to create persuasive
advertising messages; and how best to reach each audience via media. Chapter
7 examines the use of general market, multicultural, and specialty agencies in

appealing to ethnic consumers. The lack of diversity in the advertising industry is explored, as are steps that are being taken to correct this problem. Profiles of Hispanic, African American, and Asian American advertising agencies are included, and their work on behalf of clients is highlighted. Finally, in chapter 8, the role of ethics and social responsibility in selling to the multicultural consumer is addressed.

I am indebted to a number of individuals for the successful completion of this text. A manuscript does not become a book without a great deal of effort on the part of a publisher. I am grateful to several folks at Peter Lang Publishing who have been involved with this project. First and foremost, I would like to acknowledge Chris Myers, Managing Director, who was generous with his support, guidance, and understanding during the many months it took to complete this project. This is the third time I have had the great fortune to work with him, so I speak from experience when I say that an author couldn't ask for a better editor than Chris. Special thanks also go to Meredith Ackroyd, who worked so diligently in editing the manuscript, as well as to Bernadette Shade for doing a superb job of managing the production process. I would also like to acknowledge Lisa Barfield, who was brilliant at pulling together a cover that really reflects the contents of this text. Thanks also to Damon Zucca for his invaluable comments and suggestions. Collectively, their efforts have made it a pleasure to work on this textbook. On a personal note, I want to thank my husband, Juergen, and my daughter, Sophie, not only for enduring my inattention but also for offering their love and encouragement—without which I could not continue to write. I am quite certain they are looking forward to our home life returning to normal.

Barbara Mueller

REFERENCES

Rose, P. (2002, Spring). The times they are a changing . . . and so should PR training. *Public Relations Quarterly, 47*(1), 14.

The Growth of Multicultural Markets

Melting Pot or Mosaic?

Back in 1915, the nation's estimated population passed the 100 million mark. Most likely, the 100 millionth person was a white baby born to a family in New York City or, perhaps, a rural family in upstate New York or Pennsylvania. At the time, nearly 90% of Americans were white, 9.9% were black, and 0.25% were Asian. Data on Hispanics were not available, but estimates suggest there were no more than 500,000 Hispanics living in the United States. In 1967, when the 200 millionth baby was to be born, *Life* magazine dispatched twenty-three photographers to locate the infant and devoted a five-page spread to its search. In the intervening five decades, the white population had dropped to 83.5%, while the black population had grown to 11.1%. Asians were 0.8% of the population, and Hispanics represented 4.5% of the population. Instead of deciding on a statistically valid symbol of the average newborn, the magazine chose the one born at precisely the appointed time (Roberts, 2006). *Life* immortalized Robert Ken Woo Jr., who was born at 11:03 A.M. on November

20, 1967, at Crawford W. Long Memorial Hospital in Atlanta, Georgia. His parents, a computer programmer and a chemical engineer, had emigrated seven years earlier from China. Employing a complex and highly subjective set of calculations, the Census Bureau set October 17, 2006, at 4:46 A.M. Eastern Standard Time as the moment the United States welcomed its 300 millionth inhabitant (Elsworth, 2006). Although the Census Bureau made no attempt to identify the 300 millionth person, demographers have suggested it could well be represented by a Hispanic baby—or an immigrant crossing the Mexican border (Pickel, 2006). The U.S. Census Bureau's most recently released data indicate that the United States is more ethnically diverse today than many ever could have imagined.

As populations of Hispanics, blacks, and Asians in the United States continue to grow, both in terms of their numbers as well as their economic clout, they draw increasing attention from producers, retailers, and service providers alike. The multitude of differences among these groups suggests that a generic product, promoted via a single advertising campaign geared to all consumers, will likely miss many potentially profitable marketing opportunities. As the U.S. market becomes increasingly diverse, it is essential that products, media, and the advertising messages that appear in those media be tailored to each of the ethnic market segments. This chapter begins the discussion of the multicultural consumer by examining the demographic changes taking place in America today.

Race and Ethnicity in the U.S. Marketplace

The U.S. Census Bureau (http://www.census.gov) is a treasure trove of information about the changing U.S. population. A question on race has been asked in the U.S. census since the late 1700s. However, a question regarding Hispanic origin has only been asked since 1970. Before presenting data from the most recent census, it is important to note that the census distinguishes between race and ethnicity. *Race* is based on self-identification by the census respondent. Groups include white, black or African American, American Indian and Alaska Native, Asian, and Native Hawaiian or other Pacific Islander. Hispanics are considered an ethnic group. *Hispanic origin* is also based on self-identification via a census question and refers to individuals who have indicated that their origin or descent was Mexican, Puerto Rican, Cuban, Central or South American, or some other Hispanic origin. It is important to note that people of Hispanic origin may be of any race. Because race and ethnicity are separate concepts, racial categories of white, black, American Indian and Alaska Native, Asian, and Pacific Islander all contain some people of Hispanic origin. The census uses the term *white non-Hispanic* to indicate the white population minus that part of the group that is of Hispanic origin. Also, a new racial standard was introduced in the 2000 census. For the first time, people had the option to identify themselves with more than one race; respondents were able to choose from an amazing 126 different combinations. The *single-race population* (also called the *alone population*) refers to people who identified only one race. The *alone-or-in-combination population* refers to a single-race population plus any people who are of that specified race in combination with any other race. As an example, the black alone-or-in-combination population would include all those who report black, in addition to the people who report black in combination with one or more races (white, American Indian and Alaska Native, Asian, or Pacific Islander). When all five alone-or-in-combination groups are added together, the sum is greater than the total population (U.S. Census Bureau, 2000b).

Census 2000 reported the largest census-to-census increase ever. In the decade between 1990 and 2000, the population exploded by some 32.7 million people to a total of 281 million, an increase of 13.2%. These figures represent the largest increase in the consumer market since the statistics of the baby boom (between 1950 and 1960). Boomer births boosted the population by just 28 million. The current population boom took demographers by surprise. After three decades of slowing growth, most experts anticipated that the U.S. population would continue this trend. A major driving force behind this boom was the larger-than-anticipated and larger-than-measured numbers of immigrants, both legal and illegal (Wellner, 2002).

In addition to conducting a census once every decade, the Census Bureau provides updates to their data, via a number of different reports. Their most recent report revealed that on July 1, 2004, 98% of all U.S. residents, or 289.2 million people, belonged to one of the five single-race groups. People who were white and no other race made up the largest group, numbering 236.1 million, as shown in Table 1.1. The single-race black population was 37.5 million, and the single-race Asian population was 12.3 million. The single-race American Indian and Alaska Native population accounted for 2.8 million people in the United States. The smallest single-race category was the Pacific Islander population, numbering just 506,000. Perhaps surprisingly, only 2% of the population listed themselves as belonging to the two-or-more-races population. The two-or-more-races population plus the five single-race populations equal the total population.

Table 1.1 reveals that, in 2004, 239.9 million people were either single-race white or white in combination with one or more races. These two groups accounted for 82% of the total U.S. population, while single-race whites represented 80%. The single-race black population and blacks in combination with one or more races equaled 39.2 million. While people who were black and no other race accounted for 12.8% of U.S. residents, those who were single-race black and black in combination with some other race represented 13.4%.

Table 1.1: U.S. Population by Race and Ethnic Origin for the United States, July 1, 2004

Race and Ethnic origin	Number (in thousands)	Percent of total population
Total population	293,655.4	100.0%
One race	289,216.7	98.5%
White	236,057.8	80.4%
Black or African American	37,502.8	12.8%
American Indian and Alaska Native	2,824.8	1.0%
Asian	12,326.2	4.2%
Native Hawaiian and other Pacific Islander	505.6	0.2%
Two or more racestable table text	4,438.8	1.5%
Race alone or in combination		
White	239,880.1	81.7%
Black	39,232.5	13.4%
American Indian and Alaska Native	4,409.4	1.5%
Asian	13,956.6	4.8%
Native Hawaiian and other Pacific Islander	976.4	0.3%
Hispanic or Latino (any race)	41,322.1	14.1%
White alone, non-Hispanic, or Latino	197,840.8	67.4%

Source: U.S. Census Bureau, Internet Release, 2004.

Asians who were one race or in combination with other races numbered 14.0 million in 2004. In terms of numbers, the Asian market has already matched or exceeded the populations of several European countries—including Portugal, Norway, Austria, Bulgaria, Greece, and others. Single-race Asians represented 4.2% of all Americans, while single-race Asians plus those in combination with one or more other races represented 4.8%. The largest Asian nationality is Chinese, followed by Filipino, Asian Indian, Vietnamese, and Korean—each with populations greater than one million.

The population of American Indians and Alaska Natives alone or in combination with other races (4.4 million) was 56% higher than the population of single-race American Indians and Alaska Natives. While single-race American Indians and Alaska Natives represented 1.0% of the U.S. total, this group in combination with their counterparts of more than one race represented 1.5%. The population of Pacific Islanders alone or in combination with other racial groups (976,000) was nearly twice as large as the single-race Pacific Islander population. The expanded group's share of the U.S. total was 0.3%, with 0.2% for single-race Pacific Islanders.

With 41.3 million people, the Hispanic population accounted for 14% of the total U.S. population in 2004. This means that nearly one out of every seven people in the U.S. today is a Latino. Nearly all Hispanics (99%) belonged to only one racial group. Among Hispanics, 92% were white, 4% were black, 1% were American Indian and Alaska Native, 0.6% were Asian, and 0.3% were Pacific Islander. About 583,000 Hispanics, 1% of all Hispanics, were more than one race. As revealed in Figure 1.1, almost 67% of U.S. Latinos noted that their place of origin was Mexico. Puerto Rico comes in at a distant second, with just 8.6%. People who were single-race non-Hispanic white numbered 197.8 million and represented 67% of all people living in the United States.

Although a relatively small percentage of the population identified themselves with more than one race, this multiracial trend is of particular interest to companies who are targeting the young. Multiracials tend to be younger people. While only 26% of the total U.S. population is under age eighteen, 42% of multiracials fall into this group. It should be noted that, as multiracials age, they will likely become an increasingly powerful segment of the adult

Figure 1.1: U.S. Latino Population by Place of Origin

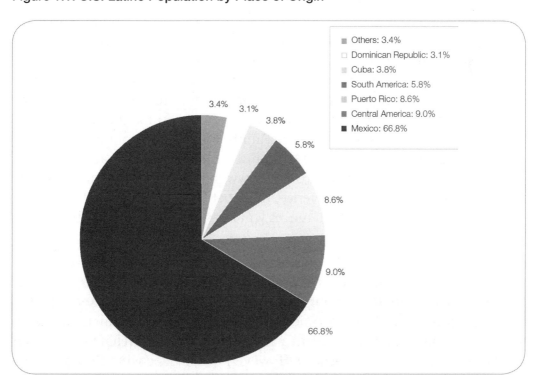

Source: *Advertising Age* (2006) Hispanic Fact Pack: Annual Guide to Hispanic Marketing and Media. Crain Communications. P. 39.

market—and it is likely that most marketers will eventually have to take this segment into account (Wellner, 2002). Subsequent discussions will primarily focus on the three largest groups: Hispanics, blacks, and Asians.

Identities and Labels

The title of this text includes the term *multicultural*. *Multicultural* is defined by the *American Heritage Dictionary of the English Language* (2000) as (a) of, relating to, or including several cultures and (b) of or relating to a social or educational theory that encourages interest in many cultures within a society rather than in only the mainstream culture. And that is exactly the focus of this text—encouraging the reader's interest in Hispanic, African American, and Asian American cultures. The reader has noted that the U.S. Census Bureau has distinguished between the terms *race* and *ethnicity* in collecting data. However, more broadly defined, the term *ethnic* relates to a sizable group of people sharing a common and distinctive racial, national, religious, linguistic, or cultural heritage. Thus, the term *ethnicity* will be used throughout this text to refer to Hispanics, African Americans, and Asian Americans.

Hispanic or Latino?

The term *Hispanic* traces its roots to the U.S. Census Bureau's efforts in the 1970s to collectively label all individuals in the United States who trace their origins to Spanish-speaking countries. Some Hispanic constituencies were displeased with the label—in part because it was imposed from the outside. After much debate, the label *Latino* was suggested as an alternative, because it encompasses nearly everyone from a culture with Latin roots. Despite the controversy, a 2002 National Survey of Latinos conducted by the Pew Hispanic Center and the Kaiser Family Foundation found that over a third of Hispanics prefer the label Hispanic, while 13% prefer Latino, and the remainder have no preference (http://www.pewhispanic.org/site/docs/pdf/LatinoSurveyReportFinal.pdf). Hence, the label Hispanic will be employed in this text, though occasional references will be made to the term Latino.

African American or Black?

As with Hispanic consumers, there is concern over whether there is a preference for a specific label among African Americans. Miller and Kemp (2005, p. 8) report that in 2001, Gallup Newswire found that many sources indicated that 40% to 45% of African Americans say they have no preference between the labels *black* or *African American*. However, when asked what they preferred being called on a personal level, blacks typically show a slight preference for the term *black*. On the other hand, when asked what they preferred the race to be called, the majority of blacks said they preferred the term *African American*. In short, "black or African American racial labels made little difference in how African Americans want to be addressed" (Miller & Kemp, 2005, p. 8). Thus, these terms will be used interchangeably throughout this text.

Asian American or Asian Pacific American?

Asian American is the label used to refer to Americans descending from more than fifteen different ethnic groups, including Japanese, Chinese, Filipinos, Vietnamese, Koreans, and Asian Indians. The term *Native Hawaiian and other Pacific Islander* refers to people tracing their ancestry to any of the original peoples of Hawaii, Guam, Samoa, or other Pacific Islands. The label *Asian Pacific American* has been employed over the past few years to refer to Asians and Native Hawaiian and other Pacific Islanders collectively. However, the U.S. Census Bureau separates these two groups in collecting data, and much of the research on this market is reported for only Asian Americans. Throughout this text, data for the ethnic group *Native Hawaiian and other Pacific Islander* will only be included when specifically cited.

Population Growth: Birthrate and Immigration

Within just four years (between Census Day, April 1, 2000, and July 1, 2004), the U.S. population as a whole increased by 4%. Growth rates differed among the racial and ethnic groups. The black population increased 5%, while the Asian population increased by 16%. The Hispanic population outpaced even the Asian population—growing by 17% during this time period. In contrast, the non-Hispanic white population was the slowest-growing group—increasing by a mere 1%—just a quarter of the national rate. As a result, the population of non-Hispanic whites declined as a proportion of the entire population, falling from 70% in April 2000 to about 67% in July 2004. Overall, the black population (single race) grew from 12.7% to 12.8% of the total population. The Asian population (single race) increased from 3.8% to 4.2% of all U.S. residents. Hispanics experienced the largest percentage-point increase in share, rising from 12% of the population in 2000 to 14% in 2004. Traditionally, blacks had always been the largest minority group in the United States. Hispanics now have that distinction.

Two factors typically drive population growth: birthrates and immigration. In the early 1900s, American women gave birth to an average of about four children during their childbearing years. According to census estimates, during the past decade, the total fertility rate has fluctuated between 2.0 and 2.1 births per woman—just below the level required for natural replacement of the population. However, many demographers expect the number of births in the United States to soar to levels higher than those recorded at the peak of the baby boom, thanks primarily to two key drivers: the wave of Generation Y women (born between 1977 and 1994) who are entering their prime child-bearing years and the growing number of Hispanics who, on average, tend to have more children than white, black, and Asian families (Fetto, 2003). Based on census data reported in 2004, among the racial and ethnic groups, only Hispanic women (any race) reached the end of their childbearing years with more births than the number required for natural replacement—2.3 births by age forty to forty-four years. Black and non-Hispanic white women were below the replacement level, averaging about 1.8 to 1.9 births by that age. One in five children born in the U.S. today is Hispanic. Between 2001 and 2010, the number of Hispanic children age nine years and younger will increase by 22%, while the number of non-Hispanic children of the same age will increase by 1% (U.S. Census Bureau, 2004a).

Clearly, manufacturers of products targeting babies and children are paying attention to these trends. Toy companies' market shares, in particular, have been waning. According to the research firm the NPD Group, sales of traditional toys dipped from $21.3 billion in 2002 to $20.7 billion in 2003—reflecting the fourth consecutive drop in sales (Hoag, 2004). However, a recent marketing study reported that Hispanic parents spend considerably more on toys for their children than do non-Hispanics (Kaplan, 2004). Simmons Hispanic Study 2000 found that 67.2% of Hispanic adults had purchased games and toys within the previous twelve months, compared to 50.4% of non-Hispanics (Hoag, 2004). Fisher-Price, Inc., for example, hired a Hispanic marketing agency—Market Vision—to execute a Hispanic marketing program targeting Latino parents of preschool children. Bonnie Garcia, president of Market Vision notes,

> Our recommendation to Fisher-Price is to make a deep connection with Hispanic families. Through traditional and non-traditional marketing vehicles, we can reach the Latino mom in her home, her neighborhood, and even her pediatrician's office. The Latino mom is very young. Her child is the center of her universe, and she is very much involved with her family and her community. As a brand of toys and juvenile products, Fisher-Price is uniquely positioned to offer her everything she needs to give her family the best possible start in life. (CoActive Marketing Group, 2004)

Television and radio spots featured Fisher-Price's Peek-a-Blocks toys and LittlePeople play sets. The company's tagline was translated into Spanish and music used in the general market advertising was rearranged with a Latin flair. The brand gained additional exposure to over one million parents through targeted pediatrician's offices via Accent Health in Español, a Hispanic TV network produced by CNN. Through a sponsorship with Meredith Corporation's American Baby Group, Fisher-Price was the sole sponsor of a new Spanish-language publication *Jugando a Crecer* (Playing to Grow), which was distributed to one million parents of newborns and infants through obstetrics-gynecology

(OB-GYN) offices and hospital birthing units with high Hispanic birthrates. The free publication addressed the importance of play in the early years of life and offered tips on how to foster baby's developing cognitive and motor skills through play. Fisher-Price purchased neighborhood billboard space with the headline message *"Juega con Ellos. Rie con Ellos. Crece con Ellos,"* or "Play with Them. Laugh with Them. Grow with Them." The campaign also included participation in grassroots festivals. A 60' x 60' play area featured five different play stations for children from six months to six years. Finally, a comprehensive Web campaign carried banner ads, play tips, and information about a sweepstakes, offering participants the chance to win toys for their tots. Fisher-Price's goal is to be the leading brand of choice for Latino families.

Beyond birthrates, immigration plays a significant role in driving population figures. The maxim that the United States is a nation of immigrants is no less true today than it was three centuries ago. But the character of U.S. immigration has changed dramatically: Hispanics and Asians—not Europeans—are the predominant groups entering the country today. Recent immigration makes up a major portion of the U.S. Hispanic community. Two in five Hispanics are foreign born—more than half of whom entered the United States between 1990 and 2002, according to census reports (Lester, 2004). The Asian population is also growing more rapidly than the total population, primarily because of strong immigration, a trend that is expected to continue. Table 1.2 presents the foreign-born population of Asian Americans. Vietnamese Americans are most likely to be foreign born.

Table 1.2: Foreign-Born Population of Asian Americans	
Ethnicity	**Percent foreign born**
Japanese	45%
Chinese	65%
Indian	70%
Filipino	76%
Korean	78%
Vietnamese	91%e

Source: Foreign Born Current Population Survey, *U.S. Census 2000*, U.S. Census Bureau, retrieved from http://www.census.gov/

Another difference in immigration patterns today is the parameters of legal versus illegal, or authorized versus unauthorized, entry. A recent Pew Hispanic Center report shows that, since the mid-1990s, illegal immigration has outstripped legal entry. As of March 2005, the number of unauthorized immigrants living in the United States has grown to as many as 12 million. Over half (56% or 6.2 million) of these unauthorized immigrants are from Mexico, and 22% or 2.5 million are from other Latin American countries, with the bulk coming from Central America. In addition, 13% or 1.5 million illegal immigrants are from Asia. A little more than 6% or 0.6 million unauthorized immigrants are from Europe and Canada, while less than 0.4 million are from Africa. According to the report, efforts to curb illegal immigration have not slowed its pace ("U.S. Has As Many As 12 Million," 2006). Clearly, the bulk of illegal immigration is from Mexico. However, according to the National Population Council of Mexico (CANAPO) the total fertility rate in Mexico has dropped from over seven children per woman in 1960 to 2.4 children per woman in 2000 and is expected to drop even further to 1.85 children per woman in the near future. Based on these and similar predictions by the Census Bureau and the United Nations, demographers predict that Mexican immigration to the United States will start to decline shortly after 2010 ("Dynamic Trends," 2005). The issue of illegal immigration remains a hotly debated topic among both politicians and the public in the United States today.

Age Distribution

According to the census, in 2004, the median age for the country as a whole was thirty-six years. Table 1.3 reveals that the non-Hispanic white population has the highest median age (forty years). The black and Asian populations had median ages of 30.8 and 34.1 years, respectively. The median age for Hispanics was significantly younger—at 26.9 years, they are nearly a decade younger than the population as a whole. The proportion of people sixty-five years of age and older was highest among non-Hispanic whites—15%, compared with 12% of the total population. The next highest proportions were among the black and Asian populations. About 8% of each of these groups was sixty-five years of age and older. Only 5% of Hispanics were aged sixty-five years and older. The share of children among the racial and Hispanic-origin groups was very nearly the inverse of the share of older adults. Non-Hispanic whites had the smallest proportion of children—22% were under eighteen years of age, compared with 25% in the total population. Twenty-three percent of Asians were under eighteen years of age, while the proportion was 30% for blacks. Among Hispanics, 34% were under eighteen years of age.

Ethnic Population Distribution

While America's changing ethnic makeup suggests growing diversity across the United States, closer examination of the torrent of statistics flowing from the Census Bureau reveals that the nation's ethnic groups are still heavily clustered in selected regions and markets. Of the 3,141 counties in the United States, over three-quarters (2,419) of them have white shares greater than the nation as a whole, and well over half of all counties (1,822) are at least 85% white. In particular, counties from the upper West and Rocky Mountains to the Midwest and Northeast are mostly white, and none of the minority groups come close to approximating their national averages. In 2004, census statistics revealed that the percentage of non-Hispanic whites was highest in North Dakota, Iowa, West Virginia, Vermont, New Hampshire, and Maine, where at least 90% of the population was white. Non-Hispanic whites were also over 80% of the population in the following states: Idaho (87%), Montana (89%), Wyoming (88%), South Dakota (87%), Minnesota (86%), and Wisconsin (86%). The non-Hispanic white resident population was 50% or less in four states: Hawaii (23%), New Mexico (43%), California (45%), and Texas (50%). In the District of Columbia, 30% of residents were non-Hispanic white.

However, census figures revealed that the country's two largest ethnic groups are following strikingly different paths in terms of population distribution: Hispanics are increasingly moving to areas where few from their ethnic group reside, while African Americans are steadily moving to suburbs in the South that have large black populations (Overberg & Nasser, 2005). In the 1990s, most Hispanic immigrants came to the United States through five gateways: California, Texas, Illinois, New York, and Florida. Today, they are just as likely to go to Iowa, South Carolina, or Tennessee—following jobs. The 2004 estimates show that the share of Hispanics living in counties with large concentrations of Hispanics is slipping and that Hispanics now make up at least 5% of the population in twenty-eight states, up from sixteen states in 1990 (Overberg & Nasser, 2005). The state with the highest percentage of Hispanics was New Mexico, where more than 43% of the population was Hispanic. California and Texas had the next highest percentages, both about

Table 1.3: Age Distribution for the U.S. Population by Race and Ethnic Origin: 2004 (Percent distribution)

Race and Ethnic origin	Younger than 18 years of age	18 to 64 years of age	65 years of age and older
Total population	25.0%	62.6%	12.4%
White alone, not Hispanic, or Latino	21.8%	63.2%	15.0%
Black or African American	30.3%	61.6%	8.1%
Asian	23.1%	68.4%	8.5%
Hispanic or Latino	34.0%	60.8%	5.2%

Source: U.S. Census Bureau: Race and Hispanic Origin in 2004, Population Profile of the United States: Dynamic Version.

35%. Arizona (28%) and Nevada (23%) followed. Montana, North and South Dakota, Ohio, and Indiana were among the states where Hispanics were less than 5% of the population. States with the lowest percentage of Hispanics included Maine (1.0%) and Virginia (0.8%).

Regarding the distribution of blacks, census data suggest an exodus back to the South. In fact, the 1990s was the decade in which a surge in a black return to the South began, representing a wholesale reversal of the South-to-North migration of earlier decades. For the first time, the South gained blacks in its migration exchanges with each of the other regions of the country. The culture and heritage in the South appear to have a strong appeal among blacks, along with a strong economy. African American Generation Xers and Generation Ys tend to be less concerned by the region's history of racial discrimination than with available jobs and the chance to network with other middle-class blacks. Young black college graduates lead the way among this group of movers; however, the South is gaining blacks from almost every demographic group, including seniors (Frey, 2004). Over half of all blacks live in the eleven states that were once in the Confederacy, up by one million from 2000. States with large percentages of blacks included Mississippi (37%), Louisiana (33%), Georgia (30%), South Carolina (29%), Maryland (29%), Alabama (26%), North Carolina (21%), Virginia (19%), Florida (15%), Tennessee (16%), Arkansas (15%), and Texas (11%). States with the lowest percentage of blacks were more scattered. The percentage of blacks was less than 1% in the following states: Montana, Idaho, Vermont, North Dakota, Maine, South Dakota, Wyoming, Utah, and New Hampshire.

Over 40% of the population of Hawaii was Asian in 2004. Census statistics reveal that California came in at a distant second place, where 12% of the people living in that state were of Asian descent. The states with the next highest percentages were New Jersey (7%), New York (6%), and Washington (6%). States with the lowest percentage of Asians were South Dakota (0.7%), North Dakota (0.7%), Wyoming (0.6%), West Virginia (0.6%), and Montana (0.5%). As noted previously, the majority of Asian Americans living in the country today are foreign born. Metropolitan magnets for Asian-American immigrants are, in order of importance, New York; Los Angeles; San Francisco; Chicago; Miami; Washington, D.C.; Dallas–Fort Worth; Houston; and Boston (Frey, 2004).

Despite the nation's increasing diversity, most neighborhoods are still racially segregated, according to an analysis of census 2000 data by the Lewis Mumford Center, at the State University of New York (Wellner, 2002). There appears to be a very strong tendency for neighborhoods to swing disproportionately toward a white population or an ethnic group. The average white person lives in a neighborhood that is 83% white, 7% black, 6% Hispanic, and 3% Asian, according to John Logan, director of the Center. The average African

American lives in a neighborhood that is 54% black, and the average Hispanic person lives in a neighborhood that is 42% Hispanic. The one ethnic group that appears to be an exception to these demographic trends in neighborhood populations is Asians. The smallest of the three ethnic groups is also the most integrated. The average Asian American lives in a neighborhood that is just 19% Asian (Wellner, 2002). The ethnic distribution and migration patterns discussed above show that America still has a long way to go before it becomes a true coast-to-coast melting pot, where racial and ethnic groups are spread evenly across the land. Currently, these patterns appear to reflect something more akin to a mosaic.

Educational Attainment

The 2000 census revealed an overall trend toward a more educated society. However, significant differences exist among various population segments. Among non-Hispanic whites, 88% were high school graduates, surpassing the previous record high. Approximately three-quarters of blacks were high school graduates, also a new record for this group. Over the past decade, differences in the percentages of blacks and non-Hispanic whites who had completed high school narrowed as black high school graduation rates improved. For the population aged twenty-five years and older, the difference between the two groups decreased from sixteen percentage points in 1989 to about ten percentage points in 2000.

Among Asians, 86% held a high school diploma or better—not significantly different from the peak reached in 1998. However, Asians have the greatest proportion of college graduates. Among those aged twenty-five years and older, nearly half held a college degree or higher level of education in 2000. In contrast, 28% of non-Hispanic whites and less than one in five blacks in this age group were college graduates.

Hispanics were the least likely of the three groups to have completed high school or college. 2000 census statistics show that 57% of Hispanics aged twenty-five years and older were high school graduates—an improvement over the 1989 share of 51% but still significantly lower than the other groups. Furthermore, the percentage of Hispanics who held a bachelor's degree or higher was only 11% (U.S. Census Bureau, 2000a). A recent report from the National Center for Public Policy and Higher Education shows that because blacks and Hispanics are less likely to earn college degrees, if the current education gap continues, the proportion of the total workforce with a college education, or even a high school diploma, will, in fact, decrease. By 2020, the proportion of the workforce with less than a high school diploma would rise from 16.1% to 18.5%, and the proportion with a bachelor's degree would fall from 17% to 16.4%. This drop in the share of the workforce with college degrees would also lead to a 2% fall in personal per-capita income from $21,591 in 2000 to $21,196 in 2020 in constant dollars. While this might not seem like a significant drop, it should be noted that, during the previous twenty-year period, that figure grew by 41%. However, if the education gap could be closed so that minority students earn bachelor's degrees at the same rate as white students, the United States could see the proportion of workers with degrees increase to 20% by 2020 (Walters, 2005).

Clearly, greater educational attainment spells greater socioeconomic success. This relationship holds true not only for the population as a whole, but also for population subgroups, including racial and ethnic groups. The level of education attained has a huge impact on future earnings potential. Based on Census Bureau figures reported in 2003, average earnings for those with advanced degrees were $72,824 in 2002. This is followed by an average of $51,194 for those with bachelor's degrees, $27,280 for those with high school diplomas, and just $18,826 for nongraduates. The difference in earnings between high school and college graduates throughout their working life comes to nearly $1 million, as the average high school graduate will earn approximately $1.2 million, while the average college graduate will make $2.1 million (Brier, 2004).

Income and Ethnic Buying Power

The following information on income in 2004 was collected in the Census Bureau's 2005 Annual Social and Economic Supplement to the Current Population Survey (U.S. Census Bureau, 2004b). Income data in the U.S. Census Bureau reports are based on the amount of money people or households receive during a calendar year. In 2004, the national median household income was $44,389, marking the second year in a row in which real median income saw no change—overall, as well as within racial and ethnic groups. For non-Hispanic white households, the median was $48,977. The median for Hispanic households was significantly lower, at $34,241. However, black households had the lowest median income ($30,134). At $57,518, Asian households had the highest median income.

The Selig Center for Economic Growth's recent report "The Multicultural Economy 2003: America's Minority Buying Power" (Humphreys, 2003) projects that the nation's total buying power will rise from $4.3 trillion in 1990 to $7.1 trillion in 2000 and to $10.6 trillion in 2008. The percentage increase for the eighteen-year period between 1990 and 2008 is 147.5%, which far outstrips cumulative inflation. The Selig Center projects that the nation's black buying power will rise from $318 billion in 1990 to $585 billion in 2000 and to $921 billion in 2008—up by 189% in eighteen years—a compound annual growth rate of 6.1%. This overall percentage gain outstrips the 128% increase projected in white buying power and the 148% increase in total buying power (all races combined). In 2008, the nation's share of total buying power that is black will be 8.7%, up from 7.4% in 1990. Nationally, African American consumers account for almost nine cents out of every dollar that is spent. The collective black population in the United States will represent more than the gross domestic purchasing power of twenty-nine countries, including Canada, Spain, and Australia. The gains in black buying power reflect much more than just population growth and inflation. The Selig Center notes that, of all the diverse supporting forces, perhaps the most important is the increased number of jobs across the country. Compared to 1990, employment opportunities have improved for everyone, including African Americans. An increasing number of blacks who are starting and expanding their own businesses also contribute to gains in buying power. The *Survey of Minority-Owned Business Enterprises* released by the Census Bureau in 2001 showed that the number of black-owned firms increased almost four times faster than the number of all U.S. firms (Humphreys, 2003). Also, compared to the white population, larger proportions of blacks are either entering the workforce for the first time or moving up from entry-level positions.

The Selig Center projects that the nation's Asian buying power will more than quadruple over the eighteen-year period, climbing from $118 billion in 1990 to $526 billion in 2008. This 345% gain from 1990 to 2008 (at a compound annual rate of growth of 8.6%) is substantially higher than the increases in buying power projected for whites, the United States as a whole, and African Americans (Humphreys, 2003). The U.S. Asian population is considered the fourteenth largest economic power in the world. Although population growth and a strong economy help, Asian buying power is propelled by the previously noted fact that Asians are better educated than the average American, and, therefore, Asians hold many top-level jobs in management or professional specialties. The increasing number of successful Asian entrepreneurs also helps to increase the group's buying power. According to the U.S. Census Bureau's 2001 *Survey of Minority-Owned Business Enterprises,* the number of Asian-owned businesses—which mostly center on business services, personal services, and retailing—increased more than four times faster than the number of all U.S. firms.

However, it will be the immense buying power of the nation's Hispanic consumers that will energize the U.S. consumer market as never before. The Selig Center projections reveal that over the eighteen-year period between 1990 and 2008, the nation's Hispanic buying power will grow at a compound annual rate of 8.8% (the comparable rate of growth for non-Hispanics is 4.9%). In terms of sheer dollar power, Hispanics' economic clout will rise from $222 billion in 1990 to $1.0142 trillion in 2008. The 2008 value will exceed the 1990 value by 357%—a percentage gain that is even greater than the Asian buying power. In 2008, Hispanics will account for 9.6% of all U.S. buying power, up from 5.2% in 1990 (Humphreys, 2003). Of the many forces supporting this substantial and continued growth, the most important is favorable demographics (higher birthrates and strong immigration), but better employment opportunities also help to increase the group's buying power. A relatively young Hispanic population, with larger proportions of them either entering the workforce for the first time or moving up on their career ladders, argues for additional gains in buying power. Overall, minority buying power is expected to reach nearly $2.5 trillion by 2008. According to the U.S. Department of Commerce, minority purchasing power may surpass $3 trillion by 2030, and, by 2045, minority disposable income may reach more than $4 trillion (U.S. Department of Commerce, 2000).

Corporate America Responds

What do all these statistics mean to corporate America? The numbers have a direct influence on the products and services that will be offered to consumer groups in the future, the media used to communicate with them, and the agencies employed to create the messages appearing in those media. One example in each of these areas will quickly demonstrate this.

Products and Services

The census numbers play a significant role in what consumers will see as they wander through shopping malls, push their carts through grocery stores, or even browse through the racks at the local greeting card shop. For example, Hallmark, the greeting card giant, uses census data to decide on the product mix that local retailers will receive. When combined with psychographic research, such data provide Hallmark with a powerful marketing tool, notes Jay Dittman, the firm's vice president of consumer research. "It is our key lens into the demographics of the population," he explains (Wellner, 2002). When the first set of census 2000 statistics began to trickle out, the company increased its focus on its En Español line, given the projections of a rapidly growing Hispanic population. Hallmark first used online focus groups to create new messages for the En Español line and then turned to census data to pick the right retail markets to target. Clearly, census data are a boon to marketers interested in beefing up their ethnic marketing plans.

Media

Because immigrants account for two-thirds of the Asian American community, most retain their native language, resulting in a multitude of Asian-language media catering to them. There are over six hundred Asian-language media outlets in the United States today—whereas, in 1990, there were only about 250 such organizations (Grant, 2003). Print media have traditionally dominated these communication channels. Scores of newspapers printed in Asian languages are available in heavily populated Asian American communities. Asian Americans gravitate to these media not only because they are printed in their native tongue, but also because they offer editorial content and coverage of their countries of origin and also their local communities. The number of radio and TV broadcasters in the Asian languages is also growing quickly in regions of the United States with high concentrations of Asian population, but it is the Internet that has experienced tremendous growth in usage. According to the Pew Internet and American Life Project, Asian Americans' index is greater than the general population's in home computer usage, and they are the heaviest users of online services (Lester, 2004). Over the coming decade, it is expected that a multitude of new print, broadcast, electronic, and other media vehicles will start up to meet the needs of growing ethnic markets.

Advertising Agencies

Marketers look to Burrell Communications for insights into the African American consumer. The agency, which was founded in 1971 with just three employees, today has grown to over 130 employees and, as one of the five largest African American advertising agencies in the country, has revenues exceeding $28 million. Founded by Tom Burrell, the agency was among the first to bring the message that "black people are not dark-skinned white people" to the advertising world (Chandler, 2004). The agency has a blue-chip client base, including McDonald's, Lexus, Crest, Allstate, General Mills, Charmin, Pampers, and Bounty, among others. McDonald's, Burrell's first client in 1972, remains a special client, given the large proportion of African Americans who own or work at the company's outlets (Wentz, 2006). A recent campaign, entitled Baobab, is intended to celebrate the burger chain's contributions to the African American community, a "deeply rooted" relationship that is nurtured 365 days a year, according to Carol Sagers, director of U.S. marketing for McDonald's (Lasare, 2005). In a television ad in the campaign, the animated spot opens with images of a young girl watering a seed that grows into a giant baobab tree, a specimen native to Africa. As the tree is seen growing in an urban community, it starts to drop new seeds, from which sprout illustrations of buildings, students with caps and gowns, and children playing, all aspects of urban culture to which McDonald's, in one way or another, contributes. The spot ends with a final shot of McDonald's 365BLACK logo. The company's 365BLACK Web site (http://www.365black.com), which emphasizes that McDonald's celebrates African American culture yearlong and is one of the top three sites visited on McDonalds.com, is highlighted at the bottom of the ad. A print version of the TV spot appears in Figure 1.2. Burrell Communication's goal is to be at the forefront of research that shows that the African American culture is not a monolith but one of various subcultures with different ideas, needs, and desires that translate into marketplace behavior.

Projections for the Future

In contrast to the hoopla associated with the arrival of the 200 millionth American, this time around, because of the milestone's connection with the politically charged issue of immigration, the celebration of the arrival of the 300 millionth American was significantly more subdued. No fireworks or government-sponsored celebrations—just a written note from President Bush welcoming the milestone as "further proof that the American dream remains as bright and hopeful as ever" (Ohlemacher, 2006). Projections suggest that America in 2050—when the population is expected to reach 400 million—will be a nation with a population that is significantly larger and even less white than it is today. Census Bureau figures suggest that the nation's population will rise by 49% by 2050—to 420 million people. And Americans who are white will no longer make up the majority. Projections suggest that whites who are not Hispanic—the dominant group since this nation was founded in 1776—will see their share of the population drop from 90% in the 1950s to 50% in 2050. Increasingly, the question will be, who is a minority? Robert Lang, head of the Metropolitan Institute at Virginia Tech, notes, "The majority will be the minority and we'll re-label minorities the majority. It's just a matter of time" (Nasser & Overberg, 2004). This profound demographic shift promises to redefine American society at every level. The following Census projections are based on current immigration and birthrates:

- The number of people of Hispanic origin is expected to increase by 2050 to 102.6 million. Their share of the nation's population will almost double to 24.4%.
- The number of blacks is projected to rise by 71%. African Americans will account for 14.6% of the population, up from 12.8%.
- The Asian American population is expected to jump from 12.2 million in 2004 (4.2% of the population) to 33.4 million by 2050, becoming 8% of the population. (Seligman, 2004)

Figure 1.2: Print Ad from McDonald's Baobab Campaign Targeting Blacks

Source: *Advertising Age* (2006) Hispanic Fact Pack: Annual Guide to Hispanic Marketing and Media. Crain Communications. P. 39.

While all eyes are concentrated on the "tipping point" year of 2050, when non-Hispanic whites will no longer comprise the majority of the U.S. population, that shift is expected to occur much earlier—as soon as 2029 by some calculations—among kids. By that date, Hispanics who are two to eleven years of age will comprise 22.9% of the children's population, African Americans will comprise 15.4%, and Asian Americans will comprise 5.3%. The *other* classification will officially push the non-white total to just over 50% (Meyers, 2006).

Summary

The United States is clearly undergoing a dramatic demographic transition. Surprisingly, the size and power of the ethnic market are not yet reflected in the strategic thinking and planning of many American businesses today. Indeed, only a fraction of the Fortune 500 companies are targeting these consumer groups. But the business climate is changing. Increasingly, corporations will have to place increased emphasis on diversity as a revenue driver.

The growing multiculturalism in the United States will create both new opportunities for marketers and new challenges. In terms of the marketing mix, products and services marketed at ethnic groups must reflect their diversity and must be priced, distributed, and promoted appropriately. The advertising messages on behalf of these products and services must also be sensitive to cultural differences. These topics are the subject of chapters 2 and 3.

REFERENCES

Advertising Age (2006). Hispanic Fact Pack: Annual Guide to Hispanic Marketing and Media. Crain Communications. P. 39.

American Heritage Dictionary of the English Language (2000). 4th edition. Boston: Houghton Mifflin.

Brier, N. R. (2004, July/August). A $1 million difference. *American Demographics, 26*(6), 10.

Chandler, D. M. (2004, August). Burrell CEO steps down. *Black Enterprise, 35*(1), 23.

CoActive Marketing Group, Inc., affiliate, Market Vision, executing integrated marketing program for Fisher-Price, Inc. (2004, November 16). *PR Newswire,* p. 1.

Dynamic trends. (2005, July/August). *Hispanic Trends,* 20.

Elsworth, C. (2006, October 18). Frightening surge brings U.S. to 300 m people: 400 m expected by 2050. *National Post,* p. 16.

Fetto, J. (2003, May). Off the map: The baby business. *American Demographics, 25*(4), 40.

Frey, W. H. (2004, July/August). Zooming in on diversity. *Demographics, 26*(6), 27–32.

Grant, S. (2003). Experts highlight formula for multicultural communications. *Public Relations Tactics, 19*(19), 12.

Hoag, C. (2004, November 18). Toy-makers make pitch to U.S. Hispanic market. *Knight-Ridder/ Tribune Business News.*

Humphreys, J. M. (2003). The multicultural economy 2003: America's minority buying power. *Georgia Business and Economic Conditions, 63*(2), 1–27.

Kaplan, D. (2004, December 10). Toy makers target Hispanic youngsters. *Knight Ridder/Tribune Business News,* p. 1.

Lasare, L. (2005, June 1). McDonald's draws on black ties. *Chicago Sun-Times,* p. 67.

Lester, L. Y. (2004, April). America's changing face. *Target Marketing, 27*(4), 26.

Meyers, T. (2006, March 13). Culture mosaic. *Advertising Age,* p. S-1.

Miller, P., & Kemp, H. (2005). *What's black about it.* Ithaca, NY: Paramount Market Publishing.

Nasser, H. E., & Overberg, P. (2004, September 30). Minorities majority in more areas; census shows racial, ethnic shift spreading. *USA Today,* p. A-1.

Ohlemacher, S. (2006, October 18). Hola, 300 millionth American. *San Diego Union Tribune,* p. A-3.

Overberg, P., & Nasser, H. E. (2005, August 11). Minority groups breaking patterns; census finds Hispanics fan out through USA, blacks cluster in South. *USA Today,* p. A-1.

Pew Hispanic Center. (2002). *National survey of Latinos.* Retrieved from http://www.pewhispanic.org/site/docs/pdf/LatinoSurveyReportFinal.pdf

Pickel, M. L. (2006, February 17). The growth of America: 300,000,000. *The Atlanta Journal–Constitution,* p. A-1.

Roberts, S. (2006, January 13). Come October, baby will make 300 million or so. *New York Times,* p. A-1.

Seligman, K. (2004, March 18). U.S. to look a lot like California by 2050/Hispanic and Asian populations to triple. *San Francisco Chronicle,* p. A-1.

U.S. Census Bureau. (2000a). Educational attainment, 2000. In *Profile of the United States: 2000* (Internet release). Retrieved from http://www.census.gov/population/www/pop-profile/profile2000.html.

U.S. Census Bureau. (2000b). Our diverse population: Race and Hispanic origin, 2000. In *Population profile of the United States: 2000* (Internet release). Retrieved from http://www.census.gov/population/www/pop-profile/profile.html.

U.S. Census Bureau. (2004a). The fertility of American women in 2004. In *Population profile of the United States: Dynamic version,* 1–4. Retrieved from http://www.census.gov/population/www/pop-profile/profile.html.

U.S. Census Bureau. (2004b). Money and income in 2004. In *Population profile of the United States: Dynamic version.* Retrieved from http://www.census.gov/population/www/pop-profile/profile.html.

U.S. Department of Commerce (2000, September). *The emerging minority marketplace: Minority purchasing power, 2000–2045.* Minority Business Development Agency. www.myjax-chamber.com/upload/purchasing_power.pdf.

U.S. has as many as 12 million illegal immigrants, report says. (2006, March 8). *San Diego Union-Tribune,* p. A-1.

Walters, A. K. (2005, November 18). Minority education should be a priority, report says. *The Chronicle of Higher Education,* p. A-26.

Wellner, A. S. (2002). The census report. *American Demographics, 24*(1), S-3.

Wentz, L. (2006). New CEOs boost Burrell strengths. *Advertising Age, 77*(2), S-5.

2

The Multicultural Consumer
and the Marketing Mix

The primary focus of this text is advertising. However, because an advertising campaign is part of an overall marketing strategy and must be coordinated with other marketing activities, the role of these other marketing mix elements will be reviewed. Companies targeting one or more ethnic consumer groups must decide whether to adapt their *marketing mix* to those consumers and, if so, to what degree. The concept of a marketing mix, popularized by Jerome McCarthy in *Basic Marketing* (1960), includes the following four *P*s:

1. *Product:* includes a product's design and development, as well as branding and packaging.
2. *Place* (or *distribution*): includes the channels used in moving the product from manufacturer to consumer.
3. *Price:* includes the price at which the product or service is offered for sale and establishes the level of profitability.
4. *Promotion:* includes advertising, personal selling, sales promotions, direct marketing, and publicity. Broadly defined, it also includes sponsorships

and participation in community events, product integration, and even word-of-mouth or buzz marketing efforts.

Tailoring the Marketing Mix

Traditionally, marketers, when they have considered appealing to ethnic consumers, have simply extended their general market campaigns. Virtually all experts today agree that firms should at least tailor portions of their marketing programs when targeting ethnic consumers.

The issue of marketing standardization versus specialization, as it pertains to product, price, distribution, and promotion, will be addressed in this chapter.

Product

The American Marketing Association defines a *product* as "anything that can be offered to a market for attention, acquisition, use, or consumption that might satisfy a want or need" (1960). A product can be thought of in terms of three levels. These three levels, as outlined by Philip Kotler and Gary Armstrong (1990), are illustrated in Figure 2.1.

The *core product* refers to the bundle of benefits the consumer expects to receive from purchasing the item. These benefits can be functional, psychological, social, and/or economic in nature. For example, a consumer may purchase an automobile for purposes of transportation (functional benefit), select a specific style because it is currently in fashion among his group of friends (social benefit), opt for a stick shift over an automatic because it provides better mileage (economic benefit), and choose the color red because it's his favorite (psychological benefit).

The *actual product* includes the specific features and styling of the product, its quality, the brand name, and its packaging.

Finally, the *augmented product* refers to product installation, delivery and credit provided to consumers, warranty, and postpurchase servicing.

Most products can be classified as durable goods, nondurable goods, or services. *Durable goods* are major products, often high-ticket items that tend to last for an extended period of time and, as a result, are purchased rather infrequently. Automobiles, appliances, and furniture are examples of durable goods. *Nondurable goods* are typically lower in price, consumed in a relatively short period of time, and thus purchased frequently. Examples of nondurable goods include food products and personal care items, such as shampoos and toothpaste. *Services* are defined as activities or benefits offered by one party to another that are essentially intangible and do not result in the transfer of

Figure 2.1: Three Levels of a Product

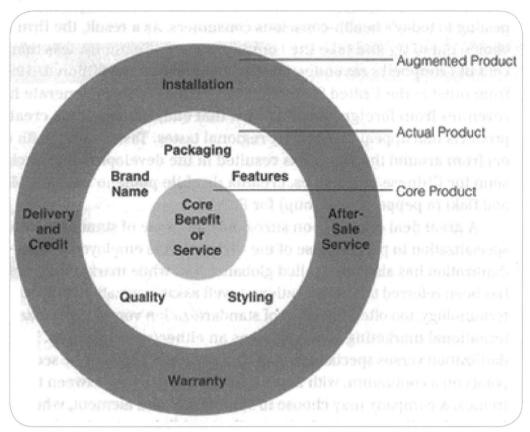

ownership of any kind. Obtaining health insurance, getting a haircut, or having an auto repaired are examples of services that consumers may purchase.

Products can be further distinguished as consumer goods and industrial goods. *Consumer goods* are items purchased by the end consumer for personal consumption. In contrast, *industrial goods* are items a firm purchases so that it may engage in business. Industrial goods include raw materials that actually become part of the end product (for example, in the garment industry, textiles purchased by a garment manufacturer that become part of its line of clothing), goods such as equipment and machinery used in the manufacturing process itself (for instance, industrial-quality sewing machines purchased to enable the creation of the fashions), and supplies and services (such as photocopier paper and long-distance telephone service).

Product planning requires that marketers explore the needs and wants of different ethnic groups and determine how those needs and wants might be satisfied by the firm's products. In addition to deciding which products should be offered, the marketer must determine whether product modifications are necessary.

Product Standardization, Adaptation, and Customization

In most cases, marketers sell exactly the same product to an ethnic consumer that they sell to the general market consumer—also known as *product standardization.* The advantages to this strategy are numerous. Selling an identical product to a number of audiences eliminates duplication of costs related to research and development, product design, and package design. For example, GMC, a division of General Motors (GM), markets its line of Denali vehicles to the general population but also targets African Americans and Hispanics. In each case, the vehicle is identical—with its 380-hp V-8 engine and premium styling appointments, including the signature chrome-plated Denali honeycomb grille as well as available rear camera and voice-assisted navigation system. However, the campaigns are tailored to the individual target groups. Figure 2.2 presents the print ad introducing the 2007 Yukon Denali to the African American consumer.

To ensure that the product is a good fit, marketers must explore differences in consumption patterns, such as whether the product is purchased by relatively the same consumer income group from one market to another, whether most consumers use the product or service for the same purpose, and whether the method of preparation is the same for all target groups. In addition, the marketer must consider the psychosocial characteristics of consumers, such as whether the same basic psychological, social, and economic factors motivate the purchase and use of the product in all target groups and whether the advantages and disadvantages of the product or service in the minds of consumers are basically the same from one segment to another. Finally, the marketer must take into account more general cultural criteria, such as whether some stigma is attached to the product or service or whether the product or service interferes with tradition in one or more of the targeted markets (Britt, 1974).

Regardless of the source of pressure for product modification, the marketer must attempt to measure the costs and revenues associated with marketing a standardized product and compare them with the costs and revenues expected in a product adaptation strategy. Band-Aid Brand bandages provide an excellent example of *product adaptation* (see Figure 2.3). While everyone's blood is red, the bandages used to cover up cuts and scrapes now come in a variety of shades. Johnson & Johnson—the industry leader with over 47% in industry sales—introduced a see-through version of its Band-Aids in the late 1980s (Burns, 1992). Representatives for the company characterized the clear strip as the best solution for people who want an inconspicuous skin color. However, even on the clear Band-Aid, the rectangle over the gauze was rendered in a Caucasian skin tone. To remedy the situation, Johnson & Johnson recently adapted their product, offering ethnic consumers bandages that are available

Figure 2.2: GMC Pitches Yukon Denali to African American Consumers

Figure 2.3: Advertisement for Band-Aid's Perfect Blend Bandages

in three different shades—light, medium and deep—to "actually blend with your skin."

Too often, marketers have attempted to sell products that, while appropriate to the general market, were not particularly well suited to the needs of ethnic consumers. Here, marketers may find that creating a completely new product is the best way to meet the needs of an ethnic market—also known as *product customization.* For example, many ethnic female consumers have different hair care concerns than Caucasian women. Among Hispanic women, 78% name frizz as their top hair care problem. While anti-frizz products are already on the market, *anti-sponge* products are specifically positioned for Hispanic women, because ingredients such as guar and silicone promise to eliminate frizz all day. In early 2006, Procter & Gamble Co. (P&G) boosted its fledgling U.S. Hispanic lineup by introducing Pantene Anti-Sponge/*Anti-Esponjado* shampoo, conditioner, and combing crème. It is also adding an Extra Straight/*Extra Liso* two-in-one shampoo and conditioner to its Extra Liso line, which was introduced in 2004. Besides targeting a fast-growing and lucrative market, the goal of the rollouts is to prevent competitor Unilever from bringing its Sunsilk Anti-Sponge products north from Mexico. WWP Group's Wing Latino, New York, was lead creative on the Pantene launch, which included Hispanic TV and print advertisements (see Figure 2.4). Publicis Groupe's Starcom Media Vest Group handled communications planning and media buying (Neff, 2005).

Packaging and Labeling Decisions

Packaging refers to the design and production of product containers or wrappings. Packaging includes the immediate container (for example, the plastic container surrounding Sure deodorant), a secondary package that is discarded after purchase (the cardboard box in which a container of Sure is sold), and any packaging necessary to ship the product to retailers (such as a cardboard carton containing dozens of packages of Sure deodorant). *Labeling* is also considered part of the packaging and consists of printed information appearing on or along with the packaging.

Packaging has promotional, as well as protective, aspects. In determining whether the same packaging can be used for ethnic markets, marketers must consider the appropriate language. The label must be written in a language that consumers will understand—and this may mean different labels for different ethnic groups. Marketers may attempt to get around this by printing multilingual labels. For example, General Mills has introduced a cereal line called *Para su Familia* (For Your Family). The line includes Frosted Corn Flakes, Frutis, Cinnamon Corn Stars, and Raisin Bran, all with bilingual packaging.

Figure 2.4: Advertisement for Pantene's Anti-Sponge Line Promising "No Frizz"

While General Mills has marketed to Hispanics in varying degrees for more than a decade, Para su Familia marks a serious attempt to capitalize on the Hispanic interest in nutritious meals (Bernstein, 2000). But just translating the language may not be enough. While some companies leave ethnic models off the packaging so that products have a more universal appeal, many more believe in featuring Hispanic, African American, and Asian American models right on the packaging, reasoning that ethnic consumers will instantly recognize that the product was created especially for them.

Place

Marketers must also determine the appropriate channels of distribution. While most consumers typically take the role of marketing intermediaries—such as wholesalers, brokers, distributors, and retailers—for granted, one of the most important decisions a company can make relates to how its products and services are made available for purchase. As Belch and Belch (2007) note, a firm can have an excellent product, at a great price, but it will be of little value unless it is available where the customer wants it, when the customer wants it, and with the proper support and service. Channels of distribution, or the *place* element of the marketing mix, essentially connect the producer of the goods with the end consumer. Some firms may choose not to employ any channel intermediaries and instead sell their products directly to the consumer. Traditionally, Avon Products Inc. has employed this approach. But, for the first time ever, in an attempt to better reach customers of all skin shades, the direct-selling company has opened storefronts in high-density Hispanic and African American markets. The step is an attempt to reach out to urban minorities who may think Avon's products don't work for them. Avon introduced the beauty kiosks in storefronts in cities, including New York, Atlanta, and Chicago, where consumers can actually try out Avon's entire array of foundation shades and Double Impact lipstick shades, as well as other products. Interested consumers then order the cosmetics directly from Avon. The company also developed an in-house multicultural beauty advisory board of twenty-four Avon associates who offer input on hair products, skin care, color, and fragrances for various skin tones (Thompson, 2003).

The vast majority of consumer products companies typically use a network of middlemen to move the product to a retailer—an institution that sells primarily to the final consumer. The country's largest retailer—Wal-Mart—has been particularly aggressive in wooing the United States' fastest-growing ethnic group. Through a program Wal-Mart calls "Store of the Community," every category buyer is responsible for tailoring merchandise to each individual store's demographic. Wal-Mart began stocking a line of bathroom and tabletop accessories from New York restaurateur and cookbook author Zarela Martinez, whose designs are inspired by Mexican folk art and culture. The retailer is also working toward bringing more Latino-flavored women's apparel to its stores, as well as devoting a larger percentage of total space to baby and children's clothing in markets with large Hispanic populations. Wal-Mart began printing its monthly advertising circulars in Spanish, as well as English, and launched its own Hispanic magazine, called *Viviendo* (Living), which it distributes for free at 1,300 stores heavily shopped by Hispanics. The glossy quarterly magazine features profiles of Latino leaders and celebrities next to ads highlighting Wal-Mart's expanding line of products and services geared toward Hispanics. The company teamed up with Sprint Corporation, as well as several other companies, to offer a new prepaid wireless service expressly targeted to Hispanics. And Wal-Mart's three-year-old financial services department offers cut-rate fees on money wire transfers, a big lure for immigrants who support family back home. In a recent study of five hundred Hispanic shoppers by NOP World, a marketing research firm, 36% of respondents chose Wal-Mart as their favorite store. J. C. Penney Company, Sears, and Target tied for second favorite, chosen by 4% of respondents (Zimmerman, 2005). Clearly, Wal-Mart's efforts appear to be paying off.

Price

In pricing products, marketers must determine whether to standardize prices across markets or to differentiate prices among target groups. In setting a *standard price,* a firm establishes a uniform price for its product all across the country. However, that price may be too high for some consumers. A marketer may opt to use a *differentiated pricing strategy* in which price is based on a number of factors and is not determined in isolation from the other marketing mix elements. For example, to appeal to the burgeoning Hispanic market, Sprint introduced a new international calling plan, allowing customers who pay an additional $4.00 monthly recurring charge the ability to call anywhere in Mexico anytime for just nine cents a minute from anywhere in the United States while on the Sprint Nationwide Personal Communications Service (PCS) Network. The competitive rates provided with this plan significantly lowered the price for wireless calls to Latin America—allowing Hispanic consumers to stay in touch with friends and loved ones ("Sprint Product Suite," 2004). One area about which ethnic marketers must be extra cautious is price discrimination—also known as race-based pricing. This issue will be dealt with in greater detail in chapter 8, which deals with ethics and social responsibility.

Pricing Objectives and Strategies

Marketers traditionally adjust pricing objectives based on the specific conditions of the markets to which they appeal. Typical pricing objectives include profit maximization, return on an investment, and increases in total sales volume or market share. In pursuing pricing objectives, a firm may select from a variety of pricing strategies. The pricing strategy adopted will, in turn, impact the other marketing factors. A firm might engage in a *market penetration* strategy, which entails establishing a relatively low price with the goal of stimulating consumer interest. The firm accepts a lower per-unit return in hopes of capturing a large share of the market and discouraging competition. Once a satisfactory level of market share is obtained, the firm typically raises prices to increase profitability. Penetration pricing is commonly employed with low-cost consumer products and tends to be most effective with price-sensitive consumers.

In a situation in which either no or very few competitors exist or in which consumers are willing to pay a high price, perhaps because a product is unique or innovative, marketers may opt to "skim the cream" from the market. The aim of a *market skimming* strategy is to obtain a premium price for a product—at least initially. This approach allows marketers to recoup research and development costs quickly as well as generate profits. Prices are typically reduced once competitors enter the market or in order to attract more price-conscious consumers.

If a number of competitors already exist in a given market or if a product is essentially undistinguishable from the competition, a firm may engage in *competitive pricing*. Here, a manufacturer sets product prices at or just below those of competitors. This approach requires constant monitoring of competitors' prices so that the marketer can prominently display a lower price in promotional messages. In contrast, with a *prestige pricing* strategy, product prices are set high and remain high. Promotional messages are aimed at a select clientele who can afford to pay the higher prices, and product quality and service are highlighted.

Clearly, the actual cost involved in manufacturing, distributing, and promoting a product will play a role in the price charged. If specific markets require product modifications, these will need to be calculated into the price of the product.

The number and nature of competitors manufacturing similar products or providing similar services will influence pricing decisions. The fewer the competitors, the greater the pricing flexibility. The intensity of demand for a certain product also impacts its price. Higher prices may be charged where demand is buoyant, and lower prices may be charged where demand is weak—even if production costs are the same in both instances. Total demand for a product is the net result of the combination of (a) consumer satisfaction derived from the product's bundle of benefits, (b) the size of the market, and (c) the market's ability to purchase the product. Consumers must not only be willing to purchase a product but also be able to purchase the product.

Promotion

Promotion is the fourth and final component in the marketing mix. Promotion includes advertising, sales promotion, public relations and publicity, and personal selling. In addition, the areas of direct marketing, sponsorships and community events, product integrations, and even word-of-mouth advertising will be addressed.

Advertising

Advertising, according to the Definitions Committee of the American Marketing Association, "is any paid form of non-personal presentation and promotion of ideas, goods or services by an identified sponsor" (*Journal of Marketing*, 1948). Several aspects of this definition deserve further explication. The "paid" aspect refers to the fact that the advertiser must purchase time and space for the message. "Non-personal" indicates that the message appears in the mass media, which means there is little opportunity for feedback from the message receiver. Because of this, advertisers utilize research to determine how a specific target audience might interpret and respond to a message prior to its distribution. Finally, the "identified" aspect refers to the fact that the media require sponsors to identify themselves.

As with the other marketing mix elements, advertising can be standardized (whereby the same advertising theme is employed for the ethnic market as is employed for the general market) or specialized (in which case the messages are adapted for ethnic markets). Increasingly, however, ethnic consumers are frustrated with general audience campaigns. A recent investigation found that nearly 50% of both Hispanics and African Americans surveyed agreed with the statement that "very little, if any, of the marketing and advertising I see has any relevance to me." Such data should raise a red flag to marketers. Nearly three-quarters of Hispanics agreed with that statement that "there should be more television or other commercials directed specifically to Hispanic consumers, while 69% of African Americans agreed that there should be more commercial messages targeted specifically at them ("Profound Shifts," 2005).

Fortunately, marketers are beginning to pay attention to such data. Over 85% of respondents to a 2004 multicultural marketing survey of its members by the Association of National Advertisers (ANA) said that they are marketing to Hispanics, up from 70% in a similar ANA study done in 2002. However, the gap is growing between the emphasis on the Hispanic market and the targeting of African Americans, with just 60% of respondents saying they market to the African American segment—a figure that is virtually unchanged from 59% in the 2002 survey. The targeting of Asian Americans is elevated somewhat, up to 35% of marketers, from 27% in 2002. Looking at how marketers define multicultural marketing, 85% said that they create separate ads for different market segments and use multicultural media. Just 7% said that they favor advertising that appeals to both the general and multicultural market. And none admitted to just translating general market ads for a multicultural audience, although many marketers do start that way before developing original, creative advertising (Wentz, 2004b).

In addition to strategic decisions, such as whether to standardize or specialize campaigns, the marketer must decide on the appropriate message content. Advertising is effective only if it is able to both gain the attention of the target audience and communicate the product benefits clearly. If the target audience is to receive the advertising message, it must appear in the appropriate medium. Media decisions include whether to employ ethnic or general audience media. Tailoring messages to Hispanics will be addressed in chapter 4. Chapter 5 is devoted to reaching African American consumers, and chapter 6 focuses on the Asian American community.

Sales Promotion

Sales promotion consists of a variety of techniques designed to support and complement both advertising and personal selling. The goal of sales promotion is to stimulate immediate consumer purchasing and/or dealer effectiveness. Sales promotion includes premiums, samples, point-of-purchase displays, and cents-off coupons. Such efforts may induce trial purchases of products, as well as maintain consumer loyalty. The perception has long been that ethnic consumers redeem significantly fewer cents-off coupons than the general population. And, when looking at overall redemption figures, one might indeed conclude that ethnic consumers really don't use coupons to a great extent. Yet, Green (1997) found that coupon use is facilitated through the media to which individuals are exposed daily. Green found that a significantly greater number of Anglo Americans report subscribing to a newspaper, the media vehicle in which a significant amount of coupons are distributed. Ethnic consumers are disproportionately exposed to print media sources in comparison to their Anglo American counterparts. Eighty-seven percent of whites sampled reported reading a daily paper, in comparison to 53% of blacks and 42% of Hispanics. These numbers are approximately the same with respect to readership of the Sunday newspaper, the newspaper day in which the majority of coupons are distributed. Furthermore, consumers who read primarily ethnic-oriented newspapers are less likely to use coupons than consumers who read general-audience newspapers, because these media are not as widely used by marketers for coupon distribution. However, no difference in coupon usage was found between Anglo American and ethnic consumers in terms of in-store coupon redemption. Thus, managers designing promotions targeting ethnic consumers would do well to focus more on in-store advertising by promoting items at the point of sale. Direct mail (discussed below) may be another way to target ethnic households with coupons and other promotions without the likely wasted coverage of newspaper advertising.

Sweepstakes and contests can create interest in and excitement about a company's product or service and can increase the likelihood that advertising campaigns will receive attention. Maggi, which manufactures soups and sauce mixes, has been a trusted name in the kitchen for generations. In appealing to the Hispanic consumer, Maggi recognized that today's Latina is more independent and concerned with current trends, yet she also wants to celebrate her culture and keep traditions alive. So Maggi made a traditional Hispanic celebration the heart of its sweepstakes. Maggi offered young Latinas an opportunity to win $5,000 toward their dream *Quinceañera*. A Quinceañera is a celebration of a young girl's fifteenth birthday and symbolizes her continuing journey into womanhood. Quinceañeras are celebrated throughout the United States and Latin America and are embraced by all Latino cultures. In a young girl's eyes, everything from the gown to the meal must be perfect. Notes Nancy Lopez-Pedroza, Maggi marketing manager

> Families have brought Maggi to the table for years and this is an opportunity to play a larger role in passing traditions and values from one generation to the next. Since the meal is an important element in the celebration and traditional dishes are often served at the reception, it makes sense for Maggi to sponsor a Quinceañera. ("Giving Latinas," 2004)

Such cultural sensitivity ensures that promotional efforts are a success with the ethnic consumer. Activities may also be directed at wholesalers, distributors, and retailers. Price deals, trade shows, and contests are typical trade promotion activities. The overall use of sales promotion efforts—whether directed at consumers or the trade—appears to be on the increase.

While many companies effectively utilize sales promotion tools to help sell their products to ethnic groups, marketers must be aware of potential pitfalls. Because of cultural differences among ethnic consumers, promotional incentives that have proven successful with one segment may not be as effective with another.

Public Relations

Public relations involves a variety of efforts to create and maintain a positive image of an organization with its various publics. *Corporate public relations* typically focuses on an organization's noncustomer publics, such as employees, stockholders, suppliers/distributors, governmental agencies, labor unions, the media, and various activist groups, as well as the public at large. When the focus is specifically an organization's interactions with current and potential consumers, this marketing-oriented aspect of public relations is called *marketing public relations,* or MPR for short. MPR is defined as "the process of planning, executing and evaluating programs that encourage purchase and consumer satisfaction through credible communication of information and impressions that identify companies and their products with the needs, wants, concerns and interests of consumers" (Harris, 1993). In short, MPR supports marketing's product and sales focus by increasing the brand and company's credibility with consumers.

MPR is often further delineated as involving either proactive or reactive public relations (J. Goldman, 1984). *Proactive MPR* is offensively, rather than defensively, oriented and opportunity seeking, rather than problem solving. Proactive MPR is a tool for communicating a brand's merits and is typically used in conjunction with advertising, sales promotion, and personal selling. Proactive MPR is also often employed when introducing a new product and announcing product revisions.

In contrast, *reactive MPR* is undertaken as a result of external pressures and challenges that might be brought on by competitive actions, shifts in consumer attitudes, changes in government policy, or other external influences. Reactive MPR generally deals with changes that have negative consequences for a company. An unanticipated marketplace event can place an organization in a vulnerable position, requiring reactive MPR (Shimp, 2003). When a major crisis strikes, judicious public relations strategies are essential to saving the brand's image. A mismanaged crisis brings on the dreaded "Seven Plagues of Unhappy Repercussions": extended duration/negative press, angry customers and shareholders, lawsuits, government investigations, public interest groups, low employee morale/productivity, and a drop in stock price and earnings (Cohen, 2000). Each plague begets another. The longer the story is covered, the bigger the bite to a company's reputation and bottom line. Denny's provides an excellent example: The company was at the forefront of one of the most widely publicized corporate crises of the last decade. Denny's problems began in early 1991, when a newspaper reported race discrimination charges by a group of students at a Denny's restaurant in San Jose, California. The story recounted how a group of eighteen African American students had been asked to prepay for their meals while a smaller group of white customers had not. The African American group quickly hired a local civil rights attorney; meanwhile, former Denny's employees began talking to the news media, disclosing that some restaurant workers in California had been instructed by their district manager to discourage African American patronage in a process known as "black-out." Explanations offered by local managers did little to douse the fire. Many Denny's restaurants in urban areas of California, often heavily populated by minorities, were experiencing loitering and safety issues related to gangs and other groups who visited in the late night and early morning hours, they argued. "Walk-outs," or customers who leave without paying bills, were also becoming a serious problem, costing Denny's more than $3 million annually. To deal with these problems, some restaurant managers implemented their own local procedures during these problem security hours. Apparently, management at corporate headquarters in Spartanburg, South Carolina, was either unaware of the growing public relations crisis or saw it as a remote issue (Randall, 1998). The situation began to snowball, with more reports of discrimination from Denny's customers around the country. In 1994, the company was required to give more than $1.5 million to civil rights groups and the United Negro College Fund (UNCF) as part of two class-action discrimination suits. By 1995, the company had paid $54 million to nearly 300,000 customers who said they were subjected to racially discriminatory behavior at at least one of the 1,600 Denny's restaurants in the United States. Company-sponsored research showed that many blacks believed Denny's managers and servers provided lower-quality service to African American customers. And so, in 1997, the restaurant chain launched a $5 million television and radio advertising campaign designed to ease lingering resentments that had kept many black customers away ("Denny's Woos," 1997). Clearly, it pays to manage a crisis well. And, while a company doesn't necessarily get off scot-free when it manages a crisis effectively, the damage is relatively short-term in contrast to damage caused by a problem that is poorly managed.

Publicity, as part of the broader function of public relations, involves seeking favorable comments on the product/service and/or firm itself via news stories, editorials, or announcements in the mass media. In contrast to advertising, publicity is not directly paid for by the company, nor does the company have control over the content or frequency of the coverage. The advantages of such free publicity are both credibility and message length. Information conveyed through nonadvertising media are generally considered more credible by the public. In addition, a news or feature treatment of an issue is typically longer than a thirty-second spot or an advertisement in the print media. Marketers attempting to reach a Hispanic audience will find Hispanic PR Wire of value. Launched in 2000, the service offers Spanish translations of English-language news releases and sends out those releases in both languages to targeted reporters and media. Clients can choose from fourteen distribution channels focused on technology, immigration, or other fields. Or they can opt to reach nearly two hundred Latino organizations, such as the National Council of La Raza, or the five-thousand-plus elected Latino officials across the country (Hemlock & Mann, 2001).

However, caution must be exercised in the distribution of press releases. While GM and its divisions generate reams of press releases, the company is careful to pick and choose only those that make sense for the Hispanic media. The company has found that Hispanic media are mostly focused on issues that impact the community and on things that can help new immigrants adapt to this country, such as how to get a loan, a job, or a house or how to cover college tuition. Furthermore, the Hispanic community ranks family values highly, thus GM attempts to use this angle in their press releases. "When we talk about our autos, we do so from the standpoint of safety for the family," notes Brenda Rios, GM's manager of diversity communication. GM keeps Hispanic journalists and editors updated on GM news and announcements through *GM Noticiaj*—a biweekly newsletter created specifically for the Hispanic media (Schnabel, 2005).

Both press releases and newsletters are important communication tools employed in public relations, but they will surely miss their mark if they do not communicate in the correct language. The challenges of working with Asian American media differ greatly from the African American and Hispanic media. Both African American and Hispanic media, for the most part, speak in one language: English and Spanish, respectively. But the languages used by Asian American media are as diverse as the groups they serve. Before sending out press releases, they must be translated for each respective community. Most Asian newspapers are written in a specific Asian community's native language. A press release will have a much better chance of being published if it is in the appropriate language. Indeed, with the exception of Filipino American media (which prefer submissions in English), many Asian media won't even consider a news item if it is not in their native tongue. ("Angles on Appealing," 2004).

Public relations practitioners also have a number of additional tools at their disposal, such as press conferences, company-sponsored events, and participation in community activities, among others. It is the responsibility of public relations personnel to position the firm as a good corporate citizen that is involved with, and concerned about, the future of the community. According to the American Cancer Society (ACS), African American men are more likely to develop prostate cancer than men of other races, and they tend to develop it at a younger age and in more aggressive forms. For this reason, the ACS recommends that African American men begin prostate cancer testing at age forty-five, or younger if they have other risk factors. Acknowledging these worrisome statistics, Anheuser-Busch partnered with 100 Black Men of

America Inc., the National Council of Negro Women, and the Institute for the Advancement of Multicultural and Minority Medicine to create Set the Date. The two-year initiative asked African American women to urge the men in their lives to get tested for prostate cancer. To combat the crisis of prostate cancer in the African American community, Set the Date includes testing at African American events and conventions across the nation as well as public campaigns.

> At Anheuser-Busch we strongly believe in using our resources to make a difference in the community. By raising awareness about the effects of prostate cancer, we hope to increase the number of men receiving early testing and creating more prostate cancer conquerors like Bishop Long and Billy Davis Jr. ("Anheuser-Busch," 2004)

notes Johnny Furr Jr., vice president of Sales Development and Community Affairs for Anheuser-Busch Inc. Company management and employees may contribute to the community's social and economic development via participation in a variety of activities: civic and youth groups, cultural or recreational activities, charitable fundraising events, and so on.

Personal Selling

Personal selling involves individual, personal contact with the customer, with the intent of either making an immediate sale or developing a long-term relationship that will eventually result in a sale. Personal selling can take a variety of forms, including sales calls at a customer's place of business or a consumer's home or customer assistance at a retail outlet. Because it typically involves both communication and personal contact, personal selling is closely linked to the unique cultural characteristics of an ethnic group. Unilever recently formed a partnership with H-E-B, a Texas food retailer known for its appeal to ethnic shoppers, in order to attract more Hispanic women into the health and beauty aisles. The manufacturer had taken note of H-E-B's Beauty Advisor Program, in which store advisors greet shoppers and help them make selections, and saw a natural fit for its *Secretes de Belleza* (Beauty Secrets) campaign. "One area where Hispanic women like to shop is home and personal care," notes Annette Fonte, senior multicultural marketing manager at Unilever. "Personal appearance is very important to them. It's not just about making their houses smell good or their food taste good, it's also important to look great" (McTaggart, 2005). Unilever worked with H-E-B to train three hundred beauty advisors. Then, during store events, advisors provided free personal consultations and beauty demonstrations to Latina shoppers, educating them on beauty and skin care, using the Secretes de Belleza brands and products, including Dove, Pond's, Vaseline Intensive Care, Suave, Caress, and Finesse. Unilever was extraordinarily pleased with the H-E-B partnership and plans to expand the program in the future (McTaggart, 2005).

Personal selling is often the most expensive element in the promotion mix on a per-customer basis. In addition to such face-to-face contact, personal selling may also include contact through some form of telecommunication, such as telephone sales, which can help to reduce costs. To ensure that every contact with an ethnic customer pays off, many firms are instituting training programs. For example, to help employees understand different ethnic groups, Diversity Manager Clark Duncan at AT&T Universal Card Services conducts workshops on ethnic—as well as gender—differences using interactive, video-based courses designed to stimulate discussion.

> What we do in the classes transfers into everyday work in dealing with customers. We have a lot of diverse customers calling in from all over the country. The better we can understand where they are coming from, the better we can deal with them. Diversity is all about trying to see the world through other people's eyes. (Hotchkiss, 1996)

Since classes began in 1994, well over half of the company's four thousand employees have taken one or both of the classes. The classes are required for employees seeking leadership positions. Because personal selling generally involves a greater degree of feedback than advertising, the impact of the sales presentation often can be assessed directly through consumers' reactions. This provides sales representatives with the opportunity to tailor their communications.

Direct Marketing

Traditionally, direct marketing has not been considered an element in the promotion mix. However, because of the increasingly important role that direct marketing plays in the communications programs of many different kinds of organizations, it is included here. Indeed, direct marketing is currently growing faster than virtually any other form of promotion. The reasons for this are numerous. The widespread use of credit cards and the convenience of toll-free numbers have made it significantly easier for consumers in most markets to respond to direct marketing offers. From the marketer's perspective, the desire for greater accountability of the effectiveness of a promotional effort has encouraged the use of this approach. In most instances, messages are sent to a known individual, making it possible to track whether that customer did or did not respond. This is clearly a benefit that most advertising and promotions cannot offer. But probably the most significant recent advance has been the ability of firms to collect massive amounts of information about their customers via computer databases. The data are used to help marketers understand who their customers are and determine what they do and don't like and when they are most likely to purchase. Such information, of course, helps to increase the likelihood that those receiving a direct marketing offer will indeed respond.

Direct marketing refers to a way of doing business—one in which the marketer attempts to sell goods directly to the consumer without the aid of a wholesaler or retailer. Messages are designed to solicit a measurable response and/or transaction from the target audience. Direct marketing is seen as much more personal than advertising because it incorporates a degree of two-way communication. Direct marketers may employ a variety of media, placing such messages on the Internet, on radio and television, and in newspapers and magazines, as well as via catalogues.

Despite the recent competition from telemarketing, e-mail, and other direct marketing options, direct mail remains a primary advertising vehicle. However, the sheer volume of direct mail coming to the average American's household makes gaining a competitive advantage very difficult. This is of less concern when marketing to ethnic groups. Various studies have shown that racial and ethnic markets receive only a fraction of the direct mail volume received by the general population. Recent statistics show that, while the average Anglo American receives some three hundred pieces of direct mail each year, the average Asian American receives a mere one hundred (Yorgey, 1999). And Hispanic households receive even fewer direct mail pieces—just twenty per year (Barbagallo, 2003). This translates into less competition in the mailbox—for now.

Spurred by the census figures revealing the significant gains in minority population and spending power, marketers are increasingly attempting to target ethnic groups via direct mail. The heart of any direct mail campaign is the mailing list. However, in terms of reaching ethnic consumers, the list industry is an emerging market. A number of unique challenges face the direct marketers attempting to reach Hispanics, African Americans, and Asian Americans. To identify ethnic group members, many marketers use mailing lists that are based on ethnic surnames. They typically cross-check the surnames with demographic information that shows pockets of ethnic group members in locations around the nation. When direct marketers get it right, it pays off. Because Hispanics receive so little direct mail—and even less in Spanish—when they do, they tend to open it. But sometimes marketers get it wrong. Dick Seng received a mailing, printed in Chinese on one side, and English on the other, which offered calls to China for just forty-two cents per minute. While Seng found the rate great, he didn't know a soul in China and wondered why MCI had sent the piece to him. He later realized that the company thought *Seng* was a Chinese surname. In fact, Seng's ancestry is German. Clearly, surnames aren't always an accurate indicator of a person's ethnic background (Silverman,

2000). Fortunately, advances in technology will help to more accurately target ethnic consumers. Data miners are starting to cross-reference ethnic surnames with specific consumer behavior patterns, such as checking whether someone with a Hispanic surname also subscribes to a Spanish-language magazine. But such efforts obviously increase the cost of mailing lists and may take more time than marketers are willing to spend.

But even these more sophisticated techniques may not guarantee that a firm will hit its mark. For example, someone may speak Spanish but may not want materials sent in Spanish. Other consumers may have an ethnic background but not speak the language because they are third- or fourth-generation Americans. Still others may have taken an ethnic name by marriage but never learned the language to which that name is attached (Silverman, 2000). Once the ethnic list industry overcomes these growing pains, direct mail is sure to prove a particularly effective tool in reaching ethnic consumers.

Sponsorships

Sponsorships are one of the fastest-growing forms of marketing today. A number of reasons have been given for the tremendous growth in sponsorship activities: the escalating costs of traditional advertising media, the fragmentation of media audiences, the growing diversity in leisure activities, and the ability to reach targeted groups of people economically (Arens, 2002). In addition, by attaching their names to special events and causes, companies are able to avoid the clutter inherent in traditional advertising media.

> Sponsorship involves two main activities: 1) an exchange between a sponsor (such as a brand) and a sponsee (such as a sporting event) whereby the latter receives a fee and the former obtains the right to associate itself with the activity sponsored and 2) the marketing of the association by the sponsor. Both activities are necessary if the sponsorship fee is to be a meaningful investment. (Cornwell & Maignan, 1998)

The objectives of sponsorships include: increasing the awareness of a company and its brands, enhancing the corporate or brand image, and showing corporate responsibility. While the primary audience of current and potential consumers may be valuable, even more important may be the secondary audience. Sponsorships can be a powerful public relations tool. The company sponsoring an event may also be communicating with stockholders, community leaders, and employees.

Sponsorships can take a variety of forms. The bulk of sponsorship dollars go to sports events (such as golf and tennis tournaments, motor sports, professional sports leagues or teams, and, of course, the Olympics). Each year thousands of ski enthusiasts assemble for the National Brotherhood of Skiers (NBS) Summit. In 2005, six thousand participants dropped more than $3 million for lodging, lift tickets, rental equipment, and entertainment during the week-long event held in Vail, Colorado. Subaru latched on to the NBS's mission to fund development of Olympic skiers and also offered members $3,000 off a new car purchase. And Fate Clothing Co. hooked up with Bacardi's Bombay Sapphire gin and *Black Outdoorsman Magazine* (http://www.blackoutdoorsman. com) for a fashion show at the summit featuring urban-influenced skiwear (Beirne, 2005).

Sponsors may also support entertainment attractions (rock concerts, for example, or the theatre) or festivals, fairs, and annual events. An excellent way for marketers to reach out to Asian Americans is to sponsor Lunar New Year celebrations. This holiday celebrates the beginning of the New Year based on the cycles of the moon. Though many associate the holiday with the Chinese, it is also celebrated by Koreans, who call it *Solnal* for the first month of the New Year, and by the Vietnamese, who call it *Tet* to honor the first morning of the first day of the Lunar New Year. Other groups that celebrate the Lunar New Year are those from Singapore, Malaysia, and Indonesia. Cities around the United States with significant Asian populations typically have large-scale celebrations that include parades and festivals. San Francisco hosts the oldest and largest Chinese New Year parade outside of Asia. The celebration dates back to the 1860s, when recent Chinese immigrants, carrying banners and colorful flags, lit firecrackers and pounded drums to drive away evil spirits as they marched down what is now called Grant Avenue in Chinatown. Today, it has become a huge marketing event, with major corporate sponsors helping to highlight Chinese culture (Ford, 2005). The event is attended by Chinese and non-Chinese alike. In addition to becoming a sponsor or exhibitor at a community event, there are a number of other ways that organizations can participate in the Lunar New Year. For example, advertisers can send Lunar New Year's cards—Target now carries a variety, along with the traditional red gift envelope used for giving money—once found only in Asian markets. Marketers can also advertise in Asian American media and mainstream media using a Lunar New Year theme. J. C. Penney's, AT&T, and Fitzgerald Auto Malls filled the pages of Washington, D.C., area ethnic publications with ads wishing readers a prosperous New Year during that city's celebration (Ly, 2003).

Companies may also choose to form an alliance with a nonprofit. This is also known as *cause-related marketing*. Cause-related marketing allows firms to enhance their brands' images and sales, and nonprofit partners obtain additional funding by aligning their causes with corporate sponsors. While the sponsored event or organization may be nonprofit, cause-related sponsorships are not the same as philanthropy. Philanthropy is support of a cause without any commercial incentive. Cause-related marketing is used to achieve specific commercial objectives. Though there are several varieties of cause-related marketing, the most common form involves a company contributing to a designated cause every time a customer undertakes some action (such as buying a product or redeeming a coupon) that supports the company and its brands (Varadarajan & Menon, 1988). For example, for over fifty-five years, P&G has supported the UNCF and its mission in communities across the country, believing the organization makes a positive difference for countless young African Americans. P&G annually contributes more than $1 million to expand educational opportunities for the more than 65,000 students UNCF supports. In 2004, P&G enhanced its support of UNCF through a variety of activities, including the sponsorship of several regional special events and the establishment of a Back-to-School national marketing campaign. The cause-related campaign was supported by several P&G brands, including Tide, Bounty, Charmin, Pantene, Olay, and Pampers. Distributed through Sunday newspapers in the fall of 2004, the P&G Back-to-School BrandSaver coupon book was created to elevate the profile of the UNCF. Reaching more than half of the homes in the United States, or nearly 55 million Americans, proceeds from consumer purchases of participating P&G products were donated to the UNCF ("United Negro College Fund," 2003). Regardless of the form that a sponsorship takes, successful sponsorships require a meaningful fit among the brand, the event or cause, and the ethnic market.

Product Integration

Heralded by many as the next big trend in marketing, consumer-product integration into media content, such as TV, films, video games, and even music, is showing increasingly positive results. Originally known as *product placement,* the tactic is now beginning to go under the moniker of *product integration* (Fitzgerald, 2003). In the United States, product placement in television literally dates back to the 1940s, when shows, such as *Texaco Star Theatre* and the *Colgate Comedy Hour,* were advertiser funded. Back then, there were no separate commercials. Instead, the star of the show would break off to plug the sponsor's product. The system worked well as long as there were only three television networks, because advertisers were rewarded with enormous viewing figures. But, as more channels were created, the economics of solo sponsorship were undermined by fragmenting audiences and rising production costs. Eventually, the networks took over program production and introduced the concept of the multiadvertiser commercial break. Now, economics are undermining the system again. With hundreds of channels being created, heavy demand for programming is raising the cost of advertising while the number of audiences per channel decline. As a result, the financially squeezed networks are having to rethink the rules that, until recently, kept advertisers out of programs (Tomkins, 2002). Product placement is also being driven by advertiser's concerns. Advertisers' confidence in the effectiveness of the traditional thirty-second spot is waning, based in good part on the findings of a recent Roper poll. The Roper survey revealed that 39% of Americans said they "often" switch to another channel when ads come on, a figure that's up 25 points from 1985. Another 19% said they turn down the TV or mute it, a 10-point increase. In fact, one of the fastest-growing gadgets that respondents said they can't live without is the remote control; 44% of respondents consider it a necessity (only 23% did in 1992). And 76% feel that advertising is "shown in far too many places now, you can't get away from it," a response that jumped 10 points since just 1998 (Ebenkamp, 2001). Sprinkled into the mix is the fear of new technology that allows viewers to eliminate television commercials altogether. TiVo and SONICblue of the United States have introduced digital video recorders (DVRs) with internal hard drives instead of cassette tapes, allowing commercials to be skipped or eliminated with a click or two of the remote control. So far, only about 8.9% of U.S. households have a DVR device, but analysts predict that could jump to 36% of U.S. households by 2007, as satellite and cable operators incorporate the technology into their set-top boxes. Hispanics appear to have a particular appetite for DVRs. According to Simmons NCS/NHCS Spring 2004 survey of DVR ownership, 3.8% of Hispanic adults have a DVR, and 9.8% said they plan to purchase one in the next twelve months. That compares to 2.6% DVR ownership by non-Hispanic adults, of whom 4.4% said they plan to purchase one in the coming year (Wentz, 2004b).

While permissible in films, traditionally, payment in exchange for product placement on television was illegal in the United States. The federal communication code required broadcasters to acknowledge any paid promotions in their program credits. Brand name products could appear in TV shows without acknowledgment, only if the manufacturer had not paid for airtime and if the products were "reasonably related" to the content of the show (Jacobson & Mazur, 1995). But advertisers have found ways to get around the rules. Today, the deals are coming in under the euphemisms of *product integration* and *branded content*. There is increased pressure toward such ads from several sources. Advertisers are worried that DVRs are encouraging more consumers to fast-forward through commercials, and networks are eager to keep their sponsors happy because they are fighting dwindling viewership and increased competition from the Internet. Hence, viewers are seeing more and more branded content. And product placement has now come to Spanish-language television. In an effort to be more relevant to its U.S. Hispanic audience, NBC-owned Telemundo produced four of its hour-long nightly novelas rather than relying on the imports from Latin America that have always been the programming staples for Spanish-language TV networks in the United States. Verizon was one of the first to integrate its brand into the novelas. In one scene, a character uses caller ID as she waits for a call about her kidnapped father. In another scene, a woman gives an English lesson to a young man she has a crush on by showing him how to photograph a flower with her phone. For Verizon, it was a chance to show how the products are used. Linda Lane Gonzalez, chief executive officer (CEO) of Viva Partnership, a Miami-based Hispanic agency that buys media for Verizon Wireless, notes that, in meetings with the networks' marketing executives, do's and don'ts were discussed. For instance, the phone was not to be used during the novela's abduction scene or while the caller was driving in a car or in a bar. And the camera feature was to be used in a well-lit scene, so that the picture would show up. But, writers and directors don't go along with all the suggestions. Ms. Gonzalez, for instance, had hoped that a novela character would mention that Verizon had the best wireless service. That didn't happen (Wentz, 2004a). There is a growing concern among Hollywood's top TV producers regarding advertisers dictating story lines. Writers Guild of America, West, President Patric Verrone notes,

> When it goes beyond putting a can of soup on the table, when it's putting a can of soup on the table and having the characters talk about the creamy goodness of the soup, or when their next door neighbor has to hear all the recipes, that's when it encroaches into our sector. (Taylor, 2006)

Writers say they recognize that ad integration is here to stay; however, their primary concern is that they will be forced to work a product into a story line in a way that is not organic. They don't want to be compelled to have their characters use products that are inappropriate to their personalities or lifestyles. What they want is to negotiate with networks in a process that gives creators a say in what can and can't be done. Representatives of the Writers Guild of America want formal talks on the issue to begin before negotiations for a new guild contract take place.

Product placements have also appeared in films for decades. However, until relatively recently, product plugs were the result of an informal barter system between advertisers and film producers. In exchange for featuring a particular brand of auto in a movie, for example, the auto manufacturer would provide wheels for the film's stars during the shoot. Paid product placements were pioneered in the 1980s, and Steven Spielberg's 1982 film *E. T.* is widely credited with starting the trend—a trend that turned out to be quite profitable to the advertiser. When the alien on *E. T.* nibbled on Reese's Pieces candy on-screen, sales of the sweet soared by over 60%. While, in the past, a film might have one or two such sponsors, today's films boast literally dozens. The recent James Bond film *Die Another Day* features James Bond driving an Aston Martin, checking the time on his Omega Seamaster, mixing his martini with Finlandia, flying on British Airways, standing at a bar covered by the distinctive blue bottles of Welsh water company Ty Nant, and toasting with Bollinger champagne—risking allegations that the Bond films are becoming little more than extended product ads. Today, there are dozens of agencies that arrange cash deals between filmmakers and corporate sponsors. A corporation will typically retain a product-placement agency for an annual fee, then pay for each placement in a film. Placement fees vary according to the prominence of the plug. Variables include whether the product is used in the background or foreground; whether a character in the program touches the product, wears the product, or talks about the product; and whether the product is featured in a product-centered episode (such as the *Seinfeld* Junior Mints episode) (Fitzgerald, 2003). Clearly, the more prominent the placement, the greater the impact on brand name awareness and recall.

Word-of-Mouth Advertising and Buzz Marketing

Marketers increasingly recognize that in order to cut through the ever-increasing advertising clutter, they must bring their messages to consumers in new and different ways. Consumers—and ethnic consumers in particular—rely on family members, friends, neighbors, associates, and co-workers for much product-related information. Marketers have adopted this concept of word-of-mouth communication through social networks and turned it from something that typically occurs spontaneously into something deliberate. Belch and Belch explain that the "practice includes a variety of techniques, such as handing out product samples, providing products to influential people and encouraging them to talk about the brand to others, building Web communities so consumers can chat about their product experiences online, and even hiring actors to talk up a brand in public places" (2007, p. 135). Clearly, when an accepted member of a social circle talks up a product, it is seen as significantly more credible by the consumer than information provided by an advertiser. BzzAgency, an online company, recently launched the Hispanic BzzChannel, a Hispanic version of its volunteer-based marketing program. Relationships and personal connections are crucial to Hispanic populations, so word-of-mouth promotions are a natural fit. A number of marketers have already signed up for the program, including Liz Claiborne, Levi Strauss & Co.'s Dockers brand, and Cadbury Schweppes's Clamato tomato juice. BzzChannel is a bilingual Web site that allows visitors to toggle directly between English and Spanish versions of each page. Volunteers, called BzzAgents, sign up via the Web and are sent samples and background information on products from marketing campaigns that match their agency profiles. After using the product, the agents are encouraged to share their opinions of the product with friends, family, and even strangers. After posting detailed stories online about how they mentioned the products through word of mouth, agents get points that eventually earn them rewards. Clamato—the tomato-based beverage—was the first Hispanic campaign launched on BzzChannel. The brand has a large Hispanic follow-ing, partly because of its popularity in Mexico, and also because, since 2001, the brand's entire U.S. marketing budget has been targeted at the Hispanic community. George Rasinski, senior brand manager for Clamato, found the Hispanic BzzChannel an excellent way to market Clamato, because the drink had a history of spreading through word-of-mouth advertising in the Hispanic community. Clamato's BzzAgency campaign began with e-mail notification to all Hispanic BzzAgents. If agents were interested in joining the campaign, they were sent a campaign kit including a brochure about the product, a sample, coupons, and information on how to buzz the product. Aside from the brand and BzzAgent's suggestions, it is basically up to the individual agent to decide how he or she would like to spread the word. According to the Web site, BzzAgency has more than 92,000 volunteers registered to work on its cam-paigns—and more than five thousand of these have Hispanic backgrounds. About 70% of the company's agents are women; 50% are older than twenty-five years of age, and 30% are older than thirty-four years of age. Occupations range from students to CEOs. Overall, the program grows by more than one thousand agents per week. The company plans to launch more BzzChannels in other communities and even abroad (Heinemann, 2005). While traditional media remain a staple in reaching ethnic consumers, approaches such as buzz marketing often prove more effective in reaching such audiences and generat-ing the desired impact. As the economic, political, and cultural power of ethnic groups in the United States continues to grow, savvy marketers will find that adding grassroots programs to the marketing and communication mix will yield impressive results and increase both the credibility and access to these important target audiences.

Integrated Marketing Communications

Until quite recently, most firms planned and managed their marketing and promotions functions separately. Increasingly, however, companies are mov-ing toward integrated marketing communications. The American Association of Advertising Agencies defines *integrated marketing communications* (IMC) as

> a concept of marketing communications planning that recognizes the added value of a comprehensive plan that evaluates the strategic roles of a variety of commu-nication disciplines, e.g., general advertising, direct response, sales promotion and public relations—and combines these disciplines to provide clarity, consistency and maximum impact. (Duncan & Everett, 1993)

A major benefit associated with IMC is synergism, "meaning that the individual efforts are mutually reinforced with the resulting effect being greater than if each functional area had selected its own targets, chosen its own message strategy, and set its own media schedule and timing" (Novelli, 1989/1990).

However, even this view of IMC is too narrow. Researchers and practitioners alike have noted that the messages consumers receive about a company and its products are not limited to advertisements, direct marketing efforts, publicity, and sales promotions. Rather, claim Don Schultz and colleagues,

> almost everything the marketer does relates to or provides some form of communication to customers and prospects, from the design of the product through the packaging and distribution channel selected. These product contacts communicate something about the value and the person for whom the product was designed. (Schultz, Tannenbaum, & Lauterborn, 1994)

The kind of customer service that is provided after the product is purchased also sends a message to consumers. Thus, the other elements of the marketing mix—which have typically been isolated from the communication strategy—are, in fact, sources of information for the consumer as well. In addition, the target audience may gather information about a product or service from conversations with friends, relatives, and co-workers. Even retailers and the media have something to say about a manufacturer's product. According to Schultz and colleagues, "The marketer has very limited control over much of the information and data that the consumer receives. . . . That's why it's so critical for marketers to maintain some sort of control over the communication they initiate or influence" (Schultz, Tannenbaum, & Lauterborn, 1994).

IMC, then, is all about managing the various contacts a firm has with its customers, since each of these contacts potentially influences consumer behavior. In order to better manage these contacts, the firm actively solicits responses from consumers. Response solicitation devices may include a telephone call, a direct mail piece, a purchase warranty card, or some other form through which the consumer can engage in two-way communications with the manufacturer. Response information is then stored in a database (along with demographic and psychographic data), providing the marketer with the necessary feedback to adjust future communications.

Schultz and colleagues note, "In short, marketing is communication and communication is marketing. The two are inseparable. And, for that reason, the proper integration of all marketing messages is that much more important" (Schultz, Tannenbaum, & Lauterborn, 1994).

Today, ever-increasing numbers of marketers are exploring the benefits that IMC has to offer. However, respondents to a recent survey conducted for *Advertising Age* reveal that few have actually achieved integration in practice (Atkinson, 2002). The survey, which polled 208 judges of the Effies—an award presented to the most effective marketing campaigns of the year—gathered the views of ad agencies, major marketers, media companies, and specialist marketing firms. The respondents agreed that cross-discipline strategies are often a nightmare to execute and difficult to measure effectively. Interestingly, most ad agencies cited consistent execution as the biggest problem, while most clients pointed to measurement as their biggest headache.

Despite the challenges associated with implementing an IMC program, most marketers today consider themselves proponents of the approach. Unilever relied on an integrated program for the company's biggest-ever Hispanic effort for its food brands. The company played on a Latin love of cooking and the surprising dearth of food programs on Spanish-language TV in kicking off *Desafio del Sabor* (The Flavor Challenge). Research revealed that Hispanics spend almost twice as much time preparing home-cooked meals as non-Latinos do. And there is intense rivalry between Mexican, Dominican, Cuban, and Puerto Rican cuisines, and, even within these national cultures, cooks typically customize their recipes. Furthermore, while Hispanics are excellent planners when it comes to shopping and cooking, research revealed their level of satisfaction with the shopping experience was much lower than that of the general market. Hispanic shoppers indicated they would enjoy stores that are easier to get to, that offer more personalized attention and speak Spanish, and where they felt more welcome. Unilever saw this as a major opportunity for both manufacturers and retailers. And, although more than 70% of Hispanics say they are confident in their cooking abilities, according to *People en Español* magazine's Hispanic Opinion Tracker (HOT) study, the Hispanic market has no Martha Stewarts, Nigella Lawsons, or Iron or Naked Chefs. The Flavor Challenge kicked off with a call to submit favorite recipes at storefront events across the country and ended with a televised cook-off on national television. Recipes were required to use one of the ten participating Unilever brands (Ragú, Knorr, Hellmann's, Lipton tea, Lawry's barbecue sauce, Wish-Bone salad dressing, Lipton Sides, Country Crock, Lipton Noodle Soup, and Skippy peanut butter). In addition to collecting recipes at stores, Unilever readied half a dozen mobile vans to go to big grocery chains and local Hispanic festivals. Bilingual culinary students helped with demonstrations and tastings at the storefront events. Customers whose recipes were selected entered the next level of competition—cooking at Desafio del Sabor regional challenges at Hispanic festivals in five cities: Chicago, Houston, Los Angeles, Miami, and New York. Winners from each regional event competed in a cook-off aired nationally on the Spanish-language TV network Univision. The grand prize: $10,000 in cash and a trip for four to Univision's top music awards show, *Premio lo Nuestro a la Musica Latina*. The winner's recipe was also featured in a Unilever recipe book. The effort was backed by TV, radio, print, and online advertising, plus public relations, promotions, and in-store advertising, a Web site (http://www.desafiodelsabor.com), and a giveaway recipe book called *Viva*

Mejor (Live Better). Although ads were in Spanish, the Web site and promotional materials and other efforts were bilingual whenever possible. Previously, Unilever had utilized primarily a brand-by-brand approach, without internal coordination. However in 2004, Unilever reorganized its multicultural efforts and in 2006 boosted its Hispanic advertising an promotion budgets nearly 50 percent to reach this growing market (Wentz, 2006).

Summary

Though the focus of this text is on advertising to the ethnic consumer, marketers realize that decisions relating to advertising cannot be made without regard to other elements of the marketing mix. Similarly, marketing decisions cannot be made without considering cultural factors, which influence consumer behavior. Each ethnic group exhibits unique cultural characteristics that influence the needs and wants of consumers within that group, their methods of satisfying them, and the messages to which they are most likely to respond. Thus, chapter 3 examines the role of culture in marketing to Hispanics, African Americans, and Asian Americans.

REFERENCES

American Marketing Association. (1960). *Marketing definitions: A glossary of marketing terms.* Compiled by the Committee on Definitions of the American Marketing Association. Chicago: American Marketing Association.

Angles on appealing to Asian-American media. (2004, May 24). *PR News,* p. 1.

Anheuser-Busch, Inc. launches prostate cancer awareness campaign. (2004, July). *Washington Informer, 40*(37), 11.

Arens, W. F. (2002). *Contemporary advertising.* New York: McGraw-Hill Irwin.

Atkinson, C. (2002, March 10). Integration still a pipe dream for many. *Advertising Age,* p. 1.

Barbagallo, P. (2003, February). Hispanics. *Target Marketing, 26*(2), 60.

Belch, G. E., & Belch, M. A. (2007). *Advertising and promotion: An integrated marketing communications perspective.* New York: McGraw-Hill Irwin.

Beirne, M. (2005, March 14). Has the group been left behind? *Brandweek,* New York, 46(11), p. 33.

Bernstein, R. (2000, May). Food for thought. *American Demographics, 22*(5), 39.

Britt, S. H. (1974, Winter). Standardizing marketing for the international market. *Columbia Journal of World Business, 9,* 32–40.

Burns, G. (1992, September 15). Bandage firm adds shading to flesh-color. *Chicago Sun-Times,* p. 43.

Cohen, R. (2000, September). Crisis readiness: Insurance for your reputation. *Directorship*, *26*(8), 16.

Cornwell, B., & Maignan, I. (1998, Spring). An international review of sponsorship research. *Journal of Advertising*, 11.

Denny's woos black customers. (1997, June 4). *The Jacksonville Free Press*, p. 2.

Duncan, T. R., & Everett, S. E. (1993, May/June). Client perceptions of integrated marketing communications. *Journal of Advertising Research*, 30–39.

Ebenkamp, B. (2001, June 4). Return to Peyton placement. *Brandweek*, p. S-10.

Fitzgerald, K. (2003, February 3). Growing pains for placements. *Advertising Age*, p. S-2.

Ford, R. L. (2005, January). Get involved in the Lunar New Year. *Public Relations Tactics*, *12*(1), 6.

Giving Latinas the Quinceañera of their dreams. (2004, May 16). *La Prensa*, p. 3-A.

Goldman, J. (1984). *Public relations in the marketing mix*. Lincolnwood, IL: NTC Business Books.

Green, C. L. (1997, Winter). In-store vs. out-of-store coupons: An examination of Anglo-, African-, and Hispanic-American redemption. *Journal of Marketing Theory and Practice*, 113–120.

Harris, T. (1993). *The marketer's guide to public relations* (p. 12). New York: Wiley.

Heinemann, A. (2005, July 14). Bzz marketing moves into Hispanic community. *Advertising Age*. Retrieved from http://www.adage.com/news.cms?newsId=45544

Hemlock, D., & Mann, J. (2001, January 22). Spanish strategies: Top Hispanic marketers share some key traits. *South Florida Sun-Sentinel*, p. 16.

Hotchkiss, A. D. (1996, June). Weaving sensitivity into marketing. *Bank Marketing*, *28*(6), 26.

Jacobson, M., & Mazur, L. A. (1995). *Marketing madness: A survival guide for consumer society* (pp. 67–72.). Boulder, CO: Westview Press.

Journal of Marketing (1948, October 12). Report of the Definitions Committee.

Kotler, P., & Armstrong, G. (1990). *Marketing: An introduction* (p. 227). Englewood Cliffs, NJ: Prentice Hall.

Ly, P. (2003, February 1). New Year's newfound popularity; More non-Asians are among the thousands joining in Lunar celebration. *The Washington Post*, p. B-1.

McCarthy, J. (1960). *Basic marketing: A managerial approach*. Homewood, IL: Irwin.

McTaggart, J. (2005, February 15). Culture clash. *Progressive Grocer*, p. 20.

Neff, J. (2005, October 3). P & G heads into Hispanic-hair battle. [Midwest region edition]. *Advertising Age*, p. 3.

Novelli, W.D. (1989/1990). One-stop shopping: Some thoughts on integrated marketing communication. *Public Relations Quarterly*, *34*(4), p. 7–9.

Profound shifts in family dynamics, priorities underway among Hispanic, African American Consumers; Yankelovich unveils 2005 Monitor Multicultural Marketing Study. (2005, July 6). *Business Wire*, p. 1.

Randall, K. (1998, Winter). Anatomy of a nightmare: Denny's discovers diversity. *Public Relations Strategist, 3*(4), 14.

Schnabel, M. (2005, Fall). Harnessing the booming Hispanic market: GM, Wal-Mart and Ford share best practices. *Public Relations Strategist, 11*(4), 45.

Schultz, D. E., Tannenbaum, S. L., & Lauterborn, R. E. (1994). *The new marketing paradigm: Integrated marketing communications* (p. 45). Lincolnwood, IL: NTC Business Books.

Shimp, T. (2003). *Advertising, promotion & supplemental aspects of integrated marketing communications.* Mason, OH: Thompson-Southwestern.

Silverman, F. (2000, June 1). When direct marketers guess, the pitch can alienate, offend, easy for ethnic marketing to miss target. *Hartford Courant,* p. E-1.

Sprint product suite grows to accommodate burgeoning Hispanic market. (2004, June 21). *PR Newswire,* p. 1.

Taylor, L. (2006, May 18). Product integration protest from TV writers. *Advertising Age.* Retrieved from http://adage.com/print?article_id=109271

Thompson, S. (2003, September 1). Avon targets black sales reps [Midwest region edition]. *Advertising Age,* p. 16.

Tompkins, R. (2002, November 5). As television audiences tire of commercials, advertisers move into programs. *Financial Times, London,* p. 21.

The United Negro College Fund announces Procter & Gamble's efforts to increase its contribution to $1.1 million. (2003, December 19). *PR Newswire,* p. 1.

Varadarajan, P. R., & Menon, A. (1988, July). Cause-related marketing: A coalignment of marketing strategy and corporate philanthropy. *Journal of Marketing,* 58–74.

Wentz, L. (2004a, October 25). Branded content hits Hispanics TV [Midwest region edition]. *Advertising Age,* p. 16.

Wentz, L. (2004b, November 1). Marketers hone focus on minorities. *Advertising Age,* p. 55.

Wentz, L. (2006, March 8). Unilever to increase Hispanic advertising budget 47%. *Advertising Age.* Retrieved from http://www.adage.com/news.cms?newsId=48178

Yorgey, L. (1999, July). Asian Americans. *Target Marketing, 22*(8), 75.

Zimmerman, A. (2005, May 31). Wal-Mart's Hispanic outreach; retailer does more to woo U.S.'s fastest-growing minority group [Eastern edition]. *Wall Street Journal,* p. B-9.

3

The Influence of Culture on Marketing and Advertising to Multicultural Consumers

Seasoned marketers reaching out to the Hispanic American, African American, and Asian American consumers are way beyond the question, Why should we market to ethnic consumers? Instead, their focus is, How do we reach out and make connections with multicultural consumers to affect behavior change? Understanding the cultural values, attitudes, and characteristics of these target markets is central in making real connections with multicultural consumers. This chapter explores the concept of culture as it relates to marketers' attempts to communicate—both verbally and nonverbally—with the ethnic consumer. The reader should note that, in this chapter, as well as in those that follow, some generalizations will be made about Hispanic Americans, African Americans, and Asian Americans. For example, it will be suggested that Hispanic Americans generally operate on a polychronic time system, while African Americans tend to operate on *kairos* time. Clearly, not each and every Hispanic American and African American will fit into this mold. Nonetheless, it is important that such shared characteristics of these groups be addressed so that the reader can understand what makes each of the ethnic markets unique.

Concept of Culture

Culture can be conceptualized in many ways. Indeed, in the early 1950s, Kroeber and Kluckhohn (1952) identified well over 160 different definitions of *culture* in the anthropological literature. Of course, many new definitions have appeared since. A classic definition is provided by E. B. Taylor, who defined culture as "a complex whole, which includes knowledge, beliefs, art, morals, law, custom, and any other capabilities and habits acquired by individuals as members of a society" (1871, p. 1). Adamson Hoebel referred to culture as the "integrated sum total of learned behavioral traits that are manifest and shared by members of society" (1960, p. 168). Culture has also been defined as a "learned, shared, compelling, interrelated set of symbols whose meaning provides a set of orientations for members of a society" (Terpstra & David, 1991, p. 12).

Even the three definitions provided here reveal some commonalities. It is generally agreed that culture is not inherent or innate but rather is learned. Learning typically takes place in institutions, such as the family, church, and school. Samovar, Porter, and Stafani (1998) note that, in addition to these formalized institutions, individuals also learn culture from more invisible instructors, such as proverbs, folktales, legends, art forms, and, of course, the mass media. Most definitions of culture also emphasize that culture is shared by members of a group. It is this shared aspect that enables communication between individuals within that culture. Because culture is shared, it defines the boundaries between different groups. Cross-cultural communication is so difficult, in large part, because of the lack of shared symbols. Finally, all facets of culture are interrelated—if one aspect of culture is changed, all else will be influenced as well. As Edward T. Hall notes, "you touch a culture in one place and everything else is affected" (1976). Typically, when the term *culture* is employed, it refers to the dominant culture of a specific country. As Samovar et al. explain, the dominant culture clearly indicates the one in power:

> People in power are those who historically have controlled, and who still control, the major institutions within the culture: church, government, education, military, mass media, monetary systems, and the like. In the U.S., white males meet the requirements of dominance. They are in the positions of power in every single major institution in this country. They are at the center of culture, because their power enables them to determine and manipulate the content and flow of the messages produced by those institutions. By controlling most of the cultural messages, they are also controlling the images presented to the majority of the population. Whether

it be the church, mass media, or the government, the dominant culture sets goals, perpetuates customs, establishes values, and makes the major decisions affecting the bulk of the population. (1998)

So, throughout this text, references to the dominant culture are referring to the non-Hispanic white population—which, at least until the present moment, has had a major influence on what people think, what they see, what they aspire to, and, often, what they purchase.

Cocultures

It is important to recognize that variations within cultures may be even greater than variations between cultures. In each culture, there exist groups of people with shared beliefs, perceptions, and value systems based on common experiences. People belonging to various nationality groups (Italian Americans, Polish Americans, and Scandinavian Americans), religious groups (Protestants, Jews, and Catholics), political groups (Democrats, Republicans, and Socialists), geographic groups (westerners, easterners, southerners), and even specific age groups are likely to exhibit characteristic patterns of behavior that serve to distinguish them from other groups within a country. Clearly, the same can be said about people who belong to specific ethnic or racial groups. For many years, the term *subculture* was used to define such groups. Recently, however, the term has been replaced, as the prefix *sub* implies that members of these groups are somehow deficient or inadequate. Nanda notes that *subculture* also carries connotations that imply "better and worse and superior and inferior" (1994). Today, the more commonly employed term is *coculture*. It should also be noted that an individual can belong to more than one coculture. Nixon and Dawson (2002) note that communication is an interactive event during which persons assign meanings to messages and jointly create identities and social reality. In communications between cocultures, the assignment of meaning to symbols requires the interpretation of those messages and adaptation to the social aspect of each individual coculture. Effective communication is compromised when problems or misinterpretations exist between the coculture and the dominant culture in the United States. A number of problems can occur because of ethnocultural factors, such as those that reflect values, beliefs, norms, and symbolic meaning. The remainder of this chapter examines the challenges of communicating between cocultures.

Self-Reference Criterion and Ethnocentrism

When we examine cultures other than our own, we tend to view them through culturally tinted glasses. For example, if our own culture places a high value on education or cleanliness, we may assume—correctly or incorrectly—that other cultures or cocultures share these same values. James Lee terms this unconscious reference to one's own culture the *self-reference criterion* (1966). Because of this unconscious reference to one's own cultural values, marketers may behave in a culturally myopic fashion. Marketing managers and advertising professionals who believe that their personal views are typical of their customers provide many examples of misplaced marketing. Increasingly, when a target audience consists of Latinos, African Americans, and even Asian Americans, advertisers will turn the work over to an advertising agency whose owners and employees are members of that ethnic group. Yet, Rotfeld (2003) notes that, every day, advertising that works is created by people grossly dissimilar from their audience. Successful advertising can only take place within the context of understanding the target audience. While understanding does not require membership in a coculture, it does require empathy with that coculture.

Ethnocentrism poses another obstacle to understanding other cultures and cocultures. Literally defined, *ethnocentrism* means culturally centered; it refers to people's tendency to place themselves at the center of the universe and not only evaluate others by the standards of their own culture but also believe that their own culture is superior to all others. A fundamental assumption of ethnocentric people is that their way of doing things is right, proper, and normal and that the ways of culturally different people are wrong and inferior (Ferraro, 1990). Not surprisingly, this tendency toward an us-versus-them mentality is universal. People in all cultures, to some degree, display ethnocentric behaviors. Ethnocentrism limits the ability to accept cultural differences, which diminishes the chance of developing effective marketing programs. The best defense against ethnocentrism is an awareness of the tendency toward ethnocentrism.

Assimilation and Acculturation

Two terms often employed when discussing ethnic groups are *assimilation* and *acculturation*.

> Assimilation is the action of making or becoming like something else; acculturation is the adoption of an alien culture. Both terms present the same phenomenon from different points of view (assimilation from the point of view of the dominant culture; acculturation from the point of view of the minority culture). (Sheehan, 2005, p. 129)

Samovar et al. point out that,

> usually acculturation is in response to extended and intensive firsthand contact between two or more previously autonomous cultures or co-cultures. This type of change is common to immigrants, who for a variety of reasons find themselves in another culture. These people, as part of the acculturation process, need to cope with a considerable amount of cultural change. In most instances they begin to detect new patterns of thinking and behavior and to structure a personality relevant to adaptation to the host society. Inherent in acculturation is the idea that most people, as they are adapting, are also holding on to many of the values, customs, and communication patterns found in their primary culture. (1998, p. 45)

It should be noted that, while many aspects of culture are subject to change as part of the acculturation process (such as what people eat, what they wear, or what television programs they watch), the deep structure of a culture is much more resistant to change. So, individuals' ethics and morals, their religious practices, and their value systems are likely to persist over time, regardless of how long they live in a host country.

Typically, immigrant populations are divided into three basic groups: mostly acculturated, partially acculturated, and relatively unacculturated. The U.S. Hispanic population provides an excellent example of differing levels of acculturation. In the 2004 U.S. Hispanic Market Report, Synovate performed a cluster analysis on a survey of nearly 1,400 Hispanics, on a national basis (*Advertising Age,* Hispanic Fact Pack, 2005). This allowed for the Hispanic population to be segmented into six groups—rather than just three—based on level of acculturation (see Figure 3.1).

Often, there may even be different levels of acculturation interacting in the same household, with an unacculturated mother perhaps purchasing for an acculturated teen. From a marketing standpoint, it is critical that the audience's level of acculturation be taken into account when planning the marketing mix strategy for both goods and services. For example, above and beyond deciding on whether to use English or Spanish for Dr Pepper's first Hispanic campaign, the challenge was to find a concept that worked with both acculturated Hispanics who grew up drinking Dr Pepper and recent immigrants for whom it is essentially a new product. Research conducted by parent company Cadbury Schweppes found that Hispanics generally consume more fruit-flavored beverages than non-Hispanics and that acculturated Hispanics drink 62% more Dr Pepper than the general market population. The findings were eye-opening for the company. They knew Hispanic Americans were drinking lots of Dr Pepper, but they did not realize they had such a huge opportunity with unacculturated Hispanics. This group was seen as a growth opportunity for the soft drink. Cadbury Schweppes hired a Hispanic agency, the Cartel Group, based in San Antonio. The agency's Executive Vice President Jesus Ramirez rented a recreational vehicle (RV) and traveled around Texas to interview pockets of Dr Pepper lovers. "We had Dr Pepper lovers and people

Figure 3.1: Acculturation and Hispanic Americans

1. Unacculturated traditionals are foreign-born Hispanics with intermediate and high levels of cultural tension. They have been in the United States for the shortest amount of time and tend to live in key entry points. They have close ties and keep in touch regularly with family and friends in their country of origin. Thirty-three percent of this group lives in either Los Angeles or Miami.
2. The unacculturated stable segment is composed of foreign-born Hispanics with low levels of tension. They tend to live in markets with high concentrations of Hispanics, such as Miami and Los Angeles, and a large proportion are homemakers. Because of the high concentration of Hispanics and established Spanish infrastructure in these markets, people in this segment have no need or motivation to acculturate further. The acculturation process among this group is much slower than for others.
3. Traditionals are the oldest group of partially acculturated Hispanic Americans. Most are foreign born, but, as a group, they have been living in the United States for the longest period of time. They are partially acculturated, with high levels of cultural tension. They have conservative values in terms of women's roles and religion. In general, although they have an attachment to the United States, they are uncomfortable with the American way of life.
4. New Latinos are relatively young and mostly foreign born and have lived in the United States for a significant amount of time. They are partially acculturated, with intermediate levels of cultural tension. Three-quarters of them have children. They tend to live in large metro areas and consume a significant amount of Spanish-language media.
5. American Latinos are very comfortable living in both worlds—the Latin culture and the U.S. culture. They are partially acculturated, with low levels of cultural tension. They are also a very young group with an inclination to purchase electronic gadgets and sport-utility vehicles (SUVs) and eat fast-food.
6. The mostly acculturated segment of Hispanics has unique characteristics. Although they are mostly acculturated, Spanish is still spoken in many of these homes, and there is some Spanish-language media consumption.

From "Hispanic Fact Pack," 2005, *Advertising Age,* p. 48.

with no relationship with the brand. We had to figure out a bridge to get them together so we could proceed with one target," he said (Wentz, 2005a). He discovered the bridge was Dr Pepper's taste—easily distinguishable from rival cola brands that taste much alike. The agency developed a TV spot featuring those familiar with Dr Pepper as advocates for the brand. Blindfolded teens in a laboratory sipped canned drinks through a straw, rejecting each with a bored "No." When given Dr Pepper to sample, they recognized it instantly and refused to give it back. A series of radio commercials came in both acculturated and unacculturated versions. In one Spanish-language spot, Hispanics asked to try Dr Pepper on the street were surprised and delighted by the taste. In the English-language version, acculturated Hispanics were asked if they could pick out the Dr Pepper in a taste test. All were confident, agreeing to wear blindfolds and even betting money. In another pair of radio spots, a guy brought his girlfriend a soda, hoping that, in the darkened movie theater, she wouldn't realize that it wasn't Dr Pepper. She did, and other moviegoers complained about their hissed argument. Like Latinos' real lives, the English-language version was peppered with Spanish. When she tasted it and complained, a guy sitting nearby called out in English, "Dude, buy her a Dr Pepper." All ads end with the words "unmistakable" or "*inconfundible.*" By all accounts, the campaign is a success among acculturated and unacculturated Hispanics alike.

The length of time that members of a coculture have spent in this country also influences how they identify themselves. As can be seen in Table 3.1, first-generation Latinos are significantly more likely to identify themselves by their country of origin than third-generation Latinos. And over one-half of third- or higher-generation Latinos are likely to identify themselves as Americans.

Table 3.1: How Latinos Identify Themselves			
Generation	By country of origin	As Latino or Hispanic	As American
First generation	68%	24%	6%
Second generation	38%	24%	35%
Third or higher generation	21%	20%	57%

Note. This table refers to either the first term or the only term that Latino respondents to the survey used to identify themselves.

Source: Pew Hispanic Center / Kaiser Family Foundation, 2002, December, *National Survey of Latinos*, retrieved from http://www.pewhispanic.org

Culture and Communication

Many cultural differences, and their impact on elements of the marketing mix, are rather obvious. Clearly, if one wishes to communicate with a Chinese American consumer, language differences must to be taken into account, and promotional materials may need to be translated into Chinese. Many cultural differences are, however, quite subtle. The problem of communicating to people of diverse cultural backgrounds has been called one of the greatest challenges in marketing communications (Ricks, 1988). Marketers, if they are to be successful in their efforts, must become culturally sensitive—that is, tuned into the nuances of culture. Indeed, they must become students of culture. Among the important elements of culture that marketers must take into consideration are verbal communication (both spoken and written) and the various forms of nonverbal communication (among them gestures, space, time, and other signs and symbols).

Verbal Communication

Because language plays such a central role in marketing, it's crucial to understand the close relationship between culture and language. Culture and communication are inextricably linked. It has been said that it is impossible to truly understand a culture without understanding the language spoken by its people (Whorf, 1956). Conversely, a language cannot be fully understood outside its cultural context. As Gerhard Maletzke explains,

> the art and manner in which one understands the world is determined to a large extent by language; but language, at the same time, is an expression of a specific group-experiencing of the world, and therefore may itself be shaped by the Weltanschauung as well as the wishes, expectations, and motivations of the group using it. (1976, p. 74)

Put more simply, culture both influences and is influenced by language.

Language and Context

The concept of high and low context provides an understanding of different cultural orientations and explains how communication is conveyed and perceived. As defined by Edward T. Hall (1976), *low-context cultures* place high value on words, and communicators are encouraged to be direct, exact, and unambiguous. What is important is what is said, not how it is said or the environment in which it is said. In contrast, *high-context cultures* consider verbal communications to be only a part of the overall message, and communicators rely much more heavily on contextual cues. Edward and Mildred Hall wrote, "Context is the information that surrounds an event and is inextricably bound up with the meaning of that event. The elements that combine to produce a given meaning—events and context—are in different proportions depending on culture" (1987, p. 7). Thus, messages in high-context cultures tend to be a good deal more implicit and ambiguous, with communicators relying much more on nonverbal behavior, the physical setting, social circumstances, and the nature of interpersonal relationships. Edward Hall further explains that

> a high context communication or message is one in which most of the information is already in the person, while very little is in the coded, explicit, transmitted part of the message. A low context communication is vested in the explicit code. (1976, p. 16)

Cultures typically are not perceived as either high or low context but are arranged along a continuum. In part, contextuality of communication is related to whether the language itself expresses ideas and facts more or less explicitly. The dominant American culture tends to be low context. In contrast, individuals from Latin American cultures, as well as Asian cultures, such as Japan, China, and Korea, tend to be high context.

The differences between communications styles in high- versus low-context cultures have direct implications for advertisers. Messages constructed by writers from high-context cultural groups might be difficult to understand by members of low-context cultural groups, because they do not come to the point. Similarly, messages constructed by writers from low-context cultural groups may be difficult to understand by members of high-context cultural groups, because they omit essential contextual material (Wells, 1987).

> People from low-context cultures are often puzzled by high-context ads and wonder 'What's the point?' Whereas those from high-context cultures are more likely to say the ad taught them something worth remembering and made it easier for them to choose which brand to buy the next time. People from high-context cultures often find low-context ads pushy and aggressive, whereas those from low-context cultures often find them informative and persuasive. (Rossman, 1994)

Language and Hispanic Americans

The great debate in communicating with Hispanic consumers appears to be whether to use Spanish or English. Statistics supporting the use of Spanish abound. A recent study conducted by Synovate Research (Wentz, 2005b) found that, of Hispanics surveyed, just over half (55%) are classified as Hispanic dominant, meaning that they prefer Spanish and have a strong desire to maintain their culture. Only about a quarter each are bilingual (23%)—comfortable in both languages and worlds but culturally more Hispanic—or U.S. dominant (22%), a group that speaks English and mirrors general market attitudes but identifies with its Latino heritage. Interestingly, the greatest increase in Spanish-language media consumption was among the U.S.-dominant group. The 2005 Yankelovich *Monitor: Multicultural Marketing Study,* produced by the Yankelovich marketing research and consulting organization, cited that 69% of respondents noted that "the Spanish language is more important to me than it was just five years ago" (Wentz, 2005b). And, according to the U.S. Hispanic Council, ads in Spanish are 4.5 times more persuasive than ads in English and post a 61% better recall (Wilson, 2005). Furthermore, according to Simmons Market Research Bureau, more than half of the predominately Spanish speakers in the United States feel more respect for companies that advertise in Spanish, feel more loyal to companies that advertise in Spanish, and remember products that are advertised in Spanish (Fonte, 2005). Finally, advocates of using Spanish-language media argue that the continuous influx of Latin American immigrants makes Spanish necessary.

On the other hand, English-language advocates note that the younger Hispanic generation tends to be either bilingual or English speaking. A nationwide 2002 survey by the Pew Hispanic Center and the Kaiser Family Foundation found that, among adult Latinos whose parents were immigrants, only 7% relied on Spanish as their primary language. Nearly half had no Spanish skills at all, and the rest were bilingual. The corresponding figures were even lower for the U.S.-born children of those second-generation Hispanic adults: Less than a quarter were bilingual, and the number of those Latinos who spoke only Spanish was not statistically significant. "The transition from Spanish to English is virtually complete in one generation," says Pew Hispanic Center director Roberto Suro. "Hispanics are undergoing a powerful process of change no less than anyone else who has come to these shores" (Contreras, 2004). Advocates of English also argue that the most affluent Hispanics tend to be the acculturated (Wentz, 2005b).

Toyota has come up with an interesting solution to the language issue: bilingual ads (see Figure 3.2). During the 2006 Super Bowl, the company ran a thirty-second bilingual ad for its new hybrid Toyota Camry—the first time a bilingual ad has been featured on the sporting event. In the spot, a Hispanic father is driving his young son in their new Camry. When the father explains how the hybrid car switches between gas and electric power, the son compares it to the way his father can switch between English and Spanish. "Because I'm always thinking of your future," the father says, explaining why he learned English—and why he bought a hybrid. Throughout the ad, the father and son mix English with Spanish, but the words they use are familiar enough to English ears that there aren't any subtitles. The ad later reappeared on both English- and Spanish-language channels (Durban, 2006).

Figure 3.2: In a Bilingual Super Bowl Ad for the Hybrid Toyota Camry, a Hispanic Father and Son Converse in Both Spanish and English

To further complicate the situation, marketers must recognize that the Spanish language varies broadly by country and even by region. For example, in Chile, the word *guagua* means "pregnant woman." However, in other Spanish-speaking countries, the word means "bus." *Pana* in Venezuela means "good friend," yet, in Mexico, it means "velvet cloth." The list goes on and on. Using the incorrect words to convey a message can get confusing or, worse yet, embarrassing for a company. Complications are also associated with various accents and dialects. A message for Mexican Americans needs to be different from a message to Cuban Americans and different still from one targeting Puerto Ricans. Hispanic consumers are like all consumers in that they want to hear their own language used correctly ("In Chile," 2005). In situations where the prospect base is broad or when marketers are unable to identify the geographic origins of the target audience, the Spanish employed should be kept neutral. However, when targeting a specific subset of the Hispanic market, marketers should acknowledge where those targeted Hispanics come from by using the Spanish spoken in that particular country (Geller, 2003).

Language and Asian Americans

The nearly 14 million Asian Americans in the United States encompass everything from Bangladeshi Americans to Vietnamese Americans. Jeff Yang, chief executive officer (CEO) of Factor Inc., a New York City–based firm that specializes in marketing to Asians, notes, "The Asian market within itself almost comprises the same level of diversity as the U.S. at large" (Wellner, 2002). The largest group of Asian Americans are Chinese, at 23 percent, followed by Filipino (17 percent), Indian (16 percent), Vietnamese (11percent), Korean (10 percent) and Japanese (7 percent), (Mandese, 2003)" The following cite should be included in references: Mandese, J. (2003, September 15). Asian market defies classification. TelevisionWeek, Chicago, Vol. 22, Issue 37, p. 11. Much like Hispanics, studies indicate that Asian Americans want to be marketed to in their own language. Indeed, by some estimates, two-thirds of Asians are what is known as *language preferent,* meaning that they would rather speak in their own languages at home (Elliott, 2000). This is in large part because so many Asian Americans are foreign born (up to 70%, according to some figures). Indeed, four out of the top ten foreign languages spoken in U.S. households today are Asian. In fact, Chinese, with 80% native preference, is now ranked the second most-spoken language after Spanish; an astonishing 96% of Vietnamese speak their own language at home, followed by 88% of Koreans, 68% of Filipinos, and 44% of Japanese (Huang & Skriloff, 2003). Even within these groupings, there is variation. For instance, Chinese speakers in Los Angeles and New York are more likely to speak Mandarin, while Chinese speakers in San Francisco are evenly split between Mandarin and Cantonese. Overall, the Asian American segment comprises a continuous influx of immigration groups that are typically not assimilated and have a high preference for in-language communications. This group cannot be effectively reached through general media but rather must be courted via in-language media.

Language and African Americans

The current prevailing notion with regard to marketing to blacks appears to be, They speak English, don't they? Miller and Kemp (2005) argue that the absence of a language barrier has become a major rationalization for reduced spending, generic messaging, and inadequate market research when targeting African Americans. Marketers may use the language issue to rationalize blending African American budgets with general market plans, while spending more on the Latino segment. Or they may buy media directed toward African Americans, but their message does not speak effectively to this target. However, an even greater danger lies in attempting to appeal to the black consumer by employing Ebonics in an ad campaign.

> Ebonics is a colloquial speech many African Americans use, almost exclusively with each other. In an attempt to relate to the black community, marketers may try to utilize Ebonic jargon in an effort to establish a commonality—i.e., "speaking the language." More often than not, this strategy will probably backfire. African Americans have as many differences in their speech patterns as any other Americans. For example, blacks from the south speak differently than those who live in New York City. West Indians will speak differently than blacks in Detroit. Many African Americans don't even speak Ebonics, nor do they speak with a so-called "black" accent or pronunciation. Some African Americans don't even like Ebonics or other stereotypical jargon, believing that it "sounds ignorant" and reinforces a negative stereotype. Most importantly, many African Americans are deeply offended when spoken to by a white person who's trying to "talk black"—by mimicking mannerisms or slang—and many resent the implication that all blacks speak in Ebonics. (Miller & Kemp, 2005, p. 24)

However, the appropriate use of language in targeting blacks can increase the success of a campaign. For example, the Colorado Department of Transportation developed a seat belt campaign targeting African American males, because this group is twice as likely to die in a motor vehicle crash as white males. Based on focus group research, a campaign was designed to appeal to African American males by using culturally appropriate visual and content strategies, as well as cultural references. Those included providing facts on African American males and automobile usage and using language, such as slang and pop phrases provided by African American men participating in the focus groups. The campaign was called Brother Keep it Together: Don't Risk It—Just Wear It. Survey results credited the program with increasing seat belt usage among African American males by 18%. The campaign also received endorsements from community organizations, including the local chapters of the National Association for the Advancement of Colored People (NAACP), the National Urban League, and 100 Black Men of America (Grant, 2003).

Translations

No discussion of language would be complete without addressing the importance of translations. Errors in the translation of brand names, packaging copy, and advertising messages have cost businesses millions of dollars, not to mention that they have damaged their credibility and reputation. Braniff International Airways provides a classic example of a translation blooper. When the now-defunct carrier translated its Fly in Leather slogan for a Spanish-speaking audience, it intended to highlight its high-class interiors and seating. But instead of conjuring images of luxury, the message caused confusion, humor, and a little bit of unease. *Vuela en Cuero,* the literal translation of Fly in Leather, urged customers to fly in their airplanes—naked (Fonte, 2005). This often-cited example of a translation gone wrong is from the 1970s; unfortunately, awkward translations still abound today. The Hershey Company provides a more recent example. While condensed milk may seem like a benign ingredient for a candy product, Hershey's found out that it doesn't always translate well. A recent ad for Hershey's new line of Latin-inspired candy, *La Dulceria Thalia,* likely set some Spanish speakers snickering. A word for caramel flavoring made with condensed goat's milk—*cajeta*—may have been read by some Spanish speakers as an impolite term for female genitalia. The ad, which featured Latina pop idol Thalia Sodi, which ran in several Spanish-language publications in the United States and Mexico, included the slogan *Sabor a Chocolate Blanco con Cajeta.* The expected translation is "The Taste of White Chocolate with Condensed Milk." Jose Cancela, of Hispanic USA , a consulting firm that helps companies market to Hispanics, was the first to publicize the gaffe. "I saw the ad in *People en Español*—the top magazine in Hispanic USA—with the picture of Thalia and the world 'cajeta' and I'm like, 'Oh my God, what are these people thinking,'" Cancela said. "It was clear to me that whoever did that marketing was just not thinking straight. They did not do their homework." Cancela said the word might be misunderstood among Spanish speakers from countries other than Mexico. "In a lot of countries, the word has no meaning," he said. Hershey's argued that there was no miscommunication and that the product is targeted to Mexicans and Mexican Americans, who need no explanation. The company noted that, in Mexico, the term is understood in the context of a common candy treat (Kumar, 2005). TransPerfect—a New York–based translation service—found even more mistranslations or misuses in recent ads targeted to Hispanics:

- "Point" was mistranslated as *puta,* which means "whore," instead of *punta.*

- "Census" was mistranslated as *sesos,* which means "brain," instead of *censo.*

- *Huahua,* which means "bus" to people from Cuba and Puerto Rico, also means "baby" to people from Chile. (Alsever, 2004)

A 2003 survey by TransPerfect found that 57% of Hispanic respondents said they've seen advertising that is incorrectly translated from English. And nearly half of them say that, if an ad is poorly translated, they tune out the message. Worse yet, 65% interpret bad translations as evidence that the advertiser doesn't care about the consumer. Of the respondents surveyed, 35% thought ads for food products were the worst translation offenders, while 20% pointed to ads for pharmaceuticals; 13% pointed to ads for baby products, and 12% pointed to ads for soda and other beverages. About 35% of respondents said that newspaper ads were the most likely to have translation errors, while 31% pointed to television ads. Magazines were cited by 27%, billboards by 15%, and radio by 12% (Whitman, 2003).

Relying on computer translator programs to develop copy for ethnic marketing materials is a surefire means of generating translation bloopers. The problem is that such programs provide literal translations that do not always transfer the appropriate meaning of a word or phrase. That, in turn, can change the meaning of the message. Even when employing professional translators, it is not enough for the translator to merely be familiar with the native tongue. In order to avoid translation blunders, translators must also be familiar with nuances, idioms, and slang. One useful technique in revealing translation errors is called back-translation (Miracle, 1988). One individual is responsible for the initial translation of the message. A second individual then translates the message back into the original language. If the message does not translate back, it's likely that there is a translation problem. Back-translation is a helpful tool, but it's still no guarantee against translation bloopers. Hiring only speakers of the language into which the message is to be translated also helps to reduce problems, as does acknowledging that some words and phrases simply cannot be translated. Carlos Fuentes, director of multicultural marketing for Vertis in Baltimore, whose targeted advertising, media, and marketing services include a suite of tools to help marketers establish relationships with Hispanic consumers, notes,

> One of the biggest mistakes marketers make in trying to reach Hispanic consumers is to simply translate existing marketing and promotional messages into Spanish. More than a simple literal translation, we suggest taking the overall message and tone and modifying it so that it becomes more relevant to the targeted audience. (Wilson, 2005)

Clearly, the same holds true when appealing to other ethnic consumer groups.

Nonverbal Communication

People communicate not only through spoken language but also via non-verbal language. Indeed, it has been estimated that approximately 70% of all communication between two individuals within the same culture is nonverbal in nature. Nonverbal communication, often referred to as the silent language, can pose serious problems for marketers and advertisers, as well.

A number of classification systems of nonverbal language exist, some containing up to twenty-four different categories of behaviors (Hall, 1976; Condon & Yousef, 1975). Most classification systems include facial expressions, eye contact and gaze, body movement (such as hand gestures and posture), touching, smell, space usage, time symbolism, appearance or dress, color symbolism, and even silence. It is important to note that nonverbal methods of communication are no more universal than verbal methods.

Nonverbal communication regulates human interaction in several important ways: (a) It sends messages about attitudes and feelings, (b) it elaborates on verbal messages, and (c) it governs the timing and turn taking between communicators (Ferraro, 1990). A thorough discussion of all of the aspects of the silent language, as it's often called, is beyond the scope of this text. However, because of their importance to marketers, four areas will be addressed briefly: space usage; time symbolism; eye contact; and colors, symbols, and signs.

Space Usage

How humans use space is referred to as *proxemics*. Edward and Mildred Hall suggest that "each person has around him an invisible bubble of space which expands and contracts depending on his relationship to those around him, his emotional state, and the activity he is performing" (1987, p. 12). Based on his observations of North Americans, Edward Hall (1966) developed four categories of distance in human interactions:

1. *Intimate distance:* Ranging from body contact to eighteen inches, this distance is used for personal contact, comforting, and protecting. Here, olfactory and thermal sensations are at their highest.
2. *Personal distance:* Ranging from eighteen inches to four feet, depending on the closeness of the relationship, in this distancing mode, people have an invisible space bubble separating themselves from others.
3. *Social distance:* Ranging from four to twelve feet, this distance is used by acquaintances and strangers in business meetings and classrooms.

4. *Public distance:* Ranging from twelve to twenty-five feet, at this distance, recognition of others is not mandatory, and the subtle shades of meaning of voice, gesture, and facial expression are lost.

However, the use of space is culture bound—members of different cultural groups do not necessarily conform to Hall's four categories of distance. Anglo Americans tend to be ill at ease with close personal space and tend to stand apart from their conversational partners, feeling uncomfortable and even threatened when their space is violated. Research has demonstrated that, although African Americans tend to establish closer distances and tend to touch more frequently during conversations than Anglo Americans, when conversing with Anglo Americans, these tendencies do not carry over. According to Nixon and Dawson (2002), African American men frequently describe efforts to maintain a distance from non–African Americans. This distance was especially maintained when interacting with Anglo American men. In addition, African Americans tend to face their partner in communication less directly than Anglo Americans do. These differences in communication patterns might give the appearance that the African American is indifferent or uninvolved in the conversation. Hispanic people are also much more comfortable when in close physical proximity to others (Hall, 1990). It is considered insulting when another withdraws from such close physical contact. In fact, Latin Americans are likely to perceive Anglo Americans as cold, distant people, because Americans' comfort distance is greater than theirs and Americans tend to touch one another less.

Space usage has direct implications for personal selling. The fact that Hispanics are comfortable with close proximity is clearly evident in selling situations. Salespeople and their customers come very close physically. Hugging and/or kissing are common (even among men). This physical closeness is such a part of the culture that written business communications between male Hispanics may end with the phrase *"un fuerte abrazo"* (a strong hug) (Comer, 2000). A salesperson who does not understand the appropriate use of space may find it difficult to sell his or her product line.

Time Symbolism

Just as the use of space is culturally influenced, so too is the use of time. A culture's concept of time refers to the relative importance it places on time. Edward T. Hall noted that, "two time systems have evolved"—*monochronic* and *polychronic.* "Monochronic time means paying attention to and doing only one thing at a time. Polychronic time means being involved with many things at once. Like oil and water, the two systems do not mix" (1966, p. 16). In a *monochronic* time (M-time) system, schedules often take priority over everything else and are treated as sacred and unalterable. Planes and trains must always run on time. Individuals raised in M-time systems constantly check their calendars and watches, worry about being prompt for appointments, and take it as an insult if kept waiting by others. Although this may seem natural and logical, it is merely a learned product of northern European culture. Hall explains that M-time systems grew out of the Industrial Revolution in England, wherein the factory labor force was required to be on hand and in place at the appointed hour. While examples of purely monochronic societies are rare, it can safely be said that many Western cultures, and, in particular, the dominant culture in the United States, practice M-time. Anglo Americans conceive of time in discrete units and often refer to time in the same words they use to talk about money. Time is something that one can save, spend, or even waste. They tend to be future oriented and schedule their time efficiently. Punctuality is considered a virtue.

Polychronic time (P-time) systems are the antithesis of M-time systems. P-time is characterized by the simultaneous occurrence of many things and by a much greater involvement with people. In P-time systems, schedules and agendas mean very little, and appointments are often forgotten or rearranged at the last minute. No eyebrows are raised if one arrives at a meeting forty-five minutes late. Individuals from Latin American cultures often exhibit P-time behaviors. Hispanic culture adheres to this more relaxed view of time, which also tends to be present oriented. Sometimes referred to as *manses time,* the Hispanic style involves flexible attitudes toward punctuality. Hispanic people are routinely late for social events, yet do not perceive themselves to be late even when they arrive as much as twenty to thirty minutes after the appointed time. Furthermore, when involved in a task that is particularly engrossing, Hispanic people are likely to lose track of time, allowing their interest to dictate the way they use time, and may even be unaware of the amount of time expended (Comer, 2000).

Miller and Kemp note that blacks also have a different relationship with time:

> The use of time in African culture is driven by Kairos time (meaning, as it comes up) and the characteristic African American need for instant gratification vs. being clock or calendar driven. Additionally, economic and social circumstances often have a high degree of impact on the African American community, which forces them to live day-to-day and use both chronological and kairos time in their daily lives. Separate, but related, a common saying in the African American community, when describing the apparent disregard for their own punctuality and to distinguish black folks' timing vs. white folk's timing, is the phrase "CP Time" (Colored People's Time). Most likely an offshoot from kairos time theory, "CP Time" is an inside joke within the community but is an unwanted stereotype when viewed from outside the community. (2005, p. 28)

What does all this mean for marketing to ethnic groups? Differences between monochronic and polychronic peoples can affect everything from the behavior of salespeople to the timing of promotions and even advertising message content. While Hispanic sales people in the United States arrive punctually for their business appointments, their perception of time shows up in the way they apportion their time during a sales interview. For the Hispanic salesperson, relationship considerations dictate the way selling time is used. Selling objectives are subordinate to the establishment of good interpersonal relationships. As a result, interviews can be long, including much relational communication (Comer, 2000). For African Americans, advertising and promoting an event too far in advance often leaves room for blacks to forget or make other plans. For example, in 2002, the Chicago Symphony Orchestra (CSO) received a grant to reach out to underserved minority communities. The CSO's typical marketing plan includes a direct mail schedule that typically begins a full five months prior to a September opening. Advised that African Americans tend to live day-to-day with less interest in the distant future, CSO released its messages closer to opening night. In addition, it also reserved a number of tickets for last-minute purchasers. Because CSO took the kairos time characteristic into consideration, it was successful in building a relationship with this new marketing segment (Miller & Kemp, 2005). In terms of message content, a telephone company did not take time orientation into account when developing a television spot for its Latin American audience. In the ad, the wife told her husband to "run down downstairs and phone Mary. Tell her we'll be a little late." This message would not resonate with Latin Americans, because they would not feel obligated to phone to warn of tardiness, as it would be expected (Ricks, 1983, p. 70).

Eye Contact

The degree of eye contact also varies from one ethnic group to another. Some groups discourage direct or prolonged eye contact. Rossman (1994) notes that most Anglo American children in the United States are taught to look at the teacher or parent if they are being scolded. In many Asian, Latin American, and other cultures, in contrast, children are often taught to look down or away as a sign of respect for the person who is scolding them. Adults who are part of the dominant culture typically regard someone who doesn't look them in the eye as shifty or untrustworthy, yet most Asians think that looking someone in the eye is rude or even confrontational. Rossman shares an example of the role that eye contact can play in a retail setting: In an interview in Los Angeles, some African Americans discussed their angry feelings toward Korean American shop owners. They said they felt poorly treated because the Koreans didn't look them in the eye, smile at them, or put change from a purchase in their hand. The African Americans interpreted the Korean Americans' behavior as disrespectful. In fact, Koreans consider it rude or aggressive to look deeply into someone's eyes, inappropriate or false to smile at someone they don't know very well, and improper to touch a stranger. Yet, if the Korean American shopkeepers are to succeed as retailers in the United States, they must learn to adapt to the nonverbal communication patterns of their customers.

Colors and Other Signs and Symbols

Research has shown that color preferences vary between the dominant culture and various cocultures. For example, while whites tend to prefer white, green, orange, and yellow, African Americans prefer blue and violet (Lee & Barnes, 1990). A thorough understanding of how colors are perceived in each ethnic group to which a marketer is planning to appeal is clearly beneficial. Recently, Home Depot launched *Colores Origenes,* a palette featuring seventy vibrant colors that reflect Hispanic culture. The retailer partnered with Bahr Paints to create the palette, which also has Spanish names for the colors, such as *Azul Cielito Lindo* (Lovely Blue Sky) and *Chayote* (Chayote Squash). The colors in *Origenes,* which means "the origin of one's roots," were designed to create visuals of Latin America and inspire consumers looking to capture their culture in their home décor (*Home Channel News,* 2005). OPI introduced the Mexico Collection of colors to sell nail polish to Hispanic women in *People en Español* magazine. The ads headline reads "OPI. La Cultura del Color"— "The Culture of Color" (see Figure 3.3). Laurence Jacobs, Charles Keown, and Kyung-Il Ghymn note, "Like language, marketers often take color for granted, having experienced certain color associations all their lives, and do not even question whether other associations may exist" (1991, p. 21). The significance of, and meanings associated with, specific colors vary as well. For instance, an advertiser may send out a red-colored direct mail piece to indicate, "Stop—this is important." However, for some Asian cultures, while red is considered a lucky color, it simply does not carry the same sense of urgency. When the *New York Times* targeted Chinese Americans for the first time, they changed the colors of vending machines in the Chinatown section of Manhattan from blue, their standard color, to red. The reason—blue is considered the color of mourning among Chinese. Marketers need to understand what associations a specific culture has in terms of colors and how they might affect product design, packaging, logos, advertisements, and other collateral.

Numbers, shapes, and symbols can also mean different things to different ethnic groups. Eliot Kang, president of Kang & Lee Advertising in New York—an agency that specializes in targeting Asian American consumers—notes that the number four implies death in various Asian cultures. "Airline executives did not think anything of using that number," noted Kang, recalling an airline

Figure 3.3: The headline for this nail polish ad reads "The culture of color."

that briefly did use such a phone number years ago. "But it would be like having the number 1–800-FRIDAY-THE-13th in English" (Elliott, 2000). At Lunar New Year celebrations, Bank of America hands out red envelopes filled with promotional materials for its Asian American customers. Traditionally given to friends and relatives, the palm-sized envelopes are usually stuffed with money. In this case, the bank's oversized envelopes give customers the choice of two hundred free checks, free checking for six months, or an $8 bonus when they open a checking account. While $8 may seem like an arbitrary sum, it isn't to the bank's new target customers: In Cantonese, eight is a lucky number. Symbols can also be problematic. One of AT&T's competitors offered a special travel clock if a customer switched from AT&T's long-distance service to their service. The promotion was directed to the Chinese American market. The direct-mail campaign raised eyebrows in the Chinese community, because giving clocks to people is tantamount to telling your customers that you want to shorten their time for living. The word for *clock* in Chinese sounds very much like the word for *death*. Hence, it is considered bad luck to give a clock to a person of Chinese descent (Grant, 2003).

Expressions of Culture

Geert Hofstede (1990) proposed that the four basic expressions of culture are symbols, heroes, rituals, and values (see Figure 3.4). These expressions are depicted by Hofstede much like the skins of an onion, suggesting that symbols represent the most superficial layers and that values represent the deepest manifestations of culture, with heroes and rituals falling in between. Marieke de Mooij (1994) does a fine job of defining these layers. *Symbols* can be words, gestures, pictures, and objects that carry a specific meaning only recognized by members of a culture. Included here are the latest status symbols, the newest fashion trends, and the hippest hairstyles. New symbols are quickly developed, and old ones fade away. Often, the symbols from one coculture are adopted by another. Miller and Kemp note that when

> African-American youth start wearing a new style of clothing, the rest of the country soon follows. Hip-hop and rap music is heard blasting from the cars of Asians, Latinos, and white youth every day. As soon as members of the so-called dominant culture have overheard another example of African-American slang, they begin using the same phrase in mainstream communications. Witness the *Today Show's* Katie Couric's repeated use of the phrase "bling-bling" when referencing luxury items. (2005, p. 4)

Symbols are shown in the outer, most superficial layer of the diagram. *Heroes* are persons, alive or dead, real or imaginary, who possess characteristics prized in a particular culture. Thus, heroes serve as models for members of a society. Political figures (from Martin Luther King Jr. to César Chávez) can be upheld as heroes by a specific group, as can film and television stars (such as Oprah Winfrey and Penélope Cruz). Even cartoon characters can be perceived as heroes (whether it be Superman or Snoopy). *Rituals* are collective activities considered essential within a culture. Social and religious ceremonies, business and political meetings, and even sporting events are all rituals. Consider the ritualistic behavior associated with attending a football game in the United States. Tickets are purchased months in advance. Fans often paint themselves with the team's colors to show support in the stands. After the event itself, tailgate parties take place in the stadium parking lot. In the diagram, symbols, heroes, and rituals are intersected with the term *practices*. While practices are visible to nonmembers of a culture, their cultural meaning is invisible. The true meaning of practices lies in how they are interpreted by members of the culture. At the core of culture lie *values*. Values are broad tendencies to prefer certain states of affairs over others and typically embody contrasts (what is good versus evil, what is beautiful versus ugly) (Hofstede, 1990). Because cultural values are of critical importance to marketers and advertisers, they will be discussed in greater detail below.

Figure 3.4: Expressions of Culture at Different Levels

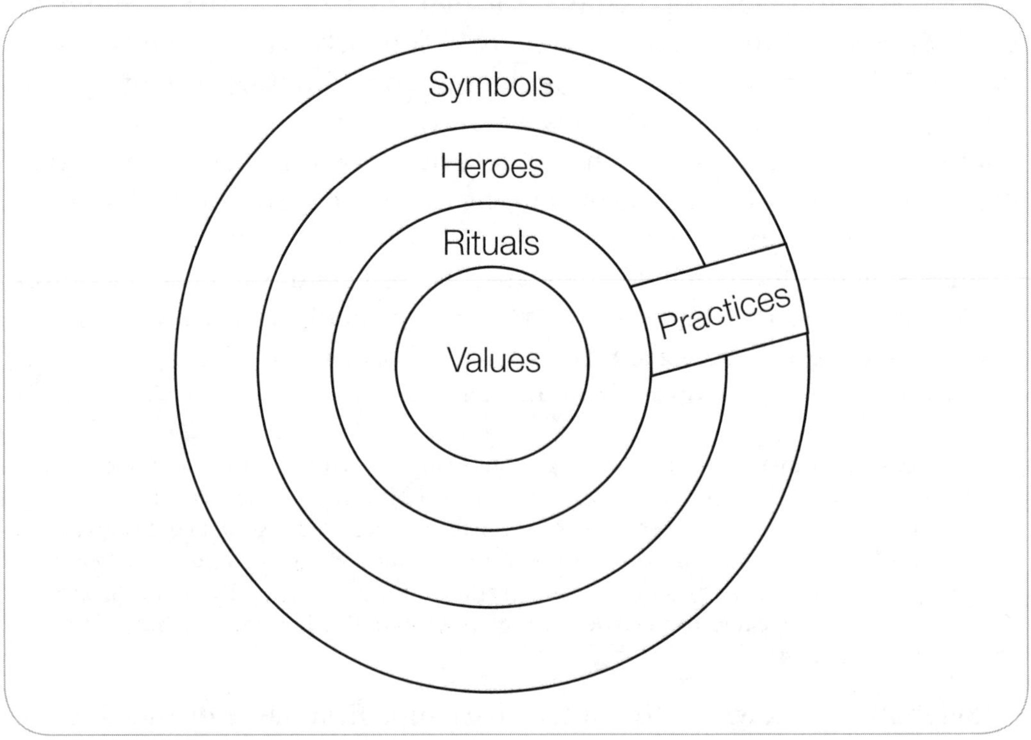

From *Expressions of Culture at Different Levels* (Working Paper No. 90–006), by Geert Hofstede, 1990, Netherlands: University of Limburg.

Values

To maximize the chances of success, marketers must examine the cultural values that dominate in a specific coculture. Milton Rokeach provides a classic definition of a *value:* "an enduring belief that a specific mode of conduct or end state of existence is personally and socially preferable to an opposite or converse mode of conduct or end state of existence" (1973). Put more simply, Edward C. Steward states that values "represent a learned organization of rules for making choices and for resolving conflicts" (1972, p. 74). Articles in scholarly journals on values and consumer behavior suggest that values may indeed be one of the most powerful explanations of and influences on consumer behavior (Rokeach, 1968).

While an examination of value systems can prove quite beneficial to a marketer, it is often fraught with problems. Though the United States is often called a cultural melting pot, in reality, it is an example of a particularly heterogeneous culture. If it is stated that a particular value is characteristic of the United States, it is not to say that each and every member of this society will possess that value. Rather, it suggests that the value is reflective of the dominant culture. However, the concept of values can prove useful in distinguishing the values of the dominant culture from those of the various cocultures. Thus, it is possible to make statements regarding the value systems that tend to distinguish one ethnic group from another.

Classifying and Assessing Values

Several classification systems have been devised for assessing the values of a culture. For example, Rokeach developed a means of quantifying personal value systems (1968). As shown in Table 3.2, the Rokeach Value Survey identifies eighteen terminal values and eighteen instrumental values. Terminal values concern desired end states of existence that are socially and personally worth striving for. Instrumental values relate to modes of conduct and represent beliefs that are socially and personally preferable in all situations with respect to all objects. Value systems are identified by having individuals complete a survey that asks them to arrange all thirty-six values in order of their importance as guiding principles in their lives.

This framework is effective in discriminating between people of culturally diverse backgrounds (Munson & McIntyre, 1978). For example, the instrumental value of *ambitious* means hardworking and aspiring. The degree to which consumers perceive themselves as hardworking (or aspiring to this value) may differ from one coculture to the next, and this may have implications for promotional efforts.

Core values go much deeper than behavior or attitudes, and they determine, at a basic level, people's choices and desires. Behavior changes with amazing

Table 3.2: Instrumental and Terminal and Instrumental Values	
Terminal values	**Instrumental values**
A comfortable life (a prosperous life)	Ambitious (hardworking, aspiring)
An exciting life (a stimulating, active life)	Broad-minded (open-minded)
A sense of accomplishment (a lasting contribution)	Capable (competent, effective)
A world at peace (free of war and conflict)	Cheerful (lighthearted, joyful)
A world of beauty (beauty of nature and the arts)	Clean (neat, tidy)
Equality (brotherhood, equal opportunity for all)	Courageous (standing up for your beliefs)
Family security (taking care of loved ones)	Forgiving (willing to pardon others)
Freedom (independence, free choice)	Helpful (working for welfare of others)
Happiness (contentedness)	Honest (sincere, truthful)
Inner harmony (freedom from inner conflict)	Imaginative (daring, creative)
Mature love (sexual and spiritual intimacy)	Independent (self-sufficient)
National security (protection from attack)	Intellectual (intelligent, reflective)
Pleasure (an enjoyable, leisurely life)	Logical (consistent, rational)
Salvation (saved, eternal life)	Loving (affectionate, tender)
Self-respect (respect, admiration)	Obedient (dutiful, respectful)
Social recognition (respect, admiration)	Polite (courteous, well-mannered)
True friendship (close companionship)	Responsible (dependent, reliable)
Wisdom (mature understanding of life)	Self-controlled (restrained, self-disciplined)

Note. From *The Nature of Human Values* (p. 28), by Milton Rokeach, 1973, New York: Free Press

speed in response to outside forces of all kinds, such as whether a person had a good night's sleep or how long the line at the grocery store was. Although slower to change, attitudes are also prone to external forces, such as, for instance, the beliefs of one's peer group. Core values, on the other hand, are intrinsic to a person's identity. By appealing to people's inner selves, it is possible to influence their outer selves—their purchase behavior (Miller, 1998).

An examination of cultural values can do more than assist marketers in segmenting consumers. With regards to the relationship between values and advertising, values may be among the major influences on human behavior. As noted in *Social Values and Social Change,*

> value-linked advertisements may animate affect, creating an affective response closer to the value-induced affect than to the product or advertisement without the value link. To the extent that affective advertisements are more influential than bland ads, values may be a mechanism to explore when trying to understand the sources of affect. (Kahle, 1983)

Indeed, numerous empirical studies have found that advertisements reflecting cultural values are, in fact, more persuasive than those that ignore them

(Gregory & Munch, 1997; Taylor & Wilson, 1997; Han & Shavitt, 1994). Research on ethnic consumers has revealed that they are, indeed, more responsive to messages that emphasize their cultures and values, such as self-fulfillment, self-respect, and accomplishment (Pitts, Whalen, O'Keefe, & Murray, 1989). If marketers hope to formulate more effective messages for ethnic consumers, they must become sensitive to the core values of that given ethnic group.

Religion, Morals, and Ethical Standards

One of the terminal values on Rokeach's list of values is salvation. Most organized religions offer a means of salvation. Robert Bartels notes that

> the foundation of culture and the most important determinant of social and business conduct are the religious and philosophic beliefs of a people. From them spring role perceptions, behavior patterns, codes of ethics and the institutionalized manner in which economic activities are performed. (1982, p. 5)

As such, knowledge of the moral and religious traditions of particular ethnic groups is essential to the marketer's understanding of why consumers behave the way they do.

Although numerous religious groups exist in the world today, Buddhism, Christianity, Hinduism, Islam, and Shinto are considered the major religions in terms of numbers of adherents. Religion can influence the value its adherents place on consumption of material goods and can have a direct impact on a number of the marketing mix elements, as well. At the heart of Buddhism, for example, is the belief that suffering is caused by attachment to material possessions and selfish enjoyment of any kind. Islam also considers an emphasis on material wealth immoral. Such views stand in direct contrast to the Protestant ethic of hard work, wherein acquisition of wealth is a measure of achievement. Yet, many bemoan the fact that the birth of Christ today is associated with a shopping frenzy. Everyone is familiar with the fervor with which American businesses gear up for the Christmas season. As early as September, many retailers begin to decorate their stores and shops with garlands and Christmas trees to stimulate holiday shopping. In December, retailers even extend their business hours in response to dramatic increases in consumer purchasing.

Religion may forbid altogether the consumption of various types of products. Drinking alcohol is frowned upon if not forbidden by Islam; strict Protestants, Jews, and Muslims do not eat pork; and Hindus do not eat beef. Not long ago, McDonald's faced a class-action lawsuit which alleged that the fast-food giant misled its customers for over a decade by advertising its French fries as vegetarian, while all the while flavoring them with beef extract. The beef flavoring was of concern to vegetarians, of course, but also to the one million Hindus in the United States who are forbidden from consuming beef or beef products. In its defense, McDonald's stated "we have never made any vegetarian claims about our French fries or any other product. When suppliers prepare the French fries and freeze them for various McDonald's stores, natural flavoring is added, which consists of minuscule amounts of beef extract" (Purewal, 2001). In 1990, McDonald's switched from preparing its fries in beef tallow to vegetable oil, in order to offer a cholesterol-free menu item. On the McDonald's Web site, where ingredients for each product are listed, there is no mention of beef being used in the fries.

Religion may provide an answer in how best to reach ethnic consumers. The vast majority (nearly three-quarters) of the Hispanic population is Catholic, and most Hispanics attend mass every Sunday morning. Some marketers have taken note of the fact that such a large segment of this population is in a certain place at a certain time. A Chase retail banking executive in Texas observed that Sunday mass had just ended at a local cathedral and that the area around the church was filled with people—many of them Hispanics. Noting that only half of U.S. Hispanics are bank customers, compared with 80% of the population as a whole, the executive recognized an opportunity and quickly ordered Chase to park its Bankmobile outside the church and open a nearby branch, which normally would be closed on Sundays. Chase's Bankmobile is a converted recreational vehicle, staffed with bilingual employees capable of bringing banking services right to potential customers (Aleshire, 2005).

A recent investigation found that religion and the intensity of religious beliefs has an effect on the attitudes towards the advertising of particular product categories. Researchers surveyed nearly 1,400 consumers across four religious groups (Buddhism, Christianity, Islam, and nonreligious believers) and four controversial product categories (gender- and sex-related products, such as female and male underwear, condoms, female contraceptives, and feminine hygiene products; social/political groups, such as religious denominations, political parties, and racially extreme groups; health and care products, such as weight loss programs, drugs for sexual diseases, and charities; and, finally, addictive products, such as cigarettes, alcohol, and gambling). Among the results, it was found that there is a significant difference between the four controversial product groups and the four religious denominations. Apparently, the Islamic followers found the advertising of gender- and sex-related products, social/political groups, and health and care products most offensive relative to the other three religions. In addition, the religiously devout respondents were more likely to find the advertising of gender- and sex-related products, health and care products, and addictive products more offensive than the less devout followers (Fam, Waller, & Erdogan, 2004). With regard to the content of advertising messages, advertisers must be careful not to offend any religious groups. In some religions, references to god or religion are taken very seriously, and such references are considered inappropriate for use on products or in promotional materials. In 2003, American Eagle Outfitters (AE) introduced a line of products, including handbags and flip-flop shoes, portraying Lord Ganesh—an auspicious deity in the Hindu religion. Heated protests followed—and the company was flooded with phone calls and e-mails. An online petition gathered 4,600 signatures in just thirty-six hours. American Hindus Against Defamation—a coalition of major Hindu organizations in North America—argued that sandals are considered dirty and to put images of a Hindu deity on them was sacrilege. In his letter of apology, Neil Bulman Jr., vice president and general counsel of AE, said,

> on behalf of American Eagle Outfitters, please accept this letter as our formal apology for our use of the image resembling Lord Ganesh on this product. Please know that the AE flip flops bearing a likeness to Lord Ganesh were designed as a fashion item. AE had no intention of offending the religious sentiments of the Hindu community. This letter confirms that we will remove these flip flop shoes from our stores in order to maintain the goodwill and our customer relations with the Hindu community. We value diversity and respect the ideal of freedom of expression of all religious and cultural beliefs. (Joseph, 2003)

The flip-flops disappeared from store shelves shortly thereafter. Victoria's Secret also learned a hard lesson when the company tried cashing in on Asian influences by using Buddha's image on a line of bikini wear. The marketing ploy sparked consumer outrage (Le, 2005).

Religion may even influence the media vehicles selected to communicate with ethnic consumers. Many African Americans consider faith an integral part of their lives. Blacks are significantly more likely to regularly attend church than either Hispanic Americans or whites. Tyson Foods recently purchased full-page ads in two magazines targeting black Christians—*Gospel Truth* and *Previous Times*. The ads, targeted to black women ages twenty-four to fifty-four, feature a black family having a picnic. The visual portrayed parents grilling and kids playing tug of war. Tyson Foods also began running commercials featuring African Americans on gospel shows on TV One, a cable channel focused on African Americans, and Black Entertainment Television. Ford Motor Company is just one major marketer running commercials on the Gospel Music Channel—featuring the Ford 500 Sedan and Explorer. Gospel radio stations are also proliferating—nationwide, there are nearly three hundred black gospel radio stations, compared with just eighty a decade ago. Although only about 15% of blacks tune in to gospel stations, according to the research firm Arbitron Inc., among those listeners, more than 70% own their own homes, and 17% have household incomes of more than $75,000—making them a particularly appealing segment of the market. Even Web sites target black Christians. ChristianHangSuite.com is an Internet portal targeted at black Christians. It hosts monthly social gatherings in hopes of getting more Web site viewers and, thus, more ads. ChristianHangSuite.com has received advertising from the Sony pictures movie *The Gospel,* gospel recording artists, and a travel agency marketing to black Christians (Williams, 2005). Note that Kraft Foods sponsors an annual Gospel Talent Search, which it promotes in its advertising (see Figure 3.5). Clearly, religion is an element of culture that pervades every aspect of a society. Understanding the impact of religion on the value system of a group and the effect of that value system on marketing should not be underestimated.

Family

The family is one of the oldest and most enduring of all human institutions. Galvin and Brommel note, "We are born into a family, mature in a family, form new families, and leave them at our death" (1991). The family is primarily responsible for transmitting a culture's values to its newest members. McGoldrick explains, "What you think, how you act, even your language, are all transmitted through the family from the wider cultural context. This context includes the culture in which you live, and those from which your ancestors have come" (1973). Clearly then, different cultures create different families. In some cultures, the *extended family* is the norm, consisting of three or more generations living together. Often, such families include not only parents, children, and grandparents, but also aunts, uncles, and cousins. In other cultures, the *nuclear family,* with mother, father, and one or more children, is more typical. *Nontraditional family structures* are more common in some cultures than others. The U.S. Census Bureau regards any occupied housing unit as a household, regardless of the relationships among the people living there. Thus, one person living alone, three roommates, or two lovers all constitute households. Families worldwide are becoming less traditional, and this is particularly so in the United States—which has the highest incidence of divorce and single-parent households of any country in the world (Solomon, 1999). A family's consumption behavior is affected by factors such as the number of people (adults and children, related and unrelated) in the family, their ages, and the number of adults employed outside the home. Families also have a lasting influence on the consumer preferences of family members. Research has shown that one of the best predictors of brands that adults use is the ones their parents used. This is apparently equally true for high-involvement products, such as autos, and low-involvement goods, such as toothpaste. As such, the family is of great interest to advertisers.

Despite the cultural differences between different Hispanic groups, one of the commonalities marketers can draw upon is the high value placed on fam-

Figure 3.5: Kraft Foods Promotes Its Annual Gospel Talent Search

ily. Familialism is an important Hispanic value (Sabogal, Marin, Otero-Sabogal, Van Oss Marin, & Perez-Stable, 1987), which involves a strong attachment for and identification with families. Hispanic people have large nuclear or extended families and are strongly attached to them. Hispanics also receive a strong sense of loyalty and solidarity from their family members (Trandis, Marin, Hui, Limansky, & Ottati, 1982), and their families serve as natural support systems for them (Valle and Martinez, 1980). Comer (2000) notes that these feelings are so strong that, when Hispanic people relocate, they typically do not move far from their families either geographically or emotionally. This deep involvement with their families permeates their lives and the lives of those in their social groups. Hispanic families are the largest of any group in the United States. There are 4.2 individuals per Hispanic family, compared to the national average of about 2.3 individuals per family. Familialism also impacts a variety of promotional activities—including, for example, advertising and personal selling. Family must be reflected in commercial messages created for the Hispanic audience. Consider the successful Got Milk campaign, which highlighted the horrors of milk deprivation. Although perceived as hilarious by the general population, Hispanics saw nothing to laugh about. The idea of a Latin mother running out of milk was offensive rather than funny. Anita Santiago, a veteran advertising executive who works exclusively in Spanish, informed the California Milk Processor Board that "being deprived of milk is not a funny spot to be in. It is worrisome for a family-oriented community. Further, the spots were not directed at the key guardian of family nutrition, Mom. And, finally, the ads questioned Mom's skills as a good housekeeper—how could she be with no milk in the house?" The Got Milk ads, if directed at Latino consumers, could have gone terribly wrong. Santiago designed the first Spanish campaign for the milk board, which carried the tagline *Y Usted les Dio Suficiente Leche Hoy?* (Have you given them enough milk today?). These ads incorporated milk recipes in Latino cooking that are passed from generation to generation and reflected the emotional and cultural bonds of Latinos to milk. They directly targeted mothers and/or grandmothers, and the campaign served the milk board's purposes well (Raine, 2001). Apparently, the aversion to the English Got Milk campaign was unique among Latinos. African Americans and Asian Americans in Milk Board focus groups appeared to appreciate the humor in the messages. Familialism is also reflected in the salesperson/customer relationship. Hispanic salespeople are typically very well acquainted with the families of their Hispanic customers and are even entertained in their homes.

While Asian Americans vary demographically by subgroup, respect for family is one value that also unites the various Asian cultures. Compared with the U.S. population as a whole, Asians tend to have more traditional arrangements. Asians are more likely to live in married-couple households and are more likely to live in a nuclear family, with a married mom and dad and related children. This cultural proclivity is so strong that advertisers who present nontraditional family images to the Asian American market find that the advertising is less than effective (Wellner, 2002). However, not every Asian household holds to tradition, according to the latest census data. In fact, for two subgroups—Japanese and Thai Americans—the share of traditional family households is not only smaller than for the Asian average, it is also smaller than for the U.S. average (see Table 3.3). Single-mother households are also less common among Asian Americans than in the population as a whole, but a larger share of Cambodian, Laotian, and Filipino households are single-mother controlled, compared with the U.S. population, as well as the Asian population as a whole. Yet, even if reality doesn't completely match the marketing images, companies are advised not to disregard the power of family values when communicating with Asian American subgroups that are less likely to live in traditional settings.

In contrast with Hispanic and Asian families, which are typically two-parent households, much media attention has been given to the decline of the black family.

Table 3.3: Asian Americans and the Traditional Family	
Ethnicity	Percent of households that are married-couple families with children younger than 18 years of age
Bangladeshi	56%
Pakistani	54%
Laotian	50%
Cambodian	50%
Vietnamese	43%
Indian	42%
Sri Lankan	42%
Filipino	36%
Asian total	36%
Chinese	33%
Korean	32%
Indonesian	29%
Malaysian	26%
Other	26%
U.S. total	25%
Thai	23%
Japanese	22%

Note. Data from *Forecast Analysis of Census 2000 Data*. Wellner, A.S. (2002, November). *Inside Asian Markets*. Forecast, Ithaca, *22*(11) p. 1

Historically, blacks have valued the institution and the traditional two-parent household. Back in 1890, 80 percent of African-American families were headed by two
parents, even though many had started life in forced family separation under slavery.
Even in the 1960s, when black Americans were in the height of civil rights strife,
only 23 percent of black infants were born out of wedlock, a modest figure compared
with 70 percent today. (Reid, 2004)

Family structures have eroded to the point where only 36% of African
American children live in two-parent homes, creating a situation where a
majority of households are headed by single women. On the bright side, more
than 75% of African Americans were middle or upper class in 2005. However,
among those who make up the 23% in poverty, an overwhelming majority are
unmarried females and their children ("More Marches," 2005). And African
Americans continue to experience a rate of joblessness that is more than twice
the national average. These conditions contribute to a median income level for
African Americans that is only 65% of that for the nation as a whole (Butler,
2000). Sensitivity regarding these statistics can go a long way with the ethnic
consumer. Consider the print ad created for a leading car company that ran in
Jet magazine, which sought to promote their vehicle to black consumers with
the slogan, "Unlike your boyfriend, it goes to work every day." The advertising
faux pas, which was rapidly withdrawn (Morley, 2003), clearly did not resonate with African American consumers. Miller and Kemp (2005, p. 27) note
that culturally sensitive, positive appeals that celebrate the culture rather than
reinforce stereotypes continue to be elements that are more likely to gain the
attention and loyalty of African Americans. Marketers are encouraged to reverse
common stereotypes by including African American family units (including
the black father as an emotionally engaged and responsible caretaker). Procter
& Gamble was much more in tune with their audience in the image of blacks
they portrayed in their campaign for Tide with Downy. Created by Burrell
Communications, the campaign featured an African American man, sleeping
on his back with a small child sleeping on his stomach. There was a shiny
gold wedding band on his left hand and neo-soul music played softly in the
background (see Figure 3.6 for a print ad from the campaign). The campaign
received rave reviews from the black community, as well as a number of
advertising awards. Because of the success of the campaign, Burrell and P&G
decided to include the ads in their general market rotation. As a result, according to P&G's Tide brand team, the commercial has the highest performance
score among Tide commercials, and the brand achieved the highest return on
investment as a result of this campaign.

Figure 3.6: Tide ad countering stereotypes of the African American family.

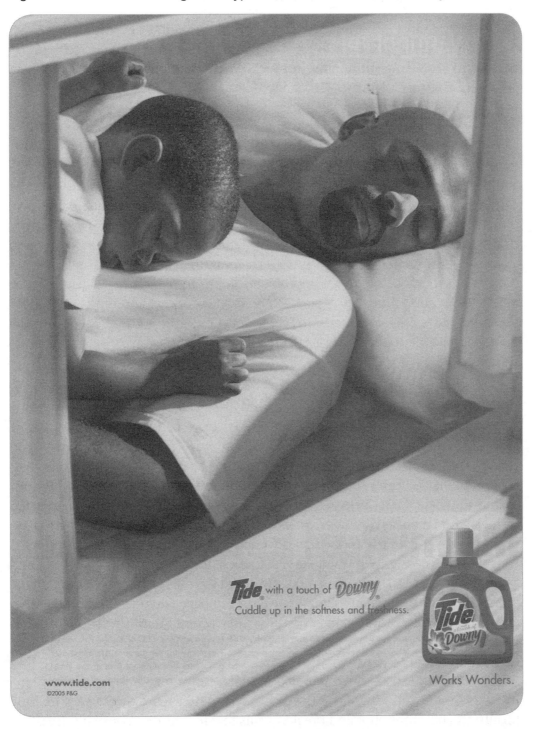

Hofstede's Dimensions of Culture

One of the most important frameworks for understanding culture in the past two decades has been Geert Hofstede's typology of cultural dimensions (1980). Based on 117,000 questionnaires from 88,000 respondents in twenty languages, reflecting sixty-six countries, Hofstede delineated four important dimensions that can be used to classify countries: *individualism,* society's preference for a group or individual orientation; *power distance,* societal desire for hierarchy or egalitarianism; *masculinity versus femininity,* a sex-role dimension; and *uncertainty avoidance,* a culture's tolerance for uncertainty. Later research resulted in the addition of a fifth dimension, *long-term orientation* (Hofstede & Bond, 1988), the cultural perspective on a long-term versus a short-term basis. Each of the five dimensions is measured on a scale from 0 to 100 (index). The scores indicate the relative differences between cultures. An increasing number of marketing and advertising researchers have recognized the potential applicability of Hofstede's dimensions to marketing research problems (for example, Albers-Miller, 1996; de Mooij, 1998; and Milner & Collins, 2000). As with context and time orientation, differences in these five dimensions can impact both the content of commercial messages and the creative strategies most likely to be effective.

Individualism versus Collectivism

Of Hofstede's five dimensions, individualism versus collectivism is the one that has received the greatest level of attention by researchers examining ethnic groups in the United States. The *individualism-versus-collectivism* dimension pertains to the importance of the group rather than the individual. A high individualism ranking indicates that individuality and individual rights are paramount within the society. Ties between individuals are loose, and everyone is expected to look after themselves. Laws, rules, and regulations are institutionalized to protect the rights of the individual. Overall, the dominant American culture is considered to be highly individualistic. Indeed, it is said that both the best and worst features of U.S. culture can be attributed to individualism. Proponents of individualism have argued that it is the basis of liberty, democracy, and freedom and serves as a protection against tyranny. On the other hand, individualism has been blamed for Americans' alienation from one another, loneliness, selfishness, and narcissism.

A low individualism ranking indicates that a culture tends to be collectivistic. In collectivistic cultures, social ties are much tighter. One owes one's lifelong loyalty to one's in-group, and breaking this loyalty has dire consequences. The supreme value is the welfare of the group. Numerous cocultures in the United States can be said to be classified as collectivistic.

Although capturing an important dimension of cultural differences, Coon and Kemmelmeier (2001) note that the simple dichotomy between individualistic and collectivistic cultures ignores large within-culture variability in individual-ism versus collectivism. They note that, while cross-cultural research focuses on members of the cultural majority, people of different ethnic groups are socialized in different traditions and possess cultural orientations that are different from the majority. Gaines et al. (1997) found that Americans of minority groups, when taken as a whole, indeed scored higher on collectivism than did Anglo Americans. However, this does not suggest that all three minority groups (Asian Americans, Hispanic Americans, and African Americans) endorse collectivism to the same degree—indeed, this hardly does justice to the diversity in the history, heritage, and status of these three groups. The cultural roots and traditions of minority populations are generally assumed to be collectivistic to match their country of origin due to socialization processes that reflect these roots. Thus, Asian Americans are thought to be collectivistic due to their Asian background. Similarly, Hispanics are seen as a collectivistic culture.

Asian cultures are typically considered to be collectivistic. For example, Japanese belong to reference groups, which vary from small to large, formal to informal, and intimate to impersonal. In identifying themselves, the Japanese stress their position in a social frame rather than their individualistic attributes. The Japanese approach to the group role is to perceive oneself as an integral part of the whole. The individual does not interact as an individual but as the son in a parent-child relationship or as a worker in an employee-employer relation-ship. A high value is placed on the harmonious integration of group members and on consensus. It is emphasized that opinions should always be held unani-mously. The Japanese see all decisions and actions as part of group consensus. Among the Japanese, this generates pressures for conformity to group norms and pressures to be like everyone else. The sense of identity anchored to in-group belongingness is sustained by going along with peers. There is restraint from expressing disagreement with whatever appears to be the majority opinion. This strong sense of belongingness as a state of self-identity calls for the individual's total commitment and loyalty to the group. This also means that the group is responsible for taking care of all the needs of its members.

Similarly, Filipino culture is considered quite collectivistic. While Western definitions identify the traditional family unit as households in which the husband, wife, and their children live together, by Filipino standards, families usually include extended family members as well. Filipino families tend to place the welfare of the family above that of the individual and the larger commu-nity. Interdependence and family loyalty are emphasized, in contrast to values of independence and individualism. Traditional Filipino values include, among others, respect for authority figures and elders, and *utang na loob*—debt of grati-tude. Even after migrating to the United States, Filipinos are expected to continue to support family members back home. Furthermore, Filipino Americans will tend to house and support relatives who migrate to the United States until they too become financially independent (Atienza, 2001). This collectivistic orientation continues to endure, generation after generation.

Hispanic culture is also rooted in collectivism. Research reveals that 61% of Hispanics, versus 46% of African Americans and only 39% of non-Hispanic whites agree with the statement that "People's main responsibility is to themselves and their families—not to making the world a better place to live in." Collectivism in a close-knit Hispanic family is fostered in large part by the lack of trust in outside institutions, which is common in Latin American businesses and government. This explains why Hispanic families look inward and depend on and trust each other. But it is fair to assume that trust will broaden with greater Hispanic consumer involvement with institutions in the United States (Suarez-Hammond, 2005).

As one might expect, advertisements for individualistic audiences should place a high value on individuality (or being unique), independence, success, and/or self-realization. In contrast, ads appealing to members of collectivistic audiences would do well to reflect the group orientation. Ads should portray people in groups rather than as individuals. *We* and *us* are effective pronouns for these ads. Message content should emphasize interdependence, family, group well-being, and concern for others.

Influence of Culture on Consumer Behavior

Culture influences why we buy. It impacts our attitudes toward consumption and our shopping behavior, what we choose to purchase, and even where we choose to purchase it. It has a direct influence on which family member is most likely to make purchase decisions and even on how we buy—with cash, check, or credit card.

Why Consumers Buy

Anthropologists, psychologists, and sociologists all have sought to explain why individuals engage in consumption behavior. In attempting to understand consumers, marketers may look at the needs that motivate purchase behavior. A useful theory of human motivation was developed by Abraham Maslow (1964), who hypothesized that people's needs can be arranged in a hierarchy reflecting their relative potency. At the base of the hierarchy are physiological needs. As humans, our need for food, water, and shelter from the elements dominates our behavior. As these fundamental or lower needs are met, higher needs emerge, such as the need for safety—for security and protection from dangers in the environment. Once these basic needs have been provided for, social needs arise—the need for affection from family and friends and the

Figure 3.7: Hennessy Ad Appealing to Social and Economic Achievement

need to belong to a group. Higher-order needs include the need for esteem (self-respect, prestige, success, and achievement) and, finally, the need for self-actualization or self-fulfillment. Miller and Kemp (2005) note that African Americans tend to have identity-shaping relationships with brands. Particular upscale, top-end brands are visible symbols of success for communicating social and economic achievement. Indeed, according to a Yankelovich study (2003), blacks were more than twice as likely as whites (30% versus 14%) to indicate that brands let others know where they are on the social ladder. Such brands function as badge items, to show others they have made it. Note how Hennessy cognac appeals to African American consumers in its copy: "I have seen Count Basie live. I have conviction. I have given back. I have 14 countries stamped on my passport. I have never forgotten where I'm from. Are you Privileged?" (see Figure 3.7). It should be noted that people are not locked into a particular level in Maslow's hierarchy; clearly, an individual attempting to fulfill esteem needs must also address basic physiological needs.

Shopping Behavior

While whites make up the majority of the shopping hordes, they are the least likely to enjoy the process. Just 35% of white consumers say they enjoy shopping, even when they don't buy anything, compared with almost half (47%) of Asian consumers, 43% of black consumers, and 42% of Hispanic shoppers who say the same. Almost two-thirds (62%) of white consumers say they go shopping only when they absolutely need something, versus 57% of Asians, 54% of Hispanics, and 47% of blacks who say they do the same. White consumers are the most likely to say they make spur-of-the-moment purchases (41%, versus 37% of Hispanics, 35% of Asians, and 34% of blacks). Yet, they are also more likely (59%) to plan far ahead to buy expensive items than are Asians (53%), Hispanics (52%), or African Americans (44%). Of the three major ethnic groups, Hispanics are more likely to make shopping a family affair. More than one-third prefer shopping with their families, and 30% report that they like shopping with their children, compared with 29% and 26%, respectively, of the total population. Asians also do not like to shop alone: 31% say they prefer shopping with their friends. African American consumers, more so than the other groups, prefer shopping individually (Gardyn & Fetto, 2003).

Brands that earn the trust of ethnic consumers are likely to find success. For example, 63% of Hispanics and 62% of African Americans, compared with 52% of non-Hispanic whites, agree with the statement, "A trusted brand name has a lot of influence on my decision to purchase an item." And it is generally recognized that ethnic consumers are brand loyal when there is trust in a brand. In fact, 62% of African Americans and 58% of Hispanics, versus 46% of non-Hispanic whites, agree with the statement, "It is risky to buy a brand you are not familiar with" (Suarez-Hammond, 2005). Of the three ethnic groups, Asian consumers tend to be the most brand conscious. Almost half (43%) say that they always look for a brand name when they shop—a significantly higher percentage than for the other ethnic groups (Gardyn & Fetto, 2003). These figures suggest that ethnic consumers should not be taken for granted.

What Consumers Buy

People purchase goods and services to meet the various needs outlined above in Maslow's model. But the exact contents of the particular market basket will differ from ethnic group to ethnic group. It should come as no great surprise that, because they are dictated by culture, consumption habits vary greatly from one coculture to the next. It pays for marketers to know the items for which ethnic consumers are shopping. See Table 3.4 for a list of favorite products by ethnic group, compiled from ACNielsen's Homescan panel of 55,000 households. The list is ranked according to the dollar volume

Table 3.4: Shopping Cart Contents Vary by Ethnic Group

Grocery item	Non-Caucasian total index	African American index	Asian American index	Hispanic American index
Vegetables (green, canned)	382	492	2	41
Hot sauce	318	354	90	182
Pickled pork products	307	355	5	70
Sandwich spreads (relish type)	280	329	39	149
Canned sausage	248	284	78	121
Corn meal	239	296	27	69
Lard	236	51	3	513
Brandy/cognac	213	253	68	122
Oriental foods (noodle ramen)	197	187	328	113
Salad and cooking oil	188	193	105	148
Fruit drinks (canned)	179	188	148	140
Beans (dry)	178	167	48	227
Lasagna (canned)	150	155	54	145
Milk (shelf stable)	148	165	146	243

Note. An index of 100 is the national average. For example, Hispanic Americans are 82% more likely than the average American to consume hot sauce but are still significantly less likely than African Americans to enjoy it. Data from ACNielsen's Homescan, 2002. Heller, W. (2002, October 15). Outlining Ethnic Preferences. Progressive Grocer, New York, 81(15), p. 24.

index for all non-Caucasian households. The national average consumption index for any product is 100. A number of the categories that index high achieve their ranking because of a strong preference by one or two ethnic groups, while generating little or no interest among the others. For example, relish-type sandwich spreads index at a whopping 329 for African Americans. Hispanics weigh in slightly below average, but Asians index at an indifferent 39 (Heller, 2002).

Hispanic households spend an average of $133 per week on groceries—significantly higher than the $91 spent by a typical non-Hispanic family. This is due, in part, to the fact that Hispanics—as previously noted—generally have larger families but also tend to eat out less often than non-Hispanic households. Preparation of authentic Hispanic meals is important for most Hispanics and is tied to values emphasizing both family and heritage. As opposed to foods promoting convenience demanded by Anglo Americans, Hispanics generally shun such products, preferring in most cases to cook from scratch. For this reason, freshness is one of the most important features sought by the Hispanic food shopper, especially in the perishable categories, such as produce, meat, and bakery ("Study Sheds Light," 2005).

Hispanics tend to like more spice in their foods than non-Hispanics do, even in American products. Several companies have taken note of this trend. Consumer research revealed that Hispanics found U.S. snacks to be too bland. Based on this information, Frito-Lay developed a line of products including such items as Cheetos Flaming Hot, Doritos Salsa Verde, and lime-flavored chips called Lay's Limon. In appealing to Hispanics, McDonald's emphasizes the spiciness of their premium chicken sandwiches (see Figure 3.8). Goya, the biggest U.S. Hispanic food company, has boosted its annual sales to nearly $700 million by tailoring its products to the tastes of Hispanics. However, Goya tailors its products even within the Hispanic segment. Goya identifies the type of Hispanics in a specific community and then caters directly to those tastes. "You can't sell Puerto Rican food to Mexican-Americans, or Mexican food to Cuban-Americans," notes company spokesperson Rafael Toro (Hemlock & Mann, 2001). So, the company targets red beans to Puerto Ricans, black beans to Cubans, and half dollar–size olives to Peruvians. To market the products, Goya highlights family and communication as key themes. Ads underscore the importance of meals as a time when family and friends come together. And, when Goya targets a specific Hispanic group, such as Mexican Americans, it tailors ads even further, to use the right words, music, dishes, and setting for those customers.

Much like Hispanic women, African American women love to cook—but also to experiment. Kraft discovered that black families like to customize products to their own taste, so a recent Kraft magazine advertisement for its macaroni and cheese product featured a black woman with the tag line, "I

Figure 3.8: McDonald's Ad Featuring a Spicy Menu Item

like to add my own special touches." The manufacturer also asked African American chefs to come up with new recipes for the product, which were run in magazines appealing to African Americans and demonstrated in stores. Kool-Aid—a powdered drinking product, which is added to water—also played up the penchant of blacks to tailor products. A TV spot for the product employed a black family talking about the ingredients they liked to add to the drink, such as fruit. The campaign led to increased purchases by this market segment (Gregory, 2001).

Even the amount or quantity of a product that consumers in different groups purchase is not constant. And the amount or quantity purchased is often directly tied to the size of the family unit. As noted previously, Hispanic households tend to be larger than those of the general population. Nearly 11% of Hispanic families have six or more members, compared to only 3.5% of the general population. This is particularly significant given the overall trend towards smaller households in the United States. While the non-Hispanic population is seeking goods and services tailored to smaller households, Hispanic families are much more likely to be interested in bulk purchases ("Marketing to Hispanics," 2004). Consumption patterns clearly have importance for advertisers in deciding how to introduce a brand. Where a group of products enjoys widespread acceptance, the message will likely be directed toward obtaining the largest share of the market. Where consumption is low or nonexistent, the marketing communications will likely have an educational character.

Where Consumers Buy

Race plays a major role in where consumers choose to shop—and why. Research has revealed variation in the number of trips ethnic consumers make annually to a various types of retailers: grocery store, drug store, mass merchants, supercenters, warehouse clubs, gas/convenience stores, and dollar stores (Gardyn & Fetto, 2003). Table 3.5 reveals that warehouse clubs, such as Costco and Sam's Club, are shopped heavily by Asian and Hispanic consumers. The typical Asian shopper, for example, makes fourteen trips a year to such stores, whereas blacks report that they shop at a warehouse just eight times a year.

NOP World—a supplier of syndicated and custom research—recently announced results from its Hispanic Retail Study. Asked which factors are most important in deciding where to shop, Hispanic Americans cited the same priorities that other Americans have when choosing retailers—low prices (77%), convenient locations (72%), and a wide range of merchandise (71%). However, a critical second tier of priorities unique to the Hispanic market was cited by about half of Hispanics as being "very important," including store employees speaking Spanish, products relevant to Hispanic consumers, and

Table 3.5: Where Ethnic Consumers Shop (Number of Trips Made Annually)

Type of store	Number of trips made annually			
	Whites	African Americans	Asian Americans	Hispanic Americans
Grocery stores	72	70	65	67
Drug stores	15	17	16	15
Mass merchants	24	20	21	24
Supercenters	19	16	12	15
Warehouse clubs	10	8	14	12
Gas/convenience stores	14	19	6	11
Dollar stores	10	16	7	10

Note. Data from ACNielsen, 2002. Gardyn, R. & Fetto, J. (2003, February). Race, Ethnicity and the Way We Shop. *American Demographics*, Ithaca, *25*(1), p. 30.

Spanish-language signage ("Hispanic Americans Choose," 2005). Digging deeper into the Hispanic market, the study uncovered significant differences between U.S.-born and foreign-born Hispanic consumers. Apparently, level of acculturation also plays a role in where consumers choose to shop. Foreign-born respondents were significantly more attracted to the tailored offerings of local stores specializing in serving Hispanic consumers, with 42 percent saying they often shopped in those stores vs. 26 percent of the U.S.-born Hispanics. Table3.6 shows a breakdown of how their shopping priorities differed based on the factors they selected as very important in deciding where to shop.

Table 3.6: Factors Influencing Where U.S.-Born versus Foreign-Born Hispanics Shop

Factor influencing where Hispanics shop	U.S.-born Hispanics	Foreign-born Hispanics
Low prices	70%	83%
Convenient location	67%	75%
Range of merchandise	68%	73%
Employees who speak Spanish	33%	69%
Products relevant to Hispanics	35%	64%
Range of payment options	35%	55%
Spanish signage	22%	65%
Product packaging/labelling in Spanish	20%	58%
Owner is member of local community	28%	40%

Note. Data from NOP World's Hispanic OmniTel Retail Survey, 2005. DSN *Retailing Today* (2005, June 27). Study Sheds Light on Latino Shopper Preferences. New York, *44*(12), p. 18.

There is one characteristic in particular that sets African Americans apart from the other ethnic and racial groups—their shared history of slavery and discrimination. African American consumers have a strong desire and need for respect—but still do not believe they are respected by society at large. Miller and Kemp (2005) note that, without respect, African Americans don't feel welcome in any environment, whether a department store, bank, or other service office, in or outside their community. Numerous research examples reflect the sentiments of African American consumers. Back in 1995, the Yankelovich research firm asked Anglo Americans and African Americans to list and rank deciding factors on where to shop. Both groups agreed that price was the number-one factor. However, the second most important factor for whites was availability of merchandise, while, for African Americans, it was respect from retail employees. In 2005, the Yankelovich *Multicultural Monitor* reported that 46% of blacks versus only 35% of whites have felt unwelcome in a store. And the Gallup poll's *2003 Race Relations* survey revealed that nearly half of blacks reported that they had experienced at least one incident of discrimination during the previous month, most often in stores (26%) but also in restaurants and theatres (18%), as well as on mass transportation (10%), (Miller & Kemp, 2005). The issue of discrimination will be discussed further in chapter 5. Research has also revealed that African American consumers, as a group, are the most likely to be willing to travel an hour or more to shop at their favorite store and almost twice as likely as average consumers to go out of their way to find new stores, especially if there is a bargain to be had. A Simmons study found that a third (34%) of black respondents will travel an hour or more to shop at a factory outlet store, compared with 27% of white consumers (Gardyn & Fetto, 2003).

Who Makes Purchase Decisions

The marketer must know who in the family is the primary decision maker and for which products. In some cultures, the female holds the purse strings, while, in others, it is the male. And, in many Anglo American households—and for an increasing number of product categories—children, teens, and young adults are the primary decision makers. Far from the *machista* myth, Hispanic American women play a very important role and are the decision makers in their family units. The same is true for African American women. As key decision makers in their households, black women exert disproportionately greater influence in spending than white women on a number of big-ticket budget items, including houses and cars. Thus, it would make sense for marketers to cultivate the African American female consumer. Yet, while they represented 3.3% of the $7.6 trillion in total buying power in the United States in 2002, less than 1% of total ad spending targeted them. If marketers had allocated a commensurate percentage on advertising that targeted the black woman, they would have spent $5.5 billion more than they did. Yin (2003) notes that advertiser reluctance to market aggressively to these consumers stems primarily from the negative image of African American women as single mothers on welfare. While there is truth to the claim that African American women have below-average spending power—as noted previously—this can be attributed, in great part, to the disparity in family structure: Black women are less likely than average to be part of a married couple. But, in recent years, African American women have made great strides: They are increasingly upwardly mobile, having made gains in education and income. Almost half of black women have attended college (46%). Black women are more likely than white women to work (62% versus 60%), and the median income of black women has grown at a faster rate during the past two decades than that of women overall. In short, African American women have become powerful consumers. A 2002 Harris Interactive poll reveals that black women are more likely to say they are independent-minded than are white women, (Miller & Kemp, 2005). Their autonomy is reflected in a greater propensity than their white counterparts to make the buying decisions in their households (see Table 3.7). Even in households headed by a married couple, African American women are more likely to control the purse strings than Caucasian women. For example, one in two married black women is the primary decision maker in buying a house, versus one in four married white women. Two-thirds of married black women choose which health care plan to carry, compared with just one-half of married white women. A similar pattern holds for autos, computers, and home electronics. According to MRI, a marketing research firm, 61% of black women say they head up their household, compared with just 45% of white

Table 3.7: Percentage of Women Who Are the Primary Decision Makers in the Household

Type of household decision	African American females	White females
Health care plans	76%	65%
Mobile/wireless phone service	65%	50%
Financial services/investments	62%	51%
Major purchases (i.e., house)	61%	43%
Home electronics	59%	46%
Computer hardware/software	58%	46%
Automobiles	58%	48%

Note. From What's Black about It? (p. 47), by P. Miller and H. Kemp, 2005, Ithaca, NY: Paramount Market Publishing, Inc.

women. The shares include women who take the lead in families headed by a married couple (Yin, 2003).

The Role of Money

Money means different things to different people. And, often, how money is perceived and used is culturally determined. Hispanic consumers, in general, are much more likely to pay cash for their purchases. Cash is the preferred method of payment for about 75% of Hispanics surveyed. Only about 15% use credit cards, compared to over 40% of the general market (Wentz, 2005c). One study found that Mexican Americans, in particular, show a significantly different attitude toward money retention than Anglo Americans. Specifically, Mexican Americans were less likely to engage in behaviors involving medium- to long-term personal saving, investing, and speculating with money at the expense of present consumption. It was also found that Mexican Americans strayed away from offers involving products/services that required planning and long-term consumption. In contrast to Mexican Americans, Cuban Americans scored higher in their attitude toward money retention (Villegas & Shah, 2005).

Interestingly, Hispanic teens appear to have significantly different attitudes toward money than do their parents. A recent study by FIND/SPV Inc. examined American teenagers' attitudes toward managing their money. The study surveyed boys and girls who were fourteen to eighteen years of age and of Caucasian, African American, Hispanic, and Asian descent. While 93% of teens said that cash was their preferred method of payment, Hispanic teens were significantly more likely to have a checking account (56%) than African American teens (29%) or Asian American teens (32%). Of teens who do use credit cards, 37% of Hispanic teens have two credit cards in their name, as compared to 16% of Caucasian teens, 25% of African American teens, and 16% of Asian teens. Nearly one-third of Hispanic teens have after-school jobs, compared to 27% of Caucasian teens, 23% of African American teens, and 22% of Asian teens ("Dynamic Trends," 2005).

Summary

To communicate effectively with ethnic markets, marketers and advertisers must recognize the pervasive influence of culture. Failure to understand the role of culture can lead, and has led, to misunderstandings, miscommunications, and marketing failures. This chapter examined only a few of the more prominent elements of culture—including verbal language, nonverbal communications, signs and symbols, cultural values, and the role of religion and family as they impact consumer behavior. The next chapter addresses effective approaches to communicating with Hispanic consumers.

REFERENCES

Albers-Miller, N. (1996). Designing cross-cultural advertising research: A closer look at paired comparisons. *International Marketing Review, 13*(5), 59–75.

Aleshire, I. (2005, January 10). For banks courting Hispanic market, thinking biculturally is key to service. *Knight Ridder/Tribune Business News,* p. 1.

Alsever, J. (2004, July 11). Latino trends fuel media, ad changes. *Denver Post,* p. K-12.

Atienza, J. (2001, June 7). Family focus: Age-old Filipino values ensure. *Filipino Reporter,* p. 59.

Bartels, R. (1982). National culture—business relations: United States and Japan contrasted. *Management International Review, 2,* 5.

Butler, J. (2000, January 19). The challenge before us on the millennium. *The Jacksonville Free Press,* p. 5.

Comer, L. (2000, Summer). Communication between Hispanic salespeople and their customers: A first look. *Journal of Personal Selling and Sales Management, 20*(3), 121–128.

Comer, L. & Nicholls, J.A.F. (2000, Summer). Communication between Hispanic salespeople and their customers: A first look. *The Journal of Personal Selling and Sales Management, 20*(3), p. 121.

Condon, J., & Yousef, M. R. (1975). *Introduction to intercultural communication* (pp. 123–124). Indianapolis, IN: Bobbs-Merrill.

Contreras, J. (2004, March 22). Two Americas: A massive wave of Hispanic immigration is raising questions about identity and integration [International edition]. *Newsweek,* p. 42.

Coon, H. M., & Kemmelmeier, M. (2001, May). Cultural orientations in the United States: (Re)examining differences among ethnic groups. *Journal of Cross-Cultural Psychology, 32*(3), 349.

De Mooij, M. (1994). *Advertising worldwide* (2nd ed.). New York: Prentice Hall.

De Mooij, M. (1998). *Global marketing and advertising: Understanding cultural paradoxes.* Thousand Oaks, CA: Sage Publications.

DSN Retailing Today (2005, June 27). Study sheds light on Latino shopper preferences. New York, *44*(12), p. 18.

Durban, D.-A. (2006, January 19). New Toyota will debut in bilingual ad. *San Diego Union-Tribune,* p. C-4.

Dynamic trends, November 2005; the latest data on Hispanic America. (2005). *Hispanic Trends, 4*(7), 18.

Elliott, S. (2000, March 6). Ads speak to Asian-Americans [Late edition—East Coast]. *New York Times,* p. C-1.

Fam, K. S., Waller, D., & Erdogan, B. Z. (2004). The influence of religion on attitudes towards the advertising of controversial products. *European Journal of Marketing, 38*(5/6), 537.

Ferraro, G. P. (1990). *The cultural dimension of international business* (p. 34). Englewood Cliffs, NJ: Prentice-Hall.

Fonte, D. (2005, October 29). Marketing firms more sophisticated in attempts to reach Spanish speakers. *Knight Ridder/Tribune Business News,* Washington, p. 1.

Gaines, S. O., Marelich, W. P., Bledsoe, K. L., Steers, W. N., Henderson, M. C., Granrose, C. S., Barajas, L., Hicks, D., Lyde, M., Takahashi, Y., Yum, N., Rios, D. L., Gracia, B. F., Farris, K. R., & Page, M. S. (1997). The link between race/ethnicity and cultural values as mediated by racial/ethnic identity and moderated by gender. *Journal of Personality and Social Psychology, 72,* 1460–1476.

Galvin, K. M., & Brommel, B. J. (1991). *Family communication: Cohesion and change* (3rd ed., p. 1). New York: HarperCollins.

Gardyn, R., & Fetto, J. (2003, February). Race, ethnicity and the way we shop. *American Demographics, 25*(1), 30.

Geller, L. K. (2003, January). Buena suerte. *Target Marketing, 21*(1), 18–20.

Grant, S. (2003, October). Experts highlight formula for multicultural communications. *Public Relations Tactics, 10*(10) 12.

Gregory, H. (2001, July 21). Positive discrimination. *Grocer,* p. 45.

Gregory, G., & Munch, J. (1997). Cultural values in international advertising: An examination of familial norms and roles in Mexico. *Psychology & Marketing, 14*(2), 99–119.

Hall, E. T. (1966). *The hidden dimension* (1st ed., p. 177). Garden City, NY: Doubleday.

Hall, E. T. (1976). *Beyond culture* (p. 13–16). New York: Doubleday.

Hall, E. T. (1990). *The hidden dimension.* New York: Anchor Books.

Hall, E. T., & Hall, M. R. (1987). *Hidden differences: Doing business with the Japanese* (p. 12). New York: Anchor Books.

Han, S., & Shavitt, S. (1994). Persuasion and culture: Advertising appeals in individualistic and collectivistic societies. *Journal of Experimental Social Psychology, 30*(4), 326–350.

Heller, W. (2002, October 15). Outlining ethnic preferences. *Progressive Grocer,* p. 24.

Hemlock, D., & Mann, J. (2001, January 22). Spanish strategies: Top Hispanic marketers share some key traits—they emphasize research, speak the language and tap media aimed at their target audience. *South Florida Sun-Sentinel,* p. 16.

Hispanic Americans choose Wal-Mart as favorite store according to NOP World study. (2005, March 28). *PR Newswire,* p. 1.

Hoebel, A. (1960). *Man, culture and society* (p. 168). New York: Oxford University Press.

Hofstede, G. (1980). *Culture's consequences: International differences in work-related values.* Beverly Hills, CA: Sage.

Hofstede, G. (1990). *Expressions of culture at different levels* (Working Paper No. 90–006). Netherlands: University of Limburg.

Hofstede, G., & Bond, M. H. (1988). The Confucius connection: From cultural roots to economic growth. *Organizational Dynamics, 16,* 5–21.

Home Channel News (2005, December 12). Homing in on Hispanics. New York, *31*(20). P. 16.

Huang, J., & Skriloff, L. (2003, January 1). Census 2000 reveals Asian Americans still have unsurpassed demographics as highly attractive consumers. *Northwest Nikkei*, p. 2-B.

In Chile, the word "guagua" means pregnant woman, in Spain it means bus; new Hispanic ad agency, Berrojo Rhoads, helps companies reach Hispanics and avoid translation nightmares. (2005, March 23). *Business Wire*, p. 1.

Jacobs, L., Keown, C., & Ghymn, K.-I. (1991). Cross-cultural color comparisons: Global marketers beware. *International Marketing Review, 8*(3), 21–30.

Joseph, G. (2003, May 9). Firm puts Ganesh image on sandal, community forces recall from stores. *India Abroad*, p. A-4.

Kahle, L. R. (Ed.). (1983). *Social values and social change: Adaptations to life in America.* New York: Praeger.

Kroeber, A. L., & Kluckhohn, C. (1952). Culture: A critical review of concepts and definitions. *Harvard University Peabody Museum of American Archaeology and Ethnology Papers, 47,* 181.

Kumar, A. (2005, May 21). Word in ad is not in bad taste, Hershey says. *The Patriot News*, p. A-1.

Le, T.-D. (2005, November 20). Tapping the ethnic marketplace without getting lost in translation. *Knight Ridder/Tribune Business News*, p. 1.

Lee, J. A. (1966, March/April). Cultural analysis in overseas operations. *Harvard Business Review, 47.*

Lee, S. & Barnes, J.H. (1990, January). Using color preferences in magazine advertising. *Journal of Advertising Research,* New York, 29(6), p. 25.

Maletzke, G. (1976). Intercultural and international communication. In H.-D. Fischer & J. C. Merrill (Eds.), *International and intercultural communication.* New York: Hastings House.

Marketing to Hispanics in the U.S. (2004, October 6). *Brand Strategy*, p. 48.

Maslow, A. (1964). A theory of human motivation. In H. Leavitt & L. Pondy (Eds.), *Readings in managerial psychology* (p. 6–24). Chicago: University of Chicago Press.

McGoldrick, M. (1973). Ethnicity, cultural diversity and normality. In F. Walalish (Ed.), *Normal family processes* (p. 331). New York: Guilford Press.

Miller, T. (1998, July 4). Global segments from 'strivers' to 'creatives.' *Marketing News*, p. 11.

Miller, P., & Kemp, H. (2005). *What's black about it?* Ithaca, NY: Paramount Market Publishing, Inc.

Milner, L., & Collins, J. (2000, Spring). Sex-role portrayals and the gender of nations. *Journal of Advertising,* 67–79.

Miracle, G. (1988). An empirical study of the usefulness of the back-translation technique for international advertising messages in print media. In J. D. Leckenby (Ed.), *Proceedings of the 1988 conference of the American Academy of Advertising,* ed. J.D. Leckenby, American Academy of Advertising, Austin, Texas, RC-51.

More marches won't put end to poverty. (2005, October 17). *Daily Breeze*, p. A-11.

Morley, H. (2003, April 11). Rule 1: Never insult the customer. *The Record*, p. B-1.

Munson, J. M., & McIntyre, S. H. (1978). Personal values and values attributed to a distant cultural stereotype. In H. K. Hunt (Ed.), *Advances in consumer research* (Vol. 5, p. 103), Ann Arbor, MI: Association for Consumer Research.

Nanda, S. (1994). *Cultural anthropology* (5th ed., p. 50). Belmont, CA: Wadsworth.

Nixon, J., & Dawson, G. (2002). Reason for cross-cultural communication training. *Corporate Communications, 7*(3), 184.

Pitts, R. E., Whalen, D. J., O'Keefe, R., & Murray, V. (1989, Winter). Black and white response to culturally targeted television commercials: A value-based approach. *Psychology and Marketing, 6,* 311–328.

Purewal, S. (2001, May 11). McDonald's sued for using beef extract in fries [New York edition]. *India Abroad,* p. 8.

Raine, G. (2001, August 25). Lost in the translation: Milk Board does without its famous slogan when it woos a Latino audience. *San Francisco Chronicle,* p. C-1.

Reid, M. (2004, April 24). First comes baby, then comes marriage? In the black community, the motivation from peers or families to get married is gone. *The Christian Science Monitor,* p. 9.

Ricks, D. (1983). *Big business blunders: Mistakes in multinational marketing.* Homewood, IL: Dow Jones–Irwin.

Ricks, D. (1988, January/February/March). International business blunders: An update. *Business and Economic Review, 34,* 11–14.

Rokeach, M. (1968). *Beliefs, attitudes and values.* San Francisco: Jossey-Bass.

Rokeach, M. (1973). *The nature of human values.* New York: Free Press.

Rossman, M. L. (1994). *Multicultural marketing: Selling to a diverse America.* New York: American Management Association.

Rotfeld, H. J. (2003). Misplaced marketing: Who do you hire when the audience isn't you? *The Journal of Consumer Marketing, 20*(2/3), 87.

Sabogal, F., Marin, G., Otero-Sabogal, R., Van Oss Marin, B., & Perez-Stable, E. (1987). Hispanic familialism and acculturation: What changes and what doesn't. *Hispanic Journal of Behavioral Sciences, 9,* 397–412.

Samovar, L., Porter, R., & Stafani, L. (1998). *Communication between cultures* (3rd ed.). Belmont, CA: Wadsworth.

Sheehan, K. (2005). *Controversies in contemporary advertising.* Thousand Oaks, CA: Sage Publications.

Solomon, M. (1999). *Consumer behavior: buying, having, and being* (4th ed.). Upper Saddle River, NJ: Prentice Hall.

Steward, E. C. (1972). *American cultural patterns: A cross cultural perspective* (p. 74). Pittsburgh: Intercultural Communications Network.

Study sheds light on Latino shopper preferences. (2005, June 27). *DSN Retailing Today,* p. 18.

Suarez-Hammond, S. (2005, September 1). Respect cultural values to connect with buyers. *Marketing News, 39*(14), 1.

Taylor, E. B. (1871). *Primitive culture* (p. 1). London: John Murray.

Taylor, E., & Wilson, D. R. (1997, Spring). Impact of information level on the effectiveness of U.S. and Korean television communication. *Journal of Advertising, 20,* 1–15.

Terpstra, V., & David, K. (1991). *The cultural environment of international business* (2nd ed.). Cincinnati, OH: Southwestern.

Trandis, H., Marin, G., Hui, C., Limansky, J., & Ottati, V. (1982, September). Role perceptions of Hispanic young adults. *Journal of Cross-Cultural Psychology, 15,* 297–320.

Valle, R., & Martinez, C. (1980). Natural networks among Mexicano elderly in the United States: Implications for mental health. In M. R. Miranda & R. A. Ruiz (Eds.), *Chicano aging and mental health.* Washington, DC: Government Printing Office.

Villegas, J., & Shah, A. (2005). Lana o Bille? Humor appeal's effects in Mexican Americans and Cuban Americans explained by their attitude toward money retention. *American Academy of Advertising Conference Proceedings, 112.*

Wellner, A. S. (2002, November). Inside Asian generations. *Forecast, 22*(11), 1.

Wells, W. (1987, February 13). Global advertisers should pay heed to contextual variations. *Marketing News,* p. 18.

Wentz, L. (2005a, June 20). Getting Hispanics to be a Pepper, too [Midwest region edition]. *Advertising Age,* p. 27.

Wentz, L. (2005b, December 5). Marketers and agencies tussle over tongues [Midwest region edition]. *Advertising Age,* p. 79.

Wentz, L. (2005c, July 18). Survey: Hispanics passionate about shopping [Midwest region edition]. *Advertising Age,* p. 29.

Whitman, J. (2003, September 19). Lost in translation: Language blunders can sully ad efforts [Europe]. *Wall Street Journal,* p. A-7.

Whorf, B. L. (1956). *Language, thought, and reality.* Cambridge, MA: Technology Press of Massachusetts Institute of Technology.

Williams, K. (2005, November 27). Advertisers embrace the power that gospel music has to offer. *The Washington Post,* p. A-1.

Wilson, M. (2005, November). Hispanic Power. *Chain Store Age, 81*(11), 74.

Yankelovich. (1995). *African American monitor.*

Yankelovich. (2003). *Monitor: Multicultural market study in collaboration with Cheskin and Images USA.*

Yin, S. (2003, September). Color bind. *American Demographer, 25*(7), 22.

4

Reaching Hispanic Consumers

Who They Are: Understanding Hispanic Identity

According to the U.S. Census Bureau's latest figures, the U.S. Hispanic population numbers more than 41 million. However, that figure includes only about one-fourth of the approximately 9 to 10 million undocumented Latinos in the United States—and the uncounted are also consumers of American goods and services (Association of Hispanic Advertising Agencies, n.d.). A fundamental error made by marketers trying to reach the Hispanic audience is to view the Hispanic community as homogeneous. Over 80% of Hispanics say they identify themselves by their country of origin or as Latino or Hispanic. But when asked which term they used first or exclusively, more than half chose their country of origin, while only a quarter use the terms *Latino* or *Hispanic*. Thus, while members of the U.S. Hispanic population understand themselves to be part of a common ethnic group, most have a stronger identification with their nationality ("Marketing to Hispanics," 2005). Because Hispanics emigrated from different countries at different times and for different reasons, demographics of specific subgroups based on country of origin can be quite different. Effective marketing and advertising to Hispanic Americans means reaching a deeper understanding of these various subgroups—Mexicans, Puerto Ricans, Cubans, Dominicans, Central Americans, and South Americans—in terms of heritage, values, customs, and preferences.

Mexicans

Mexicans make up the vast majority—nearly 67%—of the Hispanic population in the U.S. today. As Schreiber notes, "Mexican-Americans for the most part can hardly be said to have 'come here' at all. The reality is they 'were here.' As recently as 150 years ago, Mexico controlled the entire western region of our continent" (2001). Mexico lost Texas, California, New Mexico, Arizona, Utah, Nevada, and Colorado to the United States in 1848, and the Treaty of Guadalupe Hidalgo consummated the loss of these territories. Korzenny and Korzenny (2005) note that those left behind when the border crossed them constituted the first massive contingent of Mexican nationals to live in U.S. territory. Of course, the size of the Hispanic American population has grown dramatically—particularly in the past few decades—owing in great part to the proximity of Mexico to the United States. The issue of immigration—both legal and illegal—has become a sensitive topic for Hispanic and Anglo Americans alike. Many Mexican immigrants leave their families behind for economic opportunities in the United States. The United States clearly benefits from this labor pool, yet Mexico benefits as well. Latino immigrants in the United States often send money back to their families; sometimes, the money is sent to wives and children, and, other times, it is sent to help support elderly parents. Hispanic immigrants sent $53.6 billion from the United States to Latin American countries in 2005, an increase of 17% over the previous year, according to the Inter-American Development Bank. Mexico received more than $20 billion (Pesquera, 2006).

Puerto Ricans

During the Spanish-American War of 1898, the United States took over Puerto Rico, Cuba, and the Philippines from Spain. Less than twenty years later, the United States granted U.S. citizenship to Puerto Ricans, and, in 1952, Puerto Rico was granted commonwealth status. As such, Puerto Ricans are able to travel freely between their homeland and the United States. It should be noted that only those Puerto Ricans living in the United States or the District of Columbia are counted as part of the U.S. Hispanic population. Large numbers of Puerto Ricans immigrated to the United States (primarily to New York

City) in the 1950s and 1960s. Puerto Ricans living in the United States today constitute 8.6% of the total Hispanic population. A controversial issue affecting Puerto Ricans is the question of whether Puerto Rico should become a full-blown state or remain a U.S. territory. While Puerto Ricans speak Spanish, many words are different from those of Mexican Spanish. Puerto Ricans' ancestry is Spanish, African, and Native American.

Cubans

As noted previously, when the United States defeated the Spanish in the Spanish-American War, the United States took control of Cuba and, over the years, has played a dominant role in the politics of that country. However, in 1959, Fidel Castro took over power of Cuba, and the communist leader's partnership with the Soviet Union strongly influenced the island for over three decades. Large numbers of Cubans—among them doctors, lawyers, engineers, and chemists—fled Fidel Castro's regime in the 1960s. Even though there were subsequent waves of Cubans in the 1980s, their numbers were much smaller. Currently, almost nine in ten Cuban Americans in this country arrived before 1982. While some of the more recent arrivals were allowed to emigrate, others arrived illegally, and the plight of these illegal immigrants, often called boat people, has been much publicized. South Florida and, in particular, Miami have a sizable Cuban American population. Many Cuban Americans still have family in Cuba, and the country's political future is certainly a worrisome issue. Cubans constitute just 3.8% of the total Hispanic American population. However, of all the Hispanic groups in the United States, Cubans have the highest median income, as well as the highest level of education.

Dominicans

Dominicans and Puerto Ricans share a common heritage of Spanish and African backgrounds, as well as many cultural characteristics. And, like Puerto Ricans, Dominicans also speak Spanish, and their accents tend to be quite similar. However, unlike Puerto Ricans, Dominicans are not U.S. citizens, and immigration is a struggle they share with the majority of other Hispanic immigrants to the United States (Korzenny & Korzenny, 2005). Although Dominicans have been in the United States since the 1960s, when economic problems in the Dominican Republic led to a vast migration to the United States, almost half of all Dominican Americans today have arrived since 1990. Currently, the largest concentrations of Dominican Americans are in New York (the residence of over 53% of all Dominicans in the United States), Florida, and New Jersey. Approximately 3.1% of U.S. Hispanics trace their origins to the Dominican Republic.

Central Americans

The Spanish-speaking countries of Central America include Costa Rica, El Salvador, Guatemala, Honduras, Nicaragua, and Panama. Altogether, people of Central American background account for 9% of the U.S. Hispanic population. The 2000 census shows that Salvadorians (38.8%) and Guatemalans (22.1%) comprise the majority of Central Americans in the United States. Hondurans represent just 12.9% of the Central American population, and Nicaraguans represent another 10%. According to Korzenny and Korzenny (2005), in terms of heritage, about 40% of Guatemalans are Maya Indians. El Salvador, Nicaragua, and Honduras are mostly mestizo, like Mexico. Costa Rica is primarily European—with Spanish, Germans, and Italians the most prevalent countries of origin. Costa Rica has a strong component of citizens with African origin, while Panama has the largest population of African heritage among the Central American countries. Central Americans are relatively recent arrivals to the United States. Though they entered in small numbers as agricultural laborers during World War II, the largest waves of Central Americans began arriving in the late 1970s and 1980s, motivated by both economic hardship and political unrest. For example, during the 1980s, it is estimated that nearly half a million Salvadorians came to the United States either officially or unofficially as political refugees fleeing the political turmoil in their country.

South Americans

Approximately 5.3% of Hispanics in the United States trace their origins to South America. This group includes immigrants from Argentina, Bolivia, Chile, Colombia, Ecuador, Peru, Paraguay, Uruguay, and Venezuela. Of those U.S. Hispanics who trace their origins to South America, the largest groups are Colombians (37%), Ecuadorians (19%), and Peruvians (17%). Korzenny and Korzenny explain that because

> of the distance from the United States, immigrants from these countries tend to be somewhat more affluent and educated than those from countries that are closer to the United States. More affluent individuals are much more likely to afford travel to the United States. (2005)

Where to Reach Them

Despite the geographic dispersion over the past decade, Hispanic Americans living in this country are still highly geographically concentrated. Currently, they are highly concentrated in the Southwest, where half of all Hispanics live in just two states—California (with 31% of all Hispanics) and Texas (with 19%). An additional 10% live in the states of Arizona, New Mexico, and Colorado. Outside the Southwest, New York and Florida have the largest concentrations (Ahmed, 2002). As Table 4.1 reveals, in terms of reaching Hispanic consumers, Los Angeles is certainly one hot market. While just 46.7% of Los Angeles residents are Hispanic (compared to 94% in McAllen, Texas; 50.3% in Fresno-Visalia, California; or 48.6% in Miami–Fort Lauderdale, Florida), the size of Los Angeles, with its population of over 8 million, means that nearly 4 million Hispanics are clustered in just one city.

The geographic concentration of specific Hispanic populations is even more striking—three-fourths of Mexican Americans live in Texas and California, two-thirds of Puerto Ricans live in the Northeast (mostly in New York and New Jersey), and two-thirds of Cuban Americans live in Florida. This geographic concentration makes it easier to tailor marketing strategies to the particular population segment a firm decides to target. Also, advertisers should note that local demographics of Hispanics in a particular area can be quite different from the national profile of the Hispanic population (Ahmed, 2002).

Unifying Factors: Language, Religion, and Family

Language

The Spanish language unifies Mexicans, Puerto Ricans, Cubans, Dominicans, Central Americans, and South Americans. However, it is important to note that there is no such thing as pure Spanish. Though there are dialectical language variations between the countries of Latin America, a Cuban and a Peruvian are still likely to understand one another quite well. Clearly, there are also variations in the Spanish spoken within an individual Latin American country. Mexico provides an excellent example. Korzenny and Korzenny note that differences are found in

> the Spanish dialect spoken in the Atlantic coast as compared with the Pacific, Mexico City, the northern border states and the states of the south like Yucatan and Quintana Roo. Still, Mexicans can communicate with each other relatively well. Their communication is as good as the communication between people from New York and those of Georgia, each with their dialectical differences. The commonality

Table 4.1: Top Twenty-Five Hispanic Markets (by Estimated 2006 Population)

Rank	Market area	Hispanic population	Hispanics as a percentage of the total population
1.	Los Angeles	8,421,500	46.7%
2.	New York	4,389,600	20.7%
3.	Miami–Fort Lauderdale	2,141,800	48.6%
4.	Chicago	1,922,700	19.5%
5.	Houston	1,913,000	33.6%
6.	San Francisco	1,665,300	23.7%
7.	Dallas–Fort Worth	1,588,000	24.5%
8.	Phoenix-Prescott, Arizona	1,228,400	26.6%
9.	San Antonio	1,192,000	53.8%
10.	McAllen, Texas	1,115,400	94.0%
11.	San Diego	951,200	31.7%
12.	Fresno-Visalia, California	930,600	50.3%
13.	El Paso, Texas–Las Cruces, New Mexico	839,700	87.8%
14.	Sacramento-Stockton-Modesto	827,600	21.7%
15.	Albuquerque-Santa Fe, New Mexico	756,500	40.8%
16.	Denver	735,100	19.6%
17.	Palm Springs, California	704,600	36.2%
18.	Washington, D.C.–Hagerstown, Maryland	639,900	10.6%
19.	Philadelphia	563,500	7.2%
20.	Atlanta	499,800	8.9%
21.	Las Vegas	460,100	26.1%
22.	Orlando–Daytona Beach–Melbourne	456,800	13.7%
23.	Tampa–St. Petersburg–Sarasota, Florida	455,200	11.0%
24.	Boston, Massachusetts–Manchester, New Hampshire	450,200	7.2%
25.	Austin, Texas	437,500	28.1%

Note. Data from Synovate's 2006 U.S. Diversity Markets Report. Figures are 2006 estimates. From "Hispanic Fact Pack," 2006, *Advertising Age*, p. 40, retrieved from http://www.adage.com/images/random/hispfactpack06.pdf

of the Spanish languages has been one of the most salient common denominators that make the Hispanic market highly targetable. (2005, p. 23)

A central issue advertisers must address is whether to communicate with Hispanic Americans in Spanish or in English. A 2005 Yankelovich *Monitor* Multicultural Marketing Study of Hispanic consumers shows that Hispanics are using both Spanish- and English-language media and communicating in both languages. "The Spanish language is extremely important to Hispanics and they feel a need to preserve it, but they also recognize the need to master English in order to succeed and enjoy life in the U.S.," notes Sonya Suarez-Hammond, director of Yankelovich Inc. "Marketers need to use both languages in order to establish cultural and personal relevancy with the Hispanic consumer" ("Dynamic Trends," 2005). Language dominance among Latinos varies by their country or region of origin (see Table 4.2). As noted earlier, over two-thirds of U.S. Latinos originated from Mexico, and 61% of these are Spanish dominant. The only other group more likely to be Spanish dominant is the group from Central America. U.S. Latinos from Puerto Rico are most likely to be English dominant. Hispanics prefer to speak Spanish at home, with 56% speaking solely Spanish at home, and another 26% speaking Spanish and English equally ("Hispanic Fact Pack," 2006, p. 42).

Table 4.2   Language Dominance by Country or Region of Origin

Country or region of origin	Spanish dominant	Both English and Spanish dominant	English dominant
Mexico	61%	22%	17%
Puerto Rico	25%	40%	35%
Cuba	54%	29%	17%
Central America	66%	26%	8%
South America	53%	37%	10%
Dominican	54%	41%	5%

Note. Data from Synovate U.S. Hispanic Market Report 2006 via Editorial Televisa. From "Hispanic Fact Pack," 2006, *Advertising Age*, p. 43, retrieved from http://www.adage.com/images/random/hispfactpack06.pdf

The language Hispanics are most comfortable speaking is also influenced by generation. For the first time, the number of U.S.-born Hispanics—who tend to be more acculturated, are more likely to be English speaking, are better educated, and typically are more affluent than the first foreign-born generation—is growing faster than the immigrant population. By 2020, just 34% of Hispanics will be foreign-born first generation; 36% will be U.S.-born second-generation children of immigrants, and 30% will be the third-generation offspring of U.S.-born Hispanics, according to the Pew Hispanic Center (Wentz, 2005b). Even today, 88% of Hispanics younger than eighteen years of age are U.S.-born. Only 8% of foreign-born Hispanics indicated that English is the language they are most comfortable speaking; in contrast, 45% of first-generation Hispanics, 62% of second-generation Hispanics, and a full 84% of third-generation Hispanics indicated that they preferred speaking English ("Hispanic Fact Pack," 2006, p. 42). Clearly, level of acculturation has much to do with how Hispanics use media. According to the Association of Hispanic Advertising Agencies' analysis of Synovate's 2004 U.S. Hispanic Market Report (Larson, 2004), acculturated Hispanics largely subscribe to cable or satellite TV, use the Internet, and consume only about 25% of their media in Spanish. The partially acculturated population is made of up three subsets: the *American Latino,* who is comfortable in Hispanic and American culture and consumes about 49% of his media in Spanish; the *new Latino,* who is foreign born but has lived in the United States for awhile and consumes 47% of his media in Spanish; and the *traditional Hispanic,* who is older, likely male, and consumes 54% of his media in Spanish. Finally, there is the Hispanic who is not acculturated and consumes 72% of his media time in Spanish (Larson, 2004). So, what's an advertiser to do? Some advertisers believe that the best strategy is to sprinkle ad dollars in both languages and try to adjust the message to each market. However, simply translating an ad will clearly not be enough. Joe Zubizaretta, chief operating officer of Zubi Advertising Services in Miami, provides the following example: Ford Motor Company pitches its F-150 pickup trucks in English-language television ads as a "rock-hard work truck." But, in the Spanish-language ads, the truck becomes a family vehicle that takes the kids around town, allows mom to shop, and helps dad to do some hauling. In advertising to Hispanics, it's really about understanding the culture more than the language. If the commercial communications are somehow related to the culture, Latino consumers will be able to connect (Rosenblum, 2005).

Religion

Religion is a second important unifying factor. The vast majority of Latin Americans come from Christian cultures, either Catholic or Protestant. And, while not every one is equally pious—or even nominally a believer—they have all been formed in a cultural matrix that is clearly Christian (Jenkins, 2003). Catholicism is the dominant religion among Hispanics, but this too is influenced by generation. Seventy-two percent of first-generation Hispanics are Catholic, with 19% of first-generation Hispanics labeling themselves as Protestant or other Christian religion. By the second generation, the number of Catholic Hispanics has slipped to 61%, and the number of Hispanics practicing Protestant and other Christian religions has increased to 25%. Only 52% of third-generation Hispanics are Catholic, with more than 31% reporting that they are Protestant or other Christian religion (Pew Hispanic Center, 2006). This shift can be ascribed to two factors. First, the style of U.S. Catholicism is foreign to many Latinos. "Latinos bring a more practical, experiential faith with them, less doctrinal and intellectual, moving away from the European Christian emphasis on private religiosity towards a more public and communal expression of faith," explains Dr. Jesse Miranda, a professor at Vanguard University and leader of the National Evangelical Hispanic Association (Hoffmann, 2005/2006). Second, evangelical Protestants have adopted sophisticated marketing techniques, such as providing local clergy with profiles of Hispanic communities in a campaign to convert large numbers of Hispanic Catholics (Solomon, 1999). To try to reduce the continuing hemorrhage of believers, Latin Catholics in the United States have tried to import Pentecostal customs, such as traditional music and instruments during services, and to encourage emotional expressions of spontaneous praise and thanksgiving (Jenkins, 2003).

Cultures differ in the degree to which their adherents believe that life is either under one's direct control or not. This has been described in the social sciences as an orientation toward either an external or internal locus of control (Sue & Sue, 1990). Falicov explains,

> For Latinos, God, Fate, or Destiny is in charge, rather than solely oneself. Many Latinos will use phrases such as "God will provide," "God willing," or "God has willed it." When Latinos are faced with dire financial circumstances, their attitude is one of acceptance. During difficult times, faith and prayer provide a reliable source of support and strength for Latino families. Prayer and other religious practices provide coping skills during times of stress. This is in contrast to the internal locus of control. The Protestant work ethic has fostered an internal locus of control and responsibility for Anglo-Americans, who tend to feel a sense of control over their destiny. The internal belief system is one of "if I work hard, I will be rewarded in this life." Latinos, on the other hand, have more of an external locus of control. Rewards for hard work and a good life may only occur in the afterlife, rather than in the present. These rewards are often beyond one's control and expressed as "God's will." (2001)

Because of Catholic religious values, reproduction is very important to Latinos. Marriage is considered permanent and is typically based on procreation. Statistics support this. While 12% of black adults are divorced, and 10% of white adults are divorced, only 8% of adult Hispanics are divorced (Chavez, 2000). For Hispanics, the choice is not one of having fewer children in order to improve one's standard of living, as is common in nuclear Protestant American families. Instead, it is accepted to have as many children as God grants and then to stretch available financial resources in order to provide for a large family. In contrast, Anglo American couples tend to base marriage on the idea of romantic love, and the number of children a couple will have is determined by personal choice about preferred lifestyle, rather than by God's will (Falicov, 2001). The size and importance of families in the Latino community will be addressed next.

Family

A third important unifying factor is the importance of family in Latin cultures. The family and the group take precedence over the individual. This collectivistic orientation is perhaps one of the most significant differences between Latinos and Anglo Americans. The mainstream American nuclear family is generally defined as husband and wife, with approximately two children. It is uncommon for grandparents to live with their children and very unusual for other relatives to share in the daily life of an Anglo family. Falicov explains that

> this type of family is modeled by democratic and egalitarian standards that tend to promote individual expression. Examples of individualistic interactions within a nuclear family include emphasis on self-expression, direct communication, and rewarding of autonomous behaviors of children. In contrast, the nuclear Latino household is embedded in a complex extended network of families and friends based on a collectivistic belief system. From agrarian times to the present, extended families have been the prevailing form of family arrangement in Latin America. Here it is common for grandparents and other relatives to live with the extended Latino family. But there is even a broader definition of extended kin for Latinos. It may include immediate family members, distant relatives, close family friends (comadres or compadres), long-standing neighbors, in-laws, and godparents (padrinos). (2001)

An ad for American Family Insurance conveys the importance of home and family to this coculture. Both the visual aspect and the copy are intended to resonate with Hispanic consumers. The headline reads, "The Happiness in Your Heart Lives at Home." The advertiser goes on to note that, "we know that most of the best moments of your life are spent at home" (see Figure 4.1).

Almost a third of Hispanic family households—twice the proportion of the U.S. population—contain at least five members (see Table 4.3). The importance of family connectedness and cohesiveness may override the individual need for self-expression. Indeed, the English word *privacy* does not exist as a noun in Spanish, and the adjective *private* (*privado*) has connotations of secrecy and confidentiality. In other words, family togetherness is the fundamental part of the fabric of the family. The construct of *familismo* is used to describe the solidarity, family pride, loyalty, and sense of belonging that one finds in Latino families (Falicov, 2001).

Unlike the Latino extended family, the typical nuclear Anglo American family is generally less open to involvement from persons other than immediate family members. In contrast, Latinos make boundaries permeable in extended families. Emphasis is on interdependence between extended Latino family members rather than on the value of independence and self-reliance (Falicov, 2001). Latino family members may help one another materially, with money, jobs, or room and board; they also help emotionally, with advice, support, and

Figure 4.1: Advertisement for American Family Insurance Conveying the Importance of Home and Family

La alegría del corazón vive en el hogar.

En American Family Insurance sabemos que el hogar es el lugar donde usted pasa los mejores momentos de su vida. Por eso, no importa si es propietario o inquilino, contamos con una gran variedad de pólizas que podrían ofrecerle la protección que necesita. Llame hoy a uno de nuestros agentes locales o visite www.amfam.com para informarse acerca de las opciones de cobertura que existen para proteger la alegría de su corazón...el hogar.

La póliza que compre y los servicios corporativos están disponibles solamente en inglés.

American Family Mutual Insurance Company y sus subsidiarias
Oficina Central – Madison, WI 53783
www.amfam.com

Toda su protección bajo un solo techo

Table 4.3: Household Type and Size

Household type and size	United States	All Hispanics
Family households		
Two persons	41%	22%
Three persons	23%	22%
Four persons	21%	25%
Five or more persons	15%	31%
Nonfamily households		
One person	82%	74%
Two or more persons	18%	26%
Percentage of all households that are family households	69%	81%

Note. From "Current Population Survey," March 2000, U.S. Census Bureau.

reassurance. Because several generations live in the same house, few Hispanic children go to day care. Collective child rearing is common. Grandparents or aunts and uncles watch over the kids while the father and, increasingly, sometimes, the mother work. At the other end of life cycle, planning for retirement is a concept that is alien to most Hispanics. Children and grandchildren are expected to help support their parents and grandparents when they become old. Furthermore, few elderly Hispanics go to nursing homes for any length of time, and, when Hispanics do send a family member to a nursing home, the elders are far more infirm and less able to care for themselves than those from other ethnic groups. Sociologists have long viewed the strength of the Hispanic family support system as the reason for the group's underutilization of nursing homes. Hispanic families tend to be very close, and Hispanic children have great respect for their elders. They feel as though they would be letting their parents or older relatives down if they didn't do everything possible to keep them home in familiar surroundings (DiMaria, 2006).

Gender roles are typically traditional in Latino families and may be tied to the compounding effects of Roman Catholicism in a patriarchal society. Ideally, the man should be family oriented, strong, hardworking, and brave. Positive aspects of *machismo,* or the cult of manliness, include characteristics such as courage, honesty, hard work, dedication and loyalty to family, and emphasis on the role of father. The female counterpart to that concept is *marianismo.* This lesser-known stereotype refers to the ideal woman, who is considered to be submissive, self-sacrificing, and responsible for the household and children (Falicov, 1992). Many surveys show that Hispanic women list being married and having a family as the most important things in their lives, while white and African American women are more likely to rank personal happiness or job stability higher. Indeed, early marriage and childbirth are common among Hispanic cultures. A 2002 Centers for Disease Control report found that 13%

of U.S. Hispanic women were married by age eighteen, compared to 8% of white women and just 5% of black women. Interestingly, while first-generation Hispanics are more likely to aspire to marriage than second-generation Hispanics—who are assimilating to Anglo American views—third-generation Hispanics are behaving more like the first generation, getting married younger (Milano, 2006). Latino women's sense of accomplishment is very much tied to motherhood, and, as a result, they may postpone accomplishments in their career and the workplace. Even when Latino women work outside the home, they often alternate between a more assertive role at work and a more traditional one at home.

Consumption among Hispanics relates not merely to self-worth but also to the quality of family life. Latinos value time with family, and possessions may be seen as a means of enhancing those bonds. For example, Latinos may spend a considerable amount of money on a huge television that will be viewed collectively in the living room, rather than spending a similar amount on two or three smaller televisions to be used in the privacy of individual family members' rooms. Children, in particular, are doted on. It is important that children be as well dressed as the family budget will allow. According to Simmons Research, Hispanics are 57% more likely than average Americans to have purchased children's furniture in the past year. And Mexican Americans spend 93% more on children's music than the average American (Brooks, 2006). While the average Hispanic household may have less money than the average white household, they are more likely to spend what they have on their families. Hispanic income and purchasing power will be addressed next.

Hispanic Income and Buying Power

There is no denying that Hispanic Americans still lag economically. For every dollar in income earned by a white household, a Hispanic household earns just sixty-nine cents. A recently released study by the Pew Hispanic Center revealed that, while median weekly earnings increased from $423 in the second quarter of 2005 to $431 in the second quarter of 2006, wages have dropped for foreign-born Latinos, who make up nine out of every ten new Latino workers (in the study, foreign-born Hispanics are defined as both legal and illegal residents) (Delgado, 2006). It is important to note, however, that their incomes are growing faster than incomes for the mainstream population, resulting in a growing middle class among Hispanics. More Latino families have annual incomes over $40,000, increasing by 80% between 1980 and 2000—three times the rate of increase of the overall middle class (Congressional Hispanic Caucus Institute, 2005). Nearly one-third (31%) of Hispanic households earn over $50,000 per year, and over 7% earn $100,000 per year or more (see Table 4.4). The hottest markets for affluent Hispanics—in order—are Los Angeles, New York, San Antonio, San Diego, Houston, San Jose, El Paso, Dallas, San Francisco, and Phoenix (Gustke, 2006).

Table 4.4: Percentage of Households for Different Brackets of Total Income in 2002		
Income	All households	Hispanic households
Under $5,000	3.2%	4.3%
$5,000 to $9,999	5.9%	6.7%
$10,000 to $14,999	7.0%	8.1%
$15,000 to $24,999	13.2%	17.2%
$25,000 to 34,999	12.3%	15.7%
$35,000 to $49,999	15.1%	16.4%
$50,000 to $74,999	18.3%	16.9%
$75,000 to $99,999	11.0%	7.5%
$50,000 and over	43.4%	31.6%
$100,000 and over	14.1%	7.2%

Note. From "Income in the United States: 2002," U.S. Census Bureau, 2002, retrieved from http://www.census.gov/prod/2003pubs/p60-221.pdf

An increasing number of Hispanic Americans are starting or expanding their own businesses, which helps to boost their incomes. The ranks of Hispanic-owned businesses in the United States grew 43%, to 1.6 million, from 1997 to 2002—quadruple the growth of all companies. These companies generated about $222 billion in revenue, up 19%, according to a recent report on Hispanic businesses from the U.S. Census Bureau (Green, 2006). The rate of growth in Hispanic businesses exceeds the growth rate in the country's Hispanic population. The majority of Hispanic companies are in construction or service businesses, such as repair and maintenance, according to the census. Data reveal that the number of Latina-owned businesses surged 62.4% over the seven-year period that ended in 2004, while the overall number of businesses grew just 9%. According to the Center for Women's Business Research, as of 2004, Hispanic women-owned businesses numbered nearly 554,000, employed some 320,000, and generated nearly $44.4 billion in sales nationwide. Indeed, 34.9% of all Hispanic-owned firms are owned by Latinas ("U.S. Hispanics," 2005). Experts have noted that many Hispanic-owned companies have benefited from wider social and cultural acceptance in the overall marketplace.

Between 1993 and 2005, home ownership rates rose by just 5.8% among non-Hispanic whites, yet nearly double that (10.6%) among Hispanics. Despite these gains, sizable gaps in home ownership rates persist among Hispanics compared to non-Hispanic whites. As of the end of 2005, 76% of non-Hispanic whites were homeowners, compared to 50% of Hispanics. Thus, despite the rapid growth of Hispanic home ownership over the past decade, the gap between whites and Hispanics is still 26% (U.S. Department of Housing and Urban Development, 2006). However, a recent study forecasts that 60% of Latinos will own their own homes by the year 2010 and that Hispanics represent an increasing portion of the age group where most home sales occur— twenty-six to forty-six years of age (Congressional Hispanic Caucus Institute, 2005). It is expected that more than 230,000 Latino households will join the ranks of homeowners each year over the next twenty years, and projections show that U.S. Hispanics will need 4.6 million housing units over the same time period ("U.S. Hispanics," 2005).

Latino buying power drew even with African American buying power in 2006 and was expected to exceed it in 2007, according to a report by the Selig Center for Economic Growth. Hispanic buying power and black buying power each accounted for about $800 billion, or 8.4% of the total buying power in 2006. And Hispanic buying power is projected to hit $863.1 billion in 2007, according to the report (Solis, 2006). But, even as Hispanic buying power overtakes African American buying power at the national level, it is important to recognize that, in the majority of states, the African American market will continue to be much larger than the Hispanic market. This reflects the fact that Hispanics and their buying power are still much more geographically concentrated than non-Hispanics or African Americans. California accounts for 27% of Hispanic buying power in the United States, and Texas accounts for another 18%. Figure 4.2 presents the top ten states in terms of Hispanic buying power.

Hispanic Americans out-index non-Hispanic Americans in many key product areas, including food, apparel (in particular, for children), health and beauty, baby products, digital cameras, long-distance phone service, and prepaid wireless service (Association of Hispanic Advertising Agencies, n.d.). Data reveal that, in 2001, Hispanic American consumers' annual spending was spread along these lines:

- $83.3 billion on shelter and utilities
- $62.9 billion on transportation
- $38.6 billion on food consumed in the home
- $12.5 billion on apparel
- $11.1 billion on healthcare
- $10.9 billion on entertainment
- $10.3 billion on restaurant meals
- $2.2 billion on personal care products (Paulin, 2003)

Figure 4.2: Nation's Largest Hispanic Consumer Markets

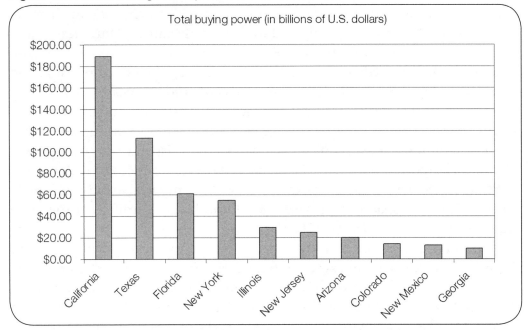

Total buying power (in billions of U.S. dollars)

Note. Data from the Selig Center for Economic Growth, Terry College of Business, University of Georgia, May 2003.

Expected to surpass $1 trillion in buying power in just a few years, Hispanics have been relabeled the "majority minority" (Pellet, 2006). Without doubt, marketers are increasingly paying attention to these numbers as well as to Hispanics' shopping behavior.

Shopping Behavior

Because Hispanics are more likely to cook from scratch than average consumers, they spend more on fresh produce and meat and tend to be heavy users of spices, seasonings, and extracts, as well as condiments, gravies, sauces, and cooking oil (Urbanski, 2003). According to "U.S. Hispanics: Insights into Grocery Preferences and Attitudes," a study that Cultural Access Group conducted for the Food Marketing Institute, Hispanics also spend more at the grocery store than the general public: $117 per week versus $87 per week. And, overall, they shop more. They make 4.3 trips to the market each month, not counting shops, such as the *panaderias* (bakeries) and *carnicerias* (butcher shops) that more than one-half of Hispanic shoppers frequent (Ebenkamp, 2002). This makes them an especially attractive target for supermarkets. For the general public, the goal of grocery shopping is primarily getting the task done—a quick in and out. In contrast, Hispanics view the supermarket as a hub of social activity—a place to spend time with the family, while selecting fresh vegetables or a pound of ground beef. "It's like a family outing," notes Thomas Tseng, director of marketing for Los Angeles–based Cultural Access Group. "Hispanics like to talk with their local butchers about cuts of meat and take time to enjoy the experience of shopping for food" (Ebenkamp, 2002). Table 4.5 provides additional insights into Hispanic shoppers.

Recently, Unilever conducted a study called "Winning the Hispanic Shopping Trip," in which it probed actual Hispanic shoppers' activities, reviewing more than 3,600 diaries and store receipts. The results showed the primacy of food and the shopping experience for this rapidly growing demographic group. "From family to community, food for Hispanic Americans has an emotional and a cultural significance that extends beyond eating," explains Mike Twitty, senior group research manager, Unilever, United States.

Table 4.5: Hispanic Shopping Characteristics

Economists	Loyalists	Price hunters	Traditionalists
Bilingual	Spanish preferred	Spanish preferred	Spanish dominant
33% born in the United States	15% born in the United States	62% born in Mexico	65% born in Mexico
Average age: 42 years	Average age: 39 years	Average age: 39 years	Average age: 40 years
Less likely to have kids at home	Young family households	Households contain kids	Households contain kids
Average household income: $29,880	Average household income: $22,420	Average household income: $23,380	Average household income: $20,880
More likely to shop	Loyal to a primary store	Shop for best price	Shop for Hispanic items
Stock up on sale items	Not influenced by ads/promotions	Try new brands if they're on sale	Least satisfied with primary store
Influenced by sale items	Risk adverse	Very price sensitive	Brand loyal, risk adverse
Do not budget for grocery shopping	Prepare shopping list and stick to it	Engage in price comparisons	Set budgets for grocery shopping
Hispanic elements are not important	Hispanic elements are important	Hispanic elements are important	Hispanic elements are very important
Spend $111 per week on groceries	Spend $112 per week on groceries	Spend $111 per week on groceries	Spend $121 per week on groceries

Note. Data from "U.S. Hispanics: Insights into Grocery Preferences and Attitudes," conducted by Cultural Access for the Food Marketing Institute. From "What's in Store," by B. Ebenkamp, May 6, 2002, *Brandweek*, p. 23.

Hence, the Hispanic shopper thinks about every aspect of food shopping and preparation. She plans her trips carefully—apparently more so than the general market shopper—and not only around what she has at home and what she needs, but around the values she can obtain. ("Hispanic Shoppers," 2006)

Other significant findings of the study include the following:

- Quick trips are just 44% of all the trips the Hispanic shopper makes, versus 62% for general market shoppers. Nonfood items spur quick trips for the Hispanic shopper.

- Hispanic women are significantly more aware (by a 48% to 36% margin) of specials before going to the store than are general market shoppers. Even inside the store, Hispanics' awareness of specials is higher than the general market populations' awareness.

- Almost one in four Hispanic shoppers walk or take public transportation (22%) compared with just one in thirty-three of general market consumers. Geography is responsible for choice as is value.

- The Hispanic shopper knows her needs beforehand, so 56% of her total grocery spending occurs on routine trips versus 22% in the general market.

- Only 2% of the Hispanic shopper's trips are urgent as opposed to 19% for the general market—a margin of one in fifty versus one in five.

- More than 50% of the respondents surveyed pay in cash, 25% use a debit card, and 11% pay by credit card. Just 2% pay by check. ("Hispanic Shoppers," 2006)

According to Steven Soto, president and chief executive officer (CEO) of the Mexican American Grocers Association (MAGA), "Hispanic Purchasing Power is said to be growing by $1 billion every six weeks—everyone will be competing for a piece of the Hispanic pie" (Dee Long, 2006). Consider the case of Super A Foods, a family-owned and -operated chain, one of several smaller grocery companies tapping into the Hispanic market and thus nipping at the heels of the big dogs in food retailing—Ralphs, Vons, Albertsons, Lucky, and Stater Bros. Super A Foods operates twelve grocery stores scattered throughout Los Angeles County and neighboring residential cities—an area that boasts one of the United States' largest Hispanic populations. Super A Foods has striven to make both its merchandise offerings and the overall shopping experience very relevant to Hispanic customers. Super A Foods offers extensive offerings in two key categories for the Hispanic customers: fresh produce and meat/fish. Their produce departments are spacious areas with aromas reminiscent of a fresh outdoor farmer's market. Mexican staples such as *nopolitos* (cactus) and bulk beans, along with such ethnic specialty items as *piloncillo* (brown sugar formed into cones and sold by the pound) are prominently displayed.

The meat/fish department offers products ranging from *carne asada,* ready to cook fajita mixtures, and plenty of *chorizo* (sausage) offerings to cuts of meat traditionally eaten in Mexico; favorites include *menudo* (tripe), pigs' feet, and pork rinds in brine. Stores also feature a *tortilleria* (tortilla factory) and *panaderia* (bakery) department. Corn and flour tortillas are made in house daily. The bakery features more than a dozen different sweet breads marketed in a self-serve glass counter, an arrangement that is very popular with Hispanic shoppers. A large showcase is filled with colorful birthday and social occasion cakes. Customers are also offered an extensive selection of packaged spices essential to Hispanic cooking. A salsa bar offers tubs of both red and green salsa, along with guacamole, freshly made each morning and priced by the pound. Because grocery shopping is a family affair, immediate hunger cravings can be satisfied with a quick-serve outlet that offers complete Mexican combo meals for just $3.99 and picnic tables placed strategically nearby to encourage customers to purchase meals hot and enjoy them right in the store as part of their shopping experience. The chain keeps advertising costs restrained by marketing via direct mail. Each week, it sends full-color circulars to nearby residents, promoting specials as well as the store's motto of Save Every Day. By knowing who their customers are, paying attention to what is important to their culture, and catering to those needs, Super A Foods continues to thrive in the competitive grocery arena (Dee Long, 2006).

Who's Talking to Hispanics?

Corporate America is beginning to respond to the phenomenal potential of the Hispanic market. Between 2000 and 2004, corporations increased their ad spending to reach the Hispanic market by a whopping 44%. According to some estimates, firms are now spending about 5% of their national advertising budgets on average to reach the Hispanic consumer according to research released by the Association of Hispanic Advertising Agencies—still just over half of the recommended 9% of national ad budgets (Machado, 2004). The study, "Ad Budget Alignment: Maximizing Impact in the Hispanic Market," revealed that, overall, only about one-fifth of product categories are currently investing near the correct levels aligned with category-specific Hispanic consumption behaviors. Retailers and direct marketing advertisers led all product categories in advertising budget allocations to reach Hispanics, shifting 7.3% of national ad spending to Hispanic media as compared to 4.8% by manufacturers and service providers. Among those spending the most ad dollars to reach the Hispanic market were consumer electronics retailers and manufacturers, food and drug retailers, and telecommunications companies. Despite the overall increase in ad spending, advertisers in some categories have been slow to recognize the buying power held by U.S. Hispanics. For example, pharmaceutical companies allocated the least advertising dollars to reach the Hispanic market, spending only 0.8% of their overall ad budgets. Companies in the categories of financial services, apparel manufacturers, and entertainment are also failing to measure up to the appropriate allocations (Machado, 2004).

In terms of specific advertisers, Lexcon Marketing Corp. ranked number one, spending nearly $180 million to reach Hispanic consumers. Procter & Gamble ranked second in Hispanic advertising spending, and Univision Communications ranked third on the list (see Table 4.6).

Table 4.6: Top Fifty Advertisers in Hispanic Media by Measured U.S. Media Spending

Rank	Marketer	2005 ad spending (in millions of U.S. dollars)	Percent change
1.	Lexcon Marketing Corp.	$179.8	2.2%
2.	Procter & Gamble Co.	$157.0	1.5%
3.	Univision Communications	$131.7	8.2%
4.	General Motors Corp.	$112.9	6.1%
5.	Sears Holdings Corp.	$84.4	−22.7%
6.	Johnson & Johnson	$74.3	11.2%
7.	McDonald's Corp.	$69.8	6.8%
8.	Ford Motor Co.	$68.5	12.0%
9.	PepsiCo	$67.3	3.2%
10.	DaimlerChrysler	$62.8	−7.5%
11.	Cisneros Group of Cos.	$61.9	4.2%
12.	Wal-Mart Stores	$61.7	11.8%
13.	Toyota Motor Corp.	$58.5	38.6%
14.	Verizon Communications	$56.8	5.6%
15.	AT&T	$53.9	−44.2%
16.	Grupo Televisa	$50.8	135.7%
17.	Hyundai Motor Co.	$47.2	22.4%
18.	Walt Disney Co.	$44.7	20.1%
19.	Home Depot	$39.6	39.8%
20.	L'Oréal Group	$38.0	13.2%
21.	Altria Group	$37.6	−0.2%
22.	SABMiller	$37.5	75.2%
23.	U.S. Government	$33.6	−9.1%
24.	Yum! Brands	$31.7	3.7%
25.	Time Warner	$30.3	−14.7%

26.	General Electric Co.	$29.7	43.8%
27.	Deutsche Telekom	$28.8	27.2%
28.	Coca-Cola Co.	$28.8	7.6%
29.	DirecTV Group	$28.0	50.4%
30.	Anheuser-Busch Cos.	$26.6	30.3%
31.	Honda Motor Co.	$26.3	18.3%
32.	Unilever	$25.8	18.6%
33.	Kellogg Co.	$25.7	5.6%
34.	Sprint Nextel Corp.	$24.5	288.9%
35.	J. C. Penney Co.	$24.4	47.8%
36.	Clorox Co.	$24.1	23.6%
37.	Ventura Entertainment Enterprises	$22.4	805.8%
38.	Bally Total Fitness Holdings Corp.	$22.3	−8.3%
39.	Allstate Corp.	$22.1	161.0%
40.	Target Corp.	$22.0	27.3%
41.	Texas Pacific Group (Burger King)	$20.8	−12.5%
42.	Americatel Corp.	$20.7	−6.2%
43.	Wendy's International	$20.2	3.7%
44.	Lowe's Cos.	$19.8	32.1%
45.	Nissan Motor Co.	$19.0	−14.9%
46.	Petrone Group	$18.0	3.7%
47.	Southwest Airlines	$17.8	4.6%
48.	Viacom	$16.4	48.0%
49.	Visa International	$16.4	63.6%
50.	EchoStar Communications Corp.	$16.4	413.6%

Note. Media are from TNS Media Intelligence and represent the sum of broadcast TV networks, Galavisión (cable), Spanish-language magazines (including four PIB-monitored Spanish-language magazines), Spanish-language newspapers, and Spanish-language spot TV.

From "Hispanic Fact Pack," 2006, *Advertising Age*, pp. 12–13, retrieved from http://www.adage.com/images/random/hispfactpack06.pdf. Reprinted with permission.

Creating Advertising That Persuades Hispanic Consumers

The 2003 Yankelovich Multicultural Monitor Study, conducted in collaboration with Cheskin and Images USA, provides information on the aspects of advertising that contribute to persuading Latino consumers (see Figure 4.3). The debate regarding whether to employ English or Spanish in commercial messages has already been addressed. Interestingly, the Yankelovich study found that, in response to the statement "the degree to which the following types of advertisements persuade you to buy or try a new product or service 'a lot,'" the most frequent response was "Ads in a language I speak at home"; a mere 38% of respondents checked this answer. Of course, these ads could be in either English or Spanish depending on the language spoken in the respondent's home. Nonetheless, this study seems to suggest that the linguistic element is not nearly as critical as some statistics would have suggested. The data reveal that information on product price is nearly as important as the language employed. A recent advertisement for Cingular long-distance telephone service does an excellent job of providing exactly such information to Hispanic consumers (see Figure 4.4). Ads that show actual results from using a product are not far behind in terms of persuasiveness.

How to Reach Them: Media

While marketers and their agencies may debate over whether the future of Hispanic media is in English or Spanish, one thing they do agree upon is the plan to increase their spending in most Hispanic media, regardless of language. An *Advertising Age* survey of nearly five hundred marketers and agencies found that 81.2% of respondents expected the Hispanic budgets for which they were responsible to grow in 2006, while just 16.8% expected them to remain the same, and a mere 2% noted that they were likely to fall (Wentz, 2005a). As

Figure 4.3: Aspects of Ads That Persuade Latino Consumers

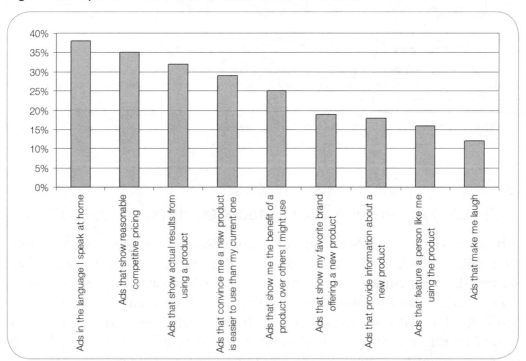

Note. Data from 2003 Yankelovich Multicultural Monitor Study (as cited in Korzenny & Korzenny, 2005, p. 112).

Figure 4.4: Cingular World Connect Ad Featuring Product Price

Tu país está al alcance dè tu mano con Cingular.

Con Cingular World Connect™ llamas a tu país desde tu teléfono móvil con nuestras tarifas internacionales más bajas. Por sólo $3.99 al mes ahorras considerablemente sobre las tarifas regulares a más de 200 países.

Llamar a tu país desde Estados Unidos es fácil, sólo marca "+" (ó el 011), el código del país y el número local al que quieres llamar.

Suscríbete hoy mismo y empieza a ahorrar.

Tarifas por minuto

países	a teléfonos fijos	a teléfonos móviles
México	9¢	9¢
Argentina	18¢	38¢
Brasil	14¢	26¢
Colombia	17¢	20¢
República Dominicana	18¢	26¢
Ecuador	35¢	36¢
Guatemala	24¢	25¢
España	7¢	34¢
Venezuela	20¢	34¢

No esperes más y llama al 1 866 Cingular
O visita www.cingular.com/espanol.

✕ cingular
adelante ▪▪▪▪▪™

Existen ciertos cargos adicionales y ciertas restricciones, según el crédito y el tiempo que el suscriptor haya sido cliente. Las llamadas que se reciben y hacen en ciertos países pueden estar bloqueadas. El listado de países bloqueados puede cambiar sin previo aviso. Para una lista completa y actualizada de países, tarifas, cargos, y términos y condiciones, visite http://www.cingular.com/customer_service/cingularWorld/cingular_world_sp. **Marcado internacional**: Se cobran cargos de tiempo de uso o roaming, además de los cargos de larga distancia. **Roaming internacional**: Se requiere un equipo compatible. No se garantiza la disponibilidad ni la calidad de cobertura o de servicio en el extranjero. ©2006 Cingular Wireless. Todos los derechos reservados.

Table 4.7: Hispanic Media Advertising Spending			
	Measured advertising spending (in millions of U.S. dollars)		
Medium	2005	2004	Percent change
Network/national TV	$1,512.0	$1,387.2	9.0%
Local TV	$638.9	$602.8	6.0%
National radio	$200.8	$191.2	5.0%
Local radio	$492.2	$473.2	4.0%
National newspapers	$113.5	$110.2	3.0%
Local newspapers	$170.8	$161.9	5.5%
Magazines	$92.8	$88.3	5.0%
Out-of-home	$80.1	$76.3	5.0%
Total	$3,301.1	$3,091.2	6.8%

Note. Data from HispanTelligence, a research arm of *Hispanic Business*. National totals are based on input from TNS Media Intelligence, media industry experts, advertising agencies, and public records. Figures are net (media-retained) ad expenditures. From "Hispanic Fact Pack," 2006, *Advertising Age*, p. 8, retrieved from http://www.adage.com/images/random/hispfactpack06.pdf

Table 4.7 shows, the bulk of Hispanic media ad spending goes to network/national TV, followed closely by local TV. Local radio is the next most important medium, followed by national radio. Both local and national papers fare slightly better than magazines.

Television

Hispanics are heavy television users. While other TV audiences are shrinking, Hispanic TV viewership just keeps on growing. Hispanic households tend to watch more TV, on average, than other viewers. Their average prime-time viewing per week, at seventeen hours, is a full 30% more than the average of all U.S. households, at thirteen hours ("Hispanic Consumers," 2002). An important benefit of television is that it lends credibility. While, for the general market, television presence does not necessarily mean that one advertiser is any more significant than another, in the Hispanic market, it provides almost instant credibility (Faura, 2004). In terms of language, a Simmons National Consumer Study shows that 76% of Hispanic adults born in the United States watch English-language TV, while only 29% of that group watches Spanish-language TV. Conversely, 81% of foreign-born Hispanics watch Spanish-language TV (Zbar, 2004). Overall, Hispanic Americans spent an average of 17.3 hours per week watching Spanish-language television, compared with

11.6 hours watching English-language television (Association of Hispanic Advertising Agencies, 2005).

Univision Communications, the leading Spanish-language media company in the United States, owns Univision Network, which covers 98% of Hispanic households in this country and commands two-thirds of the total audience watching Spanish-language TV. Univision is also the top network among all Hispanics during prime time. Looking only at adult viewers, Univision currently reaches almost 30% of Hispanics ages eighteen to forty-nine during prime time (7 to 11 P.M. in Hispanic television). *Telenovelas*—soap operas—account for the majority of Univision's programming. News, entertainment, and reality shows make up much of the remainder. Sports, and, in particular, soccer and boxing, are also very popular television fare. Univision Communications was put up for sale in early 2006 and, in June of that year, announced a $13 billion deal, scheduled to close sometime in 2007. In second place is Telemundo, which was purchased by General Electric Company's NBC network in 2001. This acquisition has made Telemundo a much more competitive entity. Like rival Univision, Telemundo has traditionally targeted new émigrés, those who are established U.S. residents but aren't fluent in English, as well as the assimilated. Prime-time programming consists primarily of novelas, while weekend

Table 4.8: Hispanic TV Network Viewership

Rank	Network	Hispanic household rating	Hispanic household share	Number of Hispanic Households (000)	Number of P2+ viewers
1.	Univision	17.7	29.0	1,989	3,456
2.	Telemundo	6.0	10.0	675	1,080
3.	FOX	4.3	7.0	478	736
4.	ABC	3.6	6.0	405	616
5.	CBS	3.0	5.0	340	490
6.	TeleFutura	2.9	5.0	325	529
7.	UPN	2.6	4.0	295	453
8.	NBC	2.6	4.0	289	419
9.	WB	1.9	3.0	214	313
10.	Azteca America	1.1	2.0	120	198

Note. Data from Nielsen Hispanic Television Index based on Hispanic prime-time viewership from 7 p.m. to 11 p.m. from September 19, 2005, to May 28, 2006. The rating is the percentage of Hispanic TV households; the share is the percentage of those households with TV sets in use who watch the network. P2+ counts the total viewing persons in thousands for those Hispanic TV households that are tuned in to the network. Viewing estimates include seven days of digital video recorder (DVR). From "Hispanic Fact Pack," 2006, *Advertising Age*, p. 33, retrieved from http://www.adage.com/images/random/hispfactpack06.pdf

Figure 4.5: Telemundo Advertisement

programming includes sports and films. Telemundo reaches 10% of prime-time viewers (see Figure 4.5 for an ad promoting Telemundo to advertisers).

TeleFutura, which was launched by Univision Communications in 2002 to reach Hispanics ages eighteen to thirty-four, is ranked number six in terms of

Table 4.9: Top Prime-Time Network TV Programs Ranked by May 2006 Ratings among Hispanic Viewers

Rank[a]	Program (day/date)	Network	Hispanic household rating	Number of average Hispanic households	Number of average Hispanic viewers
Spanish language					
1.	Bellando por un Sueno (Sunday)	Univision	23.0	2,581	4,726
2.	Fea Mas Bella (Monday)	Univision	20.1	2,259	4,066
3.	Fea Mas Bella (Thursday)	Univision	20.0	2,250	3,977
4.	Fea Mas Bella (Tuesday)	Univision	19.8	2,227	3,984
5.	Barrera de Amor (Monday)	Univision	19.6	2,202	3,833
6.	Barrera de Amor (Tuesday)	Univision	19.5	2,186	3,753
7.	Fea Mas Bella (Wednesday)	Univision	19.3	2,169	3,807
8.	Barrera de Amor (Thursday)	Univision	19.2	2,158	3,776
9.	Reyes de la Pista (Sunday)	Univision	18.9	2,119	4,012
10.	Barrera de Amor (Wednesday)	Univision	18.5	2,075	3,624
English language					
30.	American Idol (Wednesday)	FOX	8.4	944	1,756
36.	American Idol (Tuesday)	FOX	7.5	841	1,378
49.	Grey's Anatomy (Sp 2, 5/15)	ABC	6.8	762	1,218
50.	House (Tuesday)	FOX	6.5	731	1,131
54.	Desperate Housewives (Sunday)	ABC	6.1	680	1,103
55.	Family Guy (Sunday)	FOX	5.9	661	1,128
61.	So You Think You Can Dance (Thursday)	FOX	5.4	610	1,118
61.	American Dad! (Sunday)	FOX	5.4	610	1,069
63.	Family Guy (Sp Finale, 8:30 p.m., 5/21)	FOX	5.3	597	918
64.	House (Sp, 8:00 p.m., 5/21)	FOX	.2	586	862
64.	Grey's Anatomy (Sunday)	ABC	5.2	585	912

Note. Data from Nielsen Media Research, Nielsen Hispanic Television Index. Households and viewers are measured in thousands. Measurement period was 7 p.m. to 11 p.m., Monday through Sunday (May 1, 2006, through May, 28, 2006). Programs under five minutes and breakouts are excluded. Average Hispanic viewers are the number of persons in Hispanic households viewing the program. Sp indicates special. Viewing estimates include seven days of DVR. From "Hispanic Fact Pack," 2006, Advertising Age, p. 32, retrieved from http://www.adage.com/images/random/hispfactpack06.pdf. a=Rank among Hispanic viewers.

prime-time viewership. The network counterprograms against Univision, airing alternative genres during every day part. TV Azteca is a Mexican television station that began operating in Los Angeles in 2001 and has affiliate stations in several key markets. Their programming slant, with its focus on Mexico, appeals in particular to Mexican Americans. Clearly, Spanis-language media's popularity is not shrinking (see Table 4.8). Both Univision and Telemundo have also expanded into late night as a potential to draw away some of the Hispanic audience who previously viewed late night shows on the English–language networks. In addition, Univision has expanded its Saturday morning kids' block, and, along with TeleFutura and Galavisión, has bulked up their news programming in both prime time and other day parts. Despite all the new programming moves, prime-time novelas are still the bread and butter of both Univision and Telemundo.

Research shows that, over the past ten years, adult audiences aged eighteen to forty-nine watching prime-time television on Spanish-language stations grew 122%, and, during that same time, the slightly younger segment aged eighteen to thirty-four watching prime-time TV on Spanish-language networks grew 126% (Consoli, 2005). The traditional big four networks (ABC, CBS, NBC, and Fox) have been losing viewers, particularly younger ones, to cable networks, video games, and the Internet for years. Now, Spanish broadcasters are part of the threat. The numbers illustrate that the big four networks are clearly no longer the only place to reach the nation's largest TV audience and that younger Hispanic Americans are increasingly turning to Spanish-language television. For example, the young Hispanics flocking to Univision are, for the most part, bilingual, which means that they are tuning in because the programming appeals to them—not just because the actors speak Spanish. "Older viewers watch Spanish broadcasters because it's the only language they speak," notes Felix Gutierrez, a professor at the University of California's Annenberg School of Communication. "With younger Latinos, it's increasingly a choice" (Barnes & Jordan, 2005). Hispanic television viewers tend to favor reality shows and children's programming more so than do non-Hispanics (see Table 4.9).Hispanic households tend to be younger—nearly half the members are younger than age thirty. More than two-thirds, or 68%, of Hispanic households are married couples with children, according to Horizon Media's analysis of 2000 census data (Larson, 2004). Indeed, many Hispanic households tend to eat and watch TV together as a family. The data in Table 4.9 suggest more family-oriented viewing patterns, with program choices often made by younger viewers.

Among English-language networks, Fox is the most popular, reaching 7% of adult viewers, followed by ABC (6%) and CBS (5%). In response to the competition from Spanish-language networks, the big four networks have been spending time studying Univision's schedule to figure out ways to attract its audience. Some high-ranking executives at the traditional networks, at least privately, say they are concerned about Univision's growing dominance in large cities where they own highly profitable local stations. With Nielsen research showing young Hispanics spending more time watching TV than their counterparts, and the Hispanic population in the United States exploding, the big networks are waking up. In 2006, ABC hired its first U.S. Hispanic agency of record to promote its shows to the estimated 41 million U.S. Hispanics. Arenas Entertainment, a Beverly Hills, California, shop that specializes in Latino entertainment marketing, initially worked on two programs—the juggernaut *Desperate Housewives* and a new series, *Ugly Betty*. It's no coincidence, for example, that the smash primetime soap *Desperate Housewives* has two leading Hispanic characters. Arenas Entertainment's goal is to bring even more Hispanic viewers to *Desperate Housewives* and to heighten awareness of actress Eva Longoria as the feisty character Gabrielle Solis. *Ugly Betty* emerged as one of the few buzzed-about shows in the fall of 2006. The show is an adaptation of a hit Colombian telenovela called *Yo Soy Betty la Fea* that has been sold around the world. The heroine is a smart young woman whose talents are overlooked, because, unlike the stunningly beautiful characters of every other novela, she is plain, pudgy, and hideously dressed. In the United States, *Yo Soy Betty la Fea* ran a few years earlier on Telemundo, giving the NBC-owned network a big ratings boost. In early 2006, Univision started airing a Mexican

Table 4.10: Top Spanish-Language Cable Networks

Rank	Cable network	Cable coverage percentage of all Hispanic TV households	Share percentage of Hispanic cable households
1.	Galavisión	59.9%	79.8%
2.	Fox Sports en Español	36.4%	48.5%
3.	Mun2	32.8%	43.6%
4.	MTV en Español	31.4%	41.8%
5.	Discovery en Español	27.1%	36.1%
6.	CNN en Español	26.7%	35.5%
7.	Cine Latino	25.6%	34.0%
8.	Gol TV	24.8%	33.0%
9.	Canal Sur	23.2%	30.9%
10.	TV Chile International	20.6%	27.5%
10.	HITN	20.6%	27.5%

Note. Data from Nielsen Media Research's Nielsen Hispanic Television Index (NHTI) for May 2006. There are 7,930,000 Hispanic cable households out of 11,230,000 Hispanic TV households. Networks shown are those with coverage of 20% or more of Hispanic households. From "Hispanic Fact Pack," 2006, *Advertising Age*, p. 35, retrieved from http://www.adage.com/images/random/hispfactpack06.pdf. Reprinted with permission.

remake called *La Fea Mas Bella* (*The Most Beautiful Ugly Girl*), starring basically the same character but named Lety instead of Betty. ABC is hoping that U.S. Hispanics, many already familiar with the Betty character, will also become fans of the English-language version (see Figure 4.6 for an ad promoting *Ugly Betty* to Hispanics in *People en Español*). Interestingly, *Ugly Betty* will go head-to-head with Univision's *Ugly Lety*, running in the networks' top novela slot on Thursdays at 8 P.M. Hispanic ads from Arenas Entertainment appeal to Latin pride and play humorously on the idea that a Spanish-language hit has become such a phenomenon that a major network is remaking the series in English. The ads feature actress America Ferrera in her full Betty regalia—thick glasses, shiny braces, bushy eyebrows, and polka dots—and the tagline *Tan Fea Que la Hicimos en Ingles* (So Ugly We Did It in English). Though the ads are mostly in Spanish to promote the English-language show, network executives note that it is not unusual even for the Spanish-dominant population to watch the general market TV networks, in part to improve their English (Atkinson & Wentz, 2006). Not to be outdone, Fox makes certain that there are songs that appeal to the Hispanic demographic in the catalog available to *American Idol* contestants. And NBC incorporates Spanish dialogue into its soap *Passions* and is trying to hire actors who have become stars on its Telemundo channel. The network signed a talent deal with Genesis Rodriguez, an actress on Telemundo's *Prisionera*, a popular telenovela. "We are hoping she will bring her Telemundo fan base to prime time on NBC," noted Marc Hirschfeld, NBC's executive vice president of casting (Barnes & Jordan, 2005).

Meanwhile, there has been an explosion of cable channels targeting Hispanics, and their efforts to acquire Hispanic subscribers have been successful. Nielsen Media Research noted that, in 2000, cable penetration among total U.S. households was 76%, compared with an impressive 61% for Hispanic households. A major advantage of cable channels for marketers is that media, as well as smaller businesses, can afford to advertise on them. Galavisión, owned by Univision Communications, is one of the older cable networks targeting Hispanics. It was launched in 1979; today, it reaches about 5.7 million Hispanic homes and ranks as the number one network among Hispanic viewers (see Table 4.10). Galavisión offers a mix of news, sports, variety/lifestyle, and comedy programming. Galavisión broadcasts the immensely popular comedy *El Chavo* (see Table 4.11). Fox Sports en Español, which ranks number two, was launched in 1996. Fox Sports en Español found success in airing its signature sports events (such as Mexican soccer tournaments), which points to the passion Hispanic viewers have for sports. Mun2 (pronounced MunDos) is the bilingual cable sibling of Telemundo and was launched in 2001 to target Hispanics aged eighteen to thirty-four. Given that the median Hispanic age is about a decade younger than that of the general U.S. population, this is a strategic move. To appeal to this audience, Mun2 hit the streets to interview

Figure 4.6: Advertisement in *People en Español* Promoting ABC's *Ugly Betty*

young Hispanics regarding their preferences for original programming in both English and Spanish. Because music was cited as a strong cultural reference point for Latinos, particularly the younger generation, Mun2's programming is very much music driven. While they plan to launch more lifestyle programming, music—hip-hop, urban, and mainstream pop—will always be at least 50% of their programming.

Mainstream programming translated into Spanish is spreading rapidly on cable. In 1998, Discovery was one of the early cable entries into the Hispanic market, launching Discovery en Español. In 2005, Discovery Communications launched two new Spanish-language networks, Discovery Kids en Español and Discovery Viajar y Vivir (Travel and Living). These two networks feature programming from Discovery Communications' Latin American networks (Discovery International operates networks in forty-six countries), as well as programming from Discovery's Anglo American networks—such as dubbed shows from *Animal Planet*. ESPN Deportes kicked off early in 2004. In many markets, there are also Spanish-language versions of Fox Sports Net, VH1, and the Weather Channel. Another recent entry is the History Channel in Español. Notes Dan Davids, the History Channel's executive vice president / general manager, "Based on feedback we've received from conversations with Hispanic viewers across the country, there seems to be an appetite to fill in the gaps on their historical background" (Larson, 2004). The History Channel's target audience is primarily male, but the focus will be on the family viewing experience, with a mix of documentaries and series on Latin America and world history. A highlight of its lineup was the series *Hakes de America* (*Roots of America*), which focuses on people and places of historical significance in Latin America. Episodes included *Cliff Mummies of the Andes Unwrapped, Machu Picchu,* and *Strange Disappearance of the Anasazi*. A number of the programs appearing on the History Channel en Español have been packaged by the History Channel Latin America, which has experienced considerable success since it was launched in 2000. The network has grown distribution 62% to reach 11.8 million homes in Central and South America (Larson, 2004). Interestingly, MTV en Español, which was launched in 1998, announced in 2006 that it would switch to a bilingual format—to better appeal to U.S.-born Hispanics. MTV Music Television president Christina Mornan announced that MTV en Español was turning into MTV Tr3s (pronounced *tres*). Research revealed that the median age of the foreign-born population is thirty-five, while the median age of the U.S.-born population is eighteen. MTV Tr3s's so-called sweet spot is viewers aged twelve to twenty-four, of which at least 70% are U.S. born. MTV Tr3s's goal is to be in 50% of Hispanic households—about 5.5 million. They will target a slightly broader group of twelve- to thirty-four-year-olds with pop-, urban-, and rock-music programming. It also plans to add lifestyle series and news documentaries about U.S. Latinos (Klaassen, 2006).

When Spanish is spoken on the network, English subtitles are provided. When watching English-language cable, for instance, the number-one channel was

Table 4.11: Top Cable TV Programs among Hispanic Viewers

Rank	Program (date)	Network	Hispanic household rating	Number of average Hispanic households	Number of average Hispanic viewers
Spanish language					
1.	*El Chavo II* (5/22)	Galavisión	3.0	337	744
2.	*El Chavo II* (5/17)	Galavisión	2.9	321	651
3.	*El Chavo II* (5/18)	Galavisión	2.8	317	507
4.	*El Chavo II* (5/08)	Galavisión	2.7	303	692
5.	*El Chavo II* (5/6)	Galavisión	2.6	291	597
6.	*Copa Libertadores*, Qtr Rd-Gm1(2) (5/09)	Fox Sports en Español	2.6	288	463
7.	*El Chavo II* (5/19)	Galavisión	2.5	278	471
7.	*El Chavo II* (5/12)	Galavisión	2.5	278	467
9.	*El Chavo II* (5/15)	Galavisión	2.4	275	457
9.	*Noticiero Con. P.Rojas*, Wed (5/17)	Galavisión	2.4	274	447
9.	*El Chavo II* (5/09)	Galavisión	2.4	270	427
9.	*El Chavo II* (5/24)	Galavisión	2.4	264	473
English language					
1.	*Drake & Josh* (5/11)	Nickelodeon	4.7	525	678
2.	*Finding Nemo* (5/05)	Disney	4.6	512	736
3.	*SpongeBob SquarePants* (5/03)	Nickelodeon	4.4	495	791
4.	*Drake & Josh* (5/15)	Nickelodeon	4.3	479	702
5.	*SpongeBob SquarePants* (5/13)	Nickelodeon	4.2	474	628
6.	*SpongeBob SquarePants* (5/27)	Nickelodeon	4.1	455	721
7.	*SpongeBob SquarePants* (5/06)	Nickelodeon	4.0	445	682
7.	*Fairly Odd Parents* (5/06)	Nickelodeon	4.0	453	666
7.	*Stuart Little* (5/02)	Disney	4.0	454	719
7.	*Adventures of Jimmy Neutron*[a] (Sp 5/03)	Nickelodeon	4.0	450	607

Note. Data from Nielsen Media Research, Nielsen Hispanic Homevideo Index. Households and viewers are measured in thousands. Measurement period was twenty-four hours, Monday through Sunday (May 1, 2006, through May 28, 2006). Programs under five minutes and breakouts are excluded. Average Hispanic viewers are the number of persons in Hispanic households viewing the program. Viewing estimates include seven days of DVR. From "Hispanic Fact Pack," 2006, Advertising Age, p. 34, retrieved from http://www.adage.com/images/random/hispfactpack06.pdf. Reprinted with permission.

a *Adventures of Jimmy Neutron: Attack of the Twonkies.* Sp indicates special.

Nickelodeon, with kid-oriented shows such as *Drake & Josh* and *SpongeBob SquarePants* (see Table 4.11).

Until the present, Hispanic viewers were included in both the National Hispanic Television Index (NHTI) and the National People Meter Service (also known as the National Television Index [NTI]), sister services offered by Nielsen. The NHTI provided a comprehensive measurement of Hispanic television viewing and Spanish-language television in the United States, using the National People Meter Service—the same measurement tool used to report total U.S. audience behavior—but with a separate sample of Hispanic households. However, the problem that many advertising executives had with the Nielsen method was that the Hispanic viewing numbers from these two national indexes didn't match. While the NHTI sampled about eight hundred homes, Nielsen had about six hundred Hispanic homes in its National People Meter Service sample. This meant that media buyers had to go back and forth between both guides—and had to subscribe to both services. But, in late 2005, Univision, Telemundo, and Azteca America joined the Nielsen Television Index (NTI). The move allowed more direct comparison with the English-language networks from which Univision, in particular, is trying to pry away viewers and ad dollars. The separate Nielsen Hispanic Television Index (NHTI) will be phased out by September 2007. At that time, NTI will serve as the single-source reporting tool to measure total audience viewership, including both Spanish- and English-language media.

As the population and its purchasing power continue to grow, the Hispanic television landscape is expected to look markedly different within just five years than it does today. It is likely that the big four networks will increasingly compete with the Spanish-language networks for audiences and advertising dollars, and, as more cable networks proliferate and attempt to reflect their communities' makeup, Hispanic viewers will hopefully see more ethnically diverse programming.

Radio

Radio is an important medium in the Hispanic community. Korzenny and Korzenny explain,

> Given that Hispanic consumers tend to be largely concentrated in the service and labor occupations of the U.S. economy, their jobs lend themselves to radio listening. Hispanic workers with outdoor occupations in construction, landscaping, transportation, and agriculture can have the radio on while working. Others in service-related occupations in food service, hospitality, and housekeeping jobs have similar opportunities for radio exposure. Radio provides companionship and information while driving to and from work, and while at work. (2005, p. 262)

Hispanic Americans spend an average of twelve hours per week listening to Spanish-language radio—versus just seven hours per week listening to English-language radio (American Association of Hispanic Advertising Agencies, 2002). See Table 4.12 for the most popular English-language and Spanish-language formats. Nine out of ten Spanish-language radio listeners (86%) are of Hispanic origin, according to Scarborough Research. Yet, immigrants aren't the only ones who tune in. Even partially acculturated Hispanic adults are more likely to listen to radio in Spanish than in English, according to Strategy Research Corporation, a market research company based in Miami. Only 12% of Hispanics listen exclusively to English broadcasts versus 32% who listen only to Spanish broadcasts (Yin, 2002). Spanish-language stations cater to Hispanics by playing regional music and by offering in-language programming that includes news from their home countries. Mexican regional is by far the most popular Spanish-language radio format. Spanish contemporary is the second most popular, while Spanish tropical is third. Hispanic radio is rapidly growing in popularity. In 2001, there were 603 Spanish-language stations in the United States—up a whopping 82% from a decade earlier. This marks a significant gain in popularity when compared with all commercial radio stations in this country, which grew by only 10% during that same time, according to M Street Corp., a New Hampshire–based publisher and data supplier to the broadcast industry (Yin, 2002).

Radio plays a different role among Hispanics than among other ethnic groups. This role is based in great part on radio's heritage in Latin America. In Latin America, there are some four thousand radio stations, making radio one of the most community-oriented mediums on the continent. Hispanics listen to the radio almost constantly, and they turn to radio not just to be entertained but also to receive advice, to locate services, or even to find jobs. In the United States, Hispanic radio personalities are revered, because they offer listeners a way to connect to their homeland or adapt to a new one. For example, on stations operated by Entravision, a Spanish-language media company based in Santa Monica, California, radio personality Gabino Ayala, takes listeners to his *Radio Tricolor* program back home to Mexico as he reminisces about life there, interspersing stories with regional music. Mexico's president, Vicente Fox, delivers a weekly message on Radio Unica, a twenty-four-hour national news/talk network based in Miami. Many radio stations offer help with immigration issues. And, apparently, no problem is off limits. When a man thought his wife was possessed by the devil, he called Renán Almendárez Coello, *El Cucuy de la Manana* (The Bogeyman of the Morning), whose show drew close to one million listeners a day, for help. A priest later performed an on-air exorcism from KSCA-FM in Los Angeles (Yin, 2002). Many Spanish-language radio stations also organize local events and promotions and assist advertisers in participating in them. This allows the advertiser to develop a

Table 4.12: Top U.S. Radio Formats by Age Group, with Top Five Spanish-Language Format Breakout

		Share percentage by age group				
Rank	Format	12 years of age and older	12 to 17 years of age	18 to 24 years of age	25 to 34 years of age	34 to 44 years of age
All formats						
1.	News, talk, info	17.1%	2.3%	3.6%	9.5%	14.2%
2.	Adult contemporary	13.3%	6.7%	8.7%	13.0%	15.5%
3.	Spanish-language	11.5%	9.2%	17.1%	18.9%	11.9%
4.	Contemporary hits	11.1%	40.2%	25.6%	14.9%	8.0%
5.	Urban	10.2%	17.5%	13.8%	11.2%	11.0%
Spanish-language formats						
1.	Mexican regional	4.0%	2.7%	7.7%	7.7%	3.9%
2.	Spanish contemporary	3.2%	4.1%	4.7%	5.1%	3.3%
3.	Spanish adult	1.6%	0.6%	1.7%	2.7%	2.0%
4.	Spanish tropical	1.6%	1.3%	2.3%	2.3%	1.7%
5.	Spanish news	0.7%	0.1%	0.1%	0.3%	0.6%

Note. Formats ranked by share of the listening audience aged twelve years and older. In reading the chart, the Spanish-language format holds a 11.5% share of all radio listening aged twelve years and older and is strongest, at 18.9%, in the twenty-five-year-olds to thirty-four-year-olds age group. Data from Arbitron's American Format Listening Trends report for winter 2006, covering ninety-eight continuously measured markets. From "Hispanic Fact Pack," 2006, *Advertising Age*, p. 28, retrieved from http://www.adage.com/images/random/hispfactpack06.pdf. Reprinted with permission.

community-based relationship, which is so important to reaching the Hispanic consumer.

For a number of years, ad spending on Hispanic radio did not keep pace with the rapid growth of the Hispanic population. Many large companies may not have advertised on radio due to the false belief that Hispanic consumers could not afford to purchase their products. However, Hispanic buying power is on the rise. Research has revealed that Hispanic radio listeners are particularly receptive to packaged goods, automotive products, health care services, and insurance and real estate promotions. During the next twelve months, the mostly Hispanic households that tune into Spanish radio stations are 64% more likely than the average listener to plan on buying a primary residence or new condo, according to Scarborough Research, a New York City–based consumer market research firm (see Table 4.13). In particular, large increases in home ownership during the past decade were seen for Puerto Ricans (from 26 to 35%), Cubans (46 to 59%), and other Spanish families (37 to 61%) (Paulin, 2003). Hispanics also tend to buy more in categories, such as entertainment and communications purchases. Hispanic radio listeners also have a propensity for buying high-end electronics, including TVs, sound systems, and com-

Table 4.13: Future Acquisitions by Hispanic Consumers; Hispanic Buying Power Is up 161% from 1990

Item the household plans to buy within a year	Index[a]
Video camera	184
Primary house or condo, new construction	164
Satellite dish	147
Computer	138
Home security system	130
Primary house or condo, existing construction	128

Note. From "Look Who's Tuned In," by S. Yin, 2002 , October, *American Demographics*, *24*(9), p. 26.
[a]=An index of 100 is the national average. For example, in the next twelve months, households that listen to Hispanic radio are 64% more likely than average to buy a newly constructed house or condo. Index is based on data from Scarborough Research.

ponents that cost $500 or more. They are also more likely than the average listener to spend between $250 and $500 a year on CDs, cassette tapes, and other music (see Table 4.14) (Yin, 2002).

The Hispanic radio audience tends to be younger than average and to live in households with children. About 50% of Hispanic radio listeners are between the ages of eighteen and thirty-four, while 76% are between eigh-

Table 4.14: Hispanic Consumers Are Big Spenders

Product (price range)	Index[a]
Wireless/cell phone ($250 to $500)	209
Stereo equipment ($500 to $999)	147
Cosmetics, perfumes, or skin care items ($500 to $999)	143
VCR ($100 to $249)	133
Children's clothing (under $100)	132
Stereo equipment ($250 to $499)	131
Television ($500 to $999)	130
Television ($100 to $249)	129
CDs/cassette tapes/other music ($250 to $499)	129
Infants' clothing ($100 to $299)	128
Wireless/cell phone ($100 to $249)	128
Plan to purchase used car in twelve months	128
Television ($1,000 or more)	127
Infants' clothing (under $100)	123

Note. From "Look Who's Tuned In," by S. Yin, 2002, October, *American Demographics*, *24*(9), p. 26. [a]=An index of 100 is the national average. For example, Hispanic radio listeners are 109% more likely than the average American to spend between $250 and $499 on a cell phone. Index is based on data from Scarborough Research.

teen and forty-four, according to Scarborough Research. Slightly more than half (54%) of listeners are married, and 61% work full-time. About 76% live in households of three or more people; 40% live in households with two or more kids (Yin, 2002). Because they are in acquisition mode, starting families and establishing households, Hispanics who listen to Spanish-language radio are a potential market for categories that are not typically associated with young adults—such as baby and children's clothing and food categories, such as fruit juice. Procter & Gamble, Gerber, Sears, and Western Union all have been using radio for the last decade to communicate with this audience. More recently, national brands, such as Kohl's, a chain of discount department stores, and realtor Century 21, have begun to tap Hispanic listeners' ears and wallets.

In attempting to measure radio listenership among Hispanics, Arbitron has taken a number of steps to ensure the accuracy of its data. These efforts include increasing the Hispanic population estimates on an annual basis and improving methods for tracking race/ethnicity and language preference in its radio surveys. Because the Hispanic population is growing so quickly, each year, Abitron relies on Ithaca, New York–based Market Statistics to update their population estimates. In producing its annual revision, Market Statistics starts with the most recent census data and uses a variety of local, state, and federal data to update the estimates. As a result of Arbitron's annual update, radio stations in many markets have seen a bump in their ratings. Another way that Arbitron obtains information from a broader sample of the Hispanic radio audience is by posing a language preference question in the Hispanic markets at an earlier point in its survey process. In the past, language preference questions were asked after an individual had agreed to keep a radio diary. Now, Arbitron asks the question during the initial placement interview—enabling them to obtain language preference information from Hispanics whether or not they agree to participate in the diaries. This allows the research firm to have a broader base of Hispanic households to examine in its survey (Raymond, 2002). With these improvements, and more on the way, many marketers are convinced that methodologies and resultant data will better reflect the explosive growth of the Hispanic market.

Print Media

Overall, print media play a less dominant role in the lives of Hispanics than do the broadcast media. This is due in large part to two major factors: functional literacy and distribution. As noted previously, many Hispanics in the United States are immigrants, and these often had limited access to formal education prior to arriving in this country. Korzenny and Korzenny note that "a lack of a reading tradition in the cultures these consumers came from is reinforced by the functional illiteracy of many of these consumers" (2005, p. 267). Recent research shows that as many as 44% of Hispanic adults can be considered functionally illiterate (Mathis, 2006). Though functionally illiterate consumers may be capable of reading simple materials, they do face significant obstacles in reading at the level in which most newspapers and magazines are written—and this is true for both materials written in Spanish and English. The second factor limiting readership of printed materials is distribution. While English-language newspapers and magazines are readily accessible, Hispanics often find it difficult to locate Spanish-language media in major retail outlets, such as supermarkets or discount stores. Clearly, if Spanish-language titles are not available, they cannot be purchased. It should be noted, however, that smaller stores in neighborhoods with very high concentrations of Hispanics are more likely to carry Spanish-language publications to serve the needs of their clientele. As will be discussed subsequently, because of the explosion of the Hispanic market, the last few years have brought a flood of both Hispanic-targeted newspapers and magazines. It goes without saying that the success of these publications is dependent upon consumers being easily able to locate them.

Newspapers

Currently, Hispanic Americans spend nearly twice as much time reading English-language newspapers as Spanish-language newspapers—an average of 2.0 hours per week compared with 1.2 hours per week (Association of Hispanic Advertising Agencies, 2005). However, the growth of Hispanic newspapers is mirroring the growth of the Hispanic population itself. Daily Spanish-language newspapers grew from fourteen in 1990 to thirty-four a decade later. Spanish-language weeklies jumped from 152 to 265 by the year 2000. One-third of Hispanics read in English and Spanish, another one-third of Hispanics read only English, and another one-third of Hispanics read only Spanish. Seven out of ten Hispanics read daily or weekly newspapers (Rosica, 2004). Table 4.15 presents the twenty-five largest Hispanic newspapers in the United States. Further spurring the growth of newspapers, Mexico's media companies are looking north of the border, where nearly two-thirds of U.S. Hispanics are of Mexican descent, for expansion. In 2006, Hearst Corporation partnered with Mexico's leading newspaper publisher, Grupo Reforma, to launch a twice-weekly Spanish-language newspaper in San Antonio. "We hope San Antonio is just the first step," said Jorge Melendez, vice president of new media at Grupo Reforma. His company has researched U.S. cities and visited leading U.S. newspapers in half a dozen cities with large Mexican American populations, such as Los Angeles, San Francisco, Chicago, Houston, and Dallas. The new San Antonio paper's target is Hispanics with close ties to Mexico, who return annually to visit and, as previously noted, send some $20 billion a year

Table 4.15: Top Twenty-Five Hispanic Newspapers by Measured Advertising Revenue

Rank	Newspaper	2005 ad revenue	Percent change
1.	El Neuvo Herald (Miami)	$72,620.6	11.5%
2.	La Opinion (Los Angeles)	$51,41.7	4.4%
3.	El Diario (Ciudad Juarez, Mexico)	$30,517.7	24.1%
4.	El Diario La Prensa (New York)	$24,005.2	–1.0%
5.	Hoy (New York)	$12,289.0	–39.1%
6.	La Raza (Chicago)	$12,037.3	19.8%
7.	Hoy (Chicago)	$11,105.9	–48.1%
8.	Hoy (Los Angeles)	$8,725.6	4.5%
9.	El Norte (El Paso, Texas)	$8,688.9	10.5%
10.	Washington Hispanic	$8,485.3	68.5%
11.	La Voz de Phoenix	$7,519.9	72.7%
12.	Al Dia (Dallas)	$7,120.2	33.4%
13.	TV y Mas (Phoenix)	$7,032.9	–4.4%
14.	El Sentinel (Miami–Fort Lauderdale)	$6,312.0	–10.5%
15.	Diario Las Americas (Miami)	$6,244.6	4.9%
16.	Diario La Estrella (Dallas)	$6,017.8	20.5%
17.	Nuevo Nundo (San Jose, California)	$4,913.5	–30.3%
18.	Prensa Hispana (Phoenix)	$4,735.1	9.9%
19.	El Latino (San Diego)	$4,652.4	13.8%
20.	Lawndale News (Chicago)	$4,572.0	–13.6%
21.	Al Dia (Philadelphia)	$4,336.2	21.0%
22.	El Especial (New York)	$3,189.4	–2.2%
23.	La Voz de Houston	$3,180.9	14.2%
24.	Mundo L. A. (Los Angeles)	$3,121.7	1.5%
25.	Vida el Valle (Fresno, California)	$2,814.5	4.5%

Note. Dollars are in thousands. Measured newspaper ad spending from TNS Media Intelligence. Percent change is computed from figures for 2004. From "Hispanic Fact Pack," 2006, Advertising Age, p. 24, retrieved from http://www.adage.com/images/random/hispfactpack06.pdf

in remittances to their home country. Reforma's first U.S. partner is Hearst's *San Antonio Express-News*. San Antonio is more than 60% Hispanic, and about 182,000 of the city's 850,000 Hispanics fit the new paper's targeted readership of eighteen- to fifty-four-year-old Spanish speakers who go to Mexico frequently. Another 300,000 to 350,000 of San Antonians are English speakers, and the remaining Hispanic population is bilingual and bicultural. The *Express-News* already has a paper for English-speaking and bilingual Hispanics, a weekly paper called *Conexion*. The free Spanish-language paper is called *Cancha*

Figure 4.7: ImpreMedia Advertisement

familia

Family. No matter how assimilated, how bilingual, family matters to Latinos and Latinas. And when it's time to buy the family a little something—say, a nice new doggie bed, or a cool new car to lean one's head out of—they get their information from our family: the #1 Spanish newspaper and online news publisher in the country. So when you recommend ImpreMedia to your client, tails will be wagging. And not just on the family *perro*. **ImpreMedia. Buy us and you'll own the market.**

impreMedia

#1 Spanish Language Newspaper and Online News Publisher

www.impremedia.com

Contact: Erich Linker, Senior VP National Advertising, (212) 807-4781
erich.linker@impremedia.com

(Spanish for "soccer field"), named after Reforma's sports sections in Mexico, and will have an initial circulation of 25,000. In the United States, *Cancha's* content will be about 60% sports coverage, and the remainder will be news and entertainment from Reforma's nine newspapers in Mexico (Wentz, 2006).

ImpreMedia, a national publishing company, has made reaching Hispanic newspaper readers from coast to coast its goal. ImpreMedia was formed by combining the resources of the two largest and oldest Spanish-language daily newspapers in the United States. CKP Media, publisher of *El Diario–La Presna* in New York, joined with Los Angeles daily newspaper *La Opinion* in 2004 in order to better reach the Latino population. Later that year, ImpreMedia acquired PrensAmerica Holdings Corporation, publisher of *La Raza,* the Spanish language newspaper in Chicago. Today, ImpreMedia owns seven of the United States' top Spanish-language newspapers. See Figure 4.7 for an ad promoting ImpreMedia publications to advertisers.) Note that the ad plays on the importance of family.

Magazines

Publishers are drawn by the growth in the Hispanic population, as well as by the success of magazines already targeting it (Holt, 2004). Hispanic Americans spend roughly equal amounts of time reading Spanish-language and English-language magazines—1.6 hours per week versus 1.7 hours per week (Association of Hispanic Advertising Agencies, 2005). According to Latino Print Network, there are 118 national U.S. Hispanic magazines, plus 112 Latin American–based titles with U.S. circulation (Wentz, 2005a). Table 4.16 presents the top Hispanic magazines by circulation—many of which have been introduced in just the last few years. *People en Español* has been growing briskly since it was introduced in 1998 and, with an average paid circulation of nearly 470,000, is ranked number one among Hispanic magazines (see Figure 4.8 for an ad encouraging Hispanics to subscribe to *People en Español*). *Latina,* an English-language women's magazine, is ranked second. The U.S. version of *Reader's Digest Seleccíones* was relaunched in 2000. The magazine combines original content and stories from *Reader's Digest* translated into Spanish. In June 2003, American Media created Latino Magazine Group, which publishes the Spanish-language entertainment magazine *Mira!* That same year, the Latino Group launched *Shape en Español,* a spin-off of the English-language fitness title.

In terms of magazine readership, the Hispanic market includes people who read only English and only Spanish, as well as those who move fluidly between the languages. "It's a readership of recent immigrants trying to learn the rules of their new country and also of fourth-generation Americans who embrace their Latino heritage; of entrepreneurs looking for tax advice and teenage girls eager to know what lipstick Thalia wears" (Holt, 2004). Ranked number

Table 4.16: Top Ten Hispanic Magazines by Circulation

Rank	Magazine	Average 2005 paid circulation	Percent change
1.	People en Español	469,110	3.3%
2.	Latina	416,162	17.7%
3.	Reader's Digest Selecciónes	354,699	–2.1%
4.	TV y Novelas Estados Unidos	175,765	25.4%
5.	Vanidades	155,917	5.5%
6.	Cosmopolitan en Español	139,844	11.9%
7.	Mira!	116,866	–1.7%
8.	Hispanic Business	63,649	–1.0%
9.	TV Notas	56,666	2.1%
10.	Buenhogar	49,325	—

Note. Table includes Audit Bureau of Circulations monitored magazines only, for six months ending on December 31, 2005 versus six months ending on December 31, 2004. Dash indicates that data were not available. From "Hispanic Fact Pack," 2006, *Advertising Age*, p. 27, retrieved from http://www.adage.com/images/random/hispfactpack06.pdf

two on the list of top publications, the English-language lifestyle magazine *Latina* is written for women born, or at least raised from a young age, in the United States. According to the magazine's editorial director, Betty Cortina, its readers consider themselves "100 percent American and 100 percent Latina." "We're not from Cuba or Mexico or the Dominican Republic," says Cortina, the U.S.-born daughter of Cuban immigrants. "We're from Miami, Chicago, Los Angeles and New York, but we have this culture that is very important to us." In contrast, half of the subscribers to *Reader's Digest Selecciónes* have lived in the United States for less than ten years, and, for them, the magazine acts as an introduction to the country's customs and institutions (Holt, 2004).

Internet

Hispanic online advertising is very big business (see Table 4.17). The $100 million Spanish-language online advertising market—forecast to grow 32% in 2006—is currently dominated by the biggest Spanish-language network, Univision. Univision.com receives the lion's share of Spanish-language online ad dollars and claims that half of its online advertisers run only on Univision. But, NBC Universal's Spanish-language TV network, Telemundo, is teaming up with Internet giant Yahoo! to shake up the Hispanic online market with a new co-branded Web site called Yahoo! Telemundo (Atkinson, 2006). The joint venture between the partners replaces Telmundo.com and Yahoo! en Español's Espanol.yahoo.com. The two companies are pooling Telemundo's

Figure 4.8: Ad Encouraging Subscriptions to *People en Español*

Rank	Web site	2005 ad spending	Percent change
\multicolumn{4}{l}{**Table 4.17: Top Ten Hispanic Web Sites by Measured U.S. Web Ad Spending**}
1.	Univision.com (http://www.univision.com)	$23,267.4	10.4%
2.	StarMedia (http://starmedia.com)	$9,292.1	14.7%
3.	Yahoo! En Español (http://www.espanol.yahoo.com)	$9,003.7	267.6%
4.	MSN Latin America (http://latam.msn.com)	$3,339.9	-85.2%
5.	MSN Latino (http://latino.msn.com)	$2,416.7	-74.2%
6.	Terra Networks (http://www.terra.com)	$686.5	76.2%
7.	La Opinión Digital (http://www.laopinion.com)	$679.1	—
8.	El Nuevo Herald (http://www.elnuevaoherald.com)	$437.4	79.0%
9.	CNN en Español (http://www.cnnenespanol.com)	$102.3	7.5%
10.	Latina Magazine (http://www.latina.com)	$85.1	—

Note. Dollars are in thousands. Dash indicates that data were not available. Measured Web ad spending from TNS Media Intelligence. Percent change is compared to 2004 data. TNS monitors seventeen Hispanic Web sites. From "Hispanic Fact Pack," 2006, *Advertising Age*, p. 31, retrieved from http://www.adage.com/images/random/hispfactpack06.pdf. Reprinted with permission.

ability to create original content and Yahoo!'s knowledge of online technology and operations. Telemundo, the second-largest Spanish-language network in the United States, produces most of its own programming rather than importing it from Mexico as other Spanish-language networks do, making it easier for Telemundo to create relevant online content. The new site will focus on three areas: extending Telemundo's existing TV content online, made-for-broadband video, and user-generated content. Yahoo! brings its search tools, messenger, and mail services to the site. Programming for Yahoo! Telemundo will be created in both Spanish and English, depending on which language is most relevant. Telemundo is a Spanish-language network—although its cable channel Mun2 is mostly in English—but Yahoo! has found that most Hispanics go to Yahoo!'s English-language sites (see Table 4.18).

In examining Internet behavior, *People en Español*'s annual Hispanic Opinion Tracker (HOT) Survey found wide disparity between Hispanic dominants and more acculturated Hispanics. The survey, conducted by Synovate Research, included interviews with eight thousand people, including six thousand Hispanics and two thousand non-Hispanics. Among the Hispanic sample, just over half (55%) were classified as Hispanic dominant, meaning they prefer Spanish and have a strong desire to maintain their culture. About one-quarter each were bicultural (23%), comfortable in both languages and worlds but culturally more Hispanic, or U.S. dominant (22%), a group that mirrors general market attitudes but identifies with its Latino heritage. The study found that, although 53% of all Hispanics surveyed said they use the Internet, that figure

Table 4.18: Top Ten Web Properties among Hispanic Users by Language Preference and Number of Unique Visitors

Rank	Property	Unique visitors in thousands	Percent reach
Spanish language preferred			
1.	Yahoo! sites	2,873	84.4%
2.	MSN-Microsoft sites	2,762	81.2%
3.	Google sites	2,225	65.4%
4.	Time Warner Network	2,136	62.8%
5.	eBay	1,656	48.7%
6.	Univision.com	1,553	45.7%
7.	Terra Networks	1,216	35.7%
8.	Ask Network	1,043	30.7%
9.	Wanadoo sites	956	28.1%
10.	Amazon sites	908	26.7%
English language preferred			
1.	Yahoo! sites	6,352	77.2%
2.	Time Warner Network	6,116	74.3%
3.	MSN-Microsoft sites	5,976	72.6%
4.	Google sites	5,458	66.3%
5.	eBay	4,142	50.3%
6.	MySpace.com	3,926	47.7%
7.	Ask Network	2,588	31.5%
8.	Amazon sites	2,521	30.6%
9.	New York Times Digital	2,066	25.1%
10.	Viacom Online	2,055	25.0%

Note. Data from comScore Media Metrix. Unique visitors are in thousands. Percent reach is the percent of all Hispanic Internet users who prefer Spanish (3.4 million in the upper table) or English (8.2 million in the lower table) who visited the property for the month of May 2006. From "Hispanic Fact Pack," 2006, *Advertising Age*, p. 30, retrieved from http://www.adage.com/images/random/hispfactpack06.pdf

drops to 31% for Hispanic dominants but soars to 70% for bicultural Hispanics and to 77% for the U.S. dominant. While just 11% of the Hispanic-dominant group shops online, 52% of bicultural Hispanics and 56% of U.S.-dominant Hispanics do so (Wentz, 2005c).

According to the annual AOL/Roper Hispanic Cyberstudy, Hispanic respondents spend 9.2 hours a week online at home, compared with 8.5 hours for the general online population. Hispanics are also surpassing non-Hispanics in areas like listening to and downloading music and instant messaging. Slightly more Hispanics—52%—who use the Internet at home have a broadband connection, compared to 50% of the general online population. The high-speed connection facilitates activities such as listening to music (55% of Hispanics compared with 41% of the general population) and downloading music files (55% of Hispanics compared with 41% of the general population) (Wentz, 2005d).

Marketers should take particular note of the fact that the survey revealed that 69% of respondents said they go online to learn about features and benefits of specific brands before making a purchase—up from 61% just a year earlier. And 63% go online for advice on which brands to purchase, up from 56% in the previous year's survey. Finally, 70% regard the Internet as the best source for comparing prices, a major jump from 59% the year before. In comparison with general market consumers, 63% of online Hispanics surveyed use the Internet for information to help them decide which brand to buy, versus 52% of the general online population. Regarding language, many respondents noted that they would spend even more time online with more Spanish-language content. Fully two-thirds of respondents said it's important to have Spanish content online. Interestingly, 30% of Hispanics surveyed who noted that they speak English and Spanish equally well agreed with the statement that they "pay more attention to ads when they are in Spanish than when they're only in English." According to the survey,

> the popularity of instant messaging offers insight into the fluidity of language for many Hispanics. Not only are Hispanics somewhat more likely to use instant messaging—59 percent of online Hispanics compared to 48 percent of the general online population—but 20 percent instant message mostly in Spanish, while 34 percent say they do so just about equally in English and in Spanish. (Wentz, 2005d).

Summary

Not so very long ago, the Hispanic coculture could easily have been characterized as a sleeping giant—a segment largely ignored by both marketers and the media. Many agree that the 2000 census data quantified the influence of Hispanics in the United States and brought recognition to the significant clout, buying power, and expected growth of this population segment. A sleeping giant no more, marketers large and small are rushing to capitalize on this lucrative and largely untapped market. Carl Kravetz, chairman of the Association of Hispanic Advertising Agencies, notes that marketers need to "connect emotionally with them using the language of cultural identity rather than getting bogged down in a debate over whether to use Spanish or English. It requires a deep understanding of the Latino identity" ("Results of Hispanic Advertising," 2006). To that end, research is currently being conducted by the AHAA into the question, what makes a Latino, Latino? ("The Heart of Latino," 2006). Above and beyond language, family, and faith, marketers will need to understand what is beating deep in the heart of the Latino population in America. Findings from this and future investigations will enable firms to gain new insights and bond with Hispanic consumers—whose spending power is projected to reach $1 trillion within just a few years. The following chapters will address the two other major cocultures in the United States today: African Americans and Asian Americans.

REFERENCES

Ahmed, N. (2002, Summer). The U.S. Hispanic market. *LIMRA's MarketFacts Quarterly, 21*(3), 106.

Association of Hispanic Advertising Agencies. (n.d.). Association of Hispanic Advertising Agencies POV on the economics of integration. Retrieved from http://www.ahaa.org/media/Immigration%20Forum/Immigration%20POV.htm Association of Hispanic Advertising Agencies. (2005). *Hispanic media and marketing factoids.* Retrieved from http://www.ahaa.org/media/Finalfacts04.htm

Atkinson, C. (2006, May 10). Telemundo teams with Yahoo to create Hispanic Portal. *Advertising Age.* Retrieved from http://www.adage.com/print?article_id=109118

Atkinson, C., & Wentz, L. (2006, August 14). ABC Hires First Hispanic Agency of Record. *AdAge.com.* Retrieved from http://www.adage.com/print?article_id=111150

Barnes, B., & Jordan, M. (2005, May 2). Big Four TV networks get a wake-up call—in Spanish [Eastern Edition]. *Wall Street Journal,* p. B-1.

Brooks, D. (2006, April 4). Take pride in the immigrants. *The Grand Rapids Press,* p. A-7.

Chavez, L. (2000, June 1). Marriage needs talking up. *Chicago Tribune,* p. 17.

Congressional Hispanic Caucus Institute. (2005, September 12). *Hispanic home ownership barriers start to fall.* Retrieved from http://www.chci.org/media/05september12b.html

Consoli, J. (2005, May 30). Hispanic expansion. *Brandweek,* p. SR-28.

Dee Long, D. (2006, April). The 46.5 percent niche. *Retail Merchandiser, 46*(4), 16.

Delgado, V. (2006, October 8). Latinos large part of expanding workforce. *Knight Ridder/Tribune Business News,* p. 1.

DiMaria, F. (2006, June 5). Hispanics shun nursing homes. *The Hispanic Outlook in Higher Education,* p. 24.

Dynamic trends; July/August 2005. (2005, July/August). *Hispanic Trends,* 20.

Ebenkamp, B. (2002, May 6). What's in store. *Brandweek,* p. 23.

Falicov, C. (1992, Summer). Love and gender in the Latino marriage. *American Family Therapy Newsletter,* 30.

Falicov, C. (2001, October). The cultural meanings of money: The case of Latinos and Anglo-Americans. *The American Behavioral Scientist, 45*(2), 313.

Faura, J. (2004). *The whole enchilada: Hispanic marketing 101.* Ithaca, NY: Paramount Market Publishing, Inc.

Green, F. (2006, May 13). Hispanics set the pace in business ownership. *San Diego Union-Tribune,* p. C-1.

Gustke, C. (2006, August 17). Wider, deeper pockets; top affluent Hispanic U.S. markets, ranked by number of households. *WWD,* p. 11.

The heart of Latino identify to be unveiled by Association of Hispanic Advertising Agencies. (2006, September 20). *PR Newswire.*

Hispanic consumers responsive to TV, ads, brands. (2002, January). *Growth Strategies, 937,* 2.

Hispanic fact pack: Annual guide to Hispanic marketing and media. (2006). *Advertising Age.* Retrieved from http://www.adage.com/images/random/hispfactpack06.pdf

Hispanic shoppers looking for more. (2006, June 1). *Progressive Grocer,* p. 10.

Hoffmann, R. (2005/2006, December/January). A wave of spirituality. *Hispanic, 18/19*(12/1), 44.

Holt, K. (2004). Say Hola to your next consumer. *Folio, 33*(3) 50.

Jenkins, P. (2003, Winter). Analysis: A new spirituality; Hispanic Americans are influencing religious trends in the U.S. *Hispanic Trends,* 40.

Klaassen, A. (2006, April 4). MTV's new Hispanic network to be called TR3S. *AdAge.com.* Retrieved from http://www.adage.com/news.cms?newsId=48565

Korzenny, F., & Korzenny, B. A. (2005). *Hispanic marketing: A cultural perspective.* Burlington, MA: Elsevier Butterworth-Heinemann Press.

Larson, M. (2004). Bilingual boom. *Mediaweek, 14*(8), 26.

Machado, M. (2004). Dollars spent reaching Hispanic market vary. But show consistent growth. *Hispanic, 167*(6), 71.

Marketing to Hispanics in the U.S. (2005, October 6). *Brand Strategy,* p. 48.

Mathis, G. (2006, January 5). America must invest in adult literacy. *The Tennessee Tribune,* p. A-4.

Milano, P. (2006, August 8). Marriage is big deal for Hispanics. *Florida Times Union,* p. C-1.

Paulin, G. D. (2003, August). A changing market: Expenditures by Hispanic consumers, revisited. *Monthly Labor Review, 126*(8), 12.

Pellet, J. (2006, June). Winning in a multicultural market. *Chief Executive, 218,* 48.

Pesquera, A. (2006, July 21). Remittance companies play a growing role in lives of Hispanic immigrants. *Knight Ridder/Tribune Business News,* p. 1.

Pew Hispanic Center. (2006, April 1). 2004 national survey of Latinos. *The Grand Rapids Press,* p. D-2.

Raymond, J. (2002, March). ¿Tienen numeros? *American Demographics, 24*(3), 22.

Results of Hispanic advertising trends survey cites 2000 census data as the milestone in the US Hispanic marketing and advertising explosion. (2006, September 19). *PR Newswire.*

Rosenblum, K. (2005, October 10). Breaking down the market myths. *TelevisionWeek,* p. 17.

Rosica, C. (2004, February). Hispanic Beauty. *Global Cosmetic Industry, 172*(2) 26.

Schreiber, A. (2001). *Multicultural marketing: Selling to the new America* (p. 55). Lincolnwood, IL: NTC Business Books.

Solis, D. (2006, September 1). Latino buying power still surging: It will exceed that of Blacks in 2007, report says. *Knight Ridder/Tribune Business News,* p. 1.

Solomon, M. (1999). *Consumer behavior* (4th ed.). Upper Saddle River, NJ: PrenticeHall.

Sue, E. W., & Sue, D. (1990). *Counseling the culturally different: Theory and practice* (2nd ed.). New York: John Wiley.

Urbanski, A. (2003, April 1). The merchandising emergency kit. *Progressive Grocer,* p. 21.

U.S. Department of Housing and Urban Development. (2006, March). *Improving home owner-ship opportunities for Hispanics.* Retrieved from http://www.huduser.org/publications/PDF/hisp_homeown1.pdf

U.S. Hispanics: Homeowners, business-owners. (2005, December). *Growth Strategies, 984,* 3.

Wentz, L. (2005a, December 5). Marketers and agencies tussle over tongues [Midwest region edition]. *Advertising Age,* p. 79.

Wentz, L. (2005b, May 3). Rapid change sweeps Hispanic advertising industry. . *AdAge.com.* Retrieved from http://www.adage.com.news.cms?newsId=44923

Wentz, L. (2005c, July 18). Study: U.S. Hispanic consumers love to shop. *AdAge.com.* Retrieved from http://www.adage.com/news.cms?newsId=45575

Wentz, L. (2005d, July 18). U.S. Hispanics' online use surges. *AdAge.com.* Retrieved from http://www.adage.com/news.cms?newsId=45564

Wentz, L. (2006, June 5). Hearst, Grupo Reforma launch Spanish-language paper. *Advertising Age.* Retrieved from http://www.adage.com/print?article_id=109694

Yin, S. (2002, October). Look who's tuned in. *American Demographics, 24*(9), 26.

Zbar, J. (2004). Networks give new voice to Hispanic households [Midwest region edition]. *Advertising Age, 75*(22), S10.

5

Reaching African American Consumers

Who They Are: Understanding African American Identity

According to the latest census figures, the U.S. African American population numbers some 37 million—or nearly 13% of all Americans. Their numbers surged more than 21% between 1990 and 2000—in contrast to the general population, which grew just 13.2% during the same time period. Unlike the Hispanic and Asian American groups, the growth of the African American population comes from its birth rate, as opposed to immigration. A higher percentage of the black population (94%) than the total population (89%) is native. The majority of this population is descended from enslaved Africans transported from west and central Africa to North America and the Caribbean from 1609 through 1807 during the transatlantic slave trade. However, a fraction trace their roots more recently to either the Caribbean or Africa. The percentage of new immigrants continues to grow and contributes to the vitality of the black community. Of those whom are foreign born, 41% entered the United States between 1990 and 2000, and another 32% arrived a decade earlier. In 2000, 84% of all foreign-born blacks were from two regions—the

Caribbean (60%) and Africa (24%). Just 12% of the black foreign-born population came from Central and South America (U.S. Census Bureau, 2000). These first- and second-generation black Americans retain much of the cultural identity of their ancestral homes. For example, members of the nearly 2 million-strong Caribbean American community identify themselves first by their nationality—Jamaican, Virgin Islander, Dominican—and only then as a member of an ethnic or racial group (Fielding, 2005). Blacks from the Caribbean, Central America, and South America are demographically classified as black and/or African American by the U.S. census.

Where to Reach Them

African Americans are heavily concentrated in the South. Over 55% of blacks live in the South, while 18% live in the Northeast and Midwest. Just 9% live in the West (U.S. Census Bureau, 2002). Overall, the South gained approximately 3 million African Americans in the 1990s—roughly double the number of blacks the South gained a decade earlier. Most African American migrants to the South are of working age, and about one-fifth are college graduates, adding to the growing middle class in cities like Atlanta, Georgia, and Charlotte, North Carolina.

Over half (52%) of all blacks live in a central city within a metropolitan area, compared with just 21% of non-Hispanic whites. In contrast, 57% of non-Hispanic whites live outside the central city but within the metropolitan area, compared with 36% of blacks. Only 13% of blacks (compared to 22% of non-Hispanic whites) lived in nonmetropolitan areas (U.S. Census Bureau, 2002). Table 5.1 presents the top ten African American designated market areas (DMAs) by population. The top three metropolitan areas with the largest projected growth by absolute numbers for African Americans are Atlanta; Washington, D.C.; and New York City. Among the top ten markets, Dallas, Atlanta, and Fort Lauderdale (Miami) have the largest projected African American population growth by percent (Magazine Publishers of America, n.d.).

While significant numbers of African Americans reside in the South, the bulk of the 1.9 million Americans of West Indian descent are concentrated in large urban areas on the East Coast, particularly New York, Atlanta, and Miami. The two largest black Caribbean groups among the U.S. population are of Jamaican and Haitian descent. Together, they total 1.2 million, or nearly 69% of the total number of Caribbean Americans living in the United States. Caribbean Americans comprise nearly a quarter of New York City's black population, with growing numbers in suburban Westchester County, New York; Long Island; New Jersey; and Connecticut. The ten-county metropolitan

Atlanta region has experienced one of the largest growth spurts of the segment over the past decade—more than 323% from 1990 to 2000. And, in Miami, where more than one-third of Broward County's black residents are Caribbean American, the local population of Haitians and Bahamians leads the nation. For example, with a population of nearly 250,000, Miami-Dade, Broward, and Palm Beach countries together boast one of the fastest-growing Haitian communities in the country (Fielding, 2005).

Unifying Factors: The Black Experience, Religion and the Black Church, and Family and Community

The Black Experience

African Americans suffer a unique historical scar: the legacy of slavery, legal segregation (Miah, 2006), and discrimination. This characteristic, which sets them apart from every other cultural or racial group, influences literally every aspect of African Americans' lives. Pepper Miller and Herb Kemp, authors of *What's Black about It? Insights to Increase Your Share of a Changing African American Market* (2005) identify this unifying characteristic as *the filter*. Miller and Kemp write,

Table 5.1: Geographic Concentration of African Americans by U.S. City

Market	African American population (000)	Percentage of total U.S. black population	Percentage of African Americans of total market population
New York	3,808	10%	18%
Chicago	1,738	5%	18%
Los Angeles	1,497	4%	9%
Atlanta	1,399	4%	24%
Washington, D.C.	1,376	4%	23%
Philadelphia	1,372	4%	18%
Detroit	1,128	3%	23%
Houston	966	3%	18%
Miami	853	20%	20%
Dallas / Fort Worth	843	2%	13%

Note. Data from Synovate 2004, U.S. Census Bureau. African American Market Profile, Magazine Publishers of America. Retrieved from www.magazine.org/marketprofiles.

The Filter is the nucleus of the black experience and black culture. It is a common bond among all African Americans that has an astounding impact on how others see African Americans, and on how they see themselves, in every aspect of their lives. It explains why many African Americans want to be seen as a heterogeneous rather than homogeneous group, to desire real inclusion, to see more and see differently when it comes to marketing communication . . . to use general market media, but embrace black media, to have a high propensity for instant gratification, and be more apt to use kairos time. (2005, p. 19)

The common bond felt by members of the African American community is expressed in a variety of ways. Schreiber (2001) reports that nearly 70% of African Americans surveyed felt "the need to sustain ethnic traditions and symbols," compared with just 46% of all other respondents. Seventy-eight percent of African Americans believed that "parents should pass on ethnic traditions," versus 62% of all other respondents. And 90% of blacks agreed with the statement, "I am proud of my ethnic heritage," compared to 78% of all other respondents. More recently, the Yankelovich *Monitor* Multicultural Marketing Study 2006 revealed that 67% of African Americans say, "My roots and heritage are more important to me today than they were just five years ago." And 59% of African Americans noted that they "make a great effort to become more connected with my heritage" ("Hispanics, African Americans," 2006). These statistics suggest that African Americans are keenly protective of their cultural heritage and perhaps more critical of assimilation than other ethnic groups. This is not to say that blacks reject mainstream culture but rather that they experience a deep solidarity with other African Americans.

Miller and Kemp go on to note that

The Filter has also predisposed many African Americans to become overly sensitive about feeling stereotyped and not feeling valued, respected, included, and welcomed. The impact of *The Filter* can often foster a mindset that is either "less than" among most African American and non-African American consumers, or at least "different than" or "apart from" most African Americans. One of the fundamental outcomes of *The Filter* is the African Americans' strong desire and need for respect that spans all generations, because after all these years, many African Americans still do not believe they are respected by society at large. (2005, p. 19)

That this sensitivity exists, across the board and even at the highest social strata and economic brackets, may be difficult for white marketers, who have never experienced exclusion based on race or color, to understand. However, Sonya Suarez-Hammond, director of Yankelovich, explains, "African Americans say they are loyal to companies that reflect an understanding of this awareness and their ethnic affinity" (Beasty, 2005). Respect for African Americans as consumers must be expressed at every level of the marketing communications program, from the products offered to black consumers to the retail setting in which they are sold, as well as the commercial messages employed to promote those products. The issue of respect will be addressed throughout this chapter.

Religion and the Black Church

During the decades of slavery in America, many African Americans practiced Christianity—and sought solace—in prayer meetings, which generally took place in slave cabin rooms. However, these religious meetings symbolized a threat to members of white society and were therefore closely watched to detect plans for escape or insurrection. Slaves who chose to attend the same churches as their owners were typically relegated to the balcony. It wasn't until after the Civil War that churches were segregated. "As freedom was gained by blacks, there was an expectation that things would equalize. When that didn't happen, they left in masses and started their own churches and denominations," notes sociologist Michael Emerson (Jenkins, 2006). Since the establishment of the first independent African American church in 1773, black churches have flourished. Though many African American churches were created in response to racial segregation, what developed were more than separate places to worship. Instead, these churches became religious institutions devoted to addressing the post-emancipation needs and concerns of members of the black community. Black churches became organizational sites for social, political, and economic activities. Perhaps most critically, they provided an environment that was free of oppression and racism for blacks. By the commencement of the civil rights era, black churches had become political power bases for the African American community. And, during the civil rights movement, many of these churches functioned as meeting places where blacks could strategize their moves in the fight against racial segregation and oppression. To capture a sense of the shared historical experiences of African Americans, the phrase *the black church* evolved. The phrase has developed into a term for expressing the centrality of black churches in black communities. Indeed, in an attempt to convey the significance of black churches in black communities, scholars have repeatedly asserted that "Black history and black church history intersect at so many points as to be virtually identical" (*University of Pennsylvania Journal of Constitutional Law,* n.d.).

Even today, Sunday morning continues to be the most highly segregated time in this nation because of the large number of nearly all-white and nearly all-black congregations. Emerson (2001) estimates that more than 90% of U.S. congregations are racially separate. While, over the decades, black congregations have served as places of refuge for African Americans who were not made to feel comfortable in white congregations, they also offered a place where blacks could experience their unique culture of worship. These churches use the traditional ceremonies of the denominations, but their services are enhanced by a liveliness of music that is not widespread in white parishes. While some argue against the racial divide, others note that black congregations are essential in maintaining traditional African American worship styles and African American heritage. Sandra Gay-Chapman, program associate in the African American Catholic Ministry office at the Catholic Diocese of Cleveland, says, "If the world was like it should be, everyone would accept everyone's worship traditions. But black worship style is not always accepted by the European world. Because of that, I think there is a need for traditionally black congregations" (Jenkins, 2006).

Belief in God and religious service attendance varies greatly among different segments of the U.S. population. However, a Harris Interactive poll (Taylor, 2003) revealed that African Americans (91%) are more likely to believe in God than Hispanics (81%) and whites (78%). Table 5.2 shows that African Americans are also significantly more likely to attend services on a weekly or monthly basis than either Hispanics or whites, suggesting that religion continues to play an important role in the lives of many African Americans today.

In an effort to reach black consumers where they worship, some marketers have gone so far as to take their product to church. For example, DaimlerChrysler

Table 5.2: Frequency of Attending Religious Services

Frequency of attendance	Percent distribution by race/ethnicity		
	White	African American	Hispanic
Every week or more often / once or twice a month (net)	35%	41%	37%
Every week or more often	25%	30%	23%
Once or twice a month	10%	11%	14%
A few times a year / once a year (net)	23%	25%	28%
A few times a year	19%	24%	24%
Once a year	4%	1%	4%
Less often / never (net)	29%	29%	25%
Less often	16%	15%	15%
Never	13%	13%	10%
Not a member of a religion	13%	4%	10%

Note. From "While Most Americans Believe in God, only 36 Percent Attend a Religious Service Once a Month or More Often," by H. Taylor, October 15, 2003, Harris Interactive, retrieved from http://www.harrisinteractive.com/harris_poll/index.asp?PID=408

embarked on a campaign targeting worshipers at megachurches serving African Americans across the United States. The car makers hosted one-day vehicle test-drives at the churches—located in Chicago, Philadelphia, and Los Angeles, among other cities—in connection with a gospel concert tour by two-time Grammy award-winning artist Patti LaBelle. In exchange for trying out one of the auto manufacturer's models—such as the new, eight-seat, $31,000 Chrysler Aspen sport-utility vehicle (SUV)—participants received free tickets to one of Ms. LaBelle's concerts. Among the churches that Chrysler courted was the New Birth Missionary Baptist Church in Lithonia, Georgia—a church with 25,000 members and a campus that spans 250 acres. This effort reflects a growing sentiment within some quarters of the auto industry that companies must track down customers where they live, rather than rely solely on their dealers or on more traditional forms of marketing. "You can only do so much with advertising," explains Dave Rooney, director of marketing for Chrysler, which sponsors the Inspired Drives tour. "We're trying to get into the communities and the lifestyles of customers . . . taking our products to people rather than asking people to come to us" (Power, 2006). But Chrysler's efforts at the churches weren't entirely about selling cars. For each test-drive taken, Chrysler donated $5 to the University of Pennsylvania's Abramson Cancer Center ("Chrysler Sponsored," 2006).

Family and Community

Much like Hispanic consumers, African Americans value family. Indeed, the Yankelovich *Monitor* Multicultural Marketing Study 2006 noted that both African Americans and Hispanics seek their nuclear and extended families' advice, guidance, and support in most matters. In fact, nearly half of all African Americans and Hispanics said that "when it comes to important things in my life, I almost always seek the opinion of my extended family members," compared to 33% of non-Hispanic whites. And nearly half of African Americans (42%) and 35% of Hispanics noted, "I believe my children will take care of me when I am older, so I don't need to worry about having enough savings and investments to support myself in that stage of life," compared to just 21% of non-Hispanic whites ("Profound Shifts," 2006). However, collectivism is mostly about family dynamics for the Hispanic population—as previously noted, it is about putting the good of the family before the needs of the individual. For African Americans, collectivism is more community and neighborhood oriented. This difference in orientation can be seen in marriage rates. Statistics reveal that the marriage rate for African Americans has been dropping since the 1960s, and, today, blacks have the lowest marriage rate of any racial group in the United States (Jones, 2006). Indeed, the rate of marriage among blacks is significantly lower than among whites. Among the 26.2 million blacks ages fifteen and older, 12% were divorced—compared with 10% of the white population. However, 43% of blacks had never married, compared with 25% of non-Hispanic whites. African Americans were less likely than their white counterparts to be currently married (35% and 57%, respectively). The marital distributions of African Americans and whites vary by sex. In 2002, in both groups, women were more likely than men to be widowed, separated, or divorced and less likely to be never married or currently married. Black men were more likely than their non-Hispanic white counterparts to be never married: 45% and 28%, respectively. The comparable figures for women were 42% and 21%, respectively (U.S. Census Bureau, 2002).

In 2002, there were 8.8 million black families in the United States. Nearly half (48%) of all black families were married-couple families, 43% of black families were maintained by women with no spouse present, and 9% were maintained by black men with no spouse present. The corresponding figures for non-Hispanic white families were 82%, 13%, and 5%, respectively (U.S. Census Bureau, 2002). That such a large percentage of black families are headed by women is a fact that has not been missed by marketers. See Figure 5.1 for a MetLife advertisement employing the headline, "You Carry the Future on Your Shoulders. Plan for It." The copy is subtle: "A financial game plan for every family. MetLife knows that just as every family is unique, so are their financial planning goals."

African American families tend to be larger in size, as is revealed in Table 5.3. Among married-couple families, just one-third of African American families had two members, compared with nearly half (57%) of non-Hispanic white families. However, black married-couple families were more likely than their white counterparts to have five or more members (20% and 12%, respectively). Among black families maintained by women with no spouse present, nearly 11% had five or more members, compared to less than 5% for white families. Almost 6% of black families maintained by men with no spouse present had five or more members, compared with just over 4% of comparable white households.

While the African American family may be somewhat less than traditional, extended family plays a significant role in the black community. The Afrocentric worldview encourages strong kinship bonds, which include close relationships with extended family networks, as well as nonblood relatives. Rituals, such as reunions, serve to tie extended family networks together over the years and across the miles. African American multigenerational gatherings are hardly a new fad. "They date way back, probably to Africa, to the concept of village gatherings," explains Ione Vargus, professor emerita at Temple University and director of the Family Reunion Institute. "There is a natural tendency among people in the African American community to come together,

Figure 5.1: MetLife Ad Targeting Females

Table 5.3: Family Size by Family Type and Race of Householder, 2002				
Family type and race	Percent distribution of families			
	Two members	Three members	Four members	Five or more members
Married couple				
Black	33.2%	22.4%	24.5%	19.9%
White	47.0%	19.7%	21.2%	12.1%
Female householder, no spouse present				
Black	39.7%	31.1%	18.3%	10.9%
White	54.9%	29.6%	10.7%	4.8%
Male householder, no spouse present				
Black	57.0%	25.6%	11.6%	5.8%
White	61.2%	26.0%	8.5%	4.3%

Note. Data from "Annual Demographic Supplement to the March 2002 Current Population Survey," U.S. Census Bureau. The Black population in the United States: March 2002. U.S. Department of Commerce, Economics and Statistics Administration, U.S. Census Bureau. Retrieved from www.census.gov/population/www/socdemo/race/black.html.

swap stories, [and] devote time to bonding" (Lee, 2006). Stephen Criswell, a University of South Carolina professor who has researched the sociology of African American get-togethers, notes, "the legacy of slavery most likely contributed to the reunion tradition. So many families were divided and dispersed in the antebellum years. The tradition of regrouping grew out of that period and has continued—and grown—ever since" (Lee, 2006). Today, the tide of mega-gatherings among African Americans is high and rising. Indeed, African Americans are willing to travel halfway across the country to commune with second and third cousins once removed, whereas folks from other cultures often want to bolt out the back door when their relatives pull into the driveway. And what were once small, folksy get-togethers (see Figure 5.2 for a Doubletree Hotels ad appearing in *Black Enterprise* magazine with copy that reads, "This Summer, let Doubletree make it easy to plan an unforgettable family reunion") have evolved into full-scale, carefully orchestrated celebrations. Once hosted in private homes or churches, they are now often held in luxury hotels. Special reunion Web sites and customized T-shirts are common. Some families even form nonprofit associations and use the funds to offer scholarships, buy real estate, or assist family members in need. The interest in reunions has brought a spate of guide books, cookbooks, and Web sites, as well as other resources, and tourism officials in several cities are making special efforts to help families with reunion organizing.

Because of their collectivistic orientation, community involvement is very important to African American consumers. And one of the best ways for marketers to appeal to the black consumer is to support cause-related programs that

Figure 5.2: Ad Appearing in *Black Enterprise* Magazine Encouraging Blacks to Host their Family Reunions at Doubletree Hotels

help the communities where African Americans reside. However, advertisers are cautioned against the tokenism practiced by a number of companies that do single events for the African American community. One survey noted that more than four out of five African Americans claimed that they would be more likely to buy products from companies that have a long-standing reputation for supporting the African American community. Longevity indicates a consistent level of commitment to recognizing a particular consumer base ("How We Buy," 1998). Blacks appreciate seeing that a company cares about the things they care about—education, health issues, the arts, etc. Firms that get involved with such issues leave a positive impression in the minds of black consumers and pave the way for brand loyalty. For example, Burger King Corporation celebrated Black History Month through its annual multicultural marketing program, Everyday Heroes Past, Present, and Future, by contributing to three New Orleans-based historically black colleges and universities that were structurally devastated during Hurricane Katrina. "For decades, historically black colleges and universities have been the launching pad for some of America's best and brightest," noted Bob Levite, Burger King Corporation vice president of field marketing, North America. "Burger King takes pride in commemorating Black History Month by helping to restore these rich cultural institutions within the African American community," he noted ("Burger King Helps," 2006). The company also hosted a diversity symposium featuring the presidents of historically black colleges and universities, as well as other black educators, at its global headquarters in Miami. "African Americans are highly responsive to organizations and efforts that give something back to the community, viewing such efforts as a gateway to mutual respect, rather than an attempt to exploit the market solely as a revenue opportunity" (Schreiber, 2001, p. 48).

African American Income and Buying Power

The African American middle class is growing bigger and more prosperous. Data reveal that the still-wide gap between black and white consumers is finally narrowing. Average household income for African American families rose 1.1% annually during the 1990s, about double the average rate of increase for white households as a group. However, black household income averaged nearly $20,000 less than that of white households, as reported in the Economic Policy Institute study, "The State of Working America 2000–2001" (Emerson, 2001). Figure 5.3 presents family income by family type and race. One-third of all black families and 57% of all non-Hispanic white families had incomes of $50,000 or more. The percent of white families making $75,000 or more was over twice that of blacks: 35% compared to 16%. As the table reveals, married-couple families were significantly more likely to have incomes of $50,000 or more. Over half (52%) of black married-couple families, compared with 64% of their white counterparts, had incomes of $50,000 or greater. Just over a quarter (27%) of African American married-couple families had incomes of $75,000 or more, compared with 40% of comparable white families. Yet, in comparison with the quickly expanding Hispanic market, the census reveals that there are a greater number of African American households with yearly incomes of greater than $75,000. Both black and white families maintained by women with no spouse present were more likely to have incomes concentrated in the lower income ranges. The same held true for both black and white families maintained by men with no spouse present.

The good news is that, during the 1990s, there was a 30% decline in the black poverty rate, and, in 2000, the black poverty rate reached its lowest point ever recorded by the U.S. Census Bureau ("Black Progress," 2006). The bad news is that poverty still exists in the African American community. The poverty rate, which was 12% for the total U.S. population, was 23% for African Americans (compared to 8% for non-Hispanic whites). About one in ten men in the United States were below the official poverty line in 2001. The rate for African American men (20%) was nearly three times that for non-Hispanic

Figure 5.3: Family Income by Family Type and Race of Householder

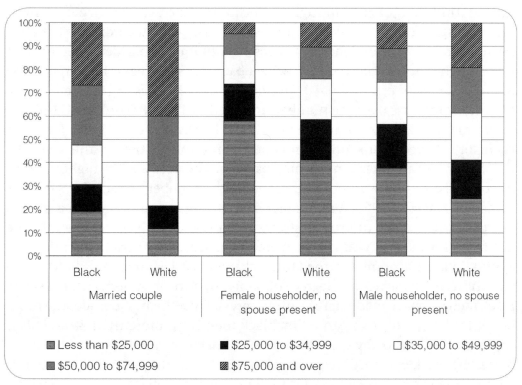

Source: Hispanic Fact Pack: Annual Guide to Hispanic Marketing and Media. *Advertising Age* (2006) Crain Communications. P. 39.

white men (7%). In 2001, 13% of all women were poor. The poverty rate for African American women (at 25%) was more than twice that for non-Hispanic white women (9%) (U.S. Census Bureau, 2002).

Increases in income among African Americans have been driven by a number of factors, among them increases in educational attainment. Education is highly valued by African Americans and is seen as crucial in improving the quality of life for the next generation. This is evidenced by the fact that African Americans' number-one financial planning concern is not retirement planning but financing children's and grandchildren's education (Buford, 2006). General Mills appeals to this value among black consumers with a promotion benefiting education. When consumers clip and send in box tops from hundreds of General Mills products, they can support schools with cash to use for computers, music programs, library books, and more. See Figure 5.4 for an ad promoting this program, with the headline "Give Him a Head Start on His Day and His Dreams."

The *Journal of Blacks in Higher Education* reports that black enrollments in college and graduate school have reached an all-time high (*The Solid Progress of African Americans in Degree Attainments,* 2006). Over half (55.1%) of all 25–29-year-old African American women in 2005 had completed some college work, while 41.9% of all 25–29-year-old African American men in 2005 had completed some college work ("Vital Signs," 2006). A more important measure of African American progress in higher education is the extent to which African Americans are completing college and earning a degree. According to the 2003 census data, of African Americans ages twenty-four and older, 72% have at least a high school diploma, 14% have a bachelor's degree or higher, and 5% hold a graduate or professional degree (see Table 5.4). These figures represent a significant increase over the numbers reported in 1980. According to the U.S. Department of Education, in the year 2004, blacks earned 131,241 four-year bachelor's degrees from American colleges and universities. In this year, the number of African Americans earning bachelor's degrees was the highest in this nation's history and was more than double the number of bachelor's degrees earned by blacks in 1990. A major factor in closing the racial gap in bachelor's degrees earned is the unusually strong performance of black women. In the 2003–2004 academic year, black women earned 87,390 bachelor's degrees, almost double the number earned by black men. Black women now hold nearly two-thirds of all bachelor's degrees obtained by African Americans. However, black men too have made significant progress. Over the past decade, the number of bachelor's degrees earned by black men is up more than 40%. This is triple the gain posted by white men but still pales in comparison to the gains posted by black women ("Solid Progress," 2006). In the 2003–2004 academic year, blacks earned 50,657 master's degrees at U.S. colleges and universities. This represents 9.1% of all master's degrees awarded that year, and the num-

Figure 5.4: General Mills Ad Promoting Their Box Tops for Education Program

ber of blacks earning this degree was up more than 14% from the previous year. Since 2000, the number of blacks earning master's degrees is up by more than 41%. Black women accounted for 71% of all master's degrees awarded to African Americans. Mention must also be made regarding the number of African Americans awarded degrees in the professions—these include degrees in medicine, law, dentistry, and several other fields. In the 2003–2004 academic year, blacks earned 5,930 professional degrees, and these made up 7.1% of all professional degrees awarded in the United States that year. The gender gap in professional degree awards is large but not as wide as in bachelor's and master's degree attainments. In 2004, black women earned 62% of all professional degrees awarded to African Americans. Finally, African Americans have also made tremendous strides in doctoral degree awards. African Americans earned 1,869 doctorates in 2004—a significant increase of more than 9% from 2003. Blacks made up 7.1% of all doctorates awarded to American citizens—this figure represents an all-time high. Thus, at all levels, from high school diplomas straight through to the doctoral level, the evidence clearly shows that large and increasing numbers of African Americans are obtaining success in education ("Solid Progress," 2006).

Another factor driving increases in income among African Americans is business ownership. An ever-increasing number of blacks own their own businesses. Revenues generated by the nation's 1.2 million black-owned businesses rose 25% between 1997 and 2002 to 88.8 billion, while the number of such firms grew by 45% in the same time period, according to a report recently released by the U.S. Census Bureau (Bergman, 2006). New York had the greatest number of black-owned firms, with 129,324, followed by California (112,873), Florida (102,079), Georgia (90,461), and Texas (88,769). These five states accounted for about 44% of all African American–owned businesses in the United States. In 2002, nearly four in ten black owned-firms operated in health care and social assistance and in services such as repair and maintenance. They owned 9.7% of all such businesses. Retail trade and health care and social assistance services accounted for 28.6% of black-owned business revenue. There were 10,727 black-owned businesses operating with receipts of $1 million or more. These firms accounted for 1% of the total number of black-owned firms and 55% of total receipts. Nearly all black-owned businesses were small—92% had no employees other than the owners. Just under one thousand black-owned firms had one hundred employees or more. These firms generated $16 billion in gross receipts. Firms of this size accounted for 24.3% of the total revenue for black-owned employer firms (Reed, 2006b).

A report issued by the Small Business Administration shows that women drove much of the growth in black entrepreneurship. Black women owned 547,341 companies in 2002, up 75% from five years earlier, when the U.S. Census Bureau last counted. The number owned by men rose a smaller 29%, to

Table 5.4: Percentages of African Americans Earning Diplomas/Degrees

Type of diploma/degree	Year earned		
	2000	1990	1980
High school diploma	72%	63%	51%
Bachelor's degree or higher	14%	11%	8%
Graduate or professional degree	5%	4%	—

Note. Dash indicates that data were not available. Data from U.S. Census Bureau, January 16, 2003. African American Market Profile. Magazine Publishers of America. Retrieved from www.magazine.org/marketprofiles.

571,670, according to the study. And, for the first time since the government began counting, black women are now more likely to own more companies than black men, assuming that growth rates stayed constant after 2002. See Figure 5.5 for an ad for body lotion that appeals to the black businesswoman with the headline "Nothing Keeps You from Handling your Business." But black women, like all female owners, still lag behind men by some key measures. The majority of their companies are part-time ventures, often run from home at night or on weekends, to supplement daytime pay. Just 5% had employees, versus 10% for companies owned by black men. Annual revenues average about $39,000 for companies owned by black women, versus $114,000 for companies owned by black men (Hopkins, 2006). Though they are increasing at a fast clip, black-owned businesses remain a small part of the economy. Though African Americans account for 13% of the population, at 5% of all businesses, African Americans lag significantly behind Hispanics and Asians in terms of business ownership. For example, Hispanics represent 40.6% of the minority population and an equal percentage of minority businesses. Blacks represent 39% of the minority population, but their rate of business ownership is just 27.1% of all minority-owned businesses. Asians, a lower percentage of the minority population than blacks, at 12.3%, own businesses at a much greater rate—30% (Reed, 2006b).

Home ownership is an important part of the American dream. Beyond providing shelter and a place where families can thrive, homes are an important financial investment. Indeed, home ownership has been called the ladder to prosperity. Approximately half of the net worth of middle-income households in the United States is in home equity. And that equity can create a variety of opportunities—money can be made available to start a business, to send children or grandchildren to college, or to invest. But while more Americans own homes today than at any time in U.S. history, fewer than half of African American families are homeowners. U.S. Census Bureau data reports that African American home ownership in the United States is 49.1%, compared to the white home ownership rate of 76% (Reed, 2006a). However, there has been an increasing percentage of African Americans renters who are saving to

Figure 5.5: Ad for Vaseline Intensive Care Total Moisture Lotion Appealing to the Black Businesswoman

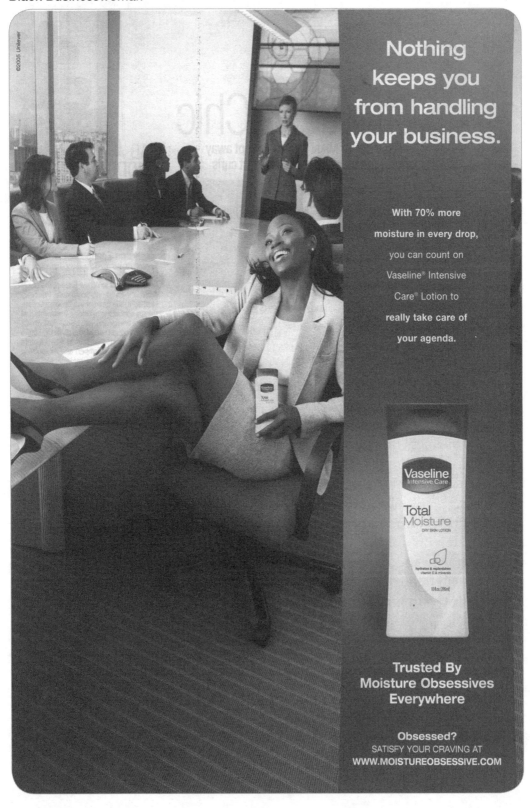

purchase a home, according to a study by the University of Southern California Lusk Center for Real Estate (Roberts, 2005). In 1983, an estimated 6.8% of African American renters were saving to buy a home, compared with 12.4% of white renters. In 2001, an estimated 16% of African American renters and 17% of white renters were saving up for a home, according to the study. More than 1.8 million black consumers intend to buy a home over the next year—a figure that is 24% above the national average ("Force of Habit," 2006). See Figure 5.6 for an ad from State Farm Insurance promoting renter's insurance to African Americans.

Marketers are keen to get their hands on the more than $760 billion black consumers currently spend annually—a sum that is greater than the gross national product of all but the top ten richest countries in the world (Ingram, 2006). By 2009, the buying power of African Americans is expected to reach $965 billion, according to the University of Georgia's Selig Center for Economic Growth. The ten states presented in Table 5.5 represent 61% of the African American population, as well as 61% of the total African American buying power.

African American Shopping Behavior

Much like their white counterparts, African American consumers spend roughly two-thirds of their incomes on housing, transportation, and food.

Table 5.5: Top Ten States in Terms of African American Buying Power

State	Black population[a]	Black buying power in 2003 (in billions of U.S. dollars)
New York	3,162,778	$65.5
California	2,439,489	$53.1
Texas	2,454,979	$50.1
Georgia	2,412,050	$46.4
Florida	2,594,770	$40.9
Maryland	1,511,665	$38.8
Illinois	1,889,267	$37.8
North Carolina	1,784,791	$31.0
Virginia	1,432,967	$29.0
Michigan	1,445,610	$28.7

Note. Data from U.S. Census Bureau: 2002 American Community Survey Profile; Selig Center for Economic Growth, 2002. *African American market profile*, Magazine Publishers of America, n.d., retrieved from http://www.magazine.org/marketprofiles [a]=Alone or in combination with at least one other ethnic group.

Figure 5.6: Ad for State Farm Insurance Appealing to African American Renters

EVEN RENTERS ARE OWNERS.

Think about it. The things you have around your apartment may seem average, but if they're damaged or stolen, replacing them will cost big time. Most renters believe their landlord's insurance covers their things. It doesn't, but State Farm® can help. Our renters insurance provides protection for pennies a day. So don't delay. Call your local State Farm agent today or visit us at *statefarm.com.*®

LIKE A GOOD NEIGHBOR STATE FARM IS THERE.®

Providing Insurance and Financial Services

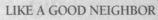

State Farm Fire and Casualty Company, State Farm General Insurance Company - Bloomington, IL; State Farm Florida Insurance Company - Winter Haven, FL; State Farm Lloyds - Dallas, TX

However, beyond that, there are differences between blacks and whites in terms of consumption priorities and marketplace behaviors that deserve marketers' attention.

Advertisers marketing to African Americans should note some of the products and services this powerful niche is likely to purchase. Table 5.6 reveals that blacks index extremely high on video game systems, home security systems, luxury vehicles, and SUVs, as well as full-sized automobiles. African Americans are significantly more likely to plan on buying a luxury vehicle over the next year, and more than 439,000 (an amount that's risen more than 20% in the last five years) intend to pay at least $35,000 for that vehicle ("Force of Habit," 2006). The Lincoln division of Ford Motor Company was so impressed with the billions blacks spent on cars that the automaker commissioned Sean "P. Diddy" Combs, the entertainment and fashion mogul, to design a limited-

Table 5.6: African American Purchasing Behavior

Items that the household plans to buy in the next twelve months	Adults in general index	African American adults index
Van or minivan	100	128
Video game system	100	181
Primary house or condo—new	100	142
Wireless/cellular service for household member	100	131
Sport utility vehicle	100	137
Any used vehicle	100	140
Any leased vehicle	100	122
Midsize car	100	122
Wireless/cellular service for self	100	148
Computer	100	130
Home security system	100	173
Primary house or condo—existing	100	122
Furniture	100	122
Mattress	100	131
Luxury vehicle	100	148
Full-size car	100	147
Digital video recorder (TiVo, etc.)	100	125

Note. An Index of 100 is the national average. For example, African Americans are 81% more likely than the average American to purchase a video game system. Data from "Top 50 Market Report" (Release 5), Scarborough Research, 2005. Prepared by NAA Business Analysis and Research Department. Retrieved from http://www.naa.org/thesource/11.asp

edition Navigator replete with six plasma screens, three DVD players, and a Sony PlayStation 2 (Young, 2004). Miller and Kemp note that

> particular upscale, top-end brands are visible symbols of success for communicating social and economic achievements. Premium brands are a reflection of aspirations in that they provide conspicuous "badges" of social status—a means for eliminating stereotypes, fulfilling emotional needs, and staying on top of the latest trends. Because of the effects of The Filter, the use or display of upscale brands confers upscale status to African American consumers. (2005, p. 25)

According to Target Market, a company that tracks black consumer spending, blacks spend a significant amount of their income on depreciable products. For example, Target Market's 2005 report noted that African American households significantly increased their expenditures on consumer electronics for the home. Products that showed the greatest one-year increase were computer hardware (+23%) and software (+75%), satellite dishes (+112%), cable TV service (+15%), and video games (+86%) ("AOL Study," 2005). Such spending is often "motivated by a desire for instant gratification and social acceptance" (Young, 2004).

Regarding the consumption behavior of female African Americans, research reveals the following:

- African American women are more likely to try new trends, compared with general market women (with data demonstrating an index of 134 for African American women versus an index of 90 for general market women).
- African American women would pay extra for products consistent with their image, compared to general market women (an index of 129 versus 94).
- African American women are more likely to believe that a brand name equals quality, compared to general market women (an index of 115 versus 95).
- More than their general market counterparts, African American women are more likely to purchase a two-family home.
- African American women are more likely to buy their first home in the coming year, compared to their general market counterparts.
- African American women are more likely to purchase homeowner/personal property insurance in the next year, compared to their general market counterparts.
- In 2005, African American women controlled $403 billion in buying power—more than Hispanic women, who controlled $346 billion in buying power.

- Over half of young African American women (eighteen to twenty-nine years of age) surveyed stated their goals were to own their own business (54%) and to own their own home (49%). (*Essence,* n.d.)

Of concern is the fact that African American households, in particular, are shown to spend larger percentages of their incomes paying credit card and other high-interest rate debt—and much of the debt they have accumulated is for those items that depreciate in value. Credit card debt has caused African American families to use critical financial resources to pay mounting monthly interest payments instead of acquiring assets, such as real estate, or saving (Sidime, 2004). According to published reports, the Ariel Mutual Funds / Charles Schwab 2003 Black Investor Survey found that, when comparing households where blacks and whites had roughly the same household incomes, whites saved nearly 20% more each month for retirement, and 30% of African Americans earning $100,000 a year had less than $5,000 in retirement savings. While 79% of whites invest in the stock market, only 61% of African Americans do so (Young, 2004).

Beyond what African American consumers buy, where they shop is very important to them. And respect is a critical part of the retail shopping experience for black consumers. According to a recent survey, 68% of African Americans (compared to 46% of non-Hispanic white consumers) say that how a store treats customers based on race is extremely important in deciding where to shop. Unfortunately, over 88% of African Americans say that discrimination is still part of most African Americans' day-to-day lives (Ragland, 2005). And over half (56%) of African Americans (compared to just 17% of non-Hispanic white consumers) agreed that, "In the past I have felt a security guard / store clerk was watching me more closely than other shoppers" (Wicks, 2005). Clearly, many African Americans feel that they are being profiled while shopping. And African American shoppers' perceptions regarding racial profiling are borne out by research conducted by Harris, Henderson, and Williams (2005). The researchers examined eighty-one federal court decisions made between 1990 and 2002 involving customers' allegations of race and/ or ethnic discrimination. The authors note that consumer racial profiling can take a number of forms, including (a) *subtle degradation,* (b) *overt degradation,* (c) *subtle denial,* and (d) *overt denial,* as well as (e) *criminal suspicion. Subtle degradation* of goods and services involves cases in which customers complain they did not receive what they expected in a particular consumption setting but do not have direct evidence that this treatment was based on their race or ethnicity. In contrast, *overt degradation* occurs when it is clear that nonwhite patrons received less by way of goods and services than white customers. *Subtle denial* refers to situations in which customers allege that they were outrightly denied access to goods and services; however, they are unable to identify white patrons who received better treatment. Conversely, *overt denial* occurs when there is clear evidence of preferential treatment of white patrons compared with nonwhite counterparts. *Criminal suspicion* cases involve allegations that customers of color were treated with suspicion or as if they were criminals. Of course, consumer racial profiling is directed not only at African American consumers but also at Hispanic and Asian consumers as well as those from other ethnic and/or racial groups.

One case of *subtle degradation* involved a black woman who was shopping at Dillard's department store. After selecting her items and paying for them, the sales associate gave her a coupon for free cologne. She proceeded to the fragrance counter and, while attempting to redeem the coupon, was stopped by a security officer who searched her belongings. Although there was no direct evidence that the security officer intentionally discriminated against her because of race, he filed a two-page security report that referred to her status as an African American twelve times (*Hampton v. Dillard Department Store,* 1998/2001/2002).

Harris, Henderson, and Williams (2005) provide the following example of Hispanic consumers who suffered *overt degradation.* Here, the customers, who are Hispanic, stopped to purchase gas and other items at a Conoco store in Fort Worth, Texas. When they presented their credit card for payment, the Conoco employee immediately asked for identification. The customers presented a valid diver's license, but the employee initially refused to accept it. After begrudgingly agreeing to the transaction, the employee shoved the customers' purchases off the counter, gestured obscenely at the customers, and announced over the store's intercom that they should "go back to where you came from, you poor Mexicans." While the customers did receive their merchandise, they were clearly verbally abused by the Conoco employee (*Arguello and Govea v. Conoco,* 2003).

A case of *subtle denial* of service occurred when a white woman took her two African American grandsons on a weekend trip to the beach. The white female entered a motel office to inquire about room availability while the remainder of the family stayed in the car. She checked into the motel and paid the bill in advance with cash. The group then deposited their bags in the room and headed for the outdoor pool. Within minutes, the desk clerk appeared and demanded that they leave immediately. When the hotel guests inquired as to why, the desk clerk said, "I want you off my premises now," without responding to their repeated requests for an explanation (*Murrell v. Ocean Mecca Motel,* 2001).

In an example of *overt denial,* a Denny's server forced African American customers to wait an extraordinarily long time to be seated. He then proceeded to make harassing gestures and directed racially charged, derogatory comments toward them. Next, a waiter refused to serve their table, informing managers that they could not make him serve "n[——]" (*Charity v. Denny's*, 1999).

Finally, a Massachusetts case provides an example of *criminal treatment*. A white female employee of the Children's Place reported that she was instructed by her employer to engage in discriminatory treatment of minority customers. For example, her supervisors asked her to shadow minority customers who were shopping in the store because of their belief that such customers were more likely to steal. She also alleged that her white supervisors directed her to refuse minority customers large shopping bags because they would likely use the bags to steal. She claimed that she and other sales associates were told to withhold credit card applications from minority customers and not to bother to inform minority customers of sales or promotions (*Commonwealth of Massachusetts v. The Children's Place Stores*, 2000).

As these cases reveal, real consumer discrimination remains a real problem in the U.S. marketplace. Firms that develop retail environments where ethnic consumers do not feel victimized, but rather respected, are likely to see increased revenues. And those who do not create discrimination-free environments will likely face the consequences. Ethnic consumers may opt to boycott the offending business. Indeed, one store's sales fell by more than 50% following a racial profiling incident (Bean, 2000). In other instances, individuals may choose to file a lawsuit, which is potentially costly to the marketer both in terms of dollars as well as negative publicity. A recent race discrimination lawsuit brought by eighteen current and former African American employees of a Niketown store in Chicago has been granted class-action status, creating a potentially damaging public relations problem for the shoe manufacturer. The suit makes embarrassing allegations that African American customers, including professional athletes, such as former Chicago Bulls basketball player Tyson Chandler and three Green Bay Packer football players, were subject to greater scrutiny and monitoring at the retail outlet. The longer the case continues and the more publicity it receives, the greater the damage to the brand, which has a huge following among African American youth. It also relies on high-profile black athletes, such as Michael Jordan and Kobe Bryant, in its marketing campaigns (Sachdev, 2006).

Who's Talking to African Americans?

Although Hispanic advertising agencies complain that most firms devote only about 3% of their ad budgets, on average, to reach Latino consumers, advertisers spend far less to target African Americans. While total advertising spending in the United States increased by 4.6% in 2005 to $276 billion, according to Insider's Report from Universal McCann, a division of the global ad agency Interpublic Group, less than 1% of total spending is targeted toward the African American market—a group that is currently similar in size to Hispanics (Alleyne & Richardson, 2006). After Hispanics zoomed past blacks to officially become the nation's largest minority group in 2000, some of the country's largest marketers went from almost ignoring Latinos to literally tripping over themselves to reach them. At the same time, some cut back on marketing to blacks (Stronger, 2006). For example, Procter & Gamble, by far the largest advertiser to both groups, spent $157 million on Hispanic advertising in 2005 but just $52.5 million in African American media outlets, according to TNS Media Intelligence. General Motors, the number-two advertiser in both rankings, spent $112 million on Hispanic advertising and only $29.4 million in African American media (Sanders, 2006). While General Motors cut ad spending in black media by about 7% from a year earlier, Ford Motor Company reduced spending to target African Americans by nearly one-third. During the same time period, General Motors increased its spending in Spanish media—excluding Spanish radio—48%, and Ford almost doubled spending on the Hispanic market (Stronger, 2006). Part of the reason that corporations haven't assigned as high a priority to the African American market as they have to the Hispanic market is because the Hispanic population is expected to grow significantly faster. While Hispanics will represent 24% of the U.S. population by 2050, blacks are expected to grow to only about 15% of the population. According to Dennis Garrett, associate professor of marketing at Marquette University, "That's why African Americans are kind of getting lost in the shuffle" (Johnson-Elie, 2006). Language, as noted in chapter 3, is also likely to be a factor. Because the vast majority of African Americans in this country speak English, it is assumed by many advertisers that, as consumers, they are a monolithic group that will respond to general market advertising. That, paired with advancements in education and increases in income, has lead many corporations to believe that blacks need no longer be segmented. So, even with the significant spending power of this market—expected to reach close to $1 trillion by 2010—many advertisers have simply overlooked the black consumer.

How to Create Ads That Persuade

Marketers will be pleased to know that African Americans appear to have an affinity for advertising. According to a survey by Simmons Market Research, just 15% of African American adults don't like advertising in general, versus 37% of all adults aged eighteen and older. And 36% of black respondents said they remembered advertised products when shopping (Price, 2005). In terms of creating messages for African American consumers, the illusion that both blacks and whites can be reached via identical advertisements through the same media is simply a myth, and marketers who ignore this crucial reality do so at their own risk. Many black consumers don't feel that much, if any, of the advertising they see has any relevance to them. According to the 2005 Yankelovich Partners and Burrell Communications Group report, 60% of black consumers feel that most television and print ads are designed only for white people. And nearly 70% of African Americans (as compared to 53% of Hispanics) say they are "extremely concerned about the practices and motives of marketers and advertisers" (Beasty, 2005). Clearly, such statistics should be a red flag to marketers and advertisers.

Most blacks agree that there is greater need for African American representation in advertising, regardless of medium. And their representation in the media has a direct impact on their consumption behavior. Over three-quarters indicate that they are more likely to buy from companies that feature African Americans using their products and services ("How We Buy," 1998). Much progress has been made in this area. Indeed, according to several academic studies, over the last fifteen years, the number of blacks appearing in commercials has been roughly proportional to their share of the American population. However, many general market advertising agencies rely on ethnic casting for their multicultural efforts—a matter of simply slipping an African American or other ethnic face into an otherwise traditional campaign. This approach typically rings false with many African Americans, as casting without tailoring the message to the distinctive aspects of the black market does not make for compelling advertising. Effectively communicating with black consumers means creating messages relevant to their lifestyle. Savvy marketers are sensitive to cultural nuances and motivators and ensure that blacks are portrayed in a positive light in their commercial messages.

Stereotypical portrayals of African Americans in advertising have drawn criticism from civil rights groups for decades. Some of the earliest and most iconic examples of blacks in commercial messages—Rastus the Cream of Wheat chef, Aunt Jemima, and Uncle Ben—showed blacks in subservient roles that recalled the days of slavery. These images have been toned down over the years (Aunt Jemima's red bandanna, for example, was replaced with pearl earrings and a lace collar in 1989) and are no longer as overtly stereotypical as they once were (Peters, 2006). For the most part, African Americans in advertising today are presented in middle-class settings and as engaging in mainstream activities. But, every now and then, another stereotypic portrayal manages to pop up. The most recent appears to be the image of the heavy, black, boisterous, and, sometimes, aggressive female, who typically finds herself in either an embarrassing or confrontational situation. Large black actresses have had recurring roles in commercials over the years and often are cast in roles where their aggressiveness is their defining trait. The heavy black spokesperson for

Pine Sol was one of the first to embrace this role. Some find the recurring use of this caricature a return to a disturbing past. "It is perpetuating a stereotype that black females are aggressive, controlling people," notes Tommy E. Whittler, a marketing professor at DePaul University. "I don't think you want to do that" (Peters, 2006). Note that the representation and stereotypic portrayal of ethnic consumers will be addressed in greater detail in chapter 8.

African Americans care not only that they are represented in advertising but also about how they are portrayed. African Americans feel a strong need to be portrayed in a positive way and will appreciate marketers who do so. Miller and Kemp offer this list of culturally sensitive and positive images that celebrate black culture rather than reinforce stereotypes:

- Upscale African American individuals and their families
- African American family united (including the black father as an emotionally engaged and responsible caretaker)
- African Americans working with and helping other African Americans
- African American women in integrated leadership roles
- African American men in integrated leadership roles
- African Americans involved in technology and healthcare (2005, p. 27)

One way marketers can convey respect for African Americans' cultural heritage is via promotional activities supporting Black History Month. Originally organized as Negro History Week in 1926 by Harvard Professor Carter G. Woodson, the intent was to bring national attention to the contributions of blacks. The week evolved into a month in 1976. Companies large and small have acknowledged Black History Month through special programming, promotions, or increased advertising in an attempt to strengthen their corporate image with blacks. Some firms do it well. For example, Procter & Gamble sponsored the PBS documentary *African American Lives* in 2006. The same year, Target created links on its Web site to black history facts and donated portions of the sales of an rhythm and blues (R&B) and gospel CD to the United Negro College Fund. Wal-Mart sponsored a *Voices of Color* film documentary series (see Figure 5.7 for an ad promoting the series) and curriculum kit, free for students in seventh through twelfth grades nationwide. According to Walter Guarino, president of Insight/SGW marketing firm, based in New Jersey,

> It's good business. Black History Month recognizes and celebrates blacks' contributions and reminds us of the hardships and injustices ethnic minorities have suffered over the years. Without some of these corporate sponsorships and special media programming, recognition of Black History Month would surely suffer. (Turner, 2006)

While some blacks say they appreciate the focus on their history and culture, others view it as pandering and question a commitment that's visible only one month a year. Marketers who only nod to blacks during the month

Figure 5.7: Wal-Mart Ad Promoting Its *Voices of Color* Film Series Saluting Black Filmmakers during Black History Month

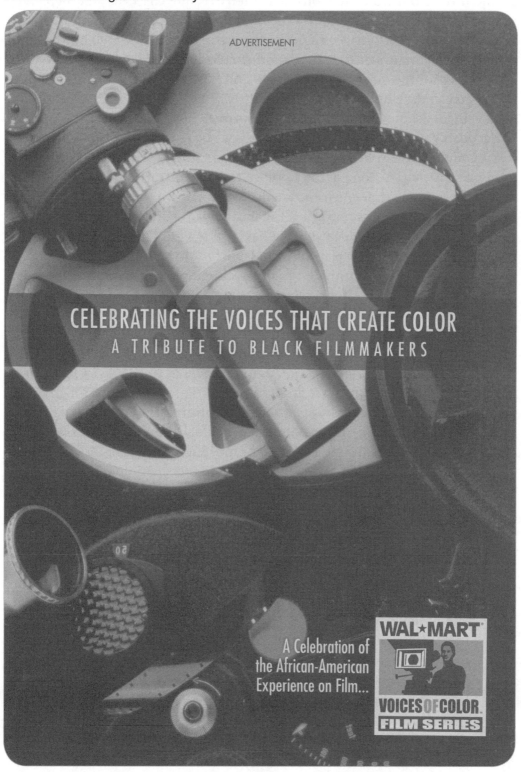

of February are seen as exploiting black history to sell products. Also, Miller and Kemp (2005) note that product-intensive messages may be perceived as disrespectful or even insulting to the very segment that the message was intended to reach. Consider the flyer from the Kmart in Maryland that proclaimed "Celebrate Black History" and then advertised "3 for $1 Jiffy Corn Muffin Mix" or the makers of Metamucil and Pepto-Bismol who ran a full-page ad in *Ebony* magazine declaring "Black History Month is a legacy of pride and achievement leading to a healthier tomorrow." The ad continued, "It's the same ideals you turn to when it comes to your GI (gastro-intestinal) health—a history of digestive solutions" (Thomas-Lester, 2006). Marketers must clearly exercise sensitivity when paying homage to black history.

To successfully attract African American shoppers—or any ethnic group, for that matter—advertisers need to get inside consumers' heads. Unfortunately, to date, there has been a dearth of behavioral research on ethnic consumers. Demographic information is readily available on African Americans, Hispanics, and Asian Americans, but the body of psychographic research for these particular ethnic groups is shockingly thin, especially compared to the voluminous amounts of data available on nonethnic consumers (Popovec, 2006). Fortunately, this is beginning to change, and the insights provided by psychographic research are invaluable. For example, recent research reveals that there is at least as much in-group variation among blacks as there is between African Americans and other consumer groups. According to McGhee Williams Osse, co-chief executive officer (co-CEO) of Burrell Communications, one of the top-ranked advertising agencies appealing to the black market, "The bottom line is that African Americans are no more homogeneous than other consumers. Understanding these differences will equip marketers with more practical and tactical methods of communicating to African Americans" (Wicks, 2005). The 2005 Yankelovich *Monitor* Multicultural Marketing Study revealed that the African American market can be broken into six sociobehavioral segments:

1. *Emulators* (11% of African Americans) are generally students, with a median age of seventeen, who identify with the young urban trendsetters within the African American culture but see themselves as unique and independent. They are trendsetters whose purchases reflect a need to be unconventional. But they also have a need for the social and emotional reassurance of brands that most reflect status or achievement.
2. *Seekers* (19% of African Americans) share some characteristics with emulators but are older and more disillusioned about life. They work part-time or are temporarily unemployed. They seek image and status brands that are popular within the culture. They are a median age of forty and have a median income of $18,000.

3. *Reachers* (24% of African Americans) are strivers who are working toward the American dream but are not on the fast track. Often single parents who care for children and/or an elderly parent, they are stressed out, and they want products and services that give them the biggest bang for their buck. They are a median age of forty and have a median income of $28,000.

4. *Attainers* (27% of African Americans) are typically married with children and have a college degree. They have a more defined sense of self and a solid plan for the future. They seek and appreciate appropriate marketing and advertising that gives them useful ideas and information about how to make their lives easier and better. They have a median income of $55,000 and are a median age of forty years old.

5. *Elites* (5% of African Americans) are upwardly mobile African Americans who live and work in a more mainstream environment but retain their cultural identity and allegiances. Marketers must appeal to them through a broader range of campaigns and executions that are generally reserved for non-Hispanic whites but can be personalized for them. They are a median age of forty-six and have a median income of $113,000.

6. *Conservers* (14% of African Americans) are an older segment with a median age of sixty-seven and an income of $38,000. This group is set in its ways and is slow to adapt to the dynamism of the African American culture. Mostly retired, their beliefs and values are deeply grounded in the experience and wisdom that helped shape their lives. Marketers must approach them in a straightforward manner. (Wicks, 2005)

A second study, commissioned by *Essence* magazine publisher Essence Communications, called "Window on Our Women: How African American Women Define Success" offers insights into what ties black women together, as well as what makes them different (Many Shades, 2006). When African American women were asked to define success, six highly segmented consumer profiles emerged:

1. *Proud Marys* represent 21% of the female black population and are connected to their cultural heritage, are involved in social and community activism, and value spiritual growth.

2. *Kays* represent 20% of the female black population. They define success in financial terms, seek the stability and security that monetary success brings, and want to retire comfortably.

3. *Amazing Graces* represent 18% of black women. They want to have it all: a career, financial success, and a happy family.

4. *Personal Beths* define interpersonal relationships as their motivation to succeed and derive satisfaction from ensuring the happiness of others. Sixteen percent of black women fall into this category.
5. *Mother Earthas* represent 13% of black women. They count raising children as the ultimate success and desire strong relationships with nuclear family and friends.
6. *Ultra Violets* represent 12% of black women. For them, financial achievement is everything. These women are focused on accomplishing financial goals and spending time with close friends.

Michelle James, director of research at *Essence* explains, "It's important to note that Amazing Graces have different consumer behavior than Mother Earthas. And, Proud Marys, for example, will be very connected to the social community. . . . Partnering with community organizations are the best way to reach her" ("Many Shades," 2006). The psychographic insights provided by these and future investigations will allow marketers to better tailor their commercial messages to black consumers.

How to Reach Them: Media

A study conducted by the Readership Institute (2002) revealed that African Americans spend more time than any other group consuming media (see Table 5.7). Much of that time is spent watching television. African Americans, on average, watch television for 1.5 hours more each day than other groups. Blacks also listen to significantly more radio than other groups—on average almost three and one-half hours per day. Although average newspaper use is lower than average, according to the Readership Institute, this reflects age, income, and education differences rather than racial or ethnic preferences. Once these three factors are accounted for, African Americans read newspapers at the same rate as the overall population.

Much like the general market, African Americans use a variety of media, but, unlike the general market, they embrace black media. Black media have more credibility than general market media—a fact that Miller and Kemp (2005) note has been underscored by research. One investigation conducted by Bendixen & Associates found that 79% of African American respondents indicated that they rely on news and information from black media sources (Cheng, 2002), and another study revealed that 56% of black respondents agreed with the statement, "I pay more attention to commercials that run during TV programs with an all-black cast" (Coleman, 2000). For these reasons, Black Entertainment Television (BET), urban radio, the *Philadelphia Tribune* (the nation's oldest

African American newspaper), and magazines such as *Ebony* and *Essence* play such an important role in reaching the black community.

Television

According to a study conducted by *Jack Myers Media Business Report*, when asked to identify the three media types that are most valuable to them among thirteen options, African Americans ranked broadcast television first and cable/satellite basic TV networks second (e-mail was ranked third). This study also

Table 5.7: Minutes per Day Spent with Media by Race/Ethnicity					
	Minutes per day spent with media				
Media type	All races	Whites	African Americans	Hispanics	Asians
Local daily newspaper	22.2	23.7	19.2	15.0	12.1
Any daily newspaper	28.2	29.7	22.1	18.8	20.6
Magazines	19.8	20.6	18.4	15.7	19.9
Internet	32.4	31.5	27.1	39.3	60.3
Television	191.3	186.1	292.7	188.5	168.4
Radio	191.4	190.0	206.1	214.5	170.7

Note. Data from "Understanding African American and Hispanic Consumers," Readership Institute, 2002, Media Management Center at Northwestern University. Retrieved from www.readership.org.

found that African Americans watch significantly more television on average—during prime time, late night, and daytime—than other ethnic groups, have more television channels on their primary TV sets, own more television sets in the home, watch more PAY TV, and are slightly more likely to own a digital video recorder (DVR) but are significantly *less* likely to skip through commercials and are more likely to stop and view selected commercials. Only 53% of African Americans who own a DVR say they skip all or most commercials, compared to 83% of Caucasian audiences (Myers, 2005).

Regardless which investigation is cited, African Americans watch more television than any other group. Yet, at the same time, there have been only a few TV outlets specifically geared toward African American viewers. Primary networks include Viacom's Black Entertainment Television (BET), Comcast-owned TV One, and the Black Family Channel, as well as newcomer, the CW Television Network. The oldest and the largest of the networks targeting black viewers, BET reaches more than 80 million households, according to

Figure 5.8: Ad for BET that "Celebrates the Beauty of Black"

Nielsen Media Research, and can be seen in the United States, Canada, and the Caribbean. See Figure 5.8 for a BET ad, that "celebrates the beauty of black." In 2005, as the network celebrated its twenty-fifth anniversary, viewership jumped an impressive 17% over 2004. Viewer favorites like *106 & Park, BET's Top 10 Live, Bobby Jones Gospel, Black Buster Cinema,* and a blend of syndicated sitcoms, highlighted by *In Living Color* and the *Jamie Foxx Show,* were consistent draws in their time slots. Long known for its hot music and great award shows (the 2005 BET Awards earned the title of most-watched program ever by African Americans in the history of cable television, with 6.6 million viewers across all demographics), the network is moving into prime time with a broader mix of shows than ever before—news, sports, reality, comedy, movies, and specials. The network recently announced it was targeting the eighteen- to thirty-four-year-old demographic, which it considers the sweet spot for African Americans. Notes Louis Carr, BET president of advertising media sales, "Whether it's technology, fashion, music, automotive or language, this demo influences so many things. It's also the magnet for every other demo" ("BET Unveils," 2006). BET offers its audience a diverse group of branded businesses, including BET.com, the number-one Internet portal for African Americans; BET Digital Networks, including BET Jazz, BET Gospel, and BET Hip-Hop; and BET Event Productions, specializing in a full range of event production services, including event management, venue selection, talent recruitment, sound, lighting, and stage production. BET has also launched a home entertainment business through a ground-breaking retail deal with Wal-Mart stores to sell BET branded content nationwide. And the company unveiled BET Mobile, a venture to access the lucrative world of ring tones, games, and video content for wireless devices ("BET Interactive," 2006).

TV One launched in January of 2004, with approximately 2.2 million subscribers. It now reaches approximately 30 million households, according to Nielsen estimates, making it one of the fastest-growing new networks this decade ("TV One Passes," 2006). The network appeals to a slightly older demographic—twenty-five to fifty-four years of age—and offers a broad range of lifestyle- and entertainment-oriented original programming, classic series, movies, fashion, and music designed to entertain and inform a diverse audience of adult African American viewers. In a comprehensive, multiyear programming agreement, TV One has acquired rights from Warner Bros. Domestic Cable Distribution to air popular movies and series. Movie titles include classic dramas, such as *The Color Purple, Malcolm X,* and *Lean on Me;* action movies, such as *Boiling Point* and *New Jack City;* comedies, such as *Uptown Saturday Night* and *Strictly Business;* and classic "blaxploitation" films, such as *Shaft* and *Superfly.* Series include *Martin, Living Single, Hangin' with Mr. Cooper,* and the *Parent 'Hood* ("TV One and Warner Bros.," 2006).

The Black Family Channel (formerly the MBC Network) offers up family values with its programming aimed at a slightly younger demographic aged eighteen to thirty-four. The twenty-four-hour digital cable network's lineup includes original programs, news, religious, music, movies, syndicated, and sports programs. The channel aims to be a more wholesome alternative to other channels targeting blacks. Indeed, almost all programming will be rated TV-PG or lower, so that it appeals to the entire family. Founded in 1998, the Black Family Channel's owners include sports figures Evander Holyfield and Cecil Fielder, as well as high-profile attorney Willie Gary and former Jackson 5 member Marlon Jackson. Viewed in just 16 million households, it is only a small fraction of the size of BET and just two-thirds of the size of TV One. However, it is in the twenty-five largest African American markets. Among its programs are *Thou$and Dollar Bee,* a spelling competition that is part of its kids' block; *Spoken,* a program about street poets; *Partners in Crime,* with standup comedians; and sports news largely focused on African American colleges. The Black Family Channel does not yet have Nielsen ratings, which has made it

Table 5.8: Top Ten Programs African Americans View during Prime Time on Network Television (Based on Ratings for the Week of October 9 through 15, 2006)

Rank	Television show and network	Live + SD household rating	Live + SD number of homes (000)	Live + SD number of viewers P2+ (000)
1	CBS NFL NATL PostGun, CBS	14.5	1956	2501
2	*CSI: NY,* CBS	13.1	1765	2545
3	*60 Minutes,* CBS	12.6	1700	2170
4	*Dancing with the Stars,* ABC	12.2	1635	2327
5	*CSI: Miami,* CBS	11.8	1586	2224
6	*Grey's Anatomy,* ABC	11.7	1572	2044
7	*CSI: Crime Scene Investigation,* CBS	10.9	1470	2005
8	*Criminal Minds,* CBS	10.7	1434	1942
9	*America's Next Top Model,* CW	10.7	1435	2089
10	*Dancing with the Stars Results,* ABC	10.3	1389	1699

Note. Live = watching a television program while it airs; SD = same day, that is, watching a television program within twenty-four hours of recording on a digital video recorder (DVR); rating = percentage of households or persons watching a TV program during the average minute; number of homes = the number of African American households in Nielsen's sample; viewers P2+ = the number of persons two years of age and older watching television. All viewing estimates include live plus same-day DVR playback. Data from Nielsen Media Research. Retrieved from http://www.nielsenmedia.com

challenging to secure advertising, although it already has a handful of top-tier brands like General Motors and McDonald's (Downey, 2006).

Recently UPN and the WB were consolidated to form the CW Television Network, which virtually eliminated half of the ethnic sitcoms that previously aired on UPN. Over the past decade, UPN had been both praised and criticized for presenting entire evenings of shows featuring predominantly black casts and aimed primarily at black viewers. Depending on one's point of view, such scheduling created programming ghettos or provided much-needed diversity to the overwhelmingly white prime-time network landscape (Zurawik, 2006).

Table 5.9: Top Twenty-Five Programs African Americans View during Prime Time on Cable TV (Based on Ratings for the Week of October 9 through 15, 2006)

Rank	Program	Network
1.	Flavor of Love 2	VH1
2.	NFL Regular Season	ESPN
3.	Flavor of Love 2	VH1
4.	Flavor of Love 2	VH1
5.	World Wrestling Entertainment (WWE)	USA
6.	WWE	USA
7.	The Wire	HBO
8.	WWE	USA
9.	Movie of the Week	BET
10.	The Suite Life of Zack & Cody	Disney
11.	Monsters, Inc.	Disney
12.	Top 25 Hottest Couples	BET
13.	Girlfriends	BET
14.	Don't Look under the Bed	Disney
15.	Beef: The Series	BET
16.	Hannah Montana	Disney
17.	Sunday Movie III	Lifetime
18.	The Replacements	Disney
19.	Beef: The Series	BET
20.	SpongeBob SquarePants	Nickelodeon
21.	The Parkers	BET
22.	Justice League Unlimited	Cartoon Network
23.	Can of Worms	Disney
24.	Danny Phantom	Nickelodeon
25.	R&R Picture Show	VH1

Note. Data from Nielsen Media Research. Retrieved from http://www.nielsenmedia.com.

Though CW Entertainment President Dawn Ostroff noted that the new joint network will offer ethnically diverse programming, media agency research executives and CW insiders say that the new network will most likely retain more WB viewers than UPN fans (Crupi & Consoli, 2006). The new lineup includes shows that exhibit the widest appeal among young viewers and thus command top advertising dollars. Many of the African American–themed programs eliminated, although popular among black viewers, never achieved the kind of crossover hit status that ensures high ad rates. For example, although UPN's *One on One* was the one hundred and seventieth most popular show among all network television viewers, it was tied for eleventh place among black viewers. *Half & Half* was ranked one hundred and sixty-seventh among weekly series in overall network viewership but was the seventh most popular show with African American viewers. As a result, there is some concern that all-black casts may have become a thing of the past, primarily because of widening efforts by executives to appeal to a broader range of viewers in an attempt to lure more advertisers, who are spending their dollars to support programs with so-called multicultural casts. As a result, top-rated shows, like *Grey's Anatomy* on ABC with its multicultural cast, represent the new gold standard for television. The show features a white female lead actress (Ellen Pompeo) and a cast of African American costars, including Chandra Wilson, Isaiah Washington, and James Pickens Jr. The show's creator, Shonda Rhimes, is black. While *Grey's Anatomy* receives high marks among most in the African American community, the prototype has caused alarm among some observers who are concerned about the disappearance of all-black casts. Other African American actors and actresses who are part of multicultural casts include Khandi Alexander, who plays the role of pathologist on *CSI: Miami.* Shemar Moore, a longtime soap opera star, now plays the role of behavioral specialist on *Criminal Minds,* and Kimberly Elise has the role of prosecutor in *Close to Home* (Holloway, 2006). Nonetheless, for the black audience, something will be missing with the cancellation of many all-black cast programs.

Representing more than 13.45 million television households in the United States, the African American television audience is the largest minority segment in Nielsen Media Research's measurement samples. While all ethnic groups are represented in Nielsen Media Research's national sample in proportion to their percent of the population, only the two largest ethnic groups—African Americans and Hispanic Americans—are reported in Nielsen Media Research's standard ratings report. Table 5.8 presents data on the top ten programs African Americans view during prime time on network TV, while Table 5.9 presents data on the top twenty-five programs African Americans view during prime time on cable TV.

Table 5.10: Radio's Reach with African Americans

Audience type	Weekly reach (percentage)	Weekly time spent listening (hours : minutes)
Persons		
12 years of age and older	95.0%	22:15
Teens		
12 to 17 years of age	95.6%	16:30
Persons		
18 years of age and older	95.0%	23:15
18 to 34 years of age	95.7%	21:45
25 to 54 years of age	96.1%	23:45
35 to 64 years of age	95.5%	24:15
65 years of age and older	90.2%	23:00
Men		
18 years of age and older	94.3%	23:30
18 to 34 years of age	94.3%	21:15
25 to 54 years of age	95.3%	23:45
35 to 64 years of age	94.9%	24:45
65 years of age and older	90.6%	24:00
Women		
18 years of age and older	95.5%	23:00
18 to 34 years of age	97.0%	22:00
25 to 54 years of age	96.8%	22:30
35 to 64 years of age	96.0%	24:00
65 years of age and older	89.9%	22:15

Note. Data are for all black markets; time spent listening estimates are for Monday through Sunday, 6 a.m. until midnight. Data from Arbitron Maximi$er Plus National Region Database, November 8, 2006. Radio's reach with African Americans. Retrieved from http://www.mediainfocenter.org.music/radio_audience/reaching_aa.asp.

Radio

Radio is an important medium in reaching African American consumers. Table 5.10 reveals that radio reaches more than 95% of all adults and that black adults spend well over twenty hours per week listening to their favorite programs.

With some 1,100 stations in the United States programmed toward African Americans, there certainly is no shortage of radio outlets aimed at black consumers—particularly in the urban markets ("Tuning In," 2006). According to Media Audit, which measures 125 different radio formats in eighty-five markets, urban radio is the number-one format in reaching African Americans. However, urban radio is an appealing format for an increasingly diverse group of listeners. The Media Audit reports that, while 52.2% of the format's listen-

Table 5.11: African American Radio Format Preferences

Format	Percent of listeners			
	18 to 34 years of age	18 to 49 years of age	25 to 54 years of age	35 years of age and older
Urban contemporary	60.8%	51.0%	43.0%	29.2%
Rhythmic/contemporary hit radio	33.4%	32.3%	34.3%	28.1%
Urban adult contemporary	29.6%	25.0%	18.9%	15.5%
Pop contemporary hit radio	22.3%	16.2%	15.5%	12.0%
Adult contemporary	11.9%	13.0%	12.8%	10.9%

Note. Data are for twelve months. Data from "Release 1," Scarborough USA, 2003. In *What's Black about It?* Miller, P. & Kemp, H., 2005, p. 62.

ers are black, 19.6% are Hispanic, 18% are Caucasian, and 4.7% are Asian ("Spotlight on R&B," 2006). Urban formats reach over 45% of African American adults, and, as Table 5.11 reveals, urban contemporary is the favored format by all demographic groups.

Newspapers

Newspapers have a strong and enduring connection with African Americans. Indeed, America's first black-owned paper was *Freedom's Journal,* founded in 1827. Fighting slavery, and then segregation, black papers were an integral part of the eventual triumph of civil rights. Over the years, these papers offered oppositional viewpoints to the mainstream press and recorded the daily activities of black communities by listing weddings, births, death, graduations, meetings, and church functions (Campbell, Martin, & Fabos, 2006). Today, local daily newspapers reach 80% of African Americans in any seven-day week, according to the Readership Institute (2006). African Americans read their local daily newspaper nineteen minutes per day, slightly less than the national average of twenty-two minutes per day, but more than the fifteen minutes per day that Hispanics spend reading the newspaper. The Readership Institute also examined the quality of time spent with newspapers. They asked respondents how often they engage in other activities while reading the newspaper, reading magazines, watching television, or listening to the radio. Overall, they found that newspapers ranked second only to magazines, with 27% of all respondents saying they rarely or never engaged in a simultaneous activity. In terms of how newspapers fit into overall information consumption, the study found that newspapers are the single most used source for news among all groups of consumers: African Americans, Hispanics, and whites. In a seven-day week, 81% of people turn to newspapers, 66% turn to their local television news, and 50% turn to national television news. Consumers turn to newspapers not only for national and local news—they are also an excellent source of commercial information. More so than white consumers, African Americans look to the paper for ads for clothing, health, and nonfood stores, as well as ads for food and groceries. Readers who spend at least a half an hour

Table 5.12: Demographic Profile of African American Newspaper Readers		
Demographic breakdown of African American adults	Daily newspaper readership (percentage)	Sunday newspaper readership (percentage)
Total	48%	57%
Gender		
Men	52%	56%
Women	46%	57%
Age		
18 to 24 years	40%	49%
25 to 34 years	42%	55%
35 to 44 years	50%	59%
45 to 54 years	54%	59%
55 to 64 years	55%	61%
65 years and older	51%	57%
Household income		
$75,000 or more	56%	63%
$50,000 or more	54%	63%
$40,000 or more	53%	61%
Less than $40,000	43%	51%
Education		
Postgraduate degree	61%	66%
College graduate	53%	63%
Some college	51%	60%
High school graduate	48%	56%
Home value		
$300,000 or more	57%	65%
$250,000 to 299,999	58%	66%
$200,000 to 249,999	55%	50%
Less than $200,000	49%	59%
Home residency		
Time in home equals less than 1 year	38%	49%
Time in home equals 1 year	45%	54%
Time in home equals 3 years	47%	54%

Note. Data from "Release 1: Top 50 Market Report," Scarborough Research, 2004. Prepared by NAA Business Analysis and Research Department. Retrieved from http://www.naa.org/thesource/11.asp.

reading ads in their Sunday paper include 39% of African Americans, 40% of Hispanics, and a comparatively low 27% of whites. This shows that, although African Americans may spend a bit less time reading the paper overall, they spend significantly more time with the advertisements. Advertisements in the black press are seen as a symbolic invitation that the company is making to the African American consumer.

While African American newspaper readership is strong among various demographics, it increases among adults with higher household incomes, more education, and longer home residency, as revealed in Table 5.12.

A recent investigation revealed that 87.6% of readers who read black newspapers do not regularly read mainstream daily newspapers. CNW Marketing Research Inc., an independent research company that designed and executed the study, found that readers of the black press generally don't trust the mainstream dailies. Those papers have traditionally been viewed by African Americans as less than fair in their reporting on the African American community. In short, editorial content is perceived to be more slanted. "Hopefully this will put to rest once and for all the mistaken assumption of many advertisers that they can reach black consumers through mainstream newspapers," noted Dorothy Leavell, chairman of Amalgamated Publishers Inc., the firm that commissioned the study ("API Black Newspaper," 2004)

A useful resource for marketers is the National Newspaper Publishers Association (NNPA), also known as the Black Press of America, a sixty-five-year-old federation of more than two hundred black community newspapers from across the United States. Since World War II, it has also served as the industry's news service, a position it has held without peer or competitor since the Associated Negro Press dissolved in 1970. In 2000, the NNPA launched NNPA Media Services, a print and Web advertising placement and press release distribution service. In 2001, in association with the NNPA Foundation, it began building the BlackPressUSA Network—the nation's premier network of local black community news and information portals. The BlackPressUSA Network is anchored by BlackPressUSA.com—the national Web portal for the Black Press of America.

Magazines

African Americans are avid consumers of magazines. According to the Magazine Publishers of America, more than eight out of ten African American adults (85%) are magazine readers—reading nearly twelve issues per month—compared with just about nine issues for all U.S. adults. And they spend nearly thirty more minutes a week reading magazines than nonblacks. African American magazine readers tend to be younger than the average U.S. maga-

Figure 5.9: Ad Promoting *Essence* Magazine to Female Readers

zine reading population and have more children at home. Nearly three out of four African American adults who read magazines are between eighteen and forty-nine years of age (compared to only 64% of the U.S. adult population) (Magazine Publishers of America, n.d.). The total number of magazine titles specifically targeting black readers has increased 40% between 1997 and 2000 to more than 150 titles, according to a report by the American Society of Magazine Editors. From 2000 to 2002 alone, the report says, there were twenty-nine new black magazine launches (the magazine industry as a whole had 745 new titles launched in 2002) (Smith, 2006). These new magazines represent a mix of categories, including business, travel, parenting, religion, and automotive.

The top five categories of magazine for African American readers are general editorial, news weeklies, women's interest, home service, and music. Unlike the average U.S. reader, music ranks among the top five categories with blacks (for the average U.S. reader, men's titles rank fifth among the top five categories) (Magazine Publishers of America, n.d.). It should come as no great surprise that blacks are the heaviest consumers of African American magazines. Some of today's top-selling magazines appealing to African Americans have been in publication for decades. *Ebony* celebrated its sixtieth anniversary, while *Jet*

Table 5.13: Top Magazine Titles by African American Audience Composition

Magazine	African Americans as a percentage of the total audience	Index
Jet	95.1%	842
Black Enterprise	92.8%	821
Ebony	89.7%	794
Essence	87.0%	770
Vibe	68.8%	609
The Source	54.0%	478
Soap Opera Weekly	34.3%	304
Entrepreneur	33.2%	294
GQ (Gentlemen's Quarterly)	27.0%	239
Soap Opera Digest	26.1%	231
Esquire	25.7%	227
O, The Oprah Magazine	23.4%	207

Note. An Index of 100 is the national average. For example, African Americans are more than twice as likely to read *O, The Oprah Magazine* as the average American. Data from Mediamark Research Inc., Spring, 2004. African American Market Profile. Magazine Publishers of America. Retrieved from www.magazine.org/marketprofiles.

is over fifty years old. *Essence,* the first successful magazine aimed at black middle-class women, was started in 1970. See Figure 5.8 for an ad promoting *Essence* magazine to female readers. *Black Enterprise* has been sharing business news with African American readers for thirty-five years. Numerous smaller titles have also been communicating with the black consumer for many years. *U.S. Black Engineer* has been around for nearly a quarter century, and *Family Digest,* which focuses on African American families and parenting, is in its tenth year. A new generation of magazines has also sprung up to meet the demands of this lucrative market, including *Vibe* and the *Source,* among others.

Table 5.13 reveals that African Americans read general market publications as well as those specifically oriented to the black market. It comes as no surprise that African Americans index significantly above the average for those publications specifically targeting blacks. The top ten advertisers in black magazines during the first half of 2006 are, in rank order, Procter & Gamble Co., General Motors, L'Oréal USA, Ford Motor Company, Colgate-Palmolive Company, Toyota Motor Corporation USA, Nissan Motor Co. North America, Wal-Mart Stores, and Kraft Foods ("Apparel, Accessories," 2006).

Computers and the Internet

According to information from the *Media Audit* ("Spotlight on R&B," 2006), computer ownership by African Americans is on the rise—72.8% of African Americans own one or more computers in the home (compared to 69.2% for Hispanics). This represents an 11.3% increase since 2001. A recently released study shows that African Americans' use of the Internet outpaces the general market in many ways. According to the 2005 AOL African American Cyberstudy, conducted for AOL by IMAGES Market Research, two-thirds of online African American households have a high-speed connection, versus 53% of the general population. Nearly 80% of African Americans have access to the Internet—close to the 88% of the general population ("AOL Study," 2005). And those African Americans currently not online are likely to get connected within the next six to twelve months. On average, African Americans spend five hours a day online, versus just 2.9 hours for the general population. They are also far more likely than the general population to use the Web to access a variety of information: news (68% versus 56%), entertainment (55% versus 26%), health-related issues (72% versus 53%), financial questions/needs (60% versus 40%), and sports (39% versus 26%). Other popular activities include using a search engine (92%), communicating with family and friends (86%), using the Internet to get driving directions (85%), opening a bank account or online banking (62%), and listening to music online (62%). In addition, 62%

of African Americans feel that the Internet is helpful with individual career advancement and is a useful education tool (80%). The survey also revealed the following:

- Online African Americans report that they use the Internet an average of six days per week, compared to five days a week for all other Internet users.
- Seventy-six percent of African Americans view the Internet as a big time saver, saying that it allows them to access large amounts of information quickly and get more things done in a day.
- Forty-nine percent of African Americans feel that the Internet is the best source of information on consumer products.
- Almost three-quarters (70%) have researched an item online and subsequently purchased it at a store.
- Forty-two percent of African Americans go online to learn about new styles and fashion information.
- Researching different vehicle types (62%) was the most common reason for automotive-related Internet usage.
- Slightly more than half (52%) of African Americans have used the Internet to price shop new cars.
- Over one-third (37%) of African Americans online plan to purchase a new or used car in the next twelve months, compared to 22% for all other Internet users.

The AOL survey found that almost three-quarters of blacks respond favorably to advertising with multiple cultures featured, and 68% favor companies that benefit the African American community. However, the study also revealed that an overwhelming number of African Americans say there isn't enough online content that speaks to them as a distinct culture with its own dynamic needs and values ("AOL Study," 2005). To that end, BET.com has established itself as the leading online media site for African American content. BET.com is the flagship product of BET Interactive, a division of BET Networks. The portal was first launched in 2000 and, today, averages over 3 million registered users and 2.6 million unique visitors per month (based on June 2006 comScore data) ("BET Interactive," 2006). BET.com has received dozens of awards from such prestigious entities as the National Association of Black Journalists, the Pew Center for Civic Journalism, and Scripps-Howard Media, along with *Interactive Design* and *Black Enterprise* magazines.

Summary

In order to tap into the power of the black consumer's dollar, marketers must recognize that race really does matter. Those who fail to fully understand that race guides everything that African American consumers think, do, and feel risk losing out on this very lucrative market. This chapter should have made clear that there are fundamental differences between African Americans and general market consumers, as well as members of other ethnic groups. To minimize these differences is to be akin to suggesting that differences between male and female consumers or between the middle aged and teenagers are irrelevant to marketing communications. *Black* is what matters to black consumers. Savvy marketers will make every attempt to move beyond demographic data and to understand the mindset of the African American consumer. Such insights will allow them to tailor every element in the marketing mix to reflect respect for this consumer segment. The next chapter explores marketing to Asian Americans.

REFERENCES

Alleyne, S., & Richardson, N. M. (2006). The 40 best companies for diversity. *Black Enterprise, 36*(12), 100.

AOL study shows Blacks outpace general market in Internet usage. (2005, October 14). *The Broward Times,* p. 4.

API Black newspaper study drops media bombshell. (2004, June 27). *Take Pride Community Magazine,* 3.

Apparel, accessories led growth in ad spending in Black magazines during August. (2006, November 10). *Target Market News.* Retrieved from http://www.targetmarketnews.com/storyid10090601.htm

Arguello and Govea v. Conoco, Inc. No. 03–324 (5th Cir. October 6, 2003).

Bean, L. (2000, December 22). Retail racial profiling charges settled by Children's Place chain. *DiversityInc.* Retrieved from http://diversityinc.com/

Beasty, C. (2005, July 7). Ethnic consumers require sensitive marketing. *Destination CRM.* Retrieved from http://www.destinationcrm.com/articles/default.asp?Articlew ID=5249

Bergman, M. (2006, April 18). Revenues for Black-owned firms near $89 billion, number of businesses up 45 percent. *U.S. Census Bureau News.* Retrieved from http:www.census.gov/press-Release/www/releases/archives/business_ownership/00671.

BET Interactive takes full control of Web power BET.com with buyout of original investment group. (2006, August 25). *PR Newswire.*

BET unveils new, original lineup. (2006, May 4). *Sacramento Observer,* p. E6.

Black Business List. (n.d.). Retrieved from http://www.blackbusinesslist.com/bisnews/national/2005/07/burrellyank.htm

Black progress being hidden. (2006, February 8). *Miami Times,* p. 3D.

Buford, H. (2006). Maximizing your share of the African American market. *Multicultural Marketing Resources*. Retrieved from http://www.multicultural.com/experts/art_aframer.html

Burger King helps damaged New Orleans universities. (2006, February 16). *The New York Beacon*, p. 25.

Campbell, R., Martin, C., & Fabos, B. (2006). *Media & culture: An introduction to mass communication* (5th ed.). Boston, MA: Bedford/St. Martin's Press.

Charity v. Denny's. WL 544687. (E.D. La. 1999).

Cheng, K. (2002, April 24). As the melting pot simmers, ethnic media reaches people of color. *DiversityInc*. Retrieved from http://diversityinc.com/

Chrysler sponsored R&B superstar's gospel tour to launch all-new Chrysler Aspen and raise funds for medical education. (2006, October 2). *PR Newswire*.

Coleman, D. (2000). *Yankelovich monitor*.

Commonwealth of Massachusetts v. The Children's Place Stores, Inc. Complaint and Consent Decree, MCAD Docket No. 00133755 (December 21, 2000).

Crupi, A., & Consoli, J. (2006, April 10). Post-UPN, ethnic GRPs are in play. *Mediaweek*, p. 6.

Downey, K. (2006, February 13). Slow build for Black Family Channel. *Broadcasting & Cable*, p. 12.

Emerson, J. (2001, September 1). African Americans. *Direct*. Retrieved from http://bg.directmag.com/ar/marketing_African_Americans/

Essence. (n.d.). Did you know? Retrieved from http://www.essence.com/mktfacts/buying-power

Fielding, M. (2005, November 15). Mistaken identity. *Marketing News*, p. 13.

Force of habit. (2006, September/October). *Marketing Management, 15*(5), 7.

Hampton v. Dillard Department Store, 985 F. Supp. 1055 (D. Kan. November 25, 1998); 247 F.3d (10th Cir. 2001); cert. denied at 122 S. Ct. 1071 (mem), 151 Led.2d 973, 70 USLW 3396, 70 USLW 3514, 534 U.S. 1131 (2002).

Harris, A.-M., Henderson, G., & Williams, J. (2005, Spring). Courting customers: Assessing consumer racial profiling and other marketplace discrimination. *Journal of Public Policy and Marketing, 24*(1), 163.

Hispanics, African Americans show strong reconnection to heritage according to Yankelovich Multicultural Marketing Study. (2006, August 11). *Business Wire*, p. 1.

Holloway, L. (2006, October). Disappearing acts. *Ebony, 61*(12), 134.

Hopkins, J. (2006, August 24). African American women step up in business world; More women of color take lead on path to entrepreneurship. *USA Today*, p. B-3.

How we buy—research says corporate reputations and trust #1 to Black America. (1998, August 26). *The Jacksonville Free Press*, p. 1.

Ingram, M. L. (2006, July 23). Marketing is influenced by minorities. *Philadelphia Tribune*, p. 8A.

Jenkins, C. (2006, September 16). Sundays still divided by race: Worship most highly segregated time in nation despite unifying identity that comes with being a Christian. *Knight Ridder/Tribune Business News*, p. 1.

Johnson-Elie, T. (2006, March 22). Opportunities: Consumers aren't all alike. *Milwaukee Journal Sentinel*, p. D-1.

Jones, J. (2006, January 8). Is marriage for White people? Blacks increasingly choose not to get married. *York Daily Record.*

Lee, G. (2006, January 22). The power of connecting; With pageantry and pride, more African American families are celebrating their ties with destination reunions. *The Record,* p. T-06.

Magazine Publishers of America. (n.d.). *MPA market profiles.* Retrieved from http://www.magazine.org/marketprofiles

The many shades of the Black shopping pattern. (2006, Fall). *Drug Store News,* 11.

Miah, M. (2006, May/June). Plight of young Black men: The scars and the crisis. *Against the Current, 21*(2), 2.

Miller, P., & Kemp, H. (2005). *What's black about it?* Ithaca, NY: Paramount Market Publishing, Inc.

Murrell v. Ocean Mecca Motel, Inc. 262 F.3d 253 (4th Cir. 2001).

Myers, J. (2005, November 9). African Americans are most media-active and advertiser-friendly audience. *Jack Myers Media Business Report.* Retrieved from http://www.media-village.com/jmr/2005/11/09/jmr-11-09-05/

Peters, J. (2006, August 1). What's so funny? [Late edition, East Coast]. *New York Times,* p. C-1.

Popovec, J. (2006, May). Role of psychographics. *National Real Estate Investor, 48*(5), 32.

Power, S. (2006, October 19). Chrysler to take its cars to church; deal with Patti LaBelle offers tickets, test drives to Sunday worshipers [Eastern edition]. *Wall Street Journal,* p. B-4.

Price, M. (2005, January 17). Some analysts expect surge in corporate spending on Black-targeted advertising. *Knight Ridder/Tribune Business News,* p. 1.

Profound shifts in family dynamics, priorities underway among Hispanic, African American consumers; Yankelovich unveils 2005 Monitor Multicultural Marketing Study. (2006, July 6). *Business Wire,* p. A.

Racial divide persists in real estate. (2005, April). *Home Buyer News, 36.* Retrieved from http://www.ahghomebuyernews.com/consumer-news.php3?IssueID=36&RowID=214

Ragland, J. (2005, August 15). Black shoppers feel they're unwelcome. *Knight Ridder/Tribune News Service,* p. 1.

Readership Institute. (2006). *How newspapers can better serve African-Americans and Hispanics.* Retrieved from http://www.readership.org/consumers/hispanic_afam/diversity_rpt.htm

Reed, W. (2006a, June 15). Advantages for African Americans in homeownership. *Washington Informer,* p. S-26.

Reed, W. (2006b, April 27). Does buying from a Black business make a difference? *The Washington Informer,* p. 12.

Roberts, G. (2005, April). Consumer News: Racial divide persists in real estate. *American Home Buyer News, 36.* Retreived from http://www.ahghomebuyernews.com/consumer-news.php3?IssueID=36&RowID=214.

Sachdev, A. (2006, March 24). Lawsuit against Niketown expands: Chicago employees allege discrimination. *Knight Ridder/Tribune Business News,* p. 1.

Sanders, L. (2006, July 3). How to target Blacks? First, you gotta spend [Midwest region edition]. *Advertising Age*, p. 19.

Schreiber, A. (2001). *Multicultural marketing: Selling to the new America.* Lincolnwood, IL: NTC Business Books.

Sidime, A. (2004, November). Credit use strangles wealth. *Black Enterprise, 35*(4), 38.

Smith, L. (2006, February 9). Paging Black readers: Publications catering to African Americans claim a small but fast growing corner of the magazine market. *Times Union*, p. C-1.

The solid progress of African Americans in degree attainments. (2006, Summer). *The Journal of Blacks in Higher Education, 52,* 54.

Spotlight on R&B urban radio: Format is valuable for many key audiences. (2006, January). *The Media Audit.*

Stronger, K. (2006, April 16). Ad dollars switching to Hispanic media; Black media outlets losing out as advertisers target the nation's new largest minority group. *Buffalo News*, p. C-1.

Taylor, H. (2003, October 15). While most Americans believe in God, only 36 percent attend a religious service once a month or more often. *Harris Interactive*. Retrieved from http://www.harrisinteractive.com/harris_poll/index.asp?PID=408

Thomas-Lester, A. (2006, March 2). Black History tie-in advertising criticized. *Miami Times*, p. 1-D.

Tuning in to a valuable audience. (2006,August 28). *PR Week*, p. 22.

Turner, T. (2006, February 1). Black History Month, brought to you by. . . . *Knight Ridder/Tribune Business News*, p. 1.

TV One and Warner Bros. Domestic Cable Distribution ink comprehensive, multi-year programming agreement for movies, series. (2006, April 10). *PR Newswire.*

TV One passes 30 million household subscriber mark, according to Nielsen Universe estimates. (2006, May 3). *PR Newswire.*

University of Pennsylvania Journal of Constitutional Law. (n.d.). The Black church. A historical background of the significance of Black churches: Beyond a monolithic construct of African-American religion and religiosity. Retrieved from http://www.law.upenn.edu/conlaw/issues/vol1/num1/simmsparris/node3_ct.html

U.S. Census Bureau. (2000). *We the people: Blacks in the United States. Census 2000 special report.* Washington, D.C.: U.S. Department of Commerce.

U.S. Census Bureau. (2002). *The black population in the United States: March, 2002.* Washington, D.C.: U.S. Department of Commerce.

Vital signs: Statistics that measure the state of racial inequality. (2006, Summer). *The Journal of Blacks in Higher Education, 52/51,* 1.

Wicks, S. (2005, July 9). New report sheds light on African American shoppers. *Black Business List.* Retrieved from http://blackbusinesslist.com

Young, Y. (2004, April 2). Tough choices for tough times. *USA Today*, p. A-09.

Zurawik, D. (2006, May 10). Black TV shows on shaky ground: Network merger could lead to demise of many sitcoms. *Knight Ridder Tribune Business News*, p. 1.

6

Reaching Asian American Consumers

Who They Are: Understanding Asian American Identity

The term *Asian American* is a bit of a misnomer in that it suggests a single, monolithic group. Nothing could be further from the truth. Asian Americans are the most diverse ethnic group in the United States today, reflecting the influence of well over fifteen distinct ethnic groups and national origins, including Bangladeshi, Cambodian, Chinese, Filipino, Indian, Indonesian, Japanese, Korean, Laotian, Malaysian, Pakistani, Sri Lankan, Taiwanese, Thai, and Vietnamese. Between 1990 and 2000, the Asian American population grew 48%, more than four times the growth rate of the U.S. population. According to the 2000 census, 10,242,998 Americans self-identified as being of Asian descent—representing 3.6% of the total U.S. population. Another 1,655,830 persons identified as being Asian in combination with one or more races, bringing the Asian American total for 2000 to 11,898,828—or 4.2% of the population at the turn of the century. And, since 2000, the Asian American population has increased faster than any other ethnic group. Asian Americans currently make up nearly 5% of the population, and this group is expected to more than triple in size, to 35 million in the next fifty years. The term *Native Hawaiian and other Pacific Islander* refers to people tracing their ancestry to any of the original peoples of Hawaii, Guam, Samoa, or other Pacific Islands. Native Hawaiian and other Pacific Islanders are a much smaller segment of the population. According to the 2000 census, a total of 874,414 Americans self-identified as being Native Hawaiian and other Pacific Islander alone or in combination. Over the past few years, it has become increasingly common to employ the label of *Asian Pacific American* to refer to Asian Hawaiian and other Pacific Islanders collectively. However, the reader should note that much of the research on this market is reported only for Asian Americans, thus, throughout this chapter, data for the ethnic group *Native Hawaiian and Pacific Islanders* are only included when specifically cited.

Eighty-seven percent of all Asian Americans come from just six countries: China, India, the Philippines, Vietnam, Korea, and Japan. Chinese Americans and Filipino Americans are the two largest groups (see Table 6.1).

In terms of growth, groups relatively new to the United States, such as Asian Indian Americans, Vietnamese, and Koreans, have increased significantly in recent years (see Table 6.2). Immigrants from India represent the fastest growing segment—more than doubling in size since 1990.

Table 6.1: Asian Americans by Top Ten Ethnicities

	Alone		Alone or in combination	
Ethnicity	Number	Percentage	Number	Percentage
Total Asian	10,242,998	100%	11,898,828	100%
Chinese	2,432,585	24%	2,865,232	24%
Filipino	1,850,314	18%	2,364,815	20%
Indian	1,678,765	16%	1,899,599	16%
Korean	1,076,872	11%	1,228,427	10%
Vietnamese	1,122,528	11%	1,223,736	10%
Japanese	796,700	8%	1,148,932	10%
Cambodian	171,937	2%	206,052	2%
Pakistani	153,533	1%	204,309	2%
Laotian	168,707	2%	198,203	2%
Hmong[a]	169,428	2%	186,310	2%

Note. From 2000 U.S. Census, Summary File 2, U.S. Census Bureau. A Profile on Asian Americans, The Asian American Advertising Federation, retrieved from www.3af.org/3AFAsianUS0305.pdf.

a=The Hmong population is defined as people inhabiting the mountainous regions of Southern China and adjacent areas of Vietnam, Laos, and Thailand.

Unlike African Americans, the majority of Asian Americans are foreign born. Less than one-third of Asian Americans were born in this country (31%—compared to 89% for the total U.S. population). In 1965, the U.S. Immigration and Naturalization Service eliminated its restrictions on Asian immigration, and, in the past twenty to twenty-five years, countries such as China, Korea, and Vietnam have relaxed barriers to emigration. As a result, more than three-quarters (75.9%) of the Asian population came to the United States during the past two decades. Rossman (1994) notes that the Asian market is highly segmented, especially when generational and assimilation issues are taken into consideration. For example, recent Chinese immigrants are likely to exhibit consumer behaviors congruent with their country of origin. They may, in fact, be similar in many ways to Chinese Americans concentrated in America's Chinatowns who may speak primarily Chinese throughout the generations, eat only traditional Chinese food, purchase goods imported from China, and use only services from Chinese American vendors and suppliers. Yet, both these groups are likely to be very different consumers from Chinese Americans living in integrated neighborhoods who are relatively assimilated by the second generation and certainly by the third generation.

Table 6.2: Countries of Origin by Foreign-Born Population with 500,000 or More Immigrants in 2000

Country of origin	Number of immigrants in 1990	Number of immigrants in 2000	Percent increase
China	921,000	1,391,000	51%
Philippines	913,000	1,222,000	34%
India	450,000	1,007,000	124%
Vietnam	543,000	863,000	59%
Korea	568,000	701,000	23%

Note. Data from U.S. Census 2000, U.S. Census Bureau. Asian American Market Profile, Magazine Publishers of America. Retrieved from www.magazine.org/marketprofiles.

Where to Reach Them

Asian Americans tend to be highly concentrated—making it somewhat easier for marketers to reach them. The U.S. Census Bureau reveals that half of Asian Americans live in just three states, and nearly three-quarters (74%) of Asian Americans live in the top ten Asian American states. Fully 89% of Asian Americans live in just twenty states (see Table 6.3).

Table 6.3: Top Twenty Asian American States

Rank	State	Number of Asian Americans (alone or in combination)	Cumulative percentage
1.	California	4,563,499	34%
2.	New York	1,336,374	44%
3.	Texas	753,105	49%
4.	Hawaii	728,945	55%
5.	New Jersey	603,396	59%
6.	Illinois	547,665	63%
7.	Washington	443,576	66%
8.	Florida	395,169	69%
9.	Virginia	354,277	72%
10.	Massachusetts	309,153	74%
11.	Pennsylvania	290,340	76%
12.	Maryland	274,886	79%
13.	Michigan	249,550	80%
14.	Georgia	238,274	82%
15.	Ohio	193,817	84%
16.	Minnesota	187,574	85%
17.	North Carolina	164,782	86%
18.	Oregon	149,080	87%
19.	Colorado	144,580	88%
20.	Arizona	144,242	89%

Note. From Data from 2003 Estimates, U.S. Census Bureau. A Profile on Asian Americans, Asian American Advertising Federation. Retrieved from www.3af.org/3AFAsianUS0305.pdf.

The top five U.S. Asian American designated market areas (DMAs), comprised of Los Angeles, New York, San Francisco, Honolulu, and Chicago, represent approximately 6 million Asians, which is nearly half of the total U.S. Asian American population (see Table 6.4). Note that four of the top ten U.S. DMAs are in California, and, together, they account for approximately one-third of the total Asian American population. The top ten U.S. cities of 100,000 or more people with the highest percentage of Asians are Honolulu, Hawaii (67.7%); Daly City, California (53.6%); Fremont, California (39.8%); Sunnyvale, California (34.2%); San Francisco, California (32.6%); Irvine, California (32.3%); Garden Grove, California (31.8%); Santa Clara, California (31.4%); Torrance, California (31.1%); and San Jose, California (28.8%). It is of interest to note that all ten cities with the highest proportion of Asians were in the West, and nine of them were in California (Améredia, 2006).

Table 6.4: Areas of Geographic Concentration by U.S. Designated Market Areas (DMAs)

DMA	Total Population	Asian AOIC	Alone or in Combination					
			Asian Indian	Chinese	Filipino	Japanese	Korean	Vietnamese
TOTAL U.S.	281,421,906	11,898,828	1,899,599	2,865,232	2,364,815	1,148,932	1,228,427	1,223,736
LOS ANGELES	17,053,236	1,914,209	126,636	479,736	448,015	204,262	274,334	253,192
NEW YORK	20,181,238	1,548,094	441,006	626,461	173,585	57,795	175,486	26,850
SAN FRANCISCO	6,908,334	1,422,378	157,518	516,078	376,367	104,006	64,511	158,034
HONOLULU	1,211,390	703,205	3,145	170,684	275,714	296,662	41,351	10,040
CHICAGO	8,820,967	426,967	123,538	76,179	94,041	23,825	49,298	17,699
WASHINGTON DC	5,629,516	379,898	81,426	72,381	49,125	16,340	61,971	47,329
SEATTLE	4,201,907	353,236	25,609	68,108	83,243	48,597	51,041	45,054
SACRAMENTO	3,208,417	313,687	42,221	66,106	75,323	31,128	11,040	28,105
SAN DIEGO	2,813,833	295,346	12,145	39,103	145,132	29,028	14,404	35,512
PHILADELPHIA	7,666,731	266,556	70,630	80,684	27,379	9,708	36,577	31,784

Source: U.S. Census Bureau, 2000 Census.

Note. AOIC = alone or in combination. From 2000 census, U.S. Census Bureau.

Over 95% of Asians and Pacific Islanders live in metropolitan areas, and many subgroups often cluster in Asian communities. Nearly one in four Asian Americans is Chinese, and Chinatowns—Chinese community enclaves—are present in nearly every large U.S. city. Major Chinatowns can be found in Chicago, Houston, Las Vegas, Los Angeles, Manhattan, Philadelphia, Portland, Oakland, San Francisco, and Washington, D.C. Similarly, Koreatowns are present in Los Angeles, New York, Atlanta, Chicago, Dallas, Oakland, and San Francisco, as well as Annandale, Virginia, and Bergen County, New Jersey. Japantowns (also known as Little Tokyos, Nihonmachis, or J-towns) are found in San Francisco, San Jose, and Los Angeles. On the other hand, Filipino Americans tend to settle in a more dispersed fashion, with somewhat less of a need to establish ties with other Filipino Americans in a given locality. Yet, Filipino community enclaves—known in the United States as Little Manila (or Manilatowns or Filipinotowns)—do exist in San Francisco, Los Angeles, and Stockton, California. Rossman (1994) explains that many of these Asian American communities can be quite insular. For example, "many people who have lived in New York's self-sufficient Chinatown all their lives, have only had rare encounters with people outside the Chinese community."

Unifying Factors: Group Orientation and the Family, Education, and Saving Money

While there is certainly a cultural divide among the different Asian segments, there are also similarities that they all share to some degree. The Cultural Access Group notes that the five main values that Asian Americans share include a group orientation, an emphasis on family, respect for elders and the community, and the importance of education and saving money (Desjardins, 2006).

Group Orientation and the Family

The traditional Asian worldview emphasizes the group, and, in particular, the family as a greater priority than the individual (Berg & Jaya, 1993). This collectivistic orientation, like so many aspects of culture, has deep historical roots. Filial piety is a major principle of Confucianism, one of the main Eastern philosophies (in addition to Buddhism and Taoism). Confucianism is the major religious influence on Chinese, Japanese, Korean, and Vietnamese cultures (although most Indians are Hindu or Moslem, and most Filipinos are Roman Catholic). *Filial* means toward the father, and *piety* means worship or reverence. The notion of filial piety places great importance on the family and defines specific rules of conduct in social relationships. Philips (1997) notes that several key concepts follow from the principle of filial piety:

- Family roles are highly structured, hierarchical, male dominated, and paternally oriented.
- The welfare and integrity of the family are of great importance. The individual is expected to submerge or repress emotions, desires, behaviors, and individual goals to further the family welfare and to maintain its reputation. The individual is obliged to save face so as not to bring shame onto the family,
- Interdependency is valued and stems from the strong sense of obligation to the family. This concept influences relationships among family members. The family provides support and assistance for each individual member; in turn, individual members provide support and assistance for the entire family. These relationships, interactions, and obligations are considered lifelong.

While all Asian subgroups may not consciously follow the principles of filial piety, it has nonetheless become ingrained in values and practices that have formed over centuries. Family is central to Asian Americans. Table 6.5 reveals that, of the Asian and Pacific Islanders and the non-Hispanic whites fifteen years and older in 2002, 57% of each population was married (note that the

Table 6.5: Marital Status of Population Aged Fifteen Years and Older for Asian and Pacific Islanders and Non-Hispanic Whites

Marital status	Asian and Pacific Islander	Non-Hispanic white
Married with spouse present	53.3%	56.3%
Married with spouse absent	4.2%	0.8%
Widowed	4.2%	6.9%
Divorced	5.0%	10.0%
Separated	1.4%	1.5%
Never married	32.9%	24.5%

Note. Data from "The Asian and Pacific Islander Population in the United States," U.S. Census Bureau, March, 2002. Retrieved from www.census.gov/population/www/socdemo/race/api.html.

designation *married* includes those with a spouse present or a spouse absent); however, the percentage of divorced Asians and Pacific Islanders was one-half that of non-Hispanic whites (5% compared with 10%, respectively).

Asians' sense of family tends to be more extended than that of the dominant culture. In addition to parents and grandparents, an extended Asian American family might include cousins, uncles, and aunts—even friends from back home or neighbors from a town or village. As a result, Asian American household sizes tend to be larger—at 3.8 persons—compared to the national average of 3.2 (Desjardins, 2006). As Table 6.6 reveals, a significantly larger percentage of Asian households consist of five or more members (19.9% versus just 12% for the non-Hispanic white population). With a greater frequency than many other immigrant groups, Asian Pacific immigrants to the United States—most especially, recent immigrants—invite members of such extended families to visit them in the United States. Advertisements incorporating images of extended families will resonate with Asian Americans. Wal-Mart used just this approach in appealing to Chinese, Filipino, and Vietnamese Americans. In their ads, Wal-Mart featured the Kwongs of Southern California, along with other real-life customers. When the Kwongs pile into the car for a

Table 6.6: Household Size for Married Couples

Household size	Asian and Pacific Islander	Non-Hispanic white
Two members	28.0%	47.0%
Three members	24.6%	19.7%
Four members	27.5%	21.2%
Five or more members	19.9%	12.1%

Note. Data from "The Asian and Pacific Islander Population in the United States, March 2002," U.S. Census Bureau, retrieved from www.census.gov/population/www/socdemo/race/api.html.

trip to Wal-Mart, it's a three-generation family affair: Grandma wants clothes, mom needs household supplies, and the kids have new video games to master. The ads show the Kwongs discussing in their native tongue how Wal-Mart has products and services that appeal to the whole family. Wal-Mart's multilanguage effort is aimed at the 100,000 to 150,000 Asian American consumers living in close proximity to Wal-Mart stores, particularly in California, Texas, New York, and New Jersey (Schmelzer, 2006). Wal-Mart is so committed to its first-ever Asian language advertising campaign that it plans to expand to additional geographic markets and population segments—including Koreans, Thais, and Cambodians. Linda Blakley, a Wal-Mart spokeswoman notes, "We've found that when we use relevant communications, we connect with the customer much more strongly" (Angrisani, 2005).

Gender roles and the relationships among family members in Asian culture tend to be quite structured. "Confucianism made men alone the structurally relevant members of the society and relegated women to social dependence" (Kim, 1993). Davis and Proctor note that, in Asian families, "Men are primarily responsible for task functions, while females attend to social and cultural tasks" (1989). In Asian families, the father tends to be the absolute authority. Care of the family and children generally falls to the mother. Samovar, Porter, and Stafani explain that the hierarchy associated with gender and age in Asian culture is rather clear: "After the father, the eldest male has most of the authority" (1998, p. 109). Such traditional gender roles are common even among Indians, whose religions are not rooted in Confucianism. Nanda notes that "Men make most of the important decisions, inheritance is through the male line, and a woman lives in her husband's village after she marries" (1994). The extent to which this is the case in Asian American families today is much influenced by level of acculturation. Children are encouraged to remain dependent for as long as possible—indeed, many parents expect children to live with them until they marry. Obligation to parents for their upbringing is lifelong, and grown children are sometimes expected to live with and take care of aging parents. Respect for elders is taught in most Asian cultures, and, in many, ancestors are revered. The honor and reputation of the family—indeed, the family's legacy—must always be protected. These last two points are clearly reflected in an American Family Insurance ad targeting Asian consumers (see Figure 6.1). The illustration portrays a father helping his daughter pack for college. The copy reads,

> Your family legacy is something to value and honor. At American Family Insurance, we feel that way, too. That's why you'll find our agents are always respectful, friendly and eager to help you select the best auto policy for you. At college, you trust her to do her best; now give us a call and find out how to best protect her on the drive there.

Figure 6.1: Ad Speaking to the Importance of Family Legacy among Asian Consumers

Protection That Goes The Distance

Your family legacy is something to value and honor. At American Family Insurance, we feel that way, too. That's why you'll find our agents are always respectful, friendly and eager to help you select the best auto policy at the best value for you. At college, you trust her to do her best; now give us a call and find out how to best protect her on the drive there. Visit us at www.amfam.com, or call today and ask about the variety of auto coverage options we have to offer.

American Family Mutual Insurance Company and its Subsidiaries
American Standard Insurance Company of Wisconsin
Home Office – Madison, WI 53783
American Family Insurance Company
American Standard Insurance Company of Ohio
Home Office – Columbus, OH 43240
www.amfam.com

0005   001633 – 4/05

AMERICAN FAMILY
INSURANCE ®

All your protection under one roof ®

Not only is the reputation of the family important, so too is that of firms. Rossman notes,

> an important selling point for most Asians Americans is the reputation of the company. Long-standing, established companies with a history of service are usually preferred over start-up operations, since age and experience are highly valued by most Asians. And if a business is family-owned, then so much the better; both tradition and respect for family count for a great deal. Once a product or service is adopted by one satisfied purchaser, it is easy to win acceptance by a larger segment of the market. (1994, p. 92)

Strong family bonds require the Asian family to provide support to all of its members. Thus, much like Hispanic Americans, Asian Americans send large amounts of money back to family members across Asia. China, Vietnam, and the Philippines are three of the largest remittance destinations in the world, accounting for 30% of the estimated $85 billion in remittance flows that Asian countries will receive in 2006 ("Wells Fargo," 2006). See Figure 6.2 for an ad promoting the services of Western Union, promising Asian consumers that they are the "fastest way to send money worldwide." In addition to Western Union, a number of banks, including Wells Fargo, have become active in the remittance market.

Asian Americans may have strong ties to their native cultures, but they are also closely connected to their Asian communities in the United States. That they strive to connect with their ethnic communities is evidenced by the fact that they actively engage in ethnic events within these communities. A recent study conducted by the interTrend Knowledge Center found that 63% of Asian Americans attended such community events in 2005 (Asian American Journalists Association, 2005). Asian Americans tend to be particularly loyal to firms that support their communities. As other marketers are just beginning to realize the potential of the Asian American market, Anheuser-Busch has already established itself as a model for outreach to Asian communities. The maker of the popular Budweiser and Michelob brands has been a pioneer in meeting the needs of the Asian community, via a long list of initiatives in the areas of leadership development, education, business and economic development, arts and culture, and health and social services, as well as women's programs. The company's comprehensive AsianBud program is more than simply an attempt to sell more beer. By recognizing and addressing the unique needs and concerns of Asian consumers, Anheuser-Busch has forged a lasting partnership with the Asian and Pacific Islander community. For example, Anheuser-Busch has partnered with Asian organizations to create the now ten-year-old Anheuser-Busch Fellows program to foster the next generation of leaders. The fellowships are designed to provide opportunities for talented young adults that will offer them the access and exposure they need to jumpstart their careers. To date, more than 150 fellowships, ranging from scholarships and grants to high-

Figure 6.2: Western Union Promotes Its Money Transfer Service to Asian Consumers

profile internships and even permanent positions with esteemed national organizations, have been awarded to young Asians who demonstrate excellence in various fields. For example, Scott Nishimoto, the first recipient of the Anheuser-Busch Frank Horton Fellowship, became the youngest member of the Hawaii State Legislature at the age of twenty-nine. Darren R. Mooko, recipient of the 1998 Anheuser-Busch March Fong Eu Community Fellowship, helped create the first Asian American studies program at Pomona College. And, after graduating from New York University's Graduate Film School, Kevin Feng Ke, the 1999 Anheuser-Busch Ang Lee Fellow, completed his first feature-length film, *Lady Shanghai*, which debuted in 2001 at the prestigious Cannes Film Festival. Anheuser-Busch also sponsors the Thomas Tang National Moot Court Competition. Anheuser-Busch awarded $10,000 in scholarships to the winners of the annual competition, in which teams of law students square off on a mock legal issue. The National Asian Pacific American Bar Association announces the winners. Among its other efforts, the company also hosted a gala dinner at the James Beard Foundation in New York, celebrating the culinary achievements of some of the country's most prominent Asian and Pacific Islander chefs. Through its various and ongoing efforts to connect with the Asian community, Anheuser-Busch has clearly established itself as a friend of the Asian community. And that friendship is one that cannot simply be measured in dollars spent. While the relationship is no doubt a good thing for the company's bottom line, it is likely even more beneficial to Asian Americans and ethnic groups in general, as it helps bring issues concerning these diverse communities to the attention of the rest of corporate America (Picture, 2006).

Education

Another important principle of Confucianism is the virtue of education. According to Sue and Okazaki (1990), Asian families tend to have high demands and expectations for educational achievement. Education is such a high priority that it is not unusual to find parents suffering more from exam anxiety than their primary school children. Asian families are likely to spend additional income on private tutors to provide their children with after-school help with homework. Children in Asian American families raised with such strong parental pressures for educational achievement pursue educational goals in order to make their parents proud and to bring honor to the family. Achievement, and, in particular, educational achievement, reflects positively on one's family and group. Research has documented that Asian American students tend to spend twice as much time each week on homework compared to non-Asian students (Steinberg, Dornbusch, & Brown, 1992). And, in high school, Asian American students exhibited the highest grade point average among any group, including African Americans, Hispanic Americans, white Americans, and others. In addition, when examining standardized test performance, Asian Americans' scores on the SAT (Scholastic Assessment Test) were much higher than the national average (Sue & Okazaki, 1990). Clearly, the hard work pays off. Almost 87% of Asians, age twenty-five and older are high school graduates, nearly the same rate as for non-Hispanic whites in this age group. Close to half of Asian Americans age twenty-five and older have a bachelor's degree or higher level of education. Indeed, Asians have the highest proportion of college graduates of any race or ethnic group in the country. The corresponding rate for all adults in this age group is just over 27%. Breaking these figures down by sex, Table 6.7 reveals that Asian and Pacific Islander men were much more likely than non-Hispanic white men to have earned at least a bachelor's degree (nearly 51% compared with 32%—a difference of 19%). Similarly, Asian and Pacific Islander women were more likely than non-Hispanic white women to have earned at least a bachelor's degree (44% compared with 27%). Among Asian subgroups, Indians lead the groups, with about 64% of the population having a bachelor's degree or higher level of education, followed by Pakistani Americans (54%) and Chinese Americans (48%). One in five Asian Americans, aged twenty-five and older, has an advanced degree (for example, a master's, doctor of philosophy

Table 6.7: Educational Attainment by Sex		
Educational attainment	Asian Pacific Islander	Non-Hispanic white
Males		
Less than high school	10.5%	11.5%
High school graduate	20.5%	31.5%
Some college or associate's degree	18.1%	25.2%
Bachelor's degree or more	50.9%	31.7%
Females		
Less than high school	14.5%	11.1%
High school graduate	23.2%	34.3%
Some college or associate's degree	18.5%	27.3%
Bachelor's degree or more	43.8%	27.3%

[Ph.D.], doctor of medicine [M.D.], or doctor of law [J.D.] degree). The corresponding rate for all adults in this age group is just 9%. The 2003 National Consumer Expenditure Survey found that Asian Americans spend about four times as much as other groups on college tuition and more than double on books, equipment, and other supplies for college (Corrie, 2005).

Saving Money

In 2005, according to the OECD, the U.S. household savings rate was negative for the first time since the Great Depression—dropping from 1.4% just a few years earlier. In comparison, Asian countries have relatively high rates of saving. China, the world's fourth largest economy, has an extraordinarily high savings rate—household savings are 25.5%. India comes in a close second at 24.3%. Thailand's household savings rate is 18.7%. Korea's rate is 10%, and Japan's rate is 7.4% (International Saving Comparisons, 2005). Thus, Asians have a tradition of saving, and, when they come to this country, they tend to remain avid savers. Asian Americans are more likely than the general market to have a bank account, with over two-thirds indicating that they had savings accounts. Overall, they save more than twice as much as the general market does. Because of the high value placed on education, many Asian families save for their children's college tuition. Lee, Hanna, and Siregar (1997) found that Asian American households were significantly more likely to have college savings as a goal than other households. Over one-third (33.9%) of Asian American households planned to save for their children's college education, versus 28.9% of Hispanic American households, 27.9% of white households, and 26.9% of black households. Asian Americans also save for other reasons. Nearly nine in ten (86%) save for emergencies, and over three-quarters save for retirement. The 2001 Minority Retirement Confidence Survey in *PR Newswire* revealed that 78% of Asian Americans say they have saved for retirement, compared to 54% of African Americans, just half of Hispanic Americans, and 69% of all workers who say they have saved for retirement. Asian Americans reported the highest level of confidence regarding various financial aspects of retirement planning, and Hispanic Americans tend to report the lowest levels of confidence. Seventy-two percent of Asian Americans feel confident that they will have enough money to live comfortably in retirement, compared with 54% of African Americans, 45% of Hispanic Americans, and 63% of all workers in the United States. In addition to saving for the short term, Asians are more likely to save for the long term. Although there are differences between Asian subgroups, Hofstede and Bond argue that most rank high in "Confucian Dynamism," which emphasizes a "future-oriented mentality" (1988). Unlike Americans, Asians are motivated to accumulate wealth for use beyond their own lifetimes. "An American might think in terms of saving for their own retirement, but an Asian will think of accumulating resources in terms of saving for their family, for multiple generations in the future" (Plumberg, 2006).

Asian American Income and Buying Power

As a group, Asian Americans tend to be a wealthy segment of the U.S. population. Forty percent of all Asian and Pacific Islander families had incomes of $75,000 or more, compared with 35% of non-Hispanic white families. As Table 6.8 reveals, among married-couple families, 44% of Asians and Pacific Islanders had incomes of $75,000 or more, about 4% higher than their non-Hispanic white counterparts. The median household income for Asians in 2004 was $57,518—the highest among all race groups. However, median household

Table 6.8: Married-Couple Family Income

Income	Asian and Pacific Islander	Non-Hispanic white
Less than $25,000	14.3%	11.8%
$25,000 to $34,999	7.4%	9.6%
$35,000 to $49,999	13.5%	15.0%
$50,000 to $74,999	20.6%	23.5%
$75,000 and over	44.2%	40.1%

Note. Data from "The Asian and Pacific Islander Population in the United States, March 2002" U.S. Census Bureau, retrieved from www.census.gov/population/www/socdemo/race/api.html.

Table 6.9: Asian Ownership of Firms by Subgroup (2002)

Group	Number of firms	Percent of total	Receipts (in billions of U.S. dollars)	Percent of total
Asian-owned	1,104,189	100.0%	$326.4	100.0%
Chinese	290,197	26.3%	$106.3	32.6%
Indian	231,179	20.9%	$89.0	27.3%
Korean	158,031	14.3%	$46.9	14.4%
Vietnamese	147,081	13.3%	$15.7	4.8%
Filipino	128,223	11.6%	$14.6	4.5%
Japanese	86,863	7.9%	$30.6	9.4%
Other Asian	71,439	6.5%	$20.3	6.2%

Note. The 2002 Survey of Business Owners (SBC) defined Asian-owned businesses as firms in which Asians own 51% or more of the stock or equity of the business. Data from 2006 census, U.S. Census Bureau. Améredia: Asian American Business Ownership. Retrieved from htt;://www.ameredia.com/demographics/business_ownership.html.

income varied greatly by Asian group. For Indians, for example, the median income was $66,771, while, for Vietnamese Americans, it was $45,980.

The relatively high-income profile of the Asian American market is a reflection of the value of education as well as the unusually high rate of entrepreneurial activity common to this market. According to a report released in May of 2006 by the U.S. Census Bureau, the number of Asian American–owned businesses grew 24% between 1997 and 2002—approximately twice the average for all businesses. The 1.1 million businesses generated more than $326 billion in revenues, up 8% from 1997. In terms of ownership by Asian American subgroups, the majority (26.3%) were owned by Chinese Americans. Indians owned another 20.9% (see Table 6.9 for breakdowns). In total, there were 49,578 Asian American–owned firms with receipts of $1 million or more. These firms accounted for 4.5% of the total number of Asian American–owed firms and nearly 68% of their total receipts. Nearly one-third of Asian American–owned businesses had paid employees. These 319,300 firms employed more than 2.2 million people and generated nearly $291 billion in revenues. There were 1,863 Asian American–owned firms with one hundred employees or more, generating nearly $52 billion in gross receipts. Nearly half (49%) of such firms were located in California, New York, and Texas—and Los Angeles County had, by far, the largest number of Asian American–owned firms with nearly 13% of all such businesses.

In terms of industries with the most Asian-owned firms, personal, repair, and maintenance services ranked number one—accounting for 188,673 of the 1.1 million firms. However, professional, scientific, and technical services ranked second, with 154,235 companies (see Figure 6.3).

Figure 6.3: Industries with the Most Asian-Owned Firms

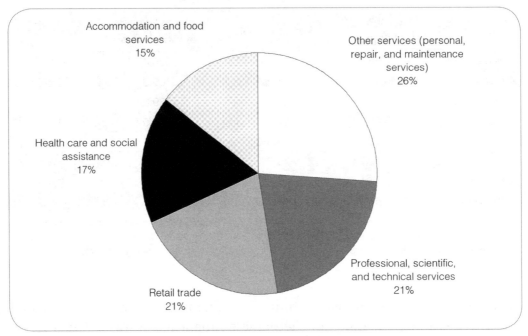

Note. Data from "Survey of Business Owners: Asian Owned Firms," U.S. Census Bureau, 2002. Revenues for Asian-owned Firms Surpass $326 Billion, Number of Businesses up 24%, U.S. Census Bureau News, May 16, 2006. Retrieved from htt;://www.census.gov/Press-Release/www/releases/archives/business_ownership/00681.

The Asian Real Estate Association of America (AREAA) and the University of California, Los Angeles (UCLA) Asian American Studies Center recently released a comprehensive analysis of home ownership trends among the Asian American consumer market ("UCLA Study," 2006). The AREAA/UCLA study found that Asian Americans have seen the fastest growth in home ownership attainment since 2000 (growing from 52% to nearly 60%) of any population, and their income and credit profile suggests that this growth will continue into the future. Yet, Asian American home ownership still lags behind owner-ship rates of the national (69%) and non-Hispanic white (76%) populations. However, home ownership rates for Asian and Pacific Islander naturalized-citizen householders (70.3%) were higher than their native-born Asian Pacific Islander householder counterparts (56.5%). Furthermore, among the natural-ized-citizen householders born in Asia, 81% of those who entered the United States in 1974 or earlier were homeowners, compared with 66% for those who entered in 1975 or later, suggesting that longer periods of residency among this group increased home ownership rates.

Asian American consumers wield disproportionately large clout in terms of their purchasing power when compared to the absolute size of the Asian popu-lation. Between 1990 and 2001, Asian Americans' spending power increased 125%, from $118 billion to $253 billion. During the same time period, the

Figure 6.4: Asian American Buying Power Compared to the Buying Power of U.S. States

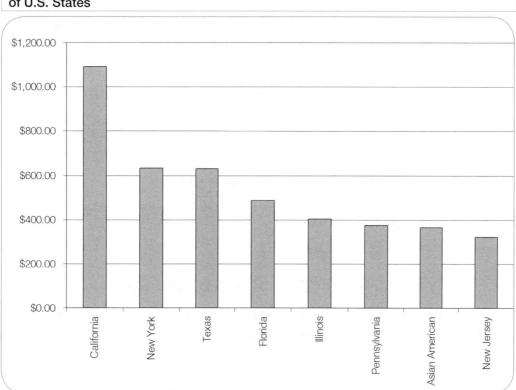

Note. Data from Selig Center for Economic Growth, 2004, University of Georgia. A Profile on Asian Americans, Asian American Advertising Federation. Retrieved from www.3af.org/3AFAsianUS0305.pdf

buying power of the United States as a whole increased by only 71%. By 2004, Asian Americans' buying power had reached $363 billion. This suggests that, as a group, Asian American consumers collectively had $41 billion more in buying power than all consumers in the state of New Jersey, the seventh most populous state in this country (see Figure 6.4) Projections from the Selig Center for Economic Growth indicate that Asian American spending power will reach $579 billion by 2010, an increase of nearly 400% since 1990—a figure that is substantially larger than the increases projected for Caucasians (164%) and African Americans (222%) and that is nearly equal to the 413% leap predicted for Hispanics ("'Invisible' Market," 2006).

The five states with the largest Asian American markets account for 62% of the group's buying power (see Table 6.12). In comparison, the five states with the largest total U.S. buying power account for only 38% of the total U.S. buying power.

Table 6.10: Top Five States in Terms of Asian American Buying Power

Rank	State	Population (in millions)	2003 buying power (in billions of U.S. dollars)	2008 buying power (in billions of U.S. dollars)[a]
1.	California	4.0	$122	$176
2.	New York	1.0	$34	$51
3.	New Jersey	0.5	$21	$34
4.	Texas	0.6	$20	$24
5.	Hawaii	0.5	$17	$21

Note. The Selig Center's data for Asians combines two categories: those who identified themselves as Asian alone or as Native Hawaiian and other Pacific Islanders alone. [a] =Projected Data from U.S. Census Bureau, 2000, and the Selig Center for Economic Growth, 2003. Asian American Market Profile, Magazine Publishers of America. Retrieved from www.magazine.org/marketprofiles.

Asian American Shopping Behavior

While whites continue to account for the majority of consumer spending in the United States, their share has been declining over the years. Consequently, understanding the unique spending and shopping habits of ethnic consumer groups is imperative for marketers. However, surprisingly little market research on Asian Americans exists, particularly when analyzing various subgroups by country of origin. And much of the research that is available is proprietary. Yet, what is known about this market makes it particularly appealing. Asian American consumers are intensely brand loyal. A survey of 1,600 Asian Americans showed that this group has a strong attraction to brand names, with 72% reporting that brand names are a strong influence on their purchase decisions, in contrast with 34% of the general population (Kaufman-Scarborough, 2000). If marketers are fortunate enough to capture a segment of the Asian American market, and those consumers become brand loyal, that loyalty will commonly be spread by word of mouth to others, including new immigrants.

As noted previously, many Asian Americans are immigrants, and, back in Asia, purchasing American brands is a sign of prestige. In China, in particular, American products have a stellar reputation. When those immigrants come to the United States, they bring with them a marked preference for the American brands they previously bought in Asia. For example, 50% of Chinese American households polled reported using Tylenol—with Advil coming in a distant second at 9%—not because Tylenol is disproportionately promoted in the Asian community, but because nearly 70% of Chinese Americans were born in China, where Tylenol is a leading brand, and Advil has yet to create a presence (Woods, 2000). Similarly, McDonald's hamburgers, Coca-Cola, Pantene shampoo, and IBM computers—all marketed heavily in China—are also popular among American Chinese immigrants (Lindorff, 1999).

Filipino Americans tend to look for the "made in the USA" mark on products when shopping. Kaufman-Scarborough (2000) notes that this can be explained by the presence of factories in the Philippines that contract the manufacturing of top name brands, such as Nike and Lacoste. The Philippine-made products are cheaper than the U.S.-made counterparts, so Filipinos tend to prefer the U.S.-made versions as a sign of status. Upon migrating to the United States, they continue this pattern and seek products made in the United States, as assurance of both quality and status. Overall, Asians also tend to be very status conscious and will spend their money on premium brands, such as Bavarian Motor Works (BMW) and Mercedes-Benz and the best French cognac and Scotch whiskey.

While brand name products are important, most Asian Americans are price-driven shoppers and, compared to U.S. adults as a whole, are often drawn by sales and coupons to stores they may not typically frequent, are willing to travel an hour or more to factory outlet stores (as they appreciate Western brand names), and often postpone purchases until items go on sale (Market Research/Packaged Facts, 2006). Kang and Lee Advertising (n.d.) note that, among the Asian American subgroups, Chinese, Vietnamese, Japanese, and Indians are among the most price and value conscious shoppers. J. C. Penney has been appealing to Asian American shoppers since 1996, when it turned to interTrend Communications for assistance in targeting Chinese and Vietnamese females in northern California—a region that boasts the highest Chinese population in the United States. The retailer relied on price promotions and in-store displays to present itself as offering quality and value to Asian shoppers. Julia Huang of interTrend notes, "women are usually the decision makers (and shoppers) in the Asian family. They are very price conscious. Sales, promotions and sweepstakes are the main forces that drive them to a store and to make purchases" ("'Invisible' Market," 2006). See Figure 6.5 for a J. C. Penney ad promoting savings of up to 50% to Asian American customers.

Research has shown that 96% of Asian Americans shop at Asian stores. For decades, small Asian grocery stores were fixtures of most Asian communities. And, until recently, a typical outing by an Asian immigrant family to purchase groceries involved at least two stops. First, a visit to an Asian store—often a smaller mom-and-pop shop—would provide the family access to Asian specialty products, including imported dry and canned goods and the freshest Asian-specific produce, seafood, and meats. Then, a second stop at a mainstream supermarket would fill in gaps on the grocery list for nonethnic products, such as household cleaners, paper products, and some mainstream packaged goods. But the retail landscape is rapidly evolving to meet the needs of the many burgeoning Asian communities around the country. The boom-

Figure 6.5: J. C. Penney Ad Promoting Huge Savings to Asian Shoppers

ing Asian population has spurred a rapid rise of Asian-owned and -operated supermarket chains, offering families one-stop shopping. Dedicated Asian staff, in-language signage, and culturally relevant promotions and advertising have enabled such stores to become the new food destinations for these communities (Gitlin, 2005). Examples include 99 Ranch Market, a large chain of Chinese supermarkets that first appeared in northern and Southern California, but have since expanded to Las Vegas, Phoenix, and Atlanta. Similarly, the Han Ah Reum chain, renamed H Mart, which directly caters to the Korean communities around the country, already boasts more than fifteen stores in New York, New Jersey, Maryland, Virginia, and Georgia. In many cases, such stores are anchors for new Asian shopping malls, which are also sprouting up across the country. For example, the Great Wall Shopping Mall in Kent, Washington, sells everything from bubble tea to *pho,* to jade necklaces to anime, to meet the needs of the diverse local Asian community. The developers strived to provide a "venue in which the Asian community can congregate." By offering authentic Asian shopping and eating experiences, the developers say the mall fosters an atmosphere that bridges the various ethnicities within the Asian community (Park, 2006). Indeed, the mall includes a variety of Asian restaurants, including Imperial Garden Seafood Restaurant, Pho To Chau, Bangkok Café, and Eddokko Japanese Restaurant. The mall is also home to a bubble tea café, a bookstore, clothing and handbag stores, and herbal and gift shops. 99 Ranch Market is also a major tenant. To further foster and promote diversity, the mall organizes six cultural festivals throughout the year. The events usually take up an entire Saturday and feature cultural performances like singing and dancing and the foods and customs of a particular community. Major grocery chains are beginning to sit up and pay attention. Albertsons, for example, has made a strong commitment to reach Asian shoppers. Albertsons has taken to printing ads in Chinese, Tagalog, and Vietnamese and has signed on to spots on ethnic television and radio shows. However, the message alone doesn't draw the clients. The grocer has studied what products for which its growing client base is looking. Store shelves display soy sauce, oyster sauce, fish sauce, coconut juice, chili paste, fermented black beans, and fifty-pound sacks of rice alongside more mainstream condiments, such as ketchup, mustard, and Worcestershire sauce. Chickens packaged with feet and head intact and head-on shrimp appeal to Asian consumers. Traditional and cultural celebrations also play a role. Albertsons offers coupons in lucky red envelopes for Lunar New Year and sells tasty moon cakes for the autumn moon festival (Soo, 2002). Other major grocery chains located in areas heavily populated by Asian groups are likely to follow suit.

The 2003 Consumer Expenditure Diary Survey (Tsai & Tan, 2006) reveals that Asian households spend, on average, $60.16 per week on food for consumption at home, nearly the same amount as all other households (who spend $59.45 per week). But what Asian American consumers buy at the supermarket is as different from the white population as where they shop. Among food categories, Asian households spend significantly more on fruits ($7.54 versus $5.30 per week for other households) and vegetables ($7.48 versus $4.84 per week for other households) and significantly less on dairy ($4.54 versus $6.36 per week for other households) and oils ($1.10 versus $1.67 per week for other households). Asian households also spend less on sweets ($1.69 versus $2.31 per week for other households) but four times more than other households on rice ($1.25 versus $0.28 per week for other house-

Table 6.11: Ranking of Food-at-Home Items by Expenditure Shares

Rank	Items purchased by Asian households	Items purchased by other households
1.	Fresh vegetables	Baked products
2.	Seafood	Beef
3.	Fresh fruit	Other dairy
4.	Baked products	Pork
5.	Poultry	Fresh fruit
6.	Beef	Fresh vegetables
7.	Pork	Other prepared foods
8.	Other dairy	Poultry
9.	Processed fruit	Carbonated drinks
10.	Cereal	Cereal
11.	Milk products	Milk products
12.	Other prepared food	Sweets
13.	Other nonalcoholic drinks	Seafood
14.	Snacks	Processed fruit
15.	Sweets	Snacks
16.	Condiments	Frozen and prepared meals
17.	Other meats	Other meats
18.	Carbonated drinks	Condiments
19.	Rice	Processed vegetables
20.	Processed vegetables	Other nonalcoholic drinks
21.	Frozen and prepared meals	Coffee
22.	Eggs	Eggs
23.	Tea	Packaged and canned soup
24.	Packaged and canned soup	Tea
25.	Coffee	Rice

Note. From "Food-at-Home Expenditures of Asian Households," by S.-L. Tsai and L. Tan, June, 2006, Monthly Labor Review, p. 23.

holds), two times more on seafood ($5.88 versus $2.28 per week for other households), and almost two times more on fresh vegetables and fresh fruits. In terms of share of total food-at-home expenditures, almost one-quarter of the Asian households' expenditures were allocated to fruits and vegetables, mostly to fresh fruits (8.8%) and fresh vegetables (10.4%). In contrast, fruits and vegetables composed only about one-sixth of other households' food-at-home expenditures. Meats made up 30.1% of Asian households' food-at-home expenditures, with seafood composing 9.8%. In contrast, meats composed 26.6% of other households' food-at-home expenditures, with a smaller share to seafood (3.8%). The shares of dairy (7.5% versus 10.7% for other households), beef (5.7% versus 8.0% for other households), and oils (1.8% versus 2.8% for other households) were significantly less for Asian households. Low levels of expenditures on dairy products were to be expected, given that 72% to 90% of Asians are lactose intolerant. Table 6.11 presents rankings of food-at-home items by expenditure shares for Asian households versus other households. Differences in weekly average expenditures between Asian American households and other households on food items suggests that race clearly plays a role in spending on grocery items.

The 2003 Consumer Expenditure Diary Survey also revealed that Asian Americans have lower expenses on entertainment, health insurance, medical services, drugs, and medical supplies. But Asian Americans do spend a larger amount on apparel and services for children younger than two years of age. And, as gift giving plays an important role in many Asian cultures, they tend to have higher expenses on gifts of goods and services. Gifts are purchased both for family within the United States, as well as relatives in their country of origin. They tend to own more expensive homes and pay higher rent than other groups. Mortgage interest, property taxes, personal insurance, and pensions take up larger portions of their budgets. They also spend more on vehicle insurance than other groups. Foreign travel back to their country of origin is also a huge expense for Asian Americans, as they value maintenance of family ties (Corrie, 2005). Table 6.12 reveals additional shopping behaviors characteristic of Asian American consumers.

Who's Talking to Asian Americans?

The Asian American market receives only a tiny fraction of the resources earmarked for multicultural marketing in the United States. As previously noted, the lion's share is geared toward the Hispanic market, with a significantly smaller portion devoted to targeting African Americans. In comparison, only a pittance is devoted to reaching Asian Americans. The Asian American Advertising Federation estimates that, in 2004, approximately $3.9 billion

Table 6.12: Asian American Consumer Behavior	
Consumer behavior	Asian index[a]
Member of private fitness club	136
Uses contact lens cleaning solutions	161
Uses facial cleansing creams, lotions, and gels	136
Has mutual fund / brokerage accounts	124
In the past three months:	
Has attended six or more movies	148
Has shopped at home electronics stores	128
Has shopped at office supply / computer stores	123
Agrees a lot with the statement:	
"I normally buy cars brand new"	148
"I prefer food presented as an art form"	211
"I go shopping frequently"	129
"I vacation somewhere different every time"	124
"I love the idea of traveling abroad"	177

Note. Data from Simmons NCS, Fall 2003. A Profile on Asian Americans, Asian American Advertising Federation. Retrieved from www.3af.org/3AFAsianUS0305.pdf.

a=An Index of 100 is the national average. For example, Asian Americans are 48% more likely than the average American to purchase a brand new car.

was spent on appealing to Hispanic consumers, and another $1.7 billion was spent on African Americans—figures that dwarf the $100 million dedicated to Asian Americans ("'Invisible' Market," 2006). Asian Americans may be just one-third the size of the Hispanic population, but their combined buying clout is well over half of that of Hispanics. In neglecting to speak directly to this audience, marketers risk ignoring a particularly appealing demographic group. Ironically, American businesses are probably spending more on marketing and branding campaigns in China than they are on marketing to the Asian American community, though America's nearly 12 million Asians are purchasing more American goods and services than all of China's 1.3 billion people put together.

Although there is no official third-party monitoring system for advertising spending in the Asian American market, Admerasia identifies the top advertising categories in rank order as financial services, telecommunications, travel, automotive, health insurance and medical facilities, and apparel (Asian American Market Profile, Magazine Publishers of America, retrieved from www.magazine.org/marketprofiles). Table 6.13 reveals the top ten advertisers in the Asian American market, according to Admerasia's internal media tracking.

That the top three advertisers are telecommunication services providers should come as no surprise, given that over 60% of Asians who live in this

Table 6.13: Top Ten Advertisers in the Asian American Market in 2002	
Rank	Company
1.	AT&T
2.	MCI
3.	Verizon
4.	Ford Motor Company
5.	General Motors
6.	New York Life Insurance Company
7.	HSBC
8.	Office of National Drug Control Policy
9.	Asiana Airlines
10.	China Airlines

Note. Data from Admerasia, 2001. Asian American Market Profile, Magazine Publishers of America. Retrieved from www.magazine.org/marketprofiles.

country are foreign born and maintain close ties with families in various parts of the world. As can be seen from Table 6.13, consumer packaged goods and, in particular, food and beverage advertisers have been slow to appeal to the Asian American market. Among the few who have are Anheuser-Busch, Hormel, and Kraft Foods, which began targeting Chinese Americans as recently as 2005. Kraft developed in-language print ads for Oreo cookies, Ritz, Kraft Barbecue Sauce, Capri Sun, and Philadelphia Cream Cheese. The ads appeared in Chinese newspapers in Los Angeles and New York and were aimed at immigrant, Chinese-speaking moms. Brand ambassadors were deployed to retailers to offer samples, give basic product information, teach shoppers where Kraft brands are merchandized in-store, and provide tips on things like which products are good to pack in lunch boxes as snacks (Reyes, 2005). Kraft also launched a Web site (http://www.krafthealthyliving.com) to promote recipes, such as Nutty Pineapple Tofu Fried Rice, which calls for Planters Peanut Oil and Planters Sliced Almonds, and Quick Veggie and Beef Noodle Bowl, made with Kraft Light Done Right Reduced-Fat Dressing ("'Invisible' Market," 2006).

How to Create Ads That Persuade

Marketers use the term *Asian American* as a default descriptor, as this audience is amazingly diverse. According to Saul Gitlin, executive vice-president of strategic services at Kang and Lee Advertising, "There is no such thing as a blanket Asian American strategy" (Dobrow, 2006). Some advertisers and agencies have defined segments of the Asian American market to strengthen their efforts in reaching this varied group (Magazine Publishers of America, n.d.).

For example, Admerasia, one of the largest advertising and multicultural marketing agencies specializing in this segment, clusters various Asian American subgroups into three broader regional groups:

> *Northeast Asians:* People coming from countries such as China, Taiwan, Japan, Korea, and Vietnam, who share linguistic and religious similarities.
> *Southeast Asians:* People coming from countries such as the Philippines, Malaysia, Indonesia, and Cambodia, who share a strong influence from the Portuguese, Spanish, and/or French.
> *South Asians:* People coming from countries such as India, Pakistan, and Bangladesh, who are either Hindu or Muslim but share a strong British influence.

Notes Gitlin,

> there may be opportunities to create a single message or platform for (North) East Asian groups—Chinese and Koreans—but anybody who tries to target Chinese Americans and Indian Americans with the same campaign is going to end up doing more harm than good. (Dobrow, 2006)

Just as it would be a huge mistake to take a campaign originally created for the general market and translate it into Hindi (ninety-nine out of one hundred times, something important will get lost in the translation), it would be equally disastrous to assume that Northeast Asians and South Asians will respond to the same message, given the significant cultural and religious differences. Even advertising to regional groupings can be problematic. For example, some marketers have targeted Koreans but inadvertently used Japanese models in their ads, and, in another instance, a footwear ad depicted Japanese women performing foot binding, a practice done exclusively in China (Solomon, 1999). Customization is clearly absolutely essential. Indeed, according to the Knowledge Center's study, seven out of ten Asian Americans agree that a company who advertises to their segment cares for their community (Asian American Journalists Association, 2005).

Language may also prove to be an obstacle. Asian American immigrants bring more languages to the United States than any other ethnic group. For example, in India alone, more than fifteen languages are spoken—including Hindi, Punjabi, Gujarati, Bengali, Telugu, Marathi, Malayalam, Tamil, Kannada, Urdu, and Kashmiri, among others. The situation is further complicated by the multitude of dialects spoken by the various subgroups of the Asian American market. However, many Asian Americans do speak a fair degree of English before moving to this country and, once they are here, typically adopt English at a rapid pace. According to the 2000 census, the majority of Asian Americans speak English "well" or "very well." Fully one-fifth (21%) of Asian Americans indicate they only speak English. As might be expected, young Asian Americans are the most likely to speak only English (see Table 6.14 for a breakdown by age group). A relatively small segment (17%) of Asian Americans says that they

Table 6.14: English Language Capability among Various Age Groups
of Asian Americans

English language capability	Percent of age group		
	Asians, 5 to 17 years of age	Asians, 18 to 64 years of age	Asians, 65 years of age and older
Speak only English	30.6%	18.9%	18.6%
Speak English "very well"	44.7%	40.1%	21.8%
Speak English "well"	17.6%	24.3%	18.7%
Speak English "not well"	6.5%	14.1%	24.3%
Speak English "not at all"	0.5%	2.7%	16.6%

Note. Data from American Demographics analysis of census 2000 data, as cited in "The A List," by K. Li, 2003, *Folio*, 32(5), p. 30.

cannot speak English "at all" or at least "not very well," (Magazine Publishers of America, n.d.).

Despite their English language capabilities, among the 9.5 million Asian Americans ages five years and older, well over three-quarters (79%) speak a language other than English at home. For example, the U.S. Department of Commerce reports that 83% of Chinese exhibit a preference to communicate in their own language. Indeed, next to Spanish, Chinese is the most widely spoken non-English language in the country (spoken by some 2.2 million Americans). Also among the top ten most frequently spoken non-English languages in this country are Tagalog (spoken by 1.3 million Filipinos), Vietnamese (1.1 million speakers), and Korean (966,959 speakers). Ninety-six percent of Vietnamese Americans and 88% of Korean Americans prefer to speak in their respective languages at home.

Kaufman-Scarborough (2000) provides the following insights into commercial communication languages preferences by Asian subgroup: Regarding Chinese Americans, Kaufman-Scarborough notes that well over three-quarters report wanting in-language advertising, yet the language issue is quite complex. For instance, recent immigrants regularly read and watch in-language media, reinforcing both reading and hearing their homeland tongues. In contrast, U.S.-born Chinese speak the language but may not read or write it. Thus, printed messages provided in Chinese may be confusing for those born in this country, while audio may be effective. While the population has several distinct language groups and dozens of dialects, Cantonese and Mandarin are the most accepted forms of Chinese in the United States. English skills are comparatively minimal among Korean Americans, therefore marketing to this group is most effective when done in the language of origin. Filipinos feel that promotional efforts to their group should include in-language media, even though a majority of them read and write English. Sixty-six percent prefer in-language media advertising. In contrast to Chinese, Koreans, and Filipinos, Indians find English to be highly acceptable for advertising. However, they also welcome use of Indian language in promotional messages, with 55% preferring in-language media. Among Japanese Americans, in-language media are preferred by 42%. Interestingly, research has shown that preference for native-language media often *increases* as Asians reside in the United States for longer periods. However, while it is safe to assume that the majority of Asian Americans groups are similar in preferring to receive advertising in their own language, advertisers are cautioned that those who are more highly acculturated and those who are second- and third-generation Asian Americans may well prefer English messages.

How to Reach Them: Media

The strong in-language preference exhibited by nearly every Asian American subgroup is further evidenced by the rapid growth in Asian-language media over the past two decades. Back in 1990, there were only 200 to 225 Asian media organizations. Today, there are some 625 nationally circulated Asian-language newspapers and magazines, as well as Asian-language cable channels and radio stations, available to advertisers (Vence, 2005). These Asian-language media typically offer much cheaper ad rates than mainstream media—for example, a thirty-second ad on a local Korean or Chinese TV station in Los Angeles could cost less than $1,000, and a full page ad in a local Chinese newspaper runs about $1,500. On the downside, however, much of Asian media is unaudited.

According to the Jack Myers Media Business Report (Myers, 2005), when asked to identify the three media types that are the most valuable to them among thirteen options, 54% of Asian Americans ranked e-mail as their most valuable medium, followed by broadcast television (51%) and Internet Web sites (46%). Cable/satellite basic television networks ranked fourth with this group (40%), and Internet search engines ranked fifth (31%). Only 12% of Asian Americans ranked pay television among their top three most valuable media, and just 8% gave the nod to radio. In terms of time spent with media, Asian Americans spent the least amount of time with television, but the most time in sending e-mails and instant messaging. While the average American spent three hours and forty-two minutes a day watching television, Asian Americans viewed just three hours of television per day but spent two hours and twelve minutes sending e-mails and instant messaging daily, plus a total of three hours and forty-eight minutes online daily (versus one hour and forty-two minutes, and three hours and thirty-six minutes, respectively, for average Americans).

Broadcast Media

Kang and Lee Advertising (n.d.) provide the following information on television and radio stations available to the six largest Asian American sub-groups—representing 87.5% of the Asian segment:

Chinese Americans

- There are twenty-five Chinese-language TV stations in the United States—including some twenty-four-hour TV stations.
- Chinese-language television programming is rapidly growing and is available through satellite and local cable, as well as UHF.
- Chinese-language TV features locally produced programming, as well as the latest news/entertainment content from Asia.
- California is the most developed of the Chinese broadcast markets.
- There are seventeen Chinese-language radio stations in the United States—including some twenty-four-hour radio stations.
- A number of programs/stations are available in each major geographic market. In most markets, radio programming is available in the two major Chinese dialects (Mandarin and Cantonese) and is available on both AM and FM frequencies.
- Availability of Chinese radio has been growing rapidly within the past five to ten years.

Filipino Americans

- There are twenty-four Filipino TV stations in the United States—including some twenty-four-hour TV stations.
- Filipino television programming is also available through satellite, local cable, and UHF.
- Filipino TV features some locally produced programs (news), as well as the latest entertainment content from the Philippines.
- As with the Chinese market, California is the most developed of the Filipino markets.
- There are eight Filipino radio stations in the United States—including some twenty-four-hour radio stations.
- One to two stations are available in major geographic markets
- Some twenty-four-hour stations are available both off-line and online.

Indian Americans

- There are twenty-six Indian-language TV stations in the United States—including some twenty-four-hour TV stations.

- Indian television programming is available through satellite and local cable, as well as UHF, although national satellite channels dominate.
- Indian TV features only a very small amount of locally produced programming (variety shows), with the majority of content coming from South Asia.
- There are seventeen Indian-language radio stations in the United States—including some twenty-four-hour radio stations.
- One to two stations are available in major geographic markets
- Some twenty-four-hour stations are available both off-line and online.

Korean Americans

- There are sixteen Korean-language TV stations in the United States—including some twenty-four-hour TV stations.
- Korean-language television programming is rapidly growing and is available through satellite, local cable, and UHF.
- Korean TV features only a very small amount of locally produced programming (news), with the majority of content produced in Korea.
- Los Angeles and New York City are the most developed of the Korean broadcast markets.
- There are thirteen Korean-language radio stations in the United States—including some twenty-four-hour radio stations.
- A number of programs/stations are available in each major geographic market. In most markets, radio programming is available on both AM and FM frequencies.
- Some twenty-four-hour stations are available both off-line and online.

Vietnamese Americans

- There are twelve Vietnamese-language TV stations in the United States.
- Vietnamese-language television programming is available through local cable, as well as UHF.
- Vietnamese-language TV features some locally produced programming, with the majority of news/entertainment content coming from Vietnam and other parts of Asia.
- California is, by far, the most developed of the Vietnamese broadcast markets.
- There are eleven Vietnamese-language radio stations in the United States—including some twenty-four-hour radio stations.
- A number of programs/stations are available in each major geographic market. Programming is available on both AM and FM frequencies.

- The availability of Vietnamese radio has been growing rapidly within the past five to ten years.

Japanese Americans

- There are twenty-three Japanese-language TV stations in the United States—including some twenty-four-hour TV stations.
- Japanese-language television programming is available through satellite, local cable, and UHF.
- Japanese TV predominantly offers programming content from Japan.
- California and New York are the most developed of the Japanese broadcast markets.
- There are five Japanese-language radio stations in the United States—including some twenty-four-hour radio stations.
- A small number of programs/stations are available in each major geographic market. In most markets, radio programming is only available on the AM frequencies.

With the dozens of different Asian languages, most of the more than 120 Asian-targeted networks position themselves as tiny premium services (Winslow, 2005). However, there has been a flurry of activity in just the past two years, as broadcasters have recognized that the third-largest ethnic group in the country is largely underserved. To fill the gap in the market, a number of new channels have been developed. In August 2004, ImaginAsian TV became the first twenty-four-hour, seven-day-a-week, Asian American channel. Programs include Japanese anime, movies from Bollywood—India's prolific film industry—Korean dramas, and cricket matches (Kalita, 2005). ImaginAsian TV will also air original English-language programming produced in the United States, such as *Uncle Morty's Dub Shack,* a comedy targeting second-generation Asian Americans, based on a group of Asian American men who work at a dubbing facility for B-grade movies. Content is either in English or subtitled. "We are trying to bridge the different Asian communities and groups, even from generation to generation, as well as the general market, which is increasingly fascinated with Asian culture," notes ImaginAsian Entertainment Chief Executive Michael Hong (Fernandez, 2005).

One of the strongest signs of growing Asian media clout came in mid-2005 when the International Channel was renamed AZN, which is short for Asian. The International Channel had previously been the United Nations of networks, featuring fare aimed at Russian, Italian, French, and Arabic viewers in their own languages, as well as a nightly three-hour *Asia Street* block. But business began to stall as pay channels catering to each ethnic group, such as TV Asia (South Asian) and SBTN (Vietnamese), began appearing on cable and satellite channels. The network decided to overhaul its programming to target Asian Americans—primarily second-generation viewers and those Asians who came to the United States as children and grew up in America, who are known as generation 1.5. AZN is looking to become the Asian equivalent of Black Entertainment Television (BET) (Sachdev, 2005). AZN Television's new lineup includes a heavy dose of Asian films, drama, anime, and originals. It will also feature Asian language news programs, pop music, documentaries, and sports. Many programs will air in their original Asian language, but subtitles in English will accommodate the more acculturated Asian Americans, as well as non-Asian viewers (Vence, 2005). Yet another network, American Desi (*Desi* is a slang term for South Asians) premiered in December 2004 on the DISH Network.

MTV has been particularly aggressive in efforts to appeal to younger Asian viewers. Nusrat Durrani, general manager / senior vice president of MTV World, spent more than two years researching Asian American channels, conducting focus groups and even house parties. He refers not just to "the need" but to "the hunger" for Asian American–targeted programming (Chang, 2006). As a result of his efforts, MTV Desi (targeting Asian Indians) was launched in July 2005, and MTV Chi—targeting Chinese Americans—was launched in December 2006. MTV K, for Korean Americans, premiered in 2006, and a fourth MTV channel targeting the Asian population is in the works. Content is custom tailored to Asian youth. For example, on MTV Chi, MTV personality and San Francisco native Suchin Pak produces and hosts *My Life,* an intimate look at issues affecting young people of color. In one episode, Pak examines Asian Americans' desire for eyelid surgery. Karen Lee, MTV Chi's first employee, produces news segments on Asian American artists and community issues. In one of her short clips, a young Chinese American talks candidly about how she perceives beauty and desirability. In another, slam poet Beau Sia declares, "There are no Asian American role models." But MTV clearly hopes to create role models and to shape how Asians Americans see themselves, and, just as importantly, how others see Asian Americans. On MTV Chi, for example, the hosts are the picture of Chinese American diversity. However, the *Top 10 Chi Countdown*—determined by online voting on the network's website—is not exclusive to Chinese and Chinese American artists. One show included New York–via–Austin indie rock from Johnny Hi-Fi, a Mandopop ballad from Jolin Tsai, Singaporean pop from Stephanie Sun, and Madonna's song "Hung Up." See Figure 6.6 for a magazine ad promoting MTV Chi. The headline reads "Find Your Chi Inside," and, inside the envelope, readers find a CD that gives them a taste of MTV Chi programming. The copy reads, "introducing MandarinDirect™ II service—get the best and latest news, info and entertainment from China, Hong Kong, and Taiwan with MTV Chi." MTV Chi is sold as part of an ethnic-specific international package on DirecTV.

Just who is watching Asian networks will become more apparent as Nielsen rolls out its local people meters. Obtaining reliable numbers in the past has been a real stumbling block for Asian television. All too often, cable channels exaggerated their numbers, which turned off advertisers. Local people meters now provide ratings for Asian American viewers in New York, Los Angeles, San Francisco, and Chicago. In January of 2005, KTSF San Francisco, a nearly thirty-year-old station operated by privately owned Lincoln Broadcasting Co., became the first Asian station to subscribe to the service. The station produces two hours of daily local programming, including newscasts produced with the *San Jose Mercury News* and spoken in Cantonese and Mandarin. It also acquires programming targeted to Indian, Filipino, Japanese, and Vietnamese viewers. Notes General Manager Michael Sherman, "The Nielsen numbers give us more credibility with advertisers" (Winslow, 2005). With numbers they can count on, major advertisers are increasingly giving the nod to Asian television. Major advertisers at KTSF include Wells Fargo and other banks, as well as General Motors, Ford Motor Company, and other major automobile manufacturers.

Print Media

Kang and Lee Advertising (n.d.) provide the following information on newspapers and magazines available to the six largest Asian American subgroups:

Chinese Americans

- There are sixty-eight Chinese-language newspapers and twenty Chinese magazines in the United States.
- The major publications among Chinese Americans have a diverse editorial focus, reflecting the various geographic origins of the community: mainland China, Hong Kong, and Taiwan. These daily publications provide the latest satellite news from Asia, coverage of U.S. national and local news, and local Chinese American community news. There are also many smaller community newspapers throughout the country, which are distributed for free.

Filipino Americans

- There are thirty-seven Filipino newspapers and eleven Filipino magazines in the United States.
- There are strong national newspapers, in addition to two to five local papers, typically available in top Filipino DMAs.
- The majority of print vehicles are published weekly.

Figure 6.6: Ad Promoting MTV Chi, Appealing to Chinese Americans

- The majority of publications reflect the Filipino culture but are printed in English, reflecting the high English-language competency within the Filipino community.

Indian Americans

- There are twenty Indian newspapers and thirteen Indian magazines in the United States.
- There are strong national newspapers and magazines, in addition to two to five free local newspapers, typically available in top Indian DMAs.
- Some print vehicles are published monthly, some are published weekly, and there are no daily publications.

Korean Americans

- There are forty-six Korean-language newspapers and sixteen Korean-language magazines in the United States.
- The major publications among Korean Americans provide the latest satellite news from Korea, coverage of U.S. national and local news, and local Korean American community news. There are also many smaller community newspapers throughout the country that are distributed for free.

Vietnamese Americans

- There are thirty-four Vietnamese-language newspapers and forty-five Vietnamese magazines in the United States.
- Typically, there are between two and ten local newspapers available in top Vietnamese DMAs.
- The majority of print vehicles are published daily, with some published weekly.

Japanese Americans

- There are twenty Japanese-language newspapers and eighteen Japanese magazines available in the United States.
- The major Japanese publications cater to Japanese expatriates, as well as Japanese Americans, and provide the latest satellite news from Japan, coverage of U.S. national and local news, and local Japanese American community news. There are also many smaller community newspapers in top Japanese DMAs.

According to a recent poll, Asian American newspapers reach a substantial percentage of Asian American adults in the United States. Approximately 80%

of all Korean, Chinese, and Vietnamese adults read an ethnic paper on a regular basis. The reach of Asian Indian, Filipino, and Japanese newspapers is smaller but still impressive—more than half of the adults in these groups read an ethnic newspaper a few times a month or more (New California Media, 2005).

One of the very few English-language newspapers appealing to the Asian community is *AsianWeek,* published in San Francisco. Founded in 1979, it is one of the most widely circulated newspapers of Pan-Asian news across all Asian ethnic groups, providing coverage of Asian American issues, such as Asian American college admissions and quotas on Chinese in competitive San Francisco examination schools.

The Asian American Journalists Association (AAJA) was founded in 1981 by a few Asian American and Pacific Islander journalists who felt a need to support one another and to encourage more Asian American and Pacific Islanders to pursue journalism at a time when there were few such faces in the media. In addition, the AAJA works for fair and accurate coverage of Asian Americans and Pacific Islanders. Today, the nonprofit organization has over two thousand members in nineteen chapters across the United States and Asia.

According to the Magazine Publishers of America (n.d.) nearly three-quarters of Asian American adults are magazine readers—a figure that is comparable to the general U.S. population. Asian Americans read, on average, eight magazine issues per month—nearly the same as the average U.S. magazine reader. Similar to the average U.S. consumer, Asian Americans read a variety of magazines in a range of categories that cater to their particular interests. The top five magazine categories ranked by a number of Asian American adult readers are news weekly, general editorial, women's, home service, and business/finance. This list differs only slightly from top categories for U.S. adults, among whom men's titles rank fifth, replacing business/finance. Table 6.15 reveals that Asian Americans index significantly above average for a number of different magazine titles.

The vast majority of Asian American publications are printed in the language of ethnic origin. English-language publications targeting the Asian American population are few and far between. In 1989, Jeff Kang created one of the first such publications targeting Asian Americans who were acculturated into the mainstream—*aMagazine* offered a mix of news, lifestyle, fashion, and politics. Most importantly, the title was distributed via major newsstands and bookstores. Initially, the publication fared well in ad sales, and major advertisers included IBM, Ford Motor Company, and Absolut Vodka. *aMagazine* jumped on the Internet bandwagon and launched a Web site, aOnline. At its peak in 1994, *aMagazine* had a circulation of around 200,000. But, during the mid-1990s, the title entered a downward spiral. After signing what appeared to be a savvy merger with Internet company Click2Asia, the magazine's very survival started to come into question. Investors encouraged the inclusion of

Table 6.15: Magazine Titles by Asian American Audience Composition

Magazine	Percent Asian American composition	Index
Percent of total U.S. adult population eighteen years of age and older	2.1%[a]	100
Fortune	6.2%	291
BusinessWeek	6.2%	287
Fast Company	5.6%	262
TENNIS Magazine	5.6%	262
Computer Shopper	5.5%	258
Popular Photography & Imaging	5.4%	250
PC Magazine	5.3%	247
W	5.3%	246
Forbes	5.0%	234
Best Life	4.8%	224
My Business	4.8%	222
Spin	4.6%	216
Entrepreneur Magazine	4.4%	206
Allure	4.4%	204
PC World	4.2%	194
Details	4.1%	193
GQ	4.1%	191

Note. Data from Mediamark Research Inc., Spring 2004. Asian American Market Profile, Magazine Publishers of America. Retrieved from www.magazine.org/marketprofiles. [a]=Census identifies Asian Americans from zero years of age and older.

more digital-sounding editorial material into the publication, and the quality of the content began to slip. As readership suffered, the magazine had difficulty attracting major investors, and these setbacks—coupled with the dot-com bust—ultimately contributed to the magazine's demise, ending a twelve-year run in 2001 (Farmer, 2004). Despite the outcome of *aMagazine,* a number of English-language Asian American magazines do continue to survive. Joining the ranks of older titles, such as *KoreAm Journal* (the nation's only English-language Korean American national magazine) and *Filipinas Magazine*—which have been in circulation for more than ten years—new magazines, including *Audrey* (appealing to Asian females) and *Noodle* (aimed at the gay Asian American audience), as well as *Yolk* and *Giant Robot* (both targeting young Asian Americans), have hit the scene with high hopes of cornering niches within the Asian American market. *Giant Robot* premiered in 1994, presenting a bento box of Asian American pop culture. The magazine includes articles on Hong Kong motion pictures, Japanese anime and toy fetishes, and U.S. indie rock. The magazine, which has spawned destination boutiques in New York, Los Angeles, and San Francisco (see Figure 6.7 for an ad promoting *Giant Robot's* Web site and stores), celebrates how much fun it is to be a young Asian American (Chang, 2006). Interestingly, the magazine's Web site notes that its readership is about half Asian, half not. The publishers of *Giant Robot* may be on to something. A new study on the cultural influence of Asian American youth, released by New American Dimensions and inter-Trend Communications, reveals that Asian American youth are increasingly generating some of the key trends in pop culture that are being embraced by the rest of mainstream American youth. According to the results of the study, "Made in America: Asian American Teens and Echo Boomers," Asian American young people are likely to see themselves as trendsetters in three distinct cultural categories: technology and gadgetry, anime and manga, and video gaming. "These results contrast with previous research we have conducted among Hispanic youth," says David Morse, president of New America Dimensions. "Whereas many second-generation Hispanic kids often exhibit their pride through their language and culture, Asian American youth seem to assert their pride in how they are shaping mainstream American culture" ("Asian American Youth," 2006).

The Internet

Lofty education and income levels have translated into a tremendous appetite for the Internet within the Asian American community. According to data collected by Améredia (2006), the integrated multicultural marketing firm, nearly three-quarters (72%) of Asian American adults have gone online, a significantly greater rate than the 58% of white adults, the 50% of Hispanic adults, and the 43% of African American adults. In addition, 70% of Asian American Internet users are online on a typical day—a figure that is much higher than it is for any other English-speaking ethnic or racial group. About half of Asian American users have been going online for more than three years, and 80% have been using the Web for two years or more, easily making Asian Americans the Web's most experienced ethnic group. It is estimated that 82% of Asian American households will be online by the end of 2007, compared to 69% of African American households and 68% of Hispanic households.

English is the most popular online language, accounting for 35.2% of the total online population; Chinese is the second most popular language at 13.7%, Japanese is the fourth most popular language at 8.4%, and Korean is the seventh most popular language at 3.9%. According to a Pew Internet and American Life Project survey (Fetto, 2002) just over one-third (34%) of Asian Americans get the day's news online, 27% seek out hobby information on a

Figure 6.7: Ad Promoting *Giant Robot's* Web Site and Stores

daily basis, 20% seek financial information on a typical day, and 19% look for political news and information on a daily basis (see Table 6.16). Yahoo!, which was used by 61% of total respondents in the past week, is most popular among Asian Americans (75%). A disproportionately high number of Asian Americans (72%) compared to the percentage of total respondents also say they use Google. In terms of buyer behavior, nearly 31% of online Asians have made five or more Internet purchases in a year, compared to 25.8% for whites, 13.8% for Hispanics, and 12.3% for African Americans.

Table 6.16: Activity Done Online on a Daily Basis[a] by Race

Activity	All races	Asians	Whites	Blacks	Hispanics
Get news	21%	34%	22%	15%	20%
Get financial information	13%	20%	14%	9%	10%
Get travel information	7%	14%	7%	7%	8%
Get hobby information	18%	27%	19%	17%	17%
Get political news and information	13%	19%	13%	9%	12%

Note. Data from the Pew Internet & American Life Project. Fetto, J. (2002, March). Cyber Tigers. American Demographics, Ithaca, 24(3), p. 9. [a]= Asked of respondents who have ever gone online.

Summary

In addition to being the fastest growing segment of the U.S. population, Asian Americans are a young, well-educated, and affluent market. As this group's size and influence continues to grow, advertisers and marketers will increasingly direct their attention to this ethnic audience. However, marketing to Asian Americans requires careful balance. While there are similarities that many Asian Americans share, such as a group orientation, high regard for family and community, and an emphasis on education and saving money, this segment should not be viewed as a single homogeneous group. The significant cultural and language differences among Asian subgroups cannot be overlooked by marketers and advertisers.

Some of the best resources providing support and guidance in developing marketing and advertising efforts targeting multicultural consumers are the advertising agencies specializing in those very markets. Such agencies are generally run by members of the ethnic group on which they concentrate and can provide invaluable insights into the culture of that market. Advertisers who avail themselves of the knowledge that these agencies bring to the table substantially increase their chances for success. Multicultural advertising agencies will be explored in the next chapter.

REFERENCES

Améredia. (2006). Asian American statistics. Retrieved from http://www.ameredia.com/resources/demographics/asian_american.html (http://www.ameredia.com/demographics/index.html).]

Angrisani, C. (2005, June 6). Wal-Mart may broaden Asian American campaign. *Supermarket News,* p. 36.

Asian American Journalists Association. (2005, November 2). Study on Asian American consumption trends. In *Community news.* Retrieved from http://www.aaja.org/news/community/2005_11_04_1

Asian American youth: America's new trendsetters; research shows youth generation's increasing influence on U.S. pop culture. (2006, July 26). *PR Newswire.*

Berg, I., & Jaya, A. (1993). Different and same: Family therapy with Asian-American families. *Journal of Marital and Family Therapy, 19,* 31–38.

Chang, J. (2006, February 24). Forget the white-bread: '80s MTV, now MTC Chi and other outlets cater to Asian Americans. *San Francisco Chronicle.*

Corrie, B. (2005, March 11). Asian Americans have big buying power. *Minneapolis St. Paul Business Journal.*

Davis, L. E., & Proctor, E. K. (1989). *Race, gender and class: Guidelines with individuals, families and groups* (p. 67). Englewood Cliffs, NJ: Prentice-Hall.

Desjardins, D. (2006, June 26). Multi-Asian sector has buying power. *Drug Store News,* p. 113.

Dobrow, L. (2006, June). Market focus: cracking the Asian conundrum. *Media Post Publications.*

Farmer, M. A. (2004, July 11). What's missing in mainstream media: Where are all the Asian American magazines? *DiversityInc.* Retrieved from http://diversityinc.com

Fernandez, M. E. (2005, January 6). Television; a united view from the East; ImaginAsian TV premiering today on Comcast cable aims to serve all Asian Americans. *Los Angeles Times,* p. E-16.

Fetto, J. (2002, March). Cyber Tigers. *American Demographics,* Ithaca, 24(3), p. 9.

Gitlin, S. (2005). Eastern influence. *Progressive Grocer, 84*(12), 34.

Hofstede, G., & Bond, M. H. (1988). The Confucius connection: From cultural roots to economic growth. *Organizational Dynamics, 16,* 5–12.

International Saving Comparisons (2005, June 29). Angry Bear. Retrieved from http://angrybear.blogspot.com/2005/06/international-saving-comparisons.html.

The 'invisible" market. (2006, February 1). *Brandweek.* Retrieved from http://www.brandweek.com/bs.news/spotlight/article_display.jsp?vnu_content_id=1001

Kalita, S. M. (2005, May 15). TV networks try to attract Asians and all their niches. *The Washington Post*, p. A-01.

Kang & Lee Advertising. (n.d.). Retrieved from http://www.kanglee.com

Kaufman-Scarborough, C. (2000). Asian American consumers as a unique market segment: fact or fallacy? *The Journal of Consumer Marketing, 17*(3), 249.

Kim, M. (1993). Transformation of family ideology in upper-middle-class families in urban South Korea. *International Journal of Cultural and Social Anthropology, 32*, 70.

Lee, S., Hanna, S., & Siregar, M. (1997). Children's college as a savings goal. *Financial Counseling and Planning, 8*(1), 33.

Li, K. (2003). The A list. *Folio, 32*(5), 30.

Lindorff, D. (1999). Marketers slowly begin to tap into U.S.'s rich Asian consumers. *Media Life*. Retrieved from http://www.medialifemagazine.com/news1999/dec99/news41220.html

Magazine Publishers of America. (n.d.). *Asian American market profile*. Retrieved from http://www.magazine.org/marketprofiles

Market Research/Packaged Facts. (2006, October 1). Consumer view: Asian Americans. *License!* Retrieved from http://www.licensemag.com/licensemag/article/articleDetail.jsp?id=377459

Myers, J. (2005, November 9). African Americans are most media-active and advertiser friendly audience. *Jack Myers MediaVillage.com*. Retrieved from http://www.mediavillage.com/jmr/2005/11/09/jmr-11–09–05/

Nanda, S. (1994). *Cultural anthropology* (5th ed., p. 349). Belmont, CA: Wadsworth Publishing.

New California Media. (2005). Ethnic media in America: The giant hidden in plain sight. *New America Media*. Retrieved from http://www.ncmonline.com

Park, Y. (2006, September 30). Kent mall becomes Asian destination. *Northwest Asian Weekly*, p. 9.

Philips, W. (1997, Winter). Culturally competent practice: Understanding Asian family values. *Children's Voice*.

Picture, B. (2006, January 5). The AsianBud-dy system. *AsianWeek*, p. 12.

Plumberg, K. (2006, March 29). Culture influences how many pennies get pinched. *Ezilon Infobase*. Retrieved from http://www.ezilon.com/information/article_16356.shtml

Reyes, S. (2005, July 25). Kraft initiative woos Asian American moms. *Brandweek*, p. 10.

Rossman, M. (1994). *Multicultural marketing: Selling to a diverse America*. New York: Amacom.

Sachdev, A. (2005, June 12). TV gains Asian flavor; as emigrants and their descendents become more numerous in the U.S. and build household incomes, more stations are tailoring programming to their tastes. *Chicago Tribune*, p. 1.

Samovar, L., Porter, R., & Stafani, L. (1998). *Communication between cultures* (3rd ed.). Belmont, CA: Wadsworth Publishing.

Schmelzer, R. (2006, March 13). The Asian answer. *PR Week*, p. 17.

Solomon, M. (1999). *Consumer behavior: Buying, having, and being.* Upper Saddle River, NJ: PrenticeHall.

Soo, J. D. (2002, September 11). Who's getting the message? Ethnic advertising finally recognized. *Asian Week,* p. 8.

Steinberg, L., Dornbusch, S.M., & Brown, B.B. (1992, June). Ethnic differences in adolescent achievement: An ecological perspective. *The American Psychologist,* Washington, 47(6), p. 723.

Sue, S., & Okazaki, S. (1990). Asian American educational achievements: A phenomenon in search of an explanation. *American Psychologist, 45*(8), 912–920.

Tsai, S.-L. S., & Tan, L. (2006, June). Food-at-home expenditures of Asian households. *Monthly Labor Review,* 15.

2001 Minority Retirement Confidence Survey: Minority groups express concerns about saving and retirement planning. (2001, May 10). *PR Newswire,* p. 1.

UCLA study predicts Asian Americans will lead future homeownership growth. (2006, May 21). *The Post Tribune,* p. G-1.

Vence, D. (2005, June 1). Asian media grow, firms take note. *Marketing News,* p. 11.

Wells Fargo becomes first major U.S. bank to offer remittance services to China, Vietnam; expands services to Philippines. (2006, October 24). *PR Newswire.*

Winslow, G. (2005, August 15). East meets local. *Broadcasting & Cable,* p. 20.

Woods, B. (2000, April 1). Asian persuasion. *PROMO.* Retrieved from http://promomagazine.com/mag/marketing_asian_persuasion/index.html

7

Advertising Agencies and Multicultural Consumers

Three types of advertising agencies are available to assist marketers in communicating with ethnic consumers. *General market* agencies are typically large agencies that work primarily on national campaigns and look at the consumer market as a whole. Some have hired ethnic professionals to provide insight into Hispanic, African American, and Asian American target audiences. *Multicultural* agencies have a more narrow focus than general market agencies but create commercials for more than one ethnic audience. For example, such a firm might have both Hispanic and African American divisions—or might even concentrate on all three of the major ethnic/racial groups. *Specialty* agencies hone their expertise on a single group. Often, the owners of these agencies are members of the target audience and have knowledge of smaller media outlets and nontraditional advertising venues. As yet another alternative, marketers may select a multicultural or specialty agency to work in tandem with their general market agency to reach the ethnic consumer.

General Market Advertising Agencies
and Ethnic Professionals

Diversify the industry to mirror the ethnic population of the United States. And do it by 2005. That was the challenge that Ed Wax, then chief executive officer (CEO) of Saatchi & Saatchi issued more than a decade ago in his last speech as chairman of the American Association of Advertising Agencies (AAAA) (Charski, 2004). Unfortunately, Wax's deadline was not met. While Hispanics, African Americans, and Asians make up 14%, 13%, and nearly 5% of the U.S. population, respectively, in advertising and related services, only the Asian population matches the nation's in percentage terms. Of the over 507,000 professionals employed in the field, Hispanics, African Americans, and Asian Americans account for only 16.7% of the total—and only 9.2% of managers, according to the U.S. Equal Employment Opportunity Commission. By comparison, the figures for other industries look significantly more positive. For example, in investment firms, ethnic employees make up 17.7% of professionals and 11.5% of managers, and the proportions for accounting firms are 23.8% for professionals and 12.9% for managers (Fernandez, 2004). Indeed, in 2004, the New York City Commission on Human Rights launched an investigation into the industry's hiring practices. After a nearly two-year investigation, which put under the microscope seventeen of the city's agencies, including BBDO, Saatchi & Saatchi, and Ogilvy & Mather, public hearings were scheduled for September of 2006—set to coincide with Advertising Week in New York, the industry's annual celebration (Sanders, 2006a). The city's Human Rights Commission's jurisdiction includes the ability to prosecute discrimination based on race, creed, color, and national origin in employment and various other areas. Those found to have violated the law would face fines as well as other penalties. An investigation of advertising's minority hiring practices was also undertaken back in the late 1960s. Of the forty agencies surveyed then, black employees represented just 3.5% of total employees. Though agencies agreed to implement improved hiring procedures, shockingly little has changed since those days (Sanders, 2006b). Now, under the threat of public embarrassment, the agencies renewed those promises. The hearings, a potential public relations disaster, were called off after the agencies signed agreements to boost minority hiring and retention (Howard, 2006). The agreements required that agencies submit to three years of monitoring by the city, under which the companies will report hiring, promotion, and retention figures to the commission each year. If they do not meet their goals, they will be required to hire an outside consultant to help them do so, among other measures. At the same time, the agencies agreed to set up diversity boards and to link progress on these issues to compensation. Executives who meet the new hiring goals will be rewarded accordingly. The agreements also require that agencies establish recruiting and internship programs through universities with large minority student populations (Cardwell & Elliott, 2006).

Clearly, mainstream agencies have a diversity problem. However, some agencies are beginning to pay attention. For example, David Bell, chairman and CEO of Interpublic Group (IPG), announced in 2003 the creation of a Diversity Task Force—IPG's first formalized effort in this area. Bell and his task force members generated the Interpublic Fellows Program, the only diversity-recruitment vehicle of its kind among the major holding companies. Bell wrote in an internal IPG memo,

> Most every brief from prospective clients now contain[s] diversity criteria. Nearly three-quarters of them require that a culturally diverse team work on the client's account. . . . We have to face up to this new reality by stepping up and setting the standard. (Charski, 2004).

Other agencies are taking steps in the right direction, as well. Each year, more and more agencies—as well as corporations—are participating in two valuable programs designed to increase the ranks of ethnic employees in ad agencies around the country. In 1996, the American Advertising Federation (AAF), which is the oldest national advertising trade organization representing some fifty thousand professionals in the advertising industry, launched its Most Promising Minority Student (MPMS) program. The program provides qualified minority candidates to corporations seeking top-tier advertising and marketing talent. In its nine-year history, the AAF's MPMS program has connected recruiters with 247 minority students who have demonstrated excellence. In a recent survey of AAF executives, more than 80% of advertising leaders said attracting and retaining multicultural talent is extremely or very important ("AAF Most Promising," 2005). Expanding on these efforts, the AAF established the Mosaic Center on Multiculturalism. This center implements all AAF multicultural and diversity initiatives and is the only national ad industry resource of its kind. The AAF Mosaic Council—which serves as the advisory board to the center—is an infrastructure of national advertisers, general market and minority advertising agencies, media organizations, and suppliers. As the advertising industry's premier think tank on diversity and multiculturalism, the council identifies best practices for achieving greater industry diversity and multiculturalism while advancing the common interest of all industry segments. The AAF's Mosaic Principles and Recommended Practices primary objective is to increase the representation of people of color throughout the business, to help companies achieve growth by leveraging multicultural and targeted ethnic marketing communications, and to promote fair competition. These voluntary guidelines have industry-wide support, including endorsements from the AAAA, the Association of National Advertisers (ANA), the Association of Hispanic Advertising Agencies (AHAA), Association of Asian American Advertising Agencies (AAAAA), the National Association of Black Owned Broadcasters (NABOB), and the National Association of Hispanic Publications (NAHP). Among the numerous companies and agencies that already have committed to adopting the principles are Procter & Gamble, DaimlerChrysler, Coca-Cola, Johnson & Johnson, Verizon Communications, and Kraft Foods. The principles and several of the recommendations are outlined in Figure 7.1. The AAF Mosaic Center also recognizes successful integrated multicultural marketing and diversity efforts that demonstrate the spirit of their Mosaic Principles and Recommended Practices through their annual Mosaic Awards. In addition, they host Mosaic Career Fairs to connect talented minority advertising, marketing, and communications students with industry professionals who are seeking entry-level candidates. Each year, students and corporate recruiters are brought together for one day to discuss potential career opportunities. Students also participate in a professional development seminar designed to increase their knowledge about resume writing, interviewing skills, and networking. More information on the MPMS program, Mosaic Career Fairs, and scholarships can be found at the AAF's Web site (http://www.aaf.org).

A second valuable program is coordinated by the AAAA. The AAAA is the national trade association of the advertising agency business. The nearly 1,200-member agency offices it serves in the United States employ some 65,000 people, offer a wide range of marketing communication services, and place 80% of all national advertising. The management-oriented association helps its members build their businesses and acts as the industry's spokesperson with government, media, and the public sector. The AAAA Multicultural Advertising Internship Program (MAIP) was launched in 1973. The internship offers promising multicultural students nationwide a chance to prove their ability in the real world with a ten-week paid summer internship at an advertising agency. Internships are offered in the following departments: account management, creative (art direction and copy writing), broadcast production, interactive technologies, media buying/planning, strategic/account planning, print product, and traffic. Agencies who have sponsored interns include BBDO New York, Campbell Mithun Advertising, DDB Worldwide, Euro RSCG Worldwide, FCB Chicago, Grey Worldwide, J. Walter Thompson (JWT) New York, Leo Burnett USA Inc., McCann Erickson, Ogilvy & Mather, Publicis Advertising, Saatchi & Saatchi, TBWA\Chiat\Day, and Young & Rubicam Chicago. Since the program was founded, more than 1,600 students have served as MAIP interns. More information about the AAAA MAIP can be found at the program's Web site (http://www.aaaa-maip.org/). Above and beyond the internship program, the AAAA has launched Operation Success, designed to increase ethnic diversity and inclusiveness in key operational areas of the advertising business. Operation Success focuses on three areas: (a) employee recruitment and retention, (b) training and development, and (c) vendor and supplier relationships.

Figure 7.1: Principles and Recommended Practices for Effective Advertising in the American Multicultural Marketplace)

Commit to identify and take advantage of growth opportunities in multicultural markets. In the advertising, marketing and media industries, we seek first to understand our markets and the communities we serve. We value a racially and culturally holistic approach to advertising and marketing. We make fully informed decisions by researching and evaluating consumer buying habits, current contributions to sales and/or profitability as well as growth potential. Our commitment includes investing sufficient financial resources commensurate with opportunities in all market segments and necessary to bring about the desired results.

Generate ideas and profits by practicing inclusiveness and fairness. We seek to promote the highest levels of creativity and success by promoting inclusiveness and fairness through the marketing and advertising process—from employment and career advancement within our organizations to competition and compensation for creative services and media buys. Collaboration between the general market agency, multicultural specialist agency and client team at the beginning of the overall planning process enhances our effectiveness and the likelihood of achieving goals.

Require accountability and measurable results. We require compliance with these principles in service to our clients, our customers, our employees and their communities, both as individual companies, and as an industry. By measuring and reporting on the effectiveness of our efforts, we can better target resources, increase return on investment and identify what works. By sharing what works, we stimulate innovation in our organizations and industries.

Regarding the second principle above, the AAF and its Business Practices Review Committee identified specific practical methods to help companies achieve this goal:

Recommendations for human resources diversity practices:
- Establish goals and accountability systems tied to the upward mobility of people of color. Tie executive compensation to achievement of diversity goals.
- Train, retain, develop and promote more multicultural professionals.
- Support and participate in industry-wide recruitment, professional development and retention efforts.
- Encourage business partners, vendors and suppliers to implement multicultural recruitment and human resource development initiatives.

Recommendations for inclusive advertising and marketing planning and execution:

- At the outset of the brand planning process involve all parties including multicultural agencies of record.
- Utilize the expertise of multicultural specialists. Ensure they are given the opportunity to perform the work and are compensated fairly for it.

Recommendations for implementation of fair business practices:

- Identify qualified multicultural staff; ensure they are considered for advancement opportunities and ensure they are evaluated using the same criteria as non-minority colleagues.
- Provide smaller minority-owned multicultural agencies with direct opportunities to compete.

From Mosaic Principles and Recommended Practices, by the American Advertising Foundation & the American Advertising Federation, 2006, retrieved from http://www.aaf.org/multi/pdf/mosaic_principles.pdf.

In terms of the first area, minority-owned recruiting firms are retained to identify candidates for employment to develop a diverse slate of candidates. A database of established minority professionals has been developed. Regarding training programs and development, the AAAA has encouraged the development of senior-level mentoring programs at agencies and has supported networking initiatives. Furthermore, the AAAA coordinated a program in conjunction with the City University of New York (CUNY) / Medgar Evers College and historically black colleges and universities and other institutions with strong minority enrollment to provide information, training, and education on advertising and careers in the advertising industry. Ad agency executives are encouraged to serve as instructors, mentors, and resources for students in the program. Finally, in terms of vendor and supplier relationships, participating agencies, in consultation with their clients, are encouraged to make coordinated efforts to increase the use of minority subcontractors. To that end, the AAAA has published a resource directory and convened a supplier trade show to facilitate the use of minority suppliers to the advertising industry. A program was designed to encourage and support the utilization of minority vendors and suppliers throughout the business ("AAAA Launches," 2004).

Despite the efforts of the AAF and the AAAA, a recent survey on recruiting and multicultural advertising trends, which complied the responses of 160 industry leaders representing all sectors of the industry, revealed the following:

- Only 15% categorized their organization as successful in recruiting and retaining minority talent.
- Internships are seen as the principal way to recruit minority talent.
- 27% do not utilize traditional minority recruitment methods like internships, award programs, minority job fairs, and on-campus recruiting.
- 37% of industry executives rate their organizations not at all or not very successful in obtaining the services of qualified minority vendors, while only 24% say they have been successful or very successful. ("AAF Surveys Reveal," 2006)

While diversity in general market agencies remains an issue, it must be stated that this has not prohibited some of these shops from developing highly effective advertising that touches ethnic consumers. Bill Duggan, executive vice president of the ANA, cites Procter & Gamble's campaign for CoverGirl as just one successful example. Created by Grey Worldwide, the campaign has featured Queen Latifah as its spokeswoman since 2001. CoverGirl's Queen Collection—a makeup line specifically formulated for women of color, which includes foundation, lip color, lip gloss, lip pencil, eye shadow quads, mascara, eyeliner, and nail color—was launched in early 2006 and is expected to gener-

Figure 7.2: Advertisement for CoverGirl's Queen Collection Created by Grey Worldwide

ate sales exceeding $10 million by the end of 2007 (Nagel, 2005). See Figure 7.2 for a sample ad from this campaign.

Multicultural and Specialty Advertising Agencies

In the 1960s and 1970s, few major advertising agencies launched campaigns directed at ethnic markets and even fewer hired minority professionals. This dearth led many African Americans and, later, Hispanics and Asian Americans to start up their own multicultural or specialty shops. Some suggest that the first black-owned agency actually dates back to 1956, when Vince Cullers Advertising was founded (Woods, 1995). UniWorld Group opened its doors in 1969 with the simple philosophy, "always show black consumers in positive situations." And Tom Burrell founded his agency in 1971. The company, now called Burrell Communications Group, offers clients advertising, promotions, and public relations services. While the majority of Hispanic agencies began to emerge in the mid-1980s, Conill opened its doors in New York City in 1968. In 1981, George San Jose founded the San Jose Group (SJG) in Chicago—to serve clients throughout the Spanish-speaking Americas. In 1985, Lopez Negrete was founded in Houston, Texas, and, two years later, Anita Santiago opened shop in Santa Monica, California. Today, there are more than seventy advertising agencies in the United States that cater exclusively to Hispanics. The majority of Hispanic shops are located in New York, Florida, California, and Texas—areas that tend to have the highest concentrations of Hispanic consumers. In comparison, most Asian American advertising agencies are relative newcomers. Dae Advertising was founded in San Francisco in 1990. InterTrend opened shop in Long Beach, California, in 1991. And, in 1997, AdAsia Communication was established in New York City. Many ethnic employees have been drawn to these ethnic shops, which are generally organized in much the same way as full-service agencies but specialize in reaching and communicating with minority markets. Ironically, as noted previously, the explosive growth in ethnic advertising has not led to similar growth in hiring among the major agencies. Most major agencies have largely relinquished ethnic markets to these newly established boutiques. Other conglomerates have taken a different approach. Rather than hiring more ethnic employees, some firms are tapping into these markets by purchasing established multicultural or specialty shops. For example, in 1987, Conill became part of Saatchi & Saatchi. The Bravo Group is Young & Rubicam's minority-oriented subsidiary. Advertising conglomerate WWP Group purchased 49% of African American firm UniWorld Group Inc. in 2000, while Omnicom Group bought a stake in Hispanic Agency Dieste Harmel and Partners in 2001. And, not long ago, Ogilvy & Mather bought the Hispanic agency Latin Works. "It appears that some would rather buy a successful multicultural firm than create these capabilities in-house," notes Saul Gitlin, executive vice president of Asian-focused Kang & Lee, which employs fifty Asian staffers in its New York office (Fernandez, 2004). The acquisition of ethnic agencies has allowed advertising conglomerates to assure their clients a standardized strategy and message for products across different audience segments—an increasingly common approach in the industry at large. In addition, given the trends reflected in the recent census figures, acquiring minority-owned advertising agencies is considered the politically correct thing to do when one's target audience is increasingly the ethnic consumer. For the multicultural or specialty agency, there are both pros and cons associated with becoming a subsidiary of a general market agency. Clearly, Hispanic, African American, and Asian American shops enjoy the resources of the larger agencies, as well as the association with a big name in the industry. In many instances, ethnic agencies are able to maintain a measure of independence from their owners and perhaps even obtain independent accounts. At the same time, their relationship has placed these shops in direct competition with the contacts and resources of the general market agencies. And some professionals complain about the peripheral position of ethnic agencies within the larger entity, which may fail to include them in their pitches to new clients, attempt to develop messages for an ethnic audience without consulting the subsidiary agency, or even relegate its role to translating ads done by the main branch (Davila, 2001).

Table 7.1 ranks the top Hispanic, African American, and Asian American advertising agencies in terms of billings in 2005.

Hispanic agencies, in particular, have benefited from the numbers reflected in the most recent census. Fifteen of the top twenty-five U.S. Hispanic advertising agencies experienced double-digit growth in 2005, and nine of those agencies grew by more than 20%, measured by gross income in *Advertising Age's* annual Agency Report (Wentz, 2006). For example, the Vidal Partnership's 84% growth to a 2005 income of $23.95 million, up from $13 million a year earlier, propelled Vidal for the first time into the top five agencies. In the previous year's ranking, Vidal was number eleven. Vidal is the only independent agency in the top five. Each of the four major holding companies—WWP Group, Publicis Groupe, Omnicom Group, and IPG—has a U.S. Hispanic agency among the top five. The five fastest-growing Hispanic agencies among the top twenty-five in 2005 were Grupo Gallegos, up 91.4%; Vidal; LatinWorks Marketing, up 34.4%; Conill, up 31.8%; and Winglatino, up 30.2%. In a sign of the continuing growth of the U.S. Hispanic Market during 2006, Latin agencies also earned spots in *Advertising Age's* first-ever A-List of ten leading agencies and a separate list of 10 Agencies to Watch (Wentz, 2007). The ten A-List agencies were selected based on growth, management stability and innovation, creative quality, and marketing effectiveness. They also had to

Table 7.1: Top Multicultural Agencies in 2005

Rank	Agency (parent)	Headquarters	Revenue (in U.S. millions of dollars)
Hispanic			
1.	Bromley Communications (Publicis)	San Antonio	$40.0
2.	Bravo Group (WPP)	New York	$39.4
3.	GlobalHue (Interpublic)	Southfield, Michigan	$36.2
4.	Dieste, Harmel & Partners (Omnicom)	Dallas	$35.0
5.	Vidal Partnership	New York	$23.9
6.	Accentmarketing (Interpublic)	Coral Gables, Florida	$21.0
7.	Lopez Negrete Communications	Houston	$20.2
8.	Lapiz (Publicis)	Chicago	$18.2
9.	Zubi Advertising Services	Coral Gables, Florida	$18.0
10.	La Agencia de Orci & Associates	Los Angeles	$15.1
African American			
1.	GlobalHue (Interpublic)	Southfield, Michigan	$34.7
2.	Carol H. Williams Advertising	Oakfield, California	$33.0
3.	Burrell Communications Group (Publicis)	Chicago	$32.2
4.	UniWorld Group (WPP)	New York	$14.3
5.	Matlock Advertising and Public Relations	Atlanta	$8.5
6.	Anderson Communications	Atlanta	$8.5
7.	E. Morris Communications	Chicago	$8.2
8.	Fuse Inc.	St. Louis	$8.0
9.	Images USA	Atlanta	$7.2
10.	Footsteps (Omnicom)	New York	$2.1
Asian American			
1.	PanCom International	Los Angeles	$10.5
2.	Kang & Lee (WPP)	New York	$10.1
3.	A Partnership	New York	$8.9
4.	Admerasia	New York	$7.9
5.	interTrend Communications	Long Beach, California	$7.1
6.	IW Group (Interpublic)	West Hollywood, California	$6.7
7.	Time Advertising	Millbrae, California	$6.1
8.	AdAsia Communications	New York	$3.8
8.	Ethnic Solutions	Los Angeles	$3.8
10.	Dae Advertising	San Francisco	$2.8

Source: "Special Report/Agency Report," May 1, 2006, *Advertising Age.* http://adage.com/datacenter/datapopup. php?article_id=108860.

be digital and direct-savvy. The Vidal Partnership made that ranking. Grupo Gallegos made the 10 to-Watch list of agencies for 2007. And Conill—the shop that created the first Hispanic spot to run on the Super Bowl for Toyota's Camry Hybrid—was named *Advertising Age's* Multicultural Agency of the year for 2007. In addition to Hispanic agencies owned by holding companies and independents like Vidal, new agencies are springing up to court Hispanic consumers, including the segment's first Hispanic branded content agency, the Lab; Black Sheep, a shop with a direct marketing focus; and Hispanicity, an advertising and promotion shop that uses a trigenerational approach to segment the first-, second-, and third-generation Hispanics. Then there's Project 2050, a new urban youth–marketing agency whose name refers to the year when non-Hispanic whites will no longer account for more than 50% of the U.S. population. And GlobalHue, the IPG-backed agency founded as an African American shop, now gets 51% of its revenue from the Hispanic market. All this has led Hispanic agencies to step up their game—not just to fend off new rivals but also to fend off traditional agencies that are increasingly trying to persuade clients that they, too, can target Hispanics. "We've come under siege from general market agencies who want to eat our pastelitos," notes Manny Machado, CEO of Machado Garcia-Serra, Miami, and past president of the AHAA. "Now they want to eat our lunch!" (Wentz, 2005b). David Diaz, creative director of Phoenix-based Grupo N Advertising, agrees that general market agencies have always been frustrated at seeing money go out the door to Hispanic agencies. "There was a time when agencies staffed at least one or two token employees to try and keep everything in-house, but clients are no longer buying that," Diaz noted. "That's why a few general-market agencies are now giving a concerted effort in creating internal Hispanic Departments with multiple qualified individuals and that is where we are seeing some strong competition" (Wentz, 2005b). And competition is not limited to the general market agencies or even other Hispanic shops. Puerto Rican agencies, for example, have begun eyeing the U.S. mainland's bigger Spanish-speaking market. Puerto Rico's San Juan–based Lopito, Ileana, & Howie started up a New York agency for the U.S. Hispanic market called *Azafran* (the Spanish word for the spice saffron). And other Spanish-speaking countries are looking at the United States, as well. Spain's Barcelona-based creative shop S,C,P,F..., owned by WPP Group, opened S,C,P,F . . . America in Miami to target the U.S. Hispanic market (Wentz, 2005a). Then there's la comunidad, an Argentine agency that set up shop in Miami just five years ago—and who already boasts clients such as Volkswagen, Best Buy, and MTV (Crouse, 2005).

The Hispanic advertising industry is growing four times faster than all other sectors of advertising. To meet the needs of these agencies, the AHAA—the national organization of Hispanic-owned and -managed firms—was founded in 1997. AHAA's mission is to grow, strengthen, and protect the Hispanic mar-

keting and advertising industry by providing leadership in raising awareness
of the value of Hispanic market opportunities and enhancing the professionalism of the industry. Full membership is open only to advertising agencies
devoted solely to the Hispanic market. Some have criticized the inclusion
of Hispanic advertising divisions of general market agencies; however these
were also accepted as full members, so long as they had 75% of total billings
in the Hispanic market, employed a significant percentage (65% or more) of
Hispanic staff, and offered full services in the Hispanic market (Davila, 2001).
AHAA agencies, which lead the industry with collective capitalized billings
exceeding $5 billion—more than 90% of the entire U.S. Hispanic advertising
industry—offer a blend of cultural understanding, market knowledge, proven
experience, and professional resources that make them uniquely qualified to
communicate with Hispanic consumers. The organization notes that AHAA
advertising campaigns ring true and are heard, seen, and understood because
they are authentically Hispanic. See Figure 7.3 for an advertisement for the
Hispanic Group, an AHAA member. The subhead reads, "At Hispanic Group
Advertising Agency we speak and know the cultural nuances of the Spanish
language. We don't translate . . . we interpret." In 2005, the AHAA launched
the first Hispanic advertising foundation. The Hispanic Advertising Agencies
Foundation (HAAF) serves as an independent, not-for-profit organization with
a twofold agenda: First, it aims to support, conduct, fund, and distribute market
research related to Hispanic consumers and advertising, and, second, it strives
to offer educational opportunities, materials, and scholarships to those seeking to pursue careers in Hispanic advertising. The move by the AHAA comes
at a time when corporations and national advertisers are increasingly looking for market data to help them better allocate funds and manage Hispanic
campaigns. The HAAF launched a research fund entitled *Comprende!* The fund
finances, creates, and promotes new ground-breaking research that provides
data for corporate advertisers and agencies to explore new markets and new
media and reach new consumers. Research on consumer behavior, Hispanic
cultural identity, and advertising methodologies and strategies is solicited and
supported by Comprende! Additional information about the AHAA and the
HAAF can be found at the AHAA's Web site (http://www.ahaa.org).

African American advertising agencies also have to contend with competitive pressures from larger, general market agencies for the opportunity to reach
black consumers. While advertising spending increased by 4.6% in 2005 to
$276 billion, according to *Insider's Report* from Universal McCann, a division
of the global ad agency IPG, many black ad agencies did not realize any tan-
gible benefits. Indeed, many have experienced a reduction in accounts, as well
as declining cash flow and profitability (Dingle & Harris, 2006). Increasingly,
mainstream agencies are convinced that they have a finger on the pulse of
the black market. These "general market agencies have sold unsophisticated

Figure 7.3: Advertisement Promoting the Hispanic Group Advertising Agency

advertisers on the notion that black consumers are monolithic or that hip-hop is synonymous with the total black experience," notes GlobalHue's CEO Don Coleman. As a result, naïve advertisers believe they can reach blacks through general market campaigns. "They think it can be done through casting, dropping a black actor into a general-market commercial, instead of developing a campaign that has relevancy to the black consumer," (Dingle & Harris, 2006). Rebecca Williams, senior vice president and chief creative officer at New York's UniWorld explains,

> Here in America, hip-hop has become part of American culture; it's not a black phenomenon but an American phenomenon. Now you have all these general market agencies telling clients that because they know hip-hop, they can talk to the urban market as well, but that's not true. (Pytlik, 2005)

Many clients, she explains, confuse *African American* with *hip-hop* and then assume that general-market agencies with urban expertise have the capacity to reach the entire demographic. "We talk to ethnic, urban, urbane, old school, new school—everything is a part of what we do," she notes.

> Clients get confused because general market agencies are walking in and telling them "Hey, we know hip-hop." It's hard to know if the clients are going to be smart enough to realize they need to get on top of this minority boom by putting their marketing in the hands of multicultural agencies instead of continuing to believe that general agencies can do it as well. (Pytlik, 2005)

But general market agencies may be the least of the problems African American agencies face. Ethnic dollars, once earmarked for campaigns to reach African American consumers, have been shifted to the growing Latino segment. Convincing clients that there is value in the African American segment has been a struggle for African American agencies from the start. But the growth in recent years of the Hispanic market has made the sales pitch even more challenging. Eugene Morris, CEO of E. Morris Communications Inc. (EMC) notes

> A lot of clients are looking at multicultural spending, but the fact that they are spending against multicultural audiences doesn't mean that they are spending against the African American segment. In fact, the Hispanic agencies are getting the lion's share of a lot of the multicultural dollars. (Dingle & Harris, 2006)

In short, clients are shifting dollars out of black campaigns and putting them into Hispanic campaigns. Chuck Morrison, executive vice president and general manager of UniWorld Group Inc., forecasts that "with the exception of a couple of regional and niche players, only the top four or five black agencies will most likely survive the changing dynamics" (Dingle & Harris, 2006). However, African American agency owners are standing their ground. Some have formed strategic partnerships with general market agencies, restructured internally, or adopted new strategies to help anchor their agencies for the long haul. To compete, Jo Muse, of Muse Communications, says black ad agencies have to go beyond solely developing black ads and attract more general market accounts—black advertising agencies have to offer more than the African American connection. Greg Head, president of HEADFIRST Market Research Inc. in Atlanta, agrees:

> When we talk to consumers, their world is not just black. Their world is becoming more and more diverse, and the interactions that they have on a daily basis are more multicultural than ever before. Those African American ad agencies or other agencies that focus on the African American consumer are in a position to get incremental ad spending when they can speak about this consumer as a part of the larger market. (Harris, 2005)

For example, the strategy of R. J. Dale Advertising and Public Relations was to "focus on more than just segment business," and it paid off. The Chicago-based agency beat thirteen other ad shops to win a $19 million—per-year general market account with the Illinois state lottery, making it the first time in the state's history that an African American–owned ad agency won such an account. Before it won the account, R. J. Dale had handled only the African American market for the state lottery. But, when DDB Chicago, the lottery's then general market agency resigned from its contract, president and CEO Robert J. Dale stepped in. His campaign, which included a series of TV spots featuring comedian Bernie Mac, resulted in record lottery sales of more than $1.7 billion for 2004 (Harris, 2005).

Realizing that part of their strength lies in working together to create a better competitive environment for their shops, in 2004, ten African American agencies formed the Association of Black-Owned Advertising Agencies Inc. (ABAA). The association intends to represent the interests of black agencies, lobby government and large corporations for increased sensitivity to black consumers, and ensure that organizations stay true to their diversity efforts while establishing opportunities for African Americans to enter the advertising and marketing communications field. ABAA's founding members are Anderson Communications, EMC, Equals Three Communications, Fuse Advertising, Lattimer Moffitt Communications, Matlock Advertising & Public Relations, Muse Communications, Prime Access, R. J. Dale Advertising & Public Relations, and SWG&M Advertising ("Black Advertising," 2005). Eugene Morris, interim chairman of the ABAA, notes,

> the formation of the ABAA was long overdue. For more than 40 years, the African American market has been the number one ethnic market in America. With the growing importance of these consumers, we need to find ways to collectively use our expertise and address critical issues facing both the market and our agencies. (Kaplan, 2005)

As the Asian market has grown, so too have the number of agencies available to help clients develop and deliver their messages to this audience. Greg Chew, creative director at Dae Advertising in San Francisco, noted, "What I learned is that advertising is a mirror reflection of the times. America has changed" (Eljera, 1996). Even so, there are still only about a dozen or so Asian American–owned advertising agencies nationwide. The Asian American Advertising Federation (3AF) was established in 1999 with the mission of growing the Asian and Pacific American advertising and marketing industry, raising public awareness of the importance of the community, and furthering the professionalism of the industry. Its goal is to have the organization serve as a focal point for information on the U.S. Asian market for corporations, businesses, media organizations, and academia, as well as others. Bill Imada, president of the 3AF, says that the Asian market is underserved, noting that "the Asian market is 10 to 15 years behind the Latino and African American markets" (Niwa, 2005). But the Asian segment is a fast-growing group, and estimates suggest that, by 2050, one of every ten Americans will be of Asian descent. Such statistics ensure that Asian consumers will be on the marketing radar screens of companies eager to expand their customer base. With an eye to the future, the 3AF is active in hosting conferences, seminars, and symposia designed to provide the latest information about the growing Asian and Pacific American market. More information about this organization can be found at its Web site (http://www.3af.org).

According to Miller and Kemp (2005), there are very real advantages to using a multicultural or specialty advertising agency:

- Access to invaluable ethnic insights.
- Ability to adapt positioning and accurately target the message.
- Execution of marketing programs and campaigns that reach the ethnic consumer efficiently.
- An ethnic agency is better equipped to provide authenticity and expertise—a claim that appears to be borne out by the 2004 ANA Multicultural Marketing Study in which 85% of marketers said they used a multicultural agency, up from 76% in 2002.

Ethnic-focused agencies add the most value through the following very distinct offerings:

- Minority ownership and diversity in staff who better understand and empathize with the targeted consumer.
- Ability to add depth to ethnic insights.
- Local community knowledge and access.
- Ethnic media connections.

- Assistance in overcoming barriers to relationships across racial and ethnic lines.
- Language skills for accurate translations. (Miller and Kemp, 2005)

In short, advertisers who partner with multicultural or specialty advertising agencies can best mitigate the challenges and risks inherent in marketing to Hispanic American, African American, and Asian American consumers. Profiles of three agencies targeting ethnic consumers follow.

Profile of a Hispanic Advertising Agency

George San Jose, founder of the SJG, notes on his agency's website that their mission is to "accomplish unprecedented marketing results for their clients through insightful and culturally relevant creative executions." SJG services include advertising, public relations, direct response, interactive communications, sales promotions, and both secondary and primary research. In addition, to better assist SJG clients in seizing growth opportunities throughout the United States and the Spanish-speaking Americas, he created the San Jose Network, a conglomerate of marketing firms with a reach of more than thirty countries. George San Jose is also a cofounder of the AHAA. The agency's domestic clients include Kraft, U.S. Cellular, the American Cancer Society, GlaxoSmithKline, and Hormel, as well as the National Pork Board. The National Pork Board decided in 2001 that the U.S. Hispanic market—growing at ten times the rate of the general population—could provide an important niche for the expansion of pork consumption. Working with the SJG, the National Pork Board conducted both qualitative and quantitative research to develop a campaign strategy. Through their qualitative work—focus groups—client and agency discovered a dichotomy of attitudes in the Hispanic market about pork. They found that Hispanics love the taste of pork, which they use in many traditional dishes, and even favor the taste over other proteins. However, they also found that this segment had health concerns about eating pork due to cholesterol and fat content, which they wrongly perceived to be high in all cuts of pork. But of even greater concern was the widespread fear of contracting not only trichinosis, but also an even longer list of wives' tales illnesses, ranging from "worms on the brain," to convulsions, to even stunting a child's growth. These fears stemmed from experiences in their countries of origin, where pork-related illnesses were more common in locations where meat was not maintained with proper refrigeration and sanitary conditions. As a result, Hispanics felt a conflict in eating this meat. Not surprisingly, the general market slogan which referred to pork as "the other white meat," held little meaning for Hispanics, not only because meat is not typically categorized according to colors in Hispanic cultures, but also because it did not address their concerns over food safety. The National Pork Board and SJG decided that they needed a strong educational campaign

Figure 7.4: Print Ad Targeting
Hispanics for the National Pork Board,
Created by the San Jose Group

Figure 7.5: Script for a radio spot for the National Pork Board

The script from a radio spot for the National Pork Board follows:

CONTROL.	(Military music.)
PIGS.	OINK, OINK, OINK.
PORKORAL.	Pigs, Swine, Hogs, hit the showers. We don't want "pigs" in the U.S. Pork barracks.
PIG 1.	Yes, Porkoral. (Corporal.)
PORKORAL.	Then to breakfast. U.S. pigs are well fed . . . with pure fiber and balanced grains.
PIG 1.	At your command. OINK, OINK, OINK.
PORKORAL.	Now, the Pork Doctor.
PORK DOCTOR.	Pork is a delicious alternative: National Pork Board studies show that roasted pork tenderloin, for example, has similar calories and cholesterol to a skinless roasted chicken breast.
PORKORAL.	(Marching.) We don't have piggly pork here, just delicious meat (song rhymes in Spanish).
PORKORAL.	An excellent source of protein.
PIG 1.	Pork is a fine/elegant food.
PORKORAL.	With every bite you take . . .
PIG 1.	. . . it makes your mouth water.
PORKORAL.	Pig, Swine, Hog.
PIG 1.	Pork is good and delicious.
PORKORAL.	Pork is good and delicious.
PIG 1.	It's U.S. Pork.
ANNOUNCER.	U.S. Pork Quality. This is a message from America's pork producers. Pork is good.

to give consumers the license to enjoy the pork they loved, without fear or guilt. They created a campaign slogan appropriate to the market—*El Cerdo Es Bueno* (Pork Is Good)—suggesting that U.S. pork is safe, delicious, and healthy. This message was the basis of all creative executions, which offered the basic promise that consumers could eat the pork they loved, guilt free. The reasons to believe the claim included the following: Pork is safe—modern methods of production have made disease from pork virtually nonexistent; pork is healthy—U.S. pork producers utilize improved genetics and production techniques to produce pork that is 31% leaner than just two decades ago; and pork is delicious—pork dishes are a mainstay in the Hispanic culture. SJC then leveraged the National Pork Board's well-established pork logo, which featured the word "pork" inside of a pork chop–shaped icon, and added a subtext that read: *Calidad U.S. Pork* (U.S. Quality Pork). This visual treatment provided reassurances by serving as a quality seal of approval. In 2002, SJG launched an integrated campaign including magazine ads, outdoor advertising, radio, and retail promotions, as well as public relations. Figure 7.4 provides an example of a magazine ad created by the SJG for the National Pork Board.

The National Pork Board conducted tracking research at the conclusion of the initial campaign, which indicated that the campaign was successful at beginning to break down barriers and generating increased pork consumption. The campaign was expanded from its original three markets to twelve of the top Hispanic markets. Television was incorporated into the media mix. Attitudes toward pork and consumption indices continued to improve even more dramatically. Results from a pre- and post-2004 tracking study revealed that, among the target audience, as a result of the campaign, there was a more than 29% increase in the perception that pork is as low in fat as chicken, a more than 21% increase in the belief that pork is low in cholesterol, and a more than 24% increase in the belief that "pork is safe to serve to my family." The percentage of consumers who believed that the quality of U.S. Pork is very good increased 64%, and, most importantly, the campaign generated a 31% increase in pork expenditures. The success of the campaign was recognized by more than six national communications awards.

Profile of an African American Advertising Agency

Ranked number seven on *Advertising Age's* list of top-ten African American advertising agencies, E. Morris Communications Inc. (EMC) was founded in 1987 in Chicago. The agency provides clients with both advertising and public relations services. In addition, it conducts market research and handles sales promotions and special events. The agency promises on its website to create truly effective advertising that will "talk to the soul of the consumer." Eugene Morris was also instrumental in leading the charge to form the ABAA. In 2005, EMC was recognized as *Black Enterprise* magazine's advertising agency of the

Figure 7.6: Advertisement for Wal-Mart Created by E. Morris Communications Inc.

year. Among its clients are American Family Insurance, Tyson Foods, and Wal-Mart. The agency worked hard on behalf of Wal-Mart to mend the tarnished reputation of the retailer. Wal-Mart, the world's largest retailer, had been hit with dozens of lawsuits alleging sexual discrimination and unfair pay practices and was forced to settle charges concerning contracting illegal alien workers. The company also continues to face opposition from community groups when it tries to open stores in cities and towns. EMC's goal was to revamp Wal-Mart's image among African Americans. One of the agency's first moves was to develop the documentary, *The Invisible Men of Honor: The Story of the Buffalo Soldiers,* which retells the story of the first African Americans recruited into a peacetime army. The documentary was promoted in all three thousand Wal-Mart stores (Sykes, 2005). EMC also gave Wal-Mart a human face by positioning Wal-Mart associates as an extension of the consumer: their neighbors, church members, and friends, who also happen to be Wal-Mart employees. Advertising was created to reinforce a sense of intimacy and kinship among African American consumers and further evolved to reflect consumers enjoying the value of the Wal-Mart shopping experience. The key message of the campaign was "Wal-Mart—a store for people like me." See Figure 7.6 for an ad from this campaign. The copy reads,

> I spent 15 years of my life working in the vision field as an assistant for another company. But, within two years of working for Wal-Mart, I furthered my education, got my optician's license and began my career as a specialist, earning more money with good benefits. But more importantly, I've earned my own respect. The sense of accomplishment I feel lets me know I can achieve whatever I can dream. That's what having a great career can do for you.

Based on national Gallup survey results, African Americans are now Wal-Mart's most aware shoppers. Wal-Mart is now mentioned as the primary discount store among African Americans, who rate the chain the highest versus competition for caring about its customers and being a store for "people like me."

Profile of an Asian American Advertising Agency

Ranked number five on *Advertising Age's* list of top-ten Asian American advertising agencies, interTrend Communications Inc. is a full-service communications agency targeting Asian American segments, including Chinese, Korean, Vietnamese, Filipino, Japanese, Asian Indian, and other Pacific Islander communities. For more than a decade, interTrend has assisted Fortune 1000 clients, including Northwest Airlines, Toyota, Nestlé, State Farm Insurance, Charles Schwab, and J. C. Penney Company, among others, in establishing and nurturing brand leadership positions in these emerging markets. Key to interTrend's success is its Integrated Asian American Communication Program, which includes various consumer touch points, including advertising, public relations, direct mail, interactive strategies via various in-language media outlets, promotions, events, and community outreach. InterTrend assisted State Farm Insurance in boosting brand awareness levels among Asian consumers. In conducting research for its client, interTrend found that, while life insurance companies had been advertising to the Asian market in the United States for over fifteen years, there was limited awareness of the State Farm Insurance brand and its products and services. In addition, the agency uncovered some confusion with other insurance brands, such as Allstate Corporation and Farmers Insurance Group. The agency uncovered differences among segments of the Asian market that could affect the marketing of State Farm Insurance. For example, the concept of insurance does not exist in mainland China nor in Vietnam. In Korea, insurance fraud is very common. And, in both Taiwan and Hong Kong, there is a high level of awareness of life insurance, but, in Taiwan, there is only an emerging awareness of auto and home insurance. InterTrend saw an opportunity to establish State Farm Insurance as the one source for automotive, homeowners, life, and health insurance for Asian consumers. The agency's goal was to establish emotional trust and highlight State Farm Insurance's knowledgeable agency, its many years in business, and its role in the community. Figure 7.7 presents two print ads from this campaign. Beyond boosting brand awareness among Asians, the campaign served to dramatically increase the focus on the Asian market at State Farm Insurance's corporate headquarters. It also realized increased involvement,

Figure 7.7: State Farm Insurance Print Ads Targeting the Asian Community, Created by interTrend

participation, and assistance from State Farm Insurance field agencies with large Chinese, Vietnamese, and Korean customer bases. Finally, the campaign received the Multicultural Creative Award of Excellence from the ANA.

Summary

Clearly, in ethnic marketing, the selection of an advertising agency to promote products and services to Hispanic, African American, and Asian American consumers is a complex issue. Choosing between a general market agency and a multicultural or specialty agency is just one of a long list of decisions a firm must make before embarking on a campaign to appeal to ethnic consumers. Marketers may also opt to employ an agency specializing in the market they wish to reach—whether exclusively or not—to work in tandem with a general market agency. A number of organizations and associations can assist in this decision, including the AAF, the AAAA, the AHAA, the ABAA, and the 3AF. Above and beyond selecting the right agency for the job, marketers appealing to ethnic consumers should strive to behave in a socially responsible manner in terms of product development, pricing, and distribution, as well as promotion. Such efforts can assist in avoiding costly legal entanglements and, even more importantly, can stem any erosion of ethnic consumer confidence in advertising. The role of social responsibility and ethical standards as it applies to marketing to multicultural consumers will be addressed in the next, and final, chapter of this text.

REFERENCES

AAAA launches initiative to increase diversity representation in advertising industry. (2004, September 22). *PR Newswire,* p. 1.

AAF most promising minority student program more than doubles in two years. (2005, February 3–9). *Westside Gazette,* p. 11.

AAF surveys reveal significant challenges in recruiting talent and retaining minority professionals; two-thirds of AAF Most Promising Minority Students Program alumni employed in field of advertising. (2006, February 9). *Business Wire,* p. 1.

Black advertising association. (2005). *Network Journal, 12*(6), 8.

Cardwell, D., & Elliott, S. (2006, September 8). Ad firms to hire more black managers in city. *The New York Times.* Retrieved from September 9, 2006 from http://www.newyork-times.com/2006/09/08/business/media/08ads.html?ei=5070&en=76538f8efd.

Charski, M. (2004). In search of diversity. *Adweek, 45*(30), 21.

Crouse, D. (2005, October). Hot shops. *Hispanic Trends,* 46.

Davila, A. (2001). *Latinos Inc.: The marketing and making of a people.* Berkeley, CA: University of California Press.

Dingle, D., & Harris, W. (2006). Advertising agencies. *Black Enterprise, 36*(11), 164.

Eljera, B. (1996, December 6). Target Asian America. *AsianWeek*. Retrieved June 19, 2006 from http://www.asianweek.com/120696/cover.html

Fernandez, T. (2004, June). Commission probes ad agency minority hiring. *Crain's New York Business, 20*(23), 3.

Harris, W. (2005). Winds of change. *Black Enterprise, 35*(11), 159.

Howard, T. (2006, September 27). N.Y. ad agencies vow to address lack of diversity; people of color hold few top jobs. *USA Today*, p. B-3.

Kaplan, D. (2005, February 25). Association of Black-Owned Advertising Agencies formed, 4A's seeks to assist. *MediaPostPublications*. Retrieved June 9, 2006 from http://publications.mediapost.com/index.cfm?fuseaction=Articles.showArticleHomePage.

Miller, P., & Kemp, H. (2005). *What's black about it? Insights to increase your share of a changing African American market*. New York: Paramount Market Publishing, Inc.

Nagel, A. (2005, December 2). CoverGirl's Royal Expansion. *Women's Wear Daily*, p. 6.

Niwa, G. (2006, March 17—March 23). Market matrix; APA advertising crosses over to the mainstream. *Asianweek*, San Francisco, 26(30), p. 14.

Pytlik, M. (2005, June). The multicultural boom: Our population is changing, but is advertising keeping pace? *Boards*, 41.

Sanders, L. (2006a, June 11). Ad agency chiefs subpoenaed for NYC diversity hearings. *Advertising Age*. Retrieved June 12, 2006 from http://adage.com/article?article_id=109760

Sanders, L. (2006b, March 6). NYC to subpoena ad agency execs in diversity probe. *Advertising Age*. Retrieved March 6, 2006 from http://adage.com/news.cms?newsID=48142

Sykes, T. (2005, June 1). Growth from within: E. Morris Communications Inc. gained market share in a less than stellar environment by turning to existing clients. *Black Enterprise*. Retrieved June 20, 2006 from http://www.keepmedia.com/pubs/BlackEnterprise/2005/06/01/1319323?extID=10032

Wentz, L. (2005a, September 6). Ingrid Otero-Smart goes to Anita Santiago Advertising. *Advertising Age*. Retrieved September 26, 2005 from http://www.adage.com/news.cms?newsId=45980

Wentz, L. (2005b, May 2). Multicultural? No, mainstream [Midwest region edition]. *Advertising Age*, p. 3.

Wentz, L. (2006, May 1). 15 of top 25 Hispanic agencies hit double-digit growth. *Advertising Age*. Retrieved May 2, 2006 from http://www.adage.com/print?article_id=108995

Wentz, L. (2007, January 8). Conill named Ad Age Multicultural Agency of the Year. *Advertising Age*. Retrieved from http://adage.com/print?article_id=114165

Woods, G. B. (1995). *Advertising and marketing to the new majority*.Belmont, CA: Wadsworth Publishing Company.

8

Ethics and Social Responsibility

Selling to the Multicultural Consumer

Introduction

Back in the 1970s, renowned economist Milton Friedman argued that, while it was important for businesses to "stay within the rules of the game" and "operate without deception or fraud," businesses did the most for society by just maximizing shareholder profits ("Rethinking," 2005). And many corporations bought into this philosophy. But much has changed in the corporate landscape over the last thirty-five years. Increasingly, firms have recognized that it takes something even more than engaging in ethical business practices and generating profits to navigate the land mines of today's marketplace. That something is the realization that companies are beholden not just to shareholders but also to their employees, their customers, and even society in general (Grow, Hamm, & Lee, 2005). Marketers must sell the message that they are "doing well by doing good" and simultaneously create high-level awareness of the connection between their brands and the social issues they support (Harris, 2005). Today, more than ever, a company's reputation in the marketplace is related to its social, as well as its ethical, performance. While interest in the ethical issues pertaining to business has grown enormously in the past few decades, research on the ethical dimensions of business and marketing has been relatively limited and generally nonempirical in nature (Taylor, Edwards, & Darling, 1989). And, while attention to ethnic marketing has been increasing in both the media and the academic literature, little attention has been devoted to potential ethics implications. Yet, targeting ethnic groups for marketing purposes is fraught with many ethical challenges, and these will be outlined in this chapter. Social responsibility as it relates to ethnic consumers will be addressed, as well.

Business Ethics

Corporations and their advertising agencies are required to make many difficult decisions. Granted, numerous laws—both at the federal and local level—govern how business can and cannot be conducted. Many marketers believe that the legal system of the country in which they operate should set the parameters for ethical behavior. The fundamental idea here is that, as long as the marketer and advertiser operate within the confines of these parameters, they need not be concerned with ethical issues. Yet, just because a particular business behavior is deemed acceptable does not necessarily make it ethical. For example, Nestlé SA is betting on Hispanic mothers to boost its share of the $3 million U.S. infant formula market—which, while perfectly legal, has many doctors and breast-feeding advocates irate. Nestlé entered the U.S. formula market back in 1988 with Carnation's Good Start line. But the Swiss marketer captured only a sliver of the market dominated by pharmaceutical companies, such as Abbott Laboratories (maker of Similac formula) and Bristol-Myers Squibb Company's Mead Johnson Nutritionals (which makes Enfamil). However, the recent explosion in the U.S. Hispanic population, with its higher-than-average birthrate, has enticed Nestlé to begin promoting Nan, a leading formula brand in Latin America. At issue is whether companies should market baby formula to low-income immigrant mothers when health experts and government officials agree that breast-feeding is healthier and saves in long-term health care costs.

Nestlé came under fire in the 1970s for the way it marketed infant formula in the developing world to poor, often illiterate women who often misused it. Health professionals at the time found that bottle-fed babies sometimes became undernourished and suffered from chronic illnesses, because their mothers were watering down the costly formula to make it go further, or they were preparing it with contaminated water. Indeed, studies revealed that the overall death rate of formula-fed babies was three times higher than among those who were breast-fed. That prompted the World Health Organization (WHO) in 1981 to devise a voluntary code whereby countries and companies agree to restrict the marketing of formula. Nestlé does not advertise in countries which follow the WHO code, such as Mexico. However, while the United States also signed the code, it never enacted laws to restrict marketing of formula in this country. Hispanic mothers in the United States tend to be less educated, and research suggests that women with lower levels of education are more likely to bottle-feed their babies. Furthermore, for many immigrant women from deprived backgrounds, bottle-feeding has an aura of acculturation and prosperity. The concern is that Nestlé is using this vulnerable population for a grab at market share (Jordan, 2004)—all in a perfectly legal fashion.

As the previous example reveals, not every issue is covered by a written rule, and, even where laws exist, there is a good deal of room for interpretation. With regard to business behavior, most marketers would agree that it is important to maintain high ethical standards. Most marketers would agree that cheating, stealing, lying, and taking or offering brides are generally considered unacceptable behaviors. But, beyond that, determining what is meant by *high ethical standards* is a good deal more complex. Many marketers turn to codes of ethics for guidance.

The goal of a code of ethics is to give expression to the actual core values of an organization and then to use these to guide management and marketing decisions. Core values are beliefs that are so fundamental to the organizational structure that they will not be compromised. (Laczniak & Murphy, 1990). The most effective codes of ethics recognize the importance of all individuals, agencies, and institutions relevant to the operation of the firm or agency, including customers, employees, the host community, relevant governmental agencies, the population at large, and so forth. A company must consider the impact of each of its decisions on these various publics. Such guides to ethical behavior are developed to assist marketers and advertisers in avoiding costly ethical mistakes. The International Chamber of Commerce (ICC)—which is represented in over 130 countries—is the most important international body influencing self-regulation of marketing and advertising. With the support of advertisers, agencies, and the media, the ICC has developed a number of important codes (see the ICC's Web site at http://www.iccwbo.org/), including the following:

- International Code of Advertising Practice
- International Code of Sales Promotion
- International Code of Direct Selling
- International Code of Direct Marketing
- Compendium of Rules for Users of the Telephone in Sales Marketing and Research
- International Code on Sponsorship

Most U.S. agencies subscribe to the American Association of Advertising Agencies' Code of Ethics (see Figure 8.1). And many professional organizations, as well as progressive firms, such as IBM, Caterpillar Inc., S. C. Johnson & Son Inc., and Citigroup, have constructed codes of ethics. Even the most detailed code, however, cannot cover each and every morally difficult situation. While most marketers and advertisers typically have little difficulty in making the correct decision with regard to health and safety issues, many other situations have no easy solutions and must be handled on a case-by-case basis. Furthermore, it must be noted that codes of ethics are based on voluntary compliance. Enron's code of ethics, for example, stated that "relations with the company's many publics—customers, stockholders, government, employees, suppliers, press, and bankers—will be conducted in honesty, candor and fairness" (Shepherd, 2003). If the leaders of Enron were familiar with their code, they certainly did not live by it. Clearly, written codes and ethics programs do not ensure ethical behavior.

Applying Ethics to the Marketing Mix

Ethical issues can creep into ethnic marketing at two different levels. First, there are ethical consequences should marketers choose to include ethnic consumers in their mainstream marketing programs. Pires and Stanton (2002) provide a number of examples: perpetuation of minority status by promoting continued invisibility of ethnic groups; discrimination against ethnic groups by providing inadequate, insufficient, misdirected, and misinterpretable information; and social responsibility issues, such as the failure to translate public interest information in the languages of the ethnic group (such as antismoking campaigns). Should marketers seek to individually target ethnic groups, a further set of potential consequences needs to be considered. For instance, the dumping of lower quality, unsuccessful, defective, untried products on ethnic markets; emotional damage to ethnic consumers via the use of stereotypes; price discrimination in relation to mainstream prices; and the limiting of access to services in order to capitalize on the lack of market experience and communication difficulties. Because of growing concern on the part of consumers, consumer organizations, and governments with the practices of marketers and advertisers, the highest standards of marketing behavior must be applied to each of the marketing mix elements—product, price, distribution, and promotion.

Figure 8.1: Example of an Advertising Industry Code of Ethics

FIRST ADOPTED OCTOBER 16, 1924—MOST RECENTLY REVISED SEPTEMBER 18, 1990

We hold that a responsibility of advertising agencies is to be a constructive force in business.

We hold that, to discharge this responsibility, advertising agencies must recognize an obligation, not only to their clients, but to the public, the media they employ, and to each other. As a business, the advertising agency must operate within the framework of competition. It is recognized that keen and vigorous competition, honestly conducted, is necessary to the growth and the health of American business. However, unethical competitive practices in the advertising agency business lead to financial waste, dilution of service, diversion of manpower, loss of prestige, and tend to weaken public confidence both in advertisements and in the institution of advertising.

We hold that the advertising agency should compete on merit and not by attempts at discrediting or disparaging a competitor agency, or its work, directly or by inference, or by circulating harmful rumors about another agency, or by making unwarranted claims of particular skill in judging or prejudging advertising copy.

To these ends, the American Association of Advertising Agencies has adopted the following *Creative Code* as being in the best interests of the public, the advertisers, the media, and the agencies themselves. The AAAA believes the Code's provisions serve as a guide to the kind of agency conduct that experience has shown to be wise, foresighted, and constructive. In accepting membership, an agency agrees to follow it.

Creative Code

We, the members of the American Association of Advertising Agencies, in addition to supporting and obeying the laws and legal regulations pertaining to advertising, undertake to extend and broaden the application of high ethical standards. Specifically, we will not knowingly create advertising that contains:

a.   False or misleading statements or exaggerations, visual or verbal

b.   Testimonials that do not reflect the real opinion of the individual(s) involved

c.   Price claims that are misleading

d.   Claims insufficiently supported or that distort the true meaning or practicable application of statements made by professional or scientific authority

e.   Statements, suggestions, or pictures offensive to public decency or minority segments of the population.

We recognize that there are areas that are subject to honestly different interpretations and judgment. Nevertheless, we agree not to recommend to an advertiser, and to discourage the use of, advertising that is in poor or questionable taste or that is deliberately irritating through aural or visual content or presentation. Comparative advertising shall be governed by the same standards of truthfulness, claim substantiation, tastefulness, etc., as apply to other types of advertising.

These Standards of Practice of the American Association of Advertising Agencies come from the belief that sound and ethical practice is good business. Confidence and respect are indispensable to success in a business embracing the many intangibles of agency service and involving relationships so dependent upon good faith.

Clear and willful violations of these Standards of Practice may be referred to the Board of Directors of the American Association of Advertising Agencies for appropriate action, including possible annulment of membership as provided by

   Article IV, Section 5, of the Constitution and By-Laws. Copyright 1990
   American Association of Advertising Agencies

From *Standards of Practice of the American Association of Advertising Agencies,* by American Association of Advertising Agencies, 1990, retrieved from http://www.aaaa.org/eweb/upload/inside/standards.pdf

The Product

With regard to product responsibility, firms should strive to produce high-quality goods that are culturally sensitive, as well as safe, for both consumers and the environment. Management at Abercrombie & Fitch was not nearly as vigilant as it should have been in the development of a t-shirt that proved to be offensive to the Asian American community. The t-shirt, complete with Asian cartoon caricatures common during World War II read "Wong Brothers Laundry Service: Two Wongs Can Make It White." Asian American consumers and organizations across the country contacted Abercrombie & Fitch, and, to their credit, the firm immediately pulled the shirts from their stores, catalogue, and website. Abercrombie & Fitch spokesman Hampton Carney noted, "It is not and never has been our intention to offend anyone. We thought they were cheeky, irreverent and funny and everyone would love them. But that has not been the case" (O'Sullivan, 2002). Indeed, the corporation, which markets its line of clothing all over the world, even thought that the Asian American community would find the shirts funny and buy them. Clearly, they did not. While the sale of such products is unquestionably offensive, at least it is not physically harmful. Unfortunately, the same cannot be said about the marketing of tobacco and alcoholic beverages to ethnic consumers.

Marketing Tobacco to Ethnic Consumers

The level of cigarette advertising is among the highest of any consumer item. Tobacco companies spend more than $6 billion a year in the United States on advertising and promotion. Although both the level of cigarette advertising and the social costs of cigarette use are substantial and well documented, the link between advertising and usage remains a controversial subject, and the research on the subject has produced mixed results (Saffer, 1988). Cigarette companies have long denied that their commercial messages encourage consumers to smoke. Instead, the industry "insists that its ads are intended to persuade existing smokers to switch brands. However, there are only six major cigarette manufacturers in the United States, and two of those (Philip Morris and RJR Nabisco) control 75 percent of the market. So if a smoker changes brands, there is a good chance he or she will switch to another brand of the same parent company" (Jacobson & Mazur, 1995). And the truth is that smokers tend to be extremely loyal to their brand of choice—only 10% of smokers ever switch brands ("Why Are They Still Targeting," 2004). The primary objective of all advertising, in fact, is market expansion. And it makes particular sense that if you market a product that kills your customers, you must recruit new ones. Public health advocates have long argued that advertising increases total consumption and, in particular, consumption among ethnic groups. Some years ago, a model named David Goerlitz, during a photo shoot for a

Winston ad, asked a group of R. J. Reynolds Tobacco Company executives if any of them smoked. One of them replied: "Are you kidding? We reserve that right for the poor, the young, the black and the stupid" (Frith & Mueller, 2003). The basic rationale behind the market segmentation strategy is

> that a variety of marketing programs (unique combinations of products, advertising, packages, pricing, distribution, etc.) each designed to better match the psychology and interests of a separable segment, will ultimately generate more sales and profit than would a single undifferentiated marketing program, so called mass marketing. But selective targeting can be benign or beneficial, only if the product is. If the product is unwholesome, even addictive and lethal, segmentation's efficiency delivers more death and disease, not more benefits, and provides a disservice, not a service. (Pollay, Lee, & Carter-Whitney, 1992)

It is death and disease that have been delivered via the target marketing efforts directed at African Americans, Hispanics, and Asians.

The targeting of ethnic groups by cigarette manufacturers is not a new phenomenon. Pollay et al. (1992) document that racial segmentation by the cigarette industry was quite well established in the 1950s. Pollay et al. noted that

> this segregation involved more than buying space in black magazines and appealing to ethnic pride with black models. Blacks were first subject to less and then to more advertising than whites. Endorsements from athletes were five times more likely to be employed for black audiences than for white audiences and blacks were not offered filtered brands until years after whites. In short, the cigarette industry treated the black and white markets separately, but not equally.

Cigarette companies in the United States have been particularly aggressive in their targeting of ethnic groups. Evidence of this, some critics say, is found in minority neighborhoods plastered with countless tobacco-touting billboards, as well as minority publications filled with cigarette ads. According to one study, in predominantly Asian neighborhoods, tobacco billboards are 17% more prevalent than in predominantly white neighborhoods (Warmbrunn, 1998). Almost 60% of the billboards in black neighborhoods advertise cigarettes or alcoholic beverages. In a study of seventy-three billboards along nineteen blocks in a black neighborhood in Philadelphia, sixty billboards advertised cigarettes or alcohol (Ellis, 2005). In addition to billboard advertisements, tobacco firms have advertised extensively in African American magazines. In fact, cigarettes advertised in African American magazines such as *Ebony, Jet,* and *Essence* account for a high percentage of the magazines' total advertising revenues. For instance, in an eight-year period, there were 1,477 tobacco ads in *Jet, Ebony,* and *Essence* (Ellis, 2005).

Many cigarette ads aimed at ethnic communities are printed in the native language of the community (Vietnamese, Chinese, or Spanish)—with the exception of the Surgeon General's Warning, which is printed in English.

The discrepancy seems too glaring to be merely an oversight. If consumers are only literate in one language, they may well be unaware of the dangers associated with smoking. A campaign to change these ads was spearheaded by the San Francisco Vietnamese American community, in large measure because of the high incidence of smokers among male Vietnamese—estimated to be 35%, about 1.5 times that of the general population. The result: The Federal Trade Commission issued a policy amendment in 1998 requiring advertising disclosures, such as the Surgeon General's Warning, to be in the language of the ad's target audience (Fernandez, 1998).

When the tobacco firms aren't creating advertising messages to sway the ethnic audience, they are wooing ethnic groups via generous donations. The tobacco industry has been a significant sponsor of athletic, civil, cultural, and entertainment events. Its donations and sponsorships of African American events and organizations date back to 1938, when William Reynolds, R. J. Reynolds's brother, donated money to institute the Kate Bitting Reynolds Hospital for Blacks in the segregated Winston-Salem, North Carolina, home of the R. J. Reynolds Tobacco Company. For example, the tobacco industry sponsored the fortieth anniversary gala of the United Negro College Fund, the Kool Achiever Awards, the *Ebony* Fashion Show, and a forum for publishers of black newspapers on preserving the freedoms in American life (Ellis, 2005).

Tobacco firms have been accused of pouring millions of dollars into creating addicts. And, apparently, they have been successful. According to the Surgeon General's Report, released in June of 1998, cigarette smoking is a major cause of disease and death among ethnic groups. African Americans currently bear the greatest health burden. More than 45,000 black Americans die each year from smoking-related illnesses, giving them a higher death rate due to lung cancer than any other race (Watson, 2000). Among Hispanic males, the national smoking rate rose from 8% in 1991 to 13.2% by 1997. Lung cancer is the leading cause of cancer deaths among Hispanics, according to the Centers for Disease Control and Prevention (Watson, 2000). Ethnic youth, in particular, have been targeted. While smoking increased 34% among Hispanic students between 1991 and 1997, it surged to a whopping 80% among black students (Centers for Disease Control and Prevention, 1998).

The tobacco industry has been particularly aggressive in developing products designed to appeal to ethnic smokers. In 1989, RJR Nabisco launched Uptown, a menthol cigarette designed to appeal to black smokers. But, when RJR Nabisco test-marketed Uptown in Philadelphia, it drew bitter protests from the National Association of African Americans for Positive Imagery (NAAAPI), as well as then Secretary of Health and Human Services Louis Sullivan, who accused the tobacco manufacturer of promoting a "culture of cancer among blacks." Ultimately, RJR Nabisco was forced to scrap its plan to introduce Uptown, at an estimated loss of nearly $10 million. However, tobacco firms have continued to develop brands to appeal to minority audiences. In 1998, Lorillard Tobacco Company began distribution of a new, low-priced brand called Maverick. The cigarettes sold for about $1.85 a pack, less than the then-current $2.25 price of generic brands and significantly less than the major brands. Advertisements cropped up in Milwaukee and other cities with large African American populations, including Philadelphia and Detroit. The Reverend Jesse Brown, acting executive director for the NAAAPI said that the ads were unfairly targeting African Americans, primarily young people (Thomas-Lynn, 1998). Industry giant Philip Morris rolled out a new cigarette— Marlboro Milds, a menthol brand. In Marlboro Milds, the tobacco burns at a cooler rate, which permits more nicotine to be absorbed into the body. Protests against Marlboro Milds were organized by the NAAAPI to encourage the manufacturer to pull the product—to no avail. While African American smokers smoke approximately 35% fewer cigarettes per day than do white smokers, they nevertheless have higher rates of most smoking-related diseases. This may be a result of the fact that African Americans smoke disproportionately more mentholated cigarettes. Studies have shown that 80% of black smokers prefer menthol cigarettes, while only 25% of white smokers smoke mentholated cigarettes. Menthol cigarettes are generally higher in tar and nicotine content than nonmentholated cigarettes and thus are more addicting and deadly. Ellis (2005) notes that the lethal preference for menthol brands by African American smokers was shaped by targeted advertising campaigns by the tobacco industry, which promotes these brands in culturally specific magazines and on billboards in predominantly black neighborhoods. In fact, the successes of menthol brands are almost entirely tied to the African American market. Menthol cigarettes were introduced in the 1930 but did not exceed 3% of the total market until 1949. In the 1960s, advertising for menthol cigarettes began appearing in *Ebony*. By 1963, the market share was 16%, and, by 1976, it was 28%. Sales to African Americans accounted for the vast majority of this increase. The three most popular brands among black smokers are Newport, Kool, and Salem, all menthol cigarettes. Researchers say menthol causes smokers to inhale more deeply and is associated with higher carbon monoxide concentrations, and menthol cigarettes create more cancer-causing agents than nonmenthol cigarettes (Ellis, 2005). A recent ad for Kool cigarettes (see Figure 8.2), appealing to African American smokers, encourages the audience to "Be authentic."

While ads for menthol cigarettes are directed at African American smokers, distinctly strong cigarettes appeal to Asian smokers. International Tobacco Group unveiled three new cigarette products designed to appeal specifically to Asian immigrants. International Tobacco Group, a Chinese company that manufactures its cigarettes in the United States, makes its cigarettes with a blend of imported Chinese and American-grown tobacco. "Americans might

Figure 8.2: Kool Cigarettes Encourage the Target Audience to "Be Authentic"

not like the strong flavors of Chinese cigarettes," notes Patrick Qian, division manager. Indeed, even the light version tastes as bold as Marlboro Reds, nick-named "cowboy killers," according to Qian (Kosareff, 2004). International Tobacco Group, based in Los Vegas, hosted a lavish feast to promote the new product to the Asian media. Flavored brands have even been designed to appeal to young smokers. Brown and Williamson introduced Kool Smooth Fusions—with names that sound like funky juice or coffee drinks: Mocha Taboo, Midnight Berry, Twista Lime, and Kauai Kolada. The marketing tactics used to appeal to minority youth include packaging that features disc jockeys, graffiti artists, and other hip-hop imagery, as well as a series of disc jockey competitions that Kool sponsors in cities across the country. Smooth Fusions's accompanying promotional CD-ROM featured hip-hop artists waxing poetic about their music and allowed users to create their own mix 'n' scratch tracks and graffiti on their computers (Bell, 2004). The Kool campaign raised the ire of legal experts. New York Attorney General Eliot Spitzer sent Brown and Williamson a letter saying that images of rappers, disc jockeys, and dancers featured on the Kool packs and in the ads "all appeal to youth." Brown and Williamson was among the companies that, in 1998, agreed to pay $206 bil-lion to settle smoking-related health claims brought by states. Under the terms of the settlement, tobacco companies are barred from targeting teens through advertising and/or marketing. Spitzer's letter was sent as the first step toward a class action suit against Brown and Williamson on behalf of thirty states ("Why are They Still Targeting," 2004). Spitzer, along with the attorney gener-als from Maryland and Illinois, subsequently sued Brown and Williamson. R. J. Reynolds Tobacco Company, which purchased Brown and Williamson in July of 2004, signed a settlement without admitting wrongdoing. As part of the settlement, the cigarette manufacturer agreed to pay $1.5 million and to cut back on hip-hop–themed advertising that targeted ethnic youth. R. J. Reynolds can still use some hip-hop marketing under the settlement—for example, it can still host disc jockey contests, but it must hold them in adult-only facili-ties and cannot broadcast them. The settlement prohibits the company from giving away merchandise, such as lighters with the words "House of Menthol" on them. Reynolds can only give out promotional CDs in adult-only venues or through direct mail to adults, and the CDs cannot contain hip-hop music or certain other features, including a graffiti spray-paint game. R. J. Reynolds also agreed to limit its retail displays and magazine advertising; ads for the flavored cigarettes can no longer appear in magazines for which 15% or more of the readership is younger than eighteen years of age (Herman, 2004). Unfortunately, the above example was simply the latest in a series of exploitive marketing efforts aimed at ethnic groups by the tobacco industry.

Marketing Alcoholic Beverages to Ethnic Consumers

Similarities are evident in the controversies that surround alcohol and tobacco advertising. Consumption of both alcoholic beverages and cigarettes has been linked with serious public health concerns. Alcohol is considered one of the United States' most serious health problems. Its complications kill one hundred thousand Americans annually. It can kill outright or lead to cancers, cirrhosis of the liver, heart disease, and fetal alcohol syndrome. Research shows that alcohol abuse literally changes the structure of the brain—programming users to return again and again to the source of pleasure even though most of them know it will ultimately harm them. Some 14 million Americans abuse alcohol, according to federal studies. Worse yet, as many as 40 million more Americans may be at risk of becoming problem drinkers (Ferraro, 1999). Alcohol is the cause of or a contributing factor in almost every community and family tragedy. Some 62% of the drowning incidents in America involve alcohol. About 70% of all homicide arrestees are involved with alcohol, and more than one-half of prison inmates used alcohol before committing their crime (Brown, 1992). Nearly two-thirds of single-vehicle accidents involve alcohol, and each year nearly twenty thousand lives are lost in alcohol-related accidents. It is estimated that alcohol abuse costs the United States more than $99 billion annually.

Interestingly enough, the two industries use highly similar defenses. Alcoholic beverage companies, like tobacco firms, argue that, until wine, beer, or liquor products are ruled illegal, they should be legally permitted to promote their sale via advertising campaigns. The alcoholic beverages industry has the support of advertising organizations, such as the American Association of Advertising Agencies, whose president argued, "If the product is legal, then both its producers and its legal users are entitled under our Constitution to the full benefit of truthful, non-deceptive advertising" (Farris & Albion, 1980). And, much like cigarette manufacturers who argue that they are not promoting smoking but rather using commercial messages to influence brand selection, the beer, wine, and liquor manufacturers suggest that, instead of encouraging people to drink more, they are inducing a preference for one brand over another via advertising. It is true that advertising does work to "shift consumers from one brand to another, but to suggest that it does not help bring in new consumers and encourage current users to consume more begs credulity" (Hacker, 1998).

The alcoholic beverages industry has frequently been criticized for targeting ethnic groups. But alcoholic beverage manufacturers defend their right to target African Americans, Hispanics, and Asian Americans by arguing that these groups should have the right to make their own decisions, including which ads they should see and what they should buy. Indeed, they have even found support for this position from an unlikely source. They quote Benjamin L. Hooks, retired executive director of the National Association for the Advancement of Colored People (NAACP), who, in response to the position that ethnic groups should be "protected" from advertising for some products, including alcoholic beverages, stated, "Buried in this line of thinking, and never really mentioned by these critics, is the rationale that blacks are not capable of making their own free choices and need some guardian angels to protect their best interests" (Castellano, 1992)

Researchers have revealed a direct relationship between alcohol advertising and alcohol-related problems. For example, a study on alcoholism and Hispanics released by CalPartners Coalition, a group of Hispanic organizations, found that 12% of Hispanic homicide victims are killed in bars; the incidence of rape and violence against women is higher in areas where alcohol advertising is most concentrated; and liver disease and cirrhosis of the liver are the sixth and seventh leading causes of death among Hispanics (Herdt, 1998). Heavy drinking is decreasing among whites but increasing among Hispanics. "Regrettably, Latinos tend to be heavier drinkers than other populations," said project director Eduardo Hernandez. "They don't drink as frequently as others, but when they drink, they drink heavily" (Herdt, 1998). And, according to the National Institute on Alcohol Abuse and Alcoholism, alcohol abuse is the leading health and safety problem in the African American community. Black consumers drink less alcohol per capita than whites, but poverty and poor health care contribute to disproportionately high rates of alcohol-related disease (Hacker, Collins, & Jacobson, 1987). To appeal to this audience, beverages with higher alcoholic content, such as malt liquors, have been developed. For example, Power Master, a beer marketed to blacks by the G. Heileman Brewing Company, contains 7.5% alcohol—about 60% higher than the alcohol content of regular beer. Much like the Wine Institute, the brewing industry's code of ethics contains a guideline that reads, "Advertising should neither state nor carry any implication of alcohol strength." But ads directed at black consumers frequently allude to the product's strength. An advertisement for St. Ides, another high-octane beer, featured black rapper Ice Cube chanting, "I usually drink it when I'm out just clowning, me and the home boys, be like downin it; Cause it's stronger but the taste is smooth; I grab me a forty [ounce bottle] when I want to act a fool." The "references to power in the ads aimed at minority communities carry a double meaning. These ads borrow the language of the civil rights movement and pretend to offer empowerment to the disenfranchised and alienated. It is a cruel bait and switch" (Jacobson & Mazur, 1995). Gangsta rap performers also tend to portray drinking malt liquors as a show of masculinity. Not only are malt liquors higher in alcohol than other beers, they also tend to be sold in larger containers. Malt liquors are often sold in 40-oz. (1 liter) containers. And rap lyrics often encourage chugging the bottles before they get warm. A recent study found that this combination resulted in malt liquor drinkers consuming 80% more alcohol per drink than average beer drinkers ("Malt Liquor," 2005).

Research has also shown that alcohol availability (measured by the number of bars and stores selling alcohol in a specific geographic area) and advertising are disproportionately concentrated in ethnic communities (Alaniz, 1998). One study found that West Oakland—an area in Oakland, California, where racial and ethnic minorities and the poor are concentrated—had one liquor outlet for every 298 residents. In contrast, Piedmont, the more affluent, predominantly white area of Oakland, had one alcohol outlet for every three thousand residents (Mack, 1997). Merchants use storefronts and interiors of alcohol outlets to advertise beer, wine, and spirits. One study found that a student walking from home to school in a predominantly Latino community in northern California may be exposed to between ten and sixty storefront alcohol advertisements, and that same study found that there are five times as many alcohol ads in Latino neighborhoods as in predominantly white neighborhoods (Alaniz & Wilkes, 1995). Studies of alcohol advertising in minority communities have focused primarily on billboards. A San Francisco–based investigation revealed that African American and Latino neighborhoods had proportionately more billboards advertising alcohol than white or Asian neighborhoods (Altman, Schooler, & Basil, 1991). Thirty-one percent of the billboards in Latino neighborhoods advertised alcohol, compared with 23% in African American neighborhoods, 13% in white neighborhoods, and 12% in Asian neighborhoods. Most of the alcohol billboards in Hispanic communities advertised beer and wine, whereas the majority of billboards in the African American neighborhoods promoted malt liquor and distilled spirits. Scores of cities and towns, including New York, Chicago, and Los Angeles, have enacted restrictions on billboard advertising, and, in 1997, Baltimore became the first city in the United States to remove all tobacco and alcohol billboards. The ban prompted lawsuits by advertisers and billboard companies, which said limits on billboards violate the advertisers' free speech rights. But, in April 1997, the U.S. Supreme Court let the ban stand, and the ads came down. However, despite the ruling in the Baltimore case, several other efforts to restrict billboards have been struck down by judges, who have found that they unfairly singled out tobacco and liquor companies. The Outdoor Advertising Association of America, the industry's trade group, established a voluntary code in 1990 that called for a prohibition on tobacco and alcohol billboards within five hundred feet of schools, churches, and playgrounds.

In terms of other media, a report by Georgetown University's Center on Alcohol Marketing and Youth found that blacks from twelve to twenty years old saw 77% more magazine ads than their nonblack peers did. This disproportionate exposure was amplified when the report broke down types of alcohol. Young blacks apparently saw 81% more magazine ads for distilled spirits. Indeed, Jack Daniel's was among the largest spenders on alcohol ads that reached black youth through magazines. The magazines that most exposed young African Americans to alcohol ads were *Sports Illustrated, Vibe, Cosmopolitan, ESPN the Magazine, Jet, Rolling Stone, Entertainment Weekly, Ebony, In Style, Playboy, GQ, Essence,* and *People.* The center noted that young blacks were overrepresented in the readership of most of these magazines. The report also found that alcohol companies spent a disproportionate amount of advertising dollars on the fifteen television shows that are most popular among black youth, including the *Bernie Mac Show,* the *Simpsons, King of the Hill,* and the *George Lopez Show.* Furthermore, young blacks were also more likely than their nonblack counterparts to hear radio ads for alcohol products. Because most radio alcohol advertising is placed locally, the report examined the information by region. Five areas—New York, Chicago, Los Angeles, Houston-Galveston, and Washington—accounted for 70% of black youth exposure to alcohol advertising on the radio (*Westside Gazette,* 2003). With figures such as these, it is hard to deny that the alcoholic beverages industry is, indeed, targeting ethnic groups.

In addition to developing alcoholic beverages targeted to minorities and creating hard-hitting and oftentimes exploitive campaigns to sell their products, alcohol companies (much like tobacco firms) insinuate themselves into ethnic communities by sponsoring ethnic events and organizations, awarding scholarships, and hiring ethnic employees to work for them. The Hiram Walker & Sons Distillery , which designates 10% of its total media advertising to blacks, supports the 100 Black Men of America (an organization that is made up of professionals who are dedicated to helping inner-city youth), the National Caucus on the Black Aged (an advocacy group that provides homes for the aged), the United Negro College Fund, and the NAACP. In addition, the company established the Hiram Walker Foundation, dedicated to the support of minority education, particularly in the food service and retail industries (Pomeroy, 1992). Facing stagnant beer sales, an aging population, and the blossoming appeal of wine, the nation's biggest brewers are aggressively courting Hispanics. In 2006, for example, Anheuser-Busch Inc., brewer of Budweiser and Bud Light, created a new division dedicated to marketing to Hispanics and boosted its 2006 advertising spending in Hispanic media by two-thirds—to more than $60 million (Jordan, 2006). Activists are raising health concerns about the beer advertising blitz on the grounds that it targets a population that is young and is disproportionately likely to abuse alcohol. One survey found that Hispanics consumed more beer in a typical month than other ethnic groups. The survey of over 23,000 people found that Hispanics drank an average of 6.1 beers in the previous thirty days, while non-Hispanic white respondents reported that they consumed 4.7 beers in the same period of time (Vranica, 2006). To counter criticism, the brewer has engaged in a variety of efforts, such as investing in local and national organizations that are working to promote business and economic opportunities for Hispanics, as well as Asian Americans, blacks, and women. In addition, it has awarded more than $5 million over the past five years to college students through its Urban Scholarship program. The scholarships have enabled at least five hundred minority students to each receive $10,000 to attend the college or university of their choice. And the firm touts their do-good efforts in commercial messages. The copy in a recent ad appearing in *People en Español* reads, "We know that the development of your community is important to you. That's why during the past 20 years, we've contributed more than $45 million to programs supporting community organizations that make a difference in your life." The tagline reads, 'Budweiser—The Sponsor of Your Dreams' (see Figure 8.3). All too often, marketers expect something in return for their sponsorships and diversity efforts. The support of both tobacco and alcoholic beverage firms may buy the silence of minority leaders regarding the dangers of these products in their communities (Jacobson, Taylor, & Baldwin, 1993).

Whether to represent a client that sells tobacco products or alcoholic beverages is a serious ethical question facing many advertising agencies today. Of even greater concern is the targeting of such products to ethnic audiences. Several agencies have resigned profitable accounts, because they accept the medical evidence regarding the harm that these products can cause.

The Price

Pricing responsibility refers to charging only what consumers can afford. In terms of pricing products for ethnic consumers, one area to which marketers must pay particular attention is price discrimination, sometimes known as *race-based pricing*. No one should have to pay more for a product or service because of their race or ethnicity. Dillard's department stores came under fire for charging black customers more than Caucasian customers ("Dillard's Sued," 2005). A class action lawsuit was filed against Dillard's Inc., alleging racial discrimination, deceptive sales practices, and unconscionable conduct relating to the marketing and sale of beauty salon services. Apparently, white customers at the Dillard's salon in Tuscaloosa, Alabama—the corporation owns and operates 340 retail department stores located in twenty-nine states—were charged $20 for salon services while the price to wash and set so-called ethnic hair was $30.00. Furthermore, the department store did not disclose the dual pricing policy to African Americans prior to providing the services. Dillard's has faced at least three lawsuits claiming racial discrimination since 1998.

In the case above, a single advertiser was accused of overcharging ethnic consumers. However, there are also entire industries that have been charged

Figure 8.3: Budweiser Ad Highlighting Support for the Hispanic Community

with such practices. The home loan industry serves as just one example. Back in 1968, the Fair Housing Act was passed, making discrimination in lending illegal in the housing market. However, in 2003, President Bush pledged $50 million to fight ongoing abuses in lending. He cited a 2002 study by the Department of Housing and Urban Development that showed that minorities receive less information, less assistance, and less favorable terms from mortgage lenders. And those abuses have continued. An analysis of records from twenty-five of the nation's largest lenders revealed that, in 2004, blacks who bought homes in communities across America were four times as likely as whites to get charged high interest rates for mortgage loans. Even African Americans with annual incomes of more than $100,000 paid high rates more often than whites with incomes below $40,000. For decades, blacks struggled to get loans at any price. Indeed, lenders ignored entire black neighborhoods, a practice called *redlining*. Also, in 2004, the nation's ten largest banks denied black applicants twice as often as whites. And, on average, they made only 5% of their home loans to blacks. A new group of companies has filled the void. Called *subprime* lenders, these companies charge higher interest rates than banks. The result is that blacks now receive twice as many home purchase loans as a decade ago—but one in four is paying a steep price. A high-rate loan requires borrowers to pay tens of thousands of dollars in additional interest while building less equity. Borrowers fail to repay these loans far more often, thus losing their homes and ruining their credit. And each foreclosure also damages a neighborhood (Heisiger, 2005). In short, the industry is simply discriminating in a new way. Race-based pricing may not only cause an ethnic group to boycott a marketer, but it will also likely result in a public relations nightmare.

Distribution

Additionally, goods must be distributed in a responsible fashion, and marketers must ensure that products and services are made available to consumers where they require them. Bank One provides an excellent example of a corporation that took risks to meet the needs of its customers. For more than twenty years, no new bank branches were opened in the troubled Los Angeles neighborhoods of Crenshaw—the heart of the city's African American community—and Boyle Heights—predominantly Latino. Gang activity and crime had plagued the areas. Residents had marched on police headquarters to demand better law enforcement. These were certainly not the kinds of neighborhoods where large banking companies were eager to open branches. But Bank One did so in both communities. Reza Aghamirzadeh, the company's manager of corporate community development, noted, "A key component of the strategy was to become part of the fabric of the community. You really have to prove you're there for the right reasons and that you really want to be there for the community" (Bach, 2002). To that end, local people were put in charge of the bank branches in both communities. Bank One also opened a community center in a renovated building behind the Crenshaw branch, where the Chamber of Commerce and other community groups hold seminars and meetings. While Mr. Aghamirzadeh acknowledged that crime was still a concern, so far there had been no problems. Such moves prove to be beneficial to the community and are golden opportunities for corporations looking to find untapped markets.

Promotion

Promotion responsibility refers not just to advertising message content, but rather to all promotional activities. Advertising's high visibility, however, makes it particularly vulnerable to criticism. An important area of concern related to advertising content is its stereotypic representation of a number of groups, including women, the disabled, the elderly, and, of course, ethnic groups. Advertising has always traded on stereotypes. Advertisements—both print and broadcast—must telegraphically sum up their characters in just a few seconds, and, unfortunately, stereotypes are the easiest way to accomplish this. For many years, blacks, Hispanics, and Asians were virtually invisible in advertising, and, when they appeared, it was in stereotypic fashion. Advertisers have come a long way over the past few decades, and most advertisers today portray ethnic groups favorably in their commercial communications, not just because of pressure from watchdog groups, but also because it makes good business sense not to offend the audience to which you are appealing. Admittedly, problems still do exist, in terms of frequency of representation of ethnic groups, the roles ethnic models portray, and the types of products for which multicultural models are employed.

Frequency of representation is a concept that looks at the number of minority models in advertisements as a proportion of all people shown in commercial messages. It suggests that, for portrayals to be at parity, ethnic representation in ads should approximate the ethnic group's proportion in the population (Taylor & Stern, 1997). As one might expect, Caucasians are the group most commonly portrayed in all types of advertising. In an examination of commercials appearing during prime-time programming, Taylor and Stern (1997) found that whites appeared in nearly all of the television ads, African Americans appeared in about 33% of the messages, Hispanics appeared in 10%, and Asians appeared in roughly 8%. At first glance, these figures appear encouraging. However, Taylor and Stern's research also revealed that, while white models played major roles in 90% of the spots, ethnic models were significantly less likely to appear as the sole or primary character. Both African Americans and Hispanic Americans appeared in major roles in only about half of the commercials. However, Asian models were even more likely than the members of the other ethnic groups to appear in background roles. A second investigation confirmed this trend of ethnic models appearing in primarily token or background roles (Green, 1999). In a more recent examination of television advertisements, Mastro and Stern (2003) found that 83.3% of the speaking characters were white, 12.4% were black, 2.3% were Asian, and a mere 1.0% were Hispanic.

Turning to print media, a study conducted by Lee and Joo (2005) revealed that both African Americans and Asians had, in fact, a much higher appearance in mass circulation magazine ads compared to their presence in the general population. African American models appeared in 17.5% of the ads. Asian models were featured in 8.3% of the ads. In contrast, however, Hispanics appeared in a mere 2.6% of the print messages. Compared with television, ethnic models are also more likely to be portrayed in dominant roles in magazine ads (Lee & Joo, 2005). According to their data, when Asian Americans did appear in mass circulation magazine ads, they were more likely to be featured in a primary role and in the foreground of the ads—suggesting that they are not marginalized. While African Americans show a pattern similar to Asian Americans, Hispanics exhibit an even split between a primary role and a secondary and background role combined. In terms of level of representation, the picture looks significantly better when examining only those publications targeting ethnic consumers. A study conducted by the Magazine Publishers of America (2001) found that, in magazines targeting African Americans (such as *Essence*), 80% of the models appearing in the ads are black. In *Latina,* a magazine targeting Hispanic women, about half of the models in the ads appeared to be Hispanic. And, in *A,* a magazine appealing to Asians, all of the ads featured Asian models.

In terms of the types of roles portrayed by ethnic models in advertising, the range of portrayals typically has been both limited and stereotypic. Examining the roles African American models play in commercial messages, males, in particular, are often depicted as athletes and entertainers in advertisements. Famous African American athletes have sold a variety of products. Michael Jordan has sold everything from underwear to hot dogs to cologne. More recently, Tiger Woods has pitched Nike, Titleist, Buick, Rolex, and American Express, among other brands (see Figure 8.4). Black entertainers are seen equally frequently in commercial messages. Everyone recalls Bill Cosby as the longtime spokesperson for JELL-O pudding. More recently, Jamie Foxx has pitched Rémy Martin cognac, and Tavis Smiley has endorsed One United Bank. Such portrayals have increased to the point that this role tends to be overrepresented in ads when compared to other ethnic groups and to whites. Lee and Joo (2005) found that, of the three ethnic groups, African Americans were least likely to be portrayed in the business setting. In analyzing television commercials portraying computer usage, Kinnick and her colleagues (2001) found mostly white males in positions of authority, while African American males were rarely represented as computer experts, scientists, or doctors—suggesting that black males must be athletes or superstars to be seen as competent. African American women in the computer ads were typically portrayed in the role of telemarketers and secretaries, rather than as bosses or business professionals. Sheehan (2004) also notes that

> blacks are often seen in ads as being in need and assisted by others: Any commercial for a cash-advance service, for example, is likely to feature blacks needing a loan and whites behind the counter. In addition, blacks are often pictured as caregivers for children. This type of portrayal could be seen as an extension of the domestic servant role.

In the 1970s and 1980s, judging from most television commercials, "Asian-Americans were either mincing stewardesses, sage mandarins, belligerent sumo wrestlers or rapacious Japanese businessmen" (Lee, 1991). Sheehan notes that "exotic character" portrayals are also common:

> The exotic image features portrayals of Asian women as dragon ladies or China dolls, women at opposite ends of the spectrum. Dragon ladies are women who are inherently scheming, untrustworthy and backstabbing. China dolls are docile and delicate women subservient to men. The Japanese geishas fall into the China doll category. Other exotic imagery includes stereotypes of Asians as martial arts fighters. (2004, p. 128)

Added to these images is the "model minority" stereotype (Taylor & Stern, 1997). This stereotype represents a number of positive qualities supposedly unique to Asian Americans, such as a superior work ethic, high levels of educational achievement, and a highly refined business and economic sensibility (Paek & Shah, 2003). Moreover, Asian American models are depicted as affluent and financially successful, as well as possessing a high level of technological skill and talent. Lee and Joo (2005) found that Asian American models are the most likely of the three ethnic groups to appear in a business setting, but they are significantly less likely to appear in other types of settings (such as at home, in a social setting, or outdoors). Indeed, of the mass-circulation magazine ads portraying Asian Americans, over 62% of portrayals occurred in the business setting, and only 12% appeared in either the home or social setting. Most often, Asian models appeared as co-workers (52.7%); Asian Americans were portrayed as family members in only 13% of the print ads and as friends in only 15% of the messages. These portrayals, according to the researchers, feed the "all work, no play" stereotype of Asian Americans.

Figure 8.4: Tiger Woods Is a Spokesperson for American Express

Luis Reyes, author of *The Mask of Zorro: Mexican Americans in Popular Media,* points out the four common Hispanic stereotypes: the bandit, the Latin lover, the Latina spitfire, and the sweet senorita (Nuiry, 1996). Back in 1967, Foote, Cone, and Belding, one of the country's largest advertising agencies, developed a TV and print campaign for the Frito-Lay corporation that featured a caricature of a fat, mustachioed Mexican bandit called the Frito Bandito. In the broadcast ads, the character had a thick Spanish accent, a long handlebar mustache, a huge sombrero, and a pair of six-shooters. The print ads warned, "He loves crunchy [*sic*] Fritos corn chips so much he'll stop at nothing to get yours. What's more, he's cunning, clever and sneaky!" The campaign sparked the ire of the Mexican American community. The Mexican American Anti-Defamation Committee called for the banning of the bandito, charging that the campaign carried the "racist message" that Mexicans are "sneaky thieves," (Nuiry, 1996). In response to protests, Frito-Lay stopped using the Frito Bandito character in 1970. While the bandit stereotype is typically limited to males, the spitfire stereotype is assigned to females. Chiquita Banana, formerly part of the United Fruit Company, began employing a character called Chiquita, who embodied the stereotypical, fun-loving Hispanic spitfire, in television campaigns in the 1960s. The sexy Chiquita wore a fruit-laden hat, à la Carmen Miranda, a ruffled shirt, and high heels; danced a rumba in the ads; and sang her famous "I'm a Chiquita Banana" jingle, complete with a heavy Spanish accent. The ubiquitous blue and yellow Chiquita sticker—complete with the Chiquita character in fruit headdress and gaudy costume—was placed on countless bananas in local grocery stores for many years. Unfortunately, stereotypes of Hispanics still exist in commercial messages today, though they tend to be more subtle. "When Hispanics appear in general market ads, they are usually in the kitchen, dancing to salsa music, playing soccer or living in modest neighborhoods," notes William Ortiz, president of the Hispanic division at Global/Works, New York (Voight, 2003). Lee and Joo (2005) confirm this perception—while Hispanic models are also portrayed in business settings, they are still significantly more likely to be shown in a home setting than Asian American models. Hispanic models were also more likely to be portrayed as a family member than as a co-worker than either Asian American or African American models. Paek and Shah (2003) found that Latino models were commonly portrayed as relatively poor, blue-collar workers.

Ethnic models also tend to be employed for some product categories more than others. African American models, for instance, appear frequently in ads for health and beauty products. African Americans are also commonly employed in food and beverage ads, as well as messages for financial services and cars, but rarely for over-the-counter medications (Taylor & Stern, 1997; Mastro & Stern, 2003). Asian models are commonly found as endorsers of high-tech products (see Figure 8.5) and banking/financial services but are found significantly less often as endorsers for apparel, food and beverages, or household supplies (Taylor & Stern, 1997; Marimoto & La Farle, 2002).[A more recent investigation (Lee & Joo, 2005) confirmed that ads for technology and business-related products/services do indeed feature Ashian American models more frequently as endorsers when compared to ads for nontechnological and nonbusiness-related products/services. Hispanic models appear in ads for the greatest range of products, including automotive products, entertainment, and clothing. Hispanics also appeared in television ads for telecommunications companies and messages for banking and finance. Latinos were particularly likely to be featured in television spots for soaps and deodorants (Mastro & Stern, 2003) but were unlikely to be portrayed using computers. Indeed, Kinnick and her colleagues (2001) found that less than 1% of models portrayed using computers were Hispanic.

Ethnic and racial stereotypes have been called the dark side of multicultural marketing (Solomon, 1999). Though there have been improvements in the portrayal of ethnic groups in advertising, stereotyping still occurs, and the consequence can be significant. For example, the portrayal of African American males primarily as athletes or entertainers may well send the message to black children that their futures are more connected to these areas than academics. And the complete lack of Hispanic models in ads portraying computer usage might convey the erroneous message to employers that Hispanics apparently are not technologically proficient. But even so-called positive stereotypes are of concern. While portraying Asian Americans as diligent, hard working, and technologically competent may seem complimentary, Lee and Joo (2005) note that it can lead to negative consequences for individuals, both inside and outside that ethnic group. Continued portrayals of Asian Americans based on the model minority stereotype and repetitive exposure to these images may create undue pressure on Asian Americans to conform to stereotype-driven expectations, consequently undermining their performance. Furthermore, when Asian Americans fail to meet such expectations, they may be more harshly penalized than others and suffer lower self-esteem. To the extent that Asian Americans are viewed as industrious, hard working, and serious, they may be prone to more negative stereotypes, such as being perceived as less sociable or even as workaholics. At best, stereotypic advertisements can be offensive and insulting to the ethnic consumer. At worst, they perpetuate distorted images that are harmful to the ethnic group, as well as the general population. In short, stereotypic portrayals of Asian Americans, African Americans, and Hispanic Americans in advertising messages serve no one. Scholars and practitioners alike suggest the need for more frequent and more positive portrayals of ethnic models in commercial communications, along with a broader range of roles and a greater degree of accuracy in their portrayals.

Figure 8.5: Asian American Featured in Print Advertisement for Windows Server

Ethical behavior relates to each of the four *P*s of the marketing mix: product, price, place (distribution), and promotion. And, in short, ethical business behavior pays off. Data from KLD Research and Analytics show that companies identified by *Business Ethics* as the one hundred best corporate citizens outperform the remaining S&P 500 companies on measures of overall performance. Rankings for the Best 100 list are based on the perspectives of multiple shareholders, including ethnic groups, women, employees, customers, investors, and representatives of environmental and overseas interest groups (Shepherd, 2003).

Key questions facing marketing and advertising practitioners on a day-to-day basis include the following:

- Who should and who should not be advertised to?
- What should and should not be advertised?
- What should and should not be the content of the advertising message?
- What should and should not be the symbolic tone or actual character of the advertising message?
- What should and should not be the relationship among clients, agencies, and the mass media?
- What should and should not be advertising's business obligations versus its societal obligations? (Rotzoll, Haefner, & Sandage, 1986)

Beyond Ethics: Corporate Social Responsibility

It can be said that ethical behavior deals primarily with doing no harm. In contrast, socially responsible behavior has more to do with doing good. Jeffrey R. Immelt, chairman and chief executive officer of General Electric (GE), ranked both as one of the world's most valuable *and* most admired companies by *Fortune* magazine, puts it this way: "Think about your neighbors," he says. "If they obey the law, if they pay their taxes, if they don't park their Winnebago on the street, are they just compliant? Now what about the neighbor who organizes the block party? Or, the one who picks the kids up after school? That's a good neighbor" (Gunther, 2004). GE wants to be known as a good company, not just in the United States, but also around the world. And expectations about what it means to be a good company are rising. Companies are increasingly expected to engage in corporate social responsibility.

A number of factors are driving corporate social responsibility: the unending parade of corporate wrongdoing—from Enron to WorldCom—that has rocked the business world, the resulting increase in regulatory scrutiny, intense twenty-four-hour-a-day worldwide media coverage, and, in particular, consumers' critical view of corporate scandals and their increasing expectations of big business. Today, more than ever, a company's reputation in the marketplace is related to its social, as well as its ethical, performance.

Research conducted in the late 1990s revealed that social actions played a far larger role than originally anticipated in forming consumers' *impressions* of companies. Half of the respondents in the study mentioned factors related to a company's broader responsibilities—labor practices, environmental protection, and a broader responsibility to society at large—as items they considered when forming an impression of companies. A follow-up study (*Brand Strategy,* 2005a) revealed that such societal expectations have only increased. A study conducted in the United States by Golin/Harris found that 74% of Americans say that corporate social responsibility is important to their trust in a company ("CSR No Longer," 2004). More significantly, consumers' impressions of corporations influence their purchase *behavior.* For example, more than 60% of Americans said they would switch brands or stores to purchase from companies that support particular social causes (Nelson, 2003).

More compelling than the positive impacts of corporate social responsibility are the consequences of negative social practices. According to a 2002 Cone Corporate Citizenship Study, 85% of Americans say they would be likely to speak out against a company among their family and friends if they learned about a company's harmful social behavior. Environics found a surge in the proportion of consumers who reported that they had punished a company they perceived as socially irresponsible in 2002 ("CSR No Longer," 2004). Another study reported that over 68% of consumers in the United States claim to have boycotted a food, drink, or personal care company's goods on ethical grounds (*Brand Strategy,* 2005b). The landscape of corporate excellence has changed. Ethics, integrity, and honesty are more a part of the definition than ever before. No longer is it enough to deliver an excellent offering, you must be an excellent offerer.

Executives and investors alike are paying attention. A survey conducted in 2004, which polled 136 senior executives and sixty-five institutional investors, found that 85% of the respondents ranked corporate responsibility as "central" or "important" to business decisions, compared with a mere five years earlier, when 44% of respondents answered similarly ("How CSR Is Driving," 2005). Fifty-two percent of the top 250 companies in the Fortune 500 list published separate reports on corporate social responsibility—up from 45% just three years ago. By one count, there are already one hundred thousand pages on corporate Web sites dealing with the topic, and more than two hundred mutual funds specialize in socially responsible investing (Pearlstein, 2005). But the attention doesn't stop there. Amazon lists more than six hundred books related to the topic. Increasingly, business schools offer courses in it. For example, master of business administration (MBA) programs at Harvard, Stanford, the University of Michigan, and the University of Virginia require students to complete ethics courses as part of their program of study. Furthermore, corporate social responsibility consultancies have cropped up around the globe. Finally, the United Nations has even hosted a summit on it.

While corporate social responsibility is certainly the current buzzword, it is hardly a new concept. Indeed, it has been around since the eighteenth century, when antislavery groups appealed to the public to buy sugar that had been produced in a country where unpaid labor was not enforced (*Strategic Directions* (Septmber, 2002). And, over the decades, numerous companies have prided themselves in looking out for their employees. However, it was only relatively recently that the actual term *corporate social responsibility* was coined. In the 1990s, it was primarily equated with environmental concerns, but, today, the expression has expanded to encompass a range of issues. Beyond a firm's commitment to its consumers (providing a quality product at a fair price, promoted in an ethical fashion) and its commitment to stockholders, businesses today must consider the interests of all of their employees, as well as their greater role in society.

A Firm's Responsibility to All Its Employees

A company must be representative of the customers and communities it serves. Given the diversity of the U.S. population, it is simply no longer acceptable for firms to recruit and hire all-white staffs to manufacture, promote, or sell their products. Companies must implement policies and programs to promote diversity and prevent race-based discrimination (or, for that matter, discrimination based on gender, age, religion, sexual orientation, or disability). These policies and programs must be applied to all aspects of employment, including recruiting, hiring, evaluation, training, discipline, career development, compensation, promotion, and termination (Toombs & Williams-Harold, 2004). Firms that do not engage in such practices will find that employees, lawyers, customers, the community, governmental bodies, and the media can all hold a company accountable. For example, Abercrombie & Fitch—a company with a workforce of 22,000 and more than 700 stores nationwide—was sued for hiring a disproportionately white sales staff and placing minorities in less visible jobs ("Abercrombie Trying," 2004). The nine original claimants, which included Asian Americans, a Latino, and an African American, were either refused sales jobs or fired based on their race or ethnicity. Their success was due largely to the support they received from such groups as the NAACP, the Asian Pacific American Legal Center, the Mexican American Legal Defense and Educational Fund, and the San Francisco–based law firm Minami, Lew, and Tamaki, as well as the U.S. Equal Employment Opportunity Commission. In the settlement, Abercrombie & Fitch agreed to pay $40 million to Asian American, Latino,

African American, and women applicants and employees who accused the company of discrimination. While Abercrombie & Fitch admitted to no wrong-doing in the settlement, it did agree to implement policies and programs to promote diversity and to prevent race- and gender-based discrimination. It was also required to hire a vice president of diversity and to include more people of color in its advertisements. Above and beyond the financial costs associated with failing to engage in nondiscriminatory practices, one must consider the fallout from the negative publicity generated by this suit.

While diversity is an indicator of good business, it must be incorporated from the boiler room all the way to the boardroom. Recently, in what it calls the "common goal of increasing representation of minorities and women on corporate boards," three leadership organizations formed the Alliance for Board Diversity. These groups include Catalyst, the Executive Leadership Council, and the Hispanic Association on Corporate Responsibility. The Alliance for Board Diversity released their first joint research, entitled "Women and Minorities on Fortune 100 Boards" (Bruzzese, 2005). In assessing diversity in the boardrooms of Fortune 100 companies, the study found the following:

- Just 14.9% of board seats are held by a minority individual, with minority women holding only 3% of board seats.
- Hispanics hold only 3.9% of board seats, followed by Asian Americans, who hold a mere 1%.
- There is a recycling of the same minority individuals—especially black men—on multiple boards.
- Very few Fortune 100 boards have representation from all groups, and, in more than 60% of the boards surveyed, less than one-third of the seats were held by women or minorities.
- In a statement issued by the Alliance for Board Diversity, Alfonso E. Martinez, president and CEO of the Hispanic Association on Corporate Responsibility, said that "good governance acknowledges the interests of stakeholders, including shareholders, employees, customers, suppliers and communities that businesses and organizations serve." "Having a diverse board sends a clear message to each of these groups," he noted (Bruzzese, 2005). Clearly, much work remains to be done.

However, colorizing the workforce is just the beginning. Diversity issues also extend to a firm's selection of suppliers, contractors, and professional service providers. Ford Motor Company has been recognized for its diversity efforts. Indeed, Ford has one of the largest groups of minority employees in corporate America. And Ford also operates a Minority Supplier and Dealer Development Program. The company spends more with minority suppliers than any other U.S. automotive manufacturer. Over the past decade,

Ford has received numerous awards in recognition of its supplier diversity—including the Corporation of the Year Award from the National Minority Supplier Development Council and the Gender and Race Excellence Award from the Charles H. Wright Museum of African American History (Moore, 2003). Ford's minority dealer program is a longtime leader in the auto industry as well. The company has 345 minority dealers in the United States among all brands, representing 6.7% of the firm's 5,127 dealers—the highest among major automakers (Webster, 2004). Above and beyond Ford's workforce, Ford Motor Company suppliers and dealers have created more than 39,000 jobs in minority communities. Copy in an ad for the Ford Motor Company (see Figure 8.6) reads,

> Henry Ford recognized the value of a skilled workforce—regardless of race. And when Ford Motor company became the first major corporation to pay African American workers equal pay for equal work, it helped give birth to the Black middle class. At Ford Motor Company, we're proud to do our part by supporting minority businesses, suppliers and dealers across the country. When every community has a chance to realize financial success, all Americans will advance together.

Valuing diversity does not just have to do with stamping out prejudice, complying with antidiscrimination laws, promoting good corporate citizenship, or doing the right thing with regard to ethnic groups. While these goals are important, diversity is also a key to business success. A company that gets the right handle on diversity, as it applies to employees and customers, will outperform companies that don't—in unsentimental measures, such as sales, profits, market share, and stock price (Gordon, 2005).

A Firm's Responsibility to Society

Good leaders, in companies large and small, are looking for ways to give back. In giving back to the ethnic community, firms must recognize exactly what is important to Hispanics, Asian Americans, and African Americans. Social responsibility efforts must resonate with the target audience. Consider General Motors' efforts to support the black community. Research, consisting of focus groups and telephone surveys, has provided evidence that entrepreneurship is important to this group. Furthermore, investigations revealed that there wasn't enough being done to support entrepreneurship among twenty-one- to thirty-year-olds. Entrepreneurship among young black professionals aged twenty-one to thirty—particularly in such categories as fashion, music, film, and restaurants—is so strong that *Black Enterprise* magazine dubbed these budding Spike Lees and Russell Simmons "hiphopreneurs" ("How CSR Is Driving," 2005). So, for the third year in a row, General Motors (GM) has partnered with *Black Enterprise* to serve as the title sponsor for the 2006 Black

Figure 8.6: Ford Motor Company Advertisement Promoting Its Diversity Program

Enterprise Entrepreneurs Conference. The 2006 event brought together more than 1,500 of the nation's leading corporate executives and minority business leaders. Themed Where Deals Are Made, the gathering serves as the nation's foremost African American business information and networking event. The conference featured three days of business, motivational, and leadership seminars designed to empower and profit emerging and established minority businesses. The event presents opportunities for African American entrepreneurs to further their business by networking with well-known corporate executives while strategizing to compete and thrive in today's ultracompetitive businesses (see Figure 8.7 for an advertisement for the Black Enterprise Entrepreneurs Conference). The conference featured sessions including Getting your Deal Financed, Landing the Multimillion-Dollar Government Contract, How to Create a Megafranchise, Surviving the Entrepreneurship Roller Coaster, and How to Protect Your Ideas and Inventions, among others. Roderick Gillum, vice president of GM Corporate Responsibility and Diversity, notes,

> For GM to win in the global auto business, we need business partners who represent the best talent. Whether it's the billions of dollars in purchases from suppliers; the employees who design, build and market our products; or the dealers who sell our great cars and trucks, African Americans are a key component to the strength of General Motors. ("2006 Black Enterprise," 2006)

Additional sponsors of the event included American Airlines, AT&T, ExxonMobil, FedEx, Frito-Lay, Hilton Anatole, IBM, Microsoft, Pepsi, State Farm Insurance, Wal-Mart, and Wendy's, among others.

Corporate social responsibility is not divorced from a company's bottom line. Based on a survey of the 250 top companies in the Fortune 500 survey, as well as the one hundred largest companies in sixteen countries, researchers revealed that businesses cited a variety of reasons for their involvement in corporate social responsibility—though, by far, the greatest number pointed to economic considerations. "The economic reasons were either directly linked to increased shareholder value or market share, or indirectly linked through increased business opportunities, innovation, reputation and reduced risk," the survey noted (Buck, 2005). In short, then, corporate social responsibility makes good business sense.

Summary

Clearly, both ethics and corporate social responsibility matter. They matter to consumers and employees of all races and ethnicities, to investors, and to governments and activist groups, whose power to influence business is growing. Benjamin W. Heineman Jr., senior vice president for law and public affairs at

Figure 8.7: General Motors Sponsors Black Enterprise Entrepreneurs Conference

General Electric—named the World's Most Admired Company for 2006 by *Fortune* magazine—argues that companies must invest in their reputations. "Just as there's goodwill on balance sheets, and just as a brand has value, reputation, broadly defined, has enormous value for companies" (Gunther, 2004). Today, it is no longer enough for a company to stand for productivity, growth, rising profits, and shareholder returns. In the marketplace today, the combination of ethics and corporate social responsibility isn't just a "nice thing" but rather a "must have" ("CSR No Longer," 2004).

REFERENCES

Abercrombie trying on diversity for size. (2004, November 27–December 3). *Northwest Asian Weekly*, p. 2.

Alaniz, M.K. (1998). Alcohol availability and targeted advertising in racial/ethnic minority communities. *Alcohol Health and Research World,* 22(4), p. 286–280.

Alaniz, M. L., & Wilkes, C. (1995). Reinterpreting Latino culture in the commodity form: The case of alcohol advertising in the Mexican American community. *Hispanic Journal of Behavioral Sciences, 17*(4), 430–451.

Altman, D. G., Schooler, C., & Basil, M. D. (1991). Alcohol and cigarette advertising on billboards. *Health Education Research: Theory and Practice,* 6(4), 487–490.

Anderson Cancer Center. (1995). *Tobacco use in America* (p. 30).

Bach, D. (2002, May 9). Bank One puts a bet on troubled neighborhoods. *American Banker,* p. 12-A.

Bell, K. (2004, August 19). Smoking foes decry lures to minority teens. *The Atlanta Journal Constitution,* p. C-4.

Brand Strategy (2005a, September 8). Corporate social responsibility and its impact on corporate reputation. London, p. 40.

Brand Strategy (2005b, June 9). Ethical marketing: A question of ethics. London, p. 24.

Brown, Rev. J. (1992, Fall). Marketing exploitation. *Business and Society Review, 83,* 17.

Bruzzese, A. (2005, May 26). Diversity can spice up a company. *Gannett News Service,* p. 1.

Buck, T. (2005, June 15). More companies reveal social policies. *Financial Times,* p. 8.

Castellano, J. P. (1992, Fall). Respecting differences. In *Distilling the Truth about Alcohol Ads.*

Business and Society Review, 83, p. 14. Centers for Disease Control and Prevention. (1998, June 10). Publication of Surgeon General's Report on smoking and health. *Journal of the American Medical Association,* p. 1776.

CSR no longer a "nice thing" but a "must have." (2004, January 19). *PR News,* p. 1.

Dillard's sued for charging Black customers more than Caucasian customers. (2005, June 2–8). *Westside Gazette,* p. 1.

Ellis, G. (2005, January 4). Cigarette companies target African Americans. *Philadelphia Tribune,* p. 5-B.

Farris, P., & Albion, M. (1980, Summer). The impact of advertising on the price of consumer products. *Journal of Marketing, 44,* 17–35.

Fernandez, E. (1998, June 28). Multilingual tobacco warning: FTC changes policy for ethnic audiences. *San Francisco Examiner,* p. A-1.

Ferraro, S. (1999, November 15). Menace in a bottle. Whether promoted by loneliness, loss or pain, frequent drinking puts millions of Americans at risk. *Journal Star,* Peoria, p. C8.

Frith, K. T. & Mueller, B. (2003). *Advertising and Societies: Global Issues.* Peter Lang: New York.

Gordon, J. (2005, May). Diversity is a business driver. *Training, 42*(5), 24.

Green, C. L. (1999). Ethnic evaluations of advertising: Interaction effects of strength of ethnic identification, media placement, and degree of racial composition. *Journal of Advertising, 28*(1), 49–64.

Grow, B., Hamm, S., & Lee, L. (2005, August 15). The debate over doing good. *Business Week,* p. 76.

Gunther, M. (2004, November 15). Money and morals at GE. *Fortune,* pp. 176–180.

Hacker, G. (1998, Spring). Liquor advertisements on television: Just say no. *Journal of Public Policy and Marketing, 17*(1), 139–142.

Hacker, G., Collins, R., & Jacobson, M. F. (1987). *Marketing booze to blacks.* Washington, DC: Center for Science in the Public Interest.

Harris, R. (2005, August 15–22). Growing responsibilities. *Marketing, 110*(27), 15–17.

Heisiger, M. (2005, September 4). Home loans costing blacks more, data find. *Las Vegas Review Journal,* p. 1-E.

Herdt, T. (1998, March 29). Hispanic groups assail alcohol ads. *Orange County Register,* p. A-37.

Herman, E. (2004, October 7). Cigarette maker cuts hip-hop ads; Kool to pay $1.5 million to settle charges it targeted Black teens. *Chicago Sun-Times,* p. 6.

How CSR is driving the way companies conduct business. (2005, June 1). *PR News,* p. 1.

Jacobson, M. F., & Mazur, L. A. (1995). *Marketing madness: A survival guide for a consumer society.* Boulder, CO: Westview Press.

Jacobson, M. F., Taylor, P., & Baldwin, D. (1993). Advertising alcohol: This brew's for you. *Medical and Health Annual,* 154.

Jordan, M. (2004, March 4). Nestlé ad tack for its formula faces U.S. fire. *The Wall Street Journal,* p. A-7.

Jordan, M. (2006, March 29). Cerveza, si o no? The beer industry's embrace of Hispanic market prompts a backlash from activists [Eastern edition]. *The Wall Street Journal,* p. B-1.

Kinnick, K., White, C. & Washington, K. (2001, October 31). Racial representation of computer users in prime-time advertising. *Race, Gender & Class,* New Orleans, 8(4), p. 96.

Kosareff, J. (2004, May 11). Las Vegas-based tobacco firm to offer cigarette products for Asians. *Knight Ridder Tribune Business Wire,* p. 1.

Laczniak, G., & Murphy, P. (1990, Fall/Winter). International marketing ethics. *Bridges: An Interdisciplinary Journal of Theology, Philosophy, History and Science, 2*(3/4), 155–177.

Lee, P. (1991, January 1). Asian Americans decry stereotypes in TV ads. *Los Angeles Times,* p. 6.

Lee, K.-Y., & Joo, S. H. (2005, Autumn). The portrayals of Asian Americans in mainstream magazine ads: An update. *Journalism and Mass Communication Quarterly, 82*(3), 654–671.

Mack, R. (1997). Bringing down the walls of state pre-emption: California cities fight for local control of alcohol outlets. *African American Law and Policy Report, 3*(1), 295–324.

Magazine Publishers of America. (2001). *Marketing to the emerging minorities.* Retrieved from http://www.magazine.org/Diversity/articles/ad_pages.html

Malt liquor market targets to black youth. (2005, March 23–29). *Miami Times,* p. 3-A.

Marimoto, M. & La Ferle, C. (2002). Representation of Asian Americans in magazine advertisements. In *Proceedings of the Conference of the American Academy of Advertising,* ed. A.M. Abernethy (Auburn, AL), p. 138–147.

Mastro, D., & Stern, S. (2003, December). Representations of race in television commercials: A content analysis of prime-time advertising. *Journal of Broadcasting and Electronic Media, 47*(4), 638–647.

Moore, M. D. (2003, June 11). Ford's minority supplier program grows. *Michigan Chronicle,* p. A-27.

Nelson, R. A. (2003). Ethics and social issues in business: An updated communication perspective. *Competitiveness Review, 13*(1), 66.

Nuiry, O. E. (1996, July). Ban the bandito! *Hispanic, 9*(7), 26.

O'Sullivan, T. (2002, April 30). Asian American affairs: The two Wongs of Abercrombie and Fitch. *Asian Reporter,* p. 6.

Paek, H. J., & Shah, M. (2003). Racial ideology, model minorities, and the not-so-silent partner: Stereotyping of Asian Americans in U.S. magazine advertising. *The Howard Journal of Communication, 14,* 225–243.

Pearlstein, S. (2005, October 5). Social responsibility doesn't much sway the balance sheet. *The Washington Post,* p. D-1.

Pires, C., & Stanton, J. (2002). Ethnic marketing ethics. *Journal of Business Ethics, 36,* 111–118.

Pollay, R. W., Lee, J. S., & Carter-Whitney, D. (1992, March). Separate but not equal: Racial segmentation in cigarette advertising. *Journal of Advertising, 21*(1), 45–57.

Pomeroy, H. (1992, Fall). Proof of commitment. *Business and Society Review, 83,* 13.

Rethinking the social responsibility of business. (2005, October). *Reason, 37*(5), 28–38.

Rotzoll, K. B., Haefner, J. E., & Sandage, C. H. (1986). *Advertising in contemporary society* (p. 147). Cincinnati: South-Western.

Saffer, H. (1998, Summer). Economic issues in cigarette and alcohol advertising. *Journal of Drug Issues,* 781–793.

Sheehan, K. (2004). *Controversies in contemporary advertising.* Thousand Oaks, CA: Sage Publications.

Shepherd, R. (2003, August 10). Business needs ethical focus. *Richmond Times Dispatch,* p. E-6.

Solomon, M. (1999). *Consumer behavior: Buying, having and being.* Upper Saddle River, NJ: PrenticeHall.

Strategic Directions (2002, September). McDonalds jumps on the CSR bandwagon. *18*(9), p. 8–11.

Taylor, C. R., & Stern, B. (1997, Summer). Asian-Americans: Television advertising and the "model minority." *Journal of Advertising, 26*(2), 47.

Taylor, R. E., Edwards, D., & Darling, J. R. (1989). The ethical dimensions of trade barriers: An exploratory study. *Columbia Journal of World Business.*

Thomas-Lynn, F. (1998, May 8). New brand's marketing upsets cigarette foes; groups don't like minority focus, defiant tone of low-priced product's ads. *Milwaukee Journal Sentinel,* p. 1.

Toombs, P., & Williams-Harold, B. (2004, May). Diversity in the retail industry; away from the limelight, little sign of commitment. *Network Journal, 11*(6), 21.

2006 Black Enterprise Entrepreneurs Conference begins May 17 in Dallas; General Motors returns to host nation's largest gathering of corporate executives and African American entrepreneurs. (2006, April 4). *PR Newswire.*

Voight, J. (2003, September 1). Realistic or offensive? *Adweek,* p. 16.

Vranica, S. (2006, October 24). Anheuser toasts Latino market amid a slowdown in beer sales: Thirsty for growth, brewer plans sharp rise in outlays for ads in Hispanic media [Eastern edition]. *The Wall Street Journal,* p. B-4.

Warmbrunn, S. (1998, September 19). Tobacco's appeal to minority youth concerns coalition, residents blame advertising. *Colorado Springs Gazette-Telegraph,* p. NEWS 1.

Watson, J. (2000, September 20). Ads target minority smokers; real life stories accent negatives. *Boston Globe,* p. B-3.

Webster, S. (2004, September 24). Jesse Jackson group to rank automakers' diversity. *Knight Ridder/Tribune Business News,* p. 1.

Westside Gazette (2003, September 17). Study: Young Blacks see more alcohol ads. Ft. Lauderdale, *32*(23), p. 1C.

Why are they still targeting us? (2004, August 13). *Recorder,* p. C-1.

Epilogue

Historically, the term *melting pot* has often been used in reference to the United States. However, this theoretical ideal, in which individuals from all nations meld into a single race sharing a common language, as well as similar values and customs, never materialized. The unique aspects of the different ethnic groups in this country have not diffused or disappeared. Despite acculturation (and varying degrees of assimilation) to the mainstream culture, Americans from varying ethnic backgrounds have maintained key elements of their country of origin, including language, worldviews and/or values, and customs. Hispanic Americans, African Americans, and Asian Americans remain distinct from the dominant culture, as well as distinct from one another. Geller and Orozco note that

> as opposed to the ideals of the melting pot perspective with the goal of a homogenized culture with the values of the dominant culture at the core, the U.S. now embraces "pluralism" as the ideal. Pluralism is a term that has been used to refer to the genuine *acceptance* of ethnic diversity, as opposed to mere *tolerance* for differences within society. Pluralism supports the respect and maintenance of diverse

ethnic identities within the dominant culture. The U.S. is increasingly becoming a multicultural society that no longer demands that individuals assimilate in order to be accepted. (1999)

As noted in chapter 1, America today is much more akin to a mosaic than a melting pot. In the face of increasing pluralism in U.S. society, it is essential that marketers and advertisers develop *cultural competency*. Cultural competence is the ability to communicate effectively with people of all cultures, races, and ethnic backgrounds in a way that recognizes, values, and respects their worth as individuals and protects and preserves their differences (Philips, 1996). Marketing and advertising to multicultural consumers requires special understanding and skills. While success in the marketplace is largely a function of having the right product at the right price in the right place and promoting it in the right fashion, the challenge is that what is *right* in terms of product, price, place, and promotion will likely not be quite the same from one ethnic group to another. Indeed, it may well vary within a specific ethnic group— savvy marketers and advertisers distinguish between the needs and wants of first-generation immigrant audiences versus second- or third-generation audiences of the same ethnic group. In short, there is no cookie-cutter or one-size-fits-all approach to engaging in successful promotions targeting multicultural consumers. To market and advertise effectively with consumers of different ethnic backgrounds, practitioners must understand the widely differing cultures of the audiences to which they are appealing. That cultural competency must then be woven into every element of the marketing program.

This text has attempted to highlight some of the many distinctive aspects of each of the three major ethnic groups in this country. However, this brief text can only serve as an introduction to communicating with Hispanic, African American, and Asian American consumers. Clearly, there is much more to be learned about these multicultural consumers, as well as other ethnic groups in the United States today. Marketers and advertisers must become lifelong students of culture if they are to communicate effectively in today's increasingly multicultural marketplace.

REFERENCES

Geller, P., & Orozco, E. (1999, Summer). Changes in cultural benchmarks in the multiethnic United States. *The International Scope Review, 1*(1), 1.

Philips, W. (1996). Culturally competent practice. *The Roundtable, 10*(1), 1.

Index

race
    categories of, 2–6
    in Census, 2–6
    and discrimination, 179–81
    vs. ethnicity, 2
    . see also ethnicity
race-based pricing, 32, 290
radio
    alcohol advertisements on, 289
    Asian-targeted, 235, 236, 237–39
    in Hispanic community, 140–44
Ramirez, Jesus, 59
Rasinski, George, 49
religion
    African Americans and, 81–82, 161–63
    attendance of services, 162
    and attitudes toward advertisements, 80
    and consumption of products, 79–80
    and determination of media vehicles used, 81–82
    Hispanics and, 114–15, 162
    and marketing mistakes, 80–81
    segregation of, 161–62
    and value of consumption of material goods, 79
    as way to reach ethnic consumer, 80
reputation
    of companies, 301
    importance to Asian Americans, 214, 216
respect, African Americans' need for, 72–73, 98, 160–61, 179
responsibility, social. see social responsibility
retailers, ethnic preferences for, 96–98, 179, 225, 227
Reyes, Luis, 297
R. J. Reynolds, 285
rituals, 76
Rokeach, Milton, 77
Rokeach Value System, 77, 78
Rooney, Dave, 163
Rossman, M. L., 72, 209, 216
Rotfeld, H. J., 58

salespeople, Hispanic, 72, 84
sales promotion, 35–36
Samovar, L., 56, 58–59, 214
San Jose, George, 267
Santiago, Anita, 84

saving of money, 100, 219–20
Schreiber, A., 108
Schultz, Don, 50
segregation
    of neighborhoods, 12–13
    of religion, 161–62
self-reference criterion, 57–58
services, 24–25
shopping behavior
    of African Americans, 92, 175
    of Asian Americans, 92, 224–29
    and brands, 92–93
    of Hispanics, 92, 122–25
    of whites, 92
shopping malls catering to Asian Americans, 227
Siregar, M., 219
smoking. see tobacco
social responsibility
    diversity, 302–4
    economic considerations, 306
    effects on reputation, 301
    to employees, 302–4
    resonation with target audience, 304
    to society, 304, 306
Social Values and Social Change (Kahle), 78
Soto, Steven, 124
South Americans, 110
    . see also Hispanics
space usage, 69–70
Spanish
    and communicating with Hispanic consumers, 63, 65, 68, 112–14, 127–28
    variations in, 65, 111–12
specialty advertising agencies
    acquisition by general market agencies, 258–59
    advantages of using, 266–67
    African American, 17, 86, 258, 260, 262, 264–65, 269–71
    Asian American, 258, 260, 266–67, 271–73
    Hispanic, 258, 259–62, 260, 267–68
Spitzer, Eliot, 285
sponsorships, 43–45
Stafani, L., 56, 58–59, 214
standard price, 32
Stanton, J., 278
State Farm Insurance, 271–73